COOKING BETTER ALL THE TIME

Katie Stewart

Cookery Editor, Woman's Journal

HAMLYN

LONDON · NEW YORK · SYDNEY · TORONTO

Contents

Published by The Hamlyn Publishing Group Limited
London · New York · Sydney · Toronto
Hamlyn House, Feltham, Middlesex, England
© 1966 Fleetway Publications Limited
Second impression 1970
Printed in Hong Kong by Lee Fung
SBN 600 00627 1

Introduction

Some good cooks are born that way, but I believe most arrive at a high standard of excellence as a result of constant practice. The virtue of patience is essential and a compelling interest in the art of good cooking equally so.

Nearly every woman I've met wants to be thought of as a good and creative cook—that goes for the bachelor girl as much as for the housewife. Even with a natural flair, however, everyone has to learn the basic recipes and working methods and be prepared to carry on learning all the time.

In *Cooking Better All The Time* I have taken sixteen subjects and in each case set out the basic recipes and working methods before moving on to progressively more challenging ideas.

Once these have been mastered I hope that readers will take the recipes and make changes themselves—for cooking, I believe, is a creative art offering the individual real opportunity to express his or her personality. The possibility for variety is infinite for those who take pleasure and pride in their cooking.

My enjoyment in writing this book has been tremendous. Every picture was taken especially for the subject it illustrates and my deepest thanks are due to the photographers Anthony Blake and David Davies for their skill and creative talent and also for their patience, kindness and advice. For their help and co-operation and for the encouragement of so many others at Fleetway and elsewhere I am truly grateful.

Katie Stewart

ALL ABOUT
Hors D'oeuvre

Hors d'oeuvre make a wonderfully colourful start to a meal, ideal in summer when cool, fresh food makes a nice contrast to a hot day and marvellous for entertaining, since they can be prepared well ahead and look devastatingly mouthwatering when presented properly. They can be just as simple or extravagant as you care to make them. It's traditional to offer a variety; this gives you a chance to arrange an attractive selection of colours and flavours. The minimum offered should be about four or six and the maximum as many as you like, according to the number of persons you wish to serve. Set out each one with a fork or spoon for serving and then guests may help themselves to a little from each plate. If you haven't a proper hors d'oeuvre tray, then arrange them neatly on matching small plates or large saucers.

The choice of colours and appearance should be planned with care. The recipe in fact can be quite simple, but the garnish or decoration is of the greatest importance. Try to arrange a selection giving some vegetable, egg, fish or meat, and some rice or pasta. For fewer or more persons, increase or reduce the number of hors d'oeuvre offered accordingly.

Simple hors d'oeuvre

YOU WILL NEED FOR 6 SERVINGS:

Sliced tomato: Plunge 6 firm tomatoes into boiling water for 1 minute. Drain and peel away the skins. Slice thinly and arrange in neat rows, sprinkle with 1 tablespoon finely chopped onion and pour over 2–3 tablespoons French dressing, *see page 91.*

8   *Simple hors d'oeuvre—sliced tomato, egg mayonnaise, sardine, cucumber and rice salad*

Egg mayonnaise: Hard boil 4 eggs, plunge into cold water and remove the shells. Slice thinly or cut in quarters and arrange in dish. Spoon over equal quantities mayonnaise and double cream blended together, approx. 2 tablespoons of each, and sprinkle with paprika pepper to decorate.

Rice salad: Add 4 oz. long grain rice to boiling, salted water and cook for 10 minutes until tender. Drain and rinse under cold water. Spoon the rice into a mixing basin and add a seasoning of salt and pepper, 1 small onion finely chopped, 1 green pepper, blanched in boiling water then deseeded and chopped, and 1 small (8 oz.) tin pineapple, (containing 4 rings), drained and chopped small. Stir in 3–4 tablespoons French dressing and mix well.

Sardine: Drain sardines from 1 large tin, remove tails and backbone. Arrange in serving dish and add to the oil from the tin ½ level teaspoon castor sugar and 2 tablespoons vinegar. Mix well and pour over the sardines, sprinkle with chopped parsley.

Cucumber: Peel and thinly slice half a cucumber. Place the slices in a small basin of salted water, using 1 tablespoon salt to ½ pint water. Leave to soak for 15 minutes, then drain and arrange in a dish. Sprinkle with freshly milled black pepper and pour over 2 tablespoons French dressing.

Sweetcorn: Drain the contents of 1 (11 oz.) tin whole kernel sweetcorn into a small mixing basin. Add a seasoning of salt and pepper and 2–3 tablespoons thick cream. Blend and spoon into a dish, sprinkle with paprika pepper.

Pickled herrings: Drain herrings from jar (8 oz.) of pickled herrings. Unroll and cut into ½ in. pieces. Arrange in dish and top with a little sliced onion from the jar.

Any of the above simple recipes could be replaced with one of these more sophisticated ones.

Mushrooms Provençale

Plunge 4–6 tomatoes into boiling water for 1 minute. Drain and peel away the skins. Cut in half, remove the seeds and then chop the tomato flesh coarsely. In a saucepan heat 1 tablespoon salad oil until hot, then add 1 tablespoon finely chopped onion, 1 clove of garlic crushed and finely chopped, and the diced tomato flesh. Cook very gently, covered with a lid, for 5 minutes. Then add ¼ lb. peeled and sliced button mushrooms, a seasoning of salt and pepper, sprig of thyme and half a bay leaf. Add just enough cold water to cover the mushrooms, recover with a lid and continue to cook very gently for a further 15 minutes.

Draw the pan off the heat, allow to cool and then serve sprinkled with freshly chopped parsley.

Spaghetti salad

Break about 2 oz. spaghetti into 1 in. lengths, add to a pan of boiling salted water and cook rapidly for 12 minutes or until quite soft. Drain and rinse under cold running water until free from stickiness and cooled.

Place the cooked spaghetti in a mixing basin and add the contents of 1 (7 oz.) tin salmon or lobster, skin and bones or sinews removed, and 1 tablespoon finely chopped onion. In a small screw topped jar measure a pinch of salt, pepper, dry mustard and sugar. Add first 1 tablespoon vinegar, then 3 tablespoons oil, shake well and add to the spaghetti salad. Toss the ingredients well and serve.

Potato mayonnaise

Scrape and plain boil about 1 lb. new potatoes, then drain and allow to cool.

Cut the potatoes in dice and place in a mixing basin along with 1 tablespoon finely chopped onion and ¼ lb. thinly sliced cooked chipolata sausages or 4 oz. peeled prawns if liked.

In a separate mixing basin combine together 3–4 tablespoons mayonnaise with 2–3 tablespoon single cream. Add to the potato salad and toss the ingredients to mix. Serve sprinkled with chopped chives.

Although most commonly presented in the manner we have shown above, on any menu in a restaurant you will notice that 'Hors d'oeuvre' covers a good selection of other recipes. These are usually sufficient served on their own with either brown bread and butter, pumpernickle bread or toast.

Shellfish cocktails, *see page* 39

Avocado pears with prawns

YOU WILL NEED FOR 4 SERVINGS:

2 ripe avocado pears
4 crisp lettuce leaves
2 tablespoons mayonnaise
2 tablespoons double cream
squeeze of lemon juice
dash of Worcestershire sauce
4 oz. peeled prawns

Cut the avocado pears in half lengthways and remove the stone. Rub the cut surfaces of the four halves with the cut side of a lemon to prevent them from discolouring. Place each pear half in a crisp lettuce leaf and arrange on a plate.

In a small mixing basin combine together the mayonnaise, cream, lemon juice and Worcestershire sauce. Add the prepared prawns and mix well. Spoon the mixture into the centre of each pear, filling the hollow. Serve with slices of brown bread and butter.

Mushroom cocktail

YOU WILL NEED FOR 4 SERVINGS:

6 oz. button mushrooms
cold water
pinch salt
nut of butter
4 lettuce leaves
paprika pepper
FOR THE DRESSING:
3 tablespoons mayonnaise
3 tablespoons double cream
1 tablespoon reduced mushroom liquor
1 teaspoon horseradish sauce
dash Worcestershire sauce
squeeze lemon juice

Rinse the mushrooms under cold water and remove the stalks. Halve or quarter any large ones. Place in a small saucepan, just cover with cold water, add a pinch of salt and a small nut of butter. Bring to the boil, cover with a lid and simmer gently for 5–10 minutes or until tender. Drain the mushrooms and chill. Continue to cook the liquor until reduced to about 1 tablespoon and allow to cool.

Shred the washed lettuce leaves and place in the base of small individual glass dishes. Combine together ingredients for the dressing and fold in the chilled mushroom caps. Pile into glasses and top each one with a pinch of paprika pepper.

Pâté

YOU WILL NEED FOR 4–6 SERVINGS:

3 rashers streaky bacon
12 oz. pig's liver, cut in slices
2 cloves garlic, crushed with salt
12 oz. pork sausagemeat
1 level teaspoon salt
1 level teaspoon nutmeg
¼ level teaspoon pepper
pinch mixed herbs
2 oz. melted butter
1 egg
2 tablespoons brandy (optional)

Well grease a 1½ pint pie or baking dish and line base with the streaky bacon. Mince the liver and chop the garlic very finely, combine together with the sausagemeat, salt, nutmeg, pepper, herbs and melted butter. Bind with lightly mixed egg and brandy if used.

Turn mixture into prepared dish and cover with a lid or square of kitchen foil. Place in the centre of a slow oven (300 deg. or Gas No. 2) and cook for 2 hours. Allow to cool, turn out and serve sliced with hot toast triangles and butter.

Mustard dip

MAKES ¾ PINT

3–4 level teaspoons freshly-made mustard
¼ level teaspoon salt
pinch of curry powder
freshly ground black pepper
1 teaspoon lemon juice
1 level teaspoon castor sugar
2 egg yolks
½ pint vegetable or corn oil
1 level teaspoon tomato purée
1 tablespoon wine vinegar
¼ pint double cream
hot sausages for serving

Measure the mustard, salt, curry powder, pepper, lemon juice, castor sugar and egg yolks into a medium-sized mixing basin. Blend together using a wire balloon whisk. Add the oil, drop by drop at first, whisking all the time until the mixture begins to thicken a little, then add it a little faster, stir whisking continuously. When all the oil has been added stir in the tomato purée and the vinegar, check seasoning, adding more mustard if required. Just before required, lightly whip the cream and fold into the mixture and serve as a dip for hot sausages.

Party dip

2 tablespoons French dressing
8 oz. cream cheese
2 tablespoons tomato ketchup
½ small onion, finely chopped
1 teaspoon anchovy essence

Gradually beat the dressing into the cream cheese and blend thoroughly. Add the remaining ingredients and mix well. Set aside until ready to serve.

Onion dip

Mix the contents of a packet of onion soup powder with 4 cartons of soured cream and mix well. Chill.

ALL ABOUT Soups

Soups from the stockpot

The basis of any soup, stew, casserole or gravy is a good stock. The extra trouble taken to make it is well rewarded by the rich flavour of the finished recipe. Use it as the base of clear soups, consommés and broths. Simmered gently for hours, these soups are easy to make and very tasty.

Basic recipe

Stock is an infusion of meat, bones and vegetables and is used mainly to flavour soups, stews and casseroles. It is made from simple ingredients often readily available in your kitchen, or otherwise bought very cheaply. Stock can be kept for 2–3 days in a refrigerator, otherwise make it fresh each time.

Suitable ingredients: Raw or cooked bones and meat scraps; carcasses of small game, animals or poultry; bacon rinds and trimmings; a few flavouring vegetables—carrot, onion, turnip, leek and celery; mushroom and tomato trimmings; small *bouquet garni* (to make it, tie together a few stalks of parsley, a bay leaf and a sprig of thyme); and salted water as required.

To make the stock: Rinse the bones (if using large, raw bones ask the butcher to chop them) and discard any surplus fat. Cut off any large pieces of lean meat and shred finely. Put the bones and shredded meat into a large saucepan and add cold salted water to cover—use 1 teaspoon salt to each quart of water. Add sliced vegetables and *bouquet garni* (see ingredients above).

Bring the stock to the boil and skim. Cover with a lid, lower the heat and simmer very gently for 3–4 hours. Strain the liquid off the bones and leave overnight. Next day skim off the fat and reboil the stock ready for use.

If you used fresh raw bones, keep them to start a second stockpot.

Brown stock

When brown stock is required, use bones and vegetables as for basic recipe but brown them before simmering.

To do this, rinse the raw bones and cut off any surplus fat. Shred and reserve lean meat. Place the fat, bones and vegetables in a roasting tin and roast in a fairly hot oven (400 deg. or Gas No. 6), turning once or twice until nicely browned—about 30–40 minutes.

Lift the bones and vegetables into the stockpot. Add the shredded meat, bacon rinds, bouquet garni and any other suitable ingredients. Add the salted water to cover, bring to the boil and skim and simmer as before.

Pressure-cooked stock

Use the ingredients as given above and cook at 15 lb. pressure for 1 hour. Read the instructions given with your pressure cooker before you start.

Soup from stock

Good stock, well prepared, can be used for a nourishing clear soup. Simply add a little carrot, leek and celery, all scrubbed and shredded into fine matchstick-sized pieces, to the finished reboiled stock. Simmer gently for 20 minutes to cook the vegetables, check the seasoning and serve.

Of course it is not essential to make soups from stock, a busy cook may find this impossible, but stock used in preference to water adds more flavour and goodness. If you can't make your own, cubes made from concentrated stock are an excellent substitute.

Scotch broth

YOU WILL NEED FOR 4–6 SERVINGS:

¼ lb. middle neck of mutton
2 pints of stock
   or water plus 1 level teaspoon salt
1 oz. pearl barley
1 large onion, finely chopped
1 carrot, diced
small piece of swede, diced
2 stalks celery, shredded
1 tablespoon finely chopped parsley

Wipe the meat and cut off any surplus fat. Remove any meat from the bones and shred it finely. Place the meat and bones in a large pan and cover with the stock (made to basic recipe) or salted water. Place the pearl barley in a small saucepan, cover with water and bring to the boil. Then strain and add the barley to the soup pot.
Bring the soup to the boil, skim, cover with a lid and simmer gently for 1 hour.
Add the prepared vegetables (except parsley) to the soup and simmer for another hour.
Remove the bones, check the seasoning and sprinkle with the chopped parsley before serving.

French onion soup

YOU WILL NEED FOR 4 SERVINGS:

1 oz. margarine
1 lb. onions
1½ pints stock or water
1 level teaspoon salt
1 oz. flour to blend with ¼ pint water (*see recipe*)

Melt the margarine in a fairly large saucepan and add the skinned and sliced onions. Cover and cook gently until soft—about 20–30 minutes. Remove the lid and continue to cook onions until they are a golden brown colour.
Stir in the stock or water and add the salt. Cover pan again and simmer for a further 30 minutes. In a small mixing basin blend together flour and a ¼ pint cold water—whisk or stir well to blend smoothly. Stir into the boiling soup and keep stirring until soup comes to the boil again.

Draw the pan off the heat and check the seasoning. Serve the soup thickly sprinkled with grated cheese, and float slices of toasted French bread on top.

Mushroom consommé

YOU WILL NEED FOR 4–6 SERVINGS:

1½ oz. butter or margarine
1 large onion, finely chopped
¼ lb. mushrooms, thickly sliced
2 pints of stock
juice of ½ lemon
2 tablespoons sherry

Melt the butter in a saucepan and gently fry the onion until tender and lightly browned. Add the mushrooms and fry a futher 5 minutes. Add the stock and lemon juice and bring just up to the boil. Draw the pan off the heat, check the seasoning, stir in the sherry and serve. This consommé makes a very suitable first course for a dinner party.

Chicken broth

YOU WILL NEED FOR 6 SERVINGS:

1 small stewing chicken, chicken joints or
   carcass
bouquet garni (*see basic stock recipe*)
2 stalks celery, shredded
1 onion, finely sliced
2 carrots, finely sliced
3 pints stock or water plus 2 level teaspoons salt
FOR THE GARNISH:
2 oz. patna rice
2 stalks celery
1 tablespoon chopped parsley

Place the chicken, bouquet garni and prepared vegetables in a large saucepan. Add the stock or water and salt and bring to the boil. Skim if necessary, cover the pan with a lid and simmer gently for 3–4 hours.
Strain the soup, and leave overnight or until quite cold, reserving any chicken meat. Later remove any fat that has risen to the surface and solidified, and reboil the soup.
To the hot soup add any chicken flesh cut in dice (if a whole chicken was used you may like to keep some of the meat to use in other dishes), 2 oz. patna rice and 2 stalks freshly-washed, diced celery. Cover pan and simmer soup for 20 minutes or until rice and celery are tender. Check seasoning, adding extra salt and pepper if necessary, and sprinkle with chopped parsley before serving.

Oxtail soup

YOU WILL NEED FOR 4–6 SERVINGS:

1 oxtail
1 oz. dripping
2 carrots, sliced
1 large onion, sliced
2 stalks celery, sliced
bouquet garni (*see basic stock recipe*)
few rashers of bacon or bacon rinds
3 pints stock
  or water plus 2 level teaspoons salt
TO FINISH THE SOUP:
sufficient cornflour to thicken (*see recipe*)
juice of ½ lemon

Wipe oxtail and divide it into joints. Blanch the joints—do this by placing them in a saucepan, cover with cold water and bring to the boil. Strain and pat dry. The oxtail is now ready for use.
Melt the dripping in a large pan and add the oxtail pieces, fry well on all sides and then remove pieces from hot fat and drain them. Add the prepared vegetables to the hot dripping and fry these until lightly browned. Return the meat to the pan along with the bouquet garni, bacon rashers or rinds and the stock or water.
Bring to the boil, cover with a lid and simmer gently for 3–4 hours. Strain the stock off the bones and set it aside in a cool place (overnight if necessary) until the stock is quite cold. Remove the meat from the oxtail bones and shred finely.
To finish the soup, remove any solidified fat from the surface and reboil the stock. In a small mixing basin blend about 2 heaped teaspoons cornflour with cold water to make a thin paste. Gradually stir this mixture into the soup and bring to the boil, so that the soup thickens slightly. Add the oxtail meat and lemon juice and check the seasoning. If liked, add a few drops of browning before serving to give the soup a rich colour, and for a special occasion add a tablespoon dry sherry.

Bacon broth

YOU WILL NEED FOR 6 SERVINGS:

¼ lb. carrots
¼ lb. onions
¼ lb. leeks
1 stalk of celery
1 oz. butter or margarine
1½ pints water
bacon knuckles or bones
bouquet garni (*see basic stock recipe*).
salt and pepper
1 oz. rice

Prepare the vegetables and cut into small dice. Cook gently in melted butter or margarine for 4–5 minutes. Then add water, bacon bones, bouquet garni and seasoning.
Cover with a lid and simmer gently for an hour. Remove bouquet garni and bacon bones. If there are small pieces of bacon meat on bones, return them to the broth. Add rice and cook for a further 10–12 minutes. Check seasoning and serve.

Beef and barley broth

YOU WILL NEED FOR 4–6 SERVINGS:

1 beef bone
4 oz. pearl barley
4 pints water
salt and pepper
1–1½ lb. mixed vegetables—carrots, onion
  and swedes

Have the butcher cut the bone in pieces and place in a large saucepan. Add the pearl barley, water and a good seasoning of salt and pepper. Bring up to the boil, lower the heat and simmer gently stirring occasionally for 1½–2 hours. About ½ hour before the end of the cooking time add the vegetables cleaned and cut into neat dice. When the soup is cooked remove the bones. If possible allow the soup to cool, skim off the fat and reheat before serving.

Clear chicken and rice soup

YOU WILL NEED FOR 4–6 SERVINGS:

1 large onion, peeled and chopped
1½ oz. butter or margarine
2 oz. long grain rice
1½ pints chicken stock—made using a chicken
  carcass or stock cubes
1 bay leaf
salt and pepper
½ pint milk
½ oz. (or 1 level tablespoon) flour

Add the onion to the melted butter or margarine in a large saucepan. Cover with a lid and fry gently for 5 minutes until tender but not browned. Stir in the rice, chicken stock and bay leaf. Bring up to the boil, then lower the heat, stir well to prevent the rice from sticking. Cover with a lid and cook very gently for 30 minutes.
Check seasoning, adding salt and pepper to taste. Measure the milk into a small mixing basin. Sieve the flour on to it and mix thoroughly using a whisk. Add to the soup and stir until boiling and thickened.

Purée and casserole soups

To welcome the family home on a cold winter's evening start the meal with a piping hot purée soup. Or serve a rich and satisfying casserole soup that almost makes a meal on its own. These can be prepared ahead of time and reheated, and you'll find them very economical.

Purée soups are made by cooking vegetables until they are quite soft and then passing the mixture through a sieve. Make them from starchy ingredients which give you a thick purée that needs little extra thickening.

Any left-over vegetables need never be wasted. It is possible to make up your own recipes using a mixture of root vegetables, such as potatoes, carrots, onions, swedes, celery or artichokes. Make sure you have 1 pint of stock or water for each pound of prepared vegetables. Cook until quite soft and add seasoning to taste.

Tomato soup

YOU WILL NEED FOR 4 SERVINGS:

1 oz. bacon trimmings
1½ oz. butter or margarine
1 medium-size carrot, diced
1 small onion, chopped
1½ oz. (or 2 level tablespoons) flour
1½ lb. tomatoes
1½ pints stock or water
1 level teaspoon sugar
salt and pepper
2 tablespoons cream or top of the milk
a little finely chopped parsley

Gently fry the bacon trimmings in a large pan to extract the fat. Add the butter or margarine, carrot and onion and cook gently for a few minutes, allowing the vegetables to brown a little. Stir in the flour and add the tomatoes, which have been cut in quarters. Cook gently for 5 minutes to allow the tomatoes to soften.

Stir in the stock or water, sugar and seasoning to taste. Bring to the boil, cover with a lid and simmer gently for 1 hour. Draw the pan off the heat and rub the soup through a fine sieve, discarding the pieces of skin and pips. Return the soup to the pan and re-heat gently. Just before serving, stir in the cream and sprinkle with a little chopped parsley.

Lentil soup

YOU WILL NEED FOR 6 SERVINGS:

3 pints stock or water
6 oz. lentils, soaked overnight
½ oz. butter or margarine
1 level tablespoon flour
2 carrots, sliced
2 onions, finely chopped
1 level teaspoon salt

Use a pint of water taken from the recipe to soak lentils overnight. To make soup, melt the fat in a large saucepan, add the carrots and onions and fry gently for a few minutes, stir in the flour. Gradually stir in the stock, salt and soaked lentils. Bring to the boil, cover with a lid and simmer gently for 1½ hours, skimming when necessary. Alternatively, this soup make be cooked more quickly in a pressure cooker —for 15 minutes at 15 lb. pressure, see the instructions with your cooker. When the lentils are quite soft, draw the pan off the heat and pass the soup through a sieve. Return to the pan and reheat before serving.

Mixed vegetable soup

YOU WILL NEED FOR 4–6 SERVINGS:

1–1½ lb. mixed vegetables—potatoes, carrots, onions, leeks, celery, parsnips or turnips
1–1½ oz. butter or margarine
1 level teaspoon sugar
1½–2 pints stock or water plus stock cube
salt and pepper
¼ pint milk
2 level tablespoons flour
chopped parsley for garnish

Prepare the vegetables and cut them up small. Melt the butter or margarine in a large saucepan, add the vegetables and cook gently for 5–6 minutes. Stir in the sugar, stock, seasoning of salt and pepper, and bring up to the boil. Lower the heat, cover with a lid and simmer gently for 40–45 minutes. Draw the pan off the heat and pass the soup through a sieve to make a purée. Return to the saucepan.

Measure the milk into a small mixing basin, sieve the flour on to it. Mix quickly using a whisk and add to the soup. Return to the heat and stir until boiling and thickened. Check seasonings and serve sprinkled with chopped parsley.

Delicious and filling Minestrone

Watercress soup

YOU WILL NEED FOR 4 SERVINGS:

1 lb. potatoes
1 bunch of watercress
1 oz. butter or margarine
1 small onion, finely chopped
1 stalk celery, finely chopped
1 pint stock or water
1 level teaspoon salt
¼ pint milk

Scrub, peel, and cut up the potatoes. Wash the watercress, set aside half the leaves for garnish, and chop up all the rest including the stalks. Melt the butter or margarine in a large saucepan and add the potatoes, onion, celery and chopped watercress. Sauté gently for 5 minutes. Stir in the stock or water, add the salt and bring to the boil. Cover with a lid and simmer gently for 1 hour.
When the vegetables are quite soft, draw the pan off the heat and rub the soup through a sieve, return the purée to the saucepan and reboil. Stir in the milk and reserved watercress and it is ready to serve.

Carrot soup

YOU WILL NEED FOR 4 SERVINGS:

1 lb. carrots
1 oz. butter or margarine
1 onion, finely chopped
1 pint stock or water
salt and pepper
1 level teaspoon sugar
2 tablespoons cream or top of the milk

Prepare carrots by scraping or peeling and then slicing thinly. In a large saucepan melt the butter or margarine and add the carrots and onion. Fry gently for a few minutes. Stir in the stock or water, seasoning to taste, and sugar. Bring to the boil, cover with a lid and simmer gently for 1 hour or until the carrots are tender.
Draw the pan off the heat and pass the soup through a sieve. Return to the pan and reheat until almost boiling. Just before serving, stir in the cream or top of the milk.

Satisfy a hungry family with a meal-in-a-dish. These casserole soups make a very filling first course, or try them steaming hot for supper—delicious with French bread. They are easy to make and tasty.

Minestrone

YOU WILL NEED FOR 6–8 SERVINGS:

1 lb. shin of beef with bone
6 oz. red or haricot beans
4 pints cold water
2 level teaspoons salt
2 tablespoons olive oil
1 onion, finely chopped
1 clove garlic, optional
2 stalks celery, diced
½ head of cabbage, shredded
½ lb. carrots, scraped and diced
1 (15 oz.) tin tomatoes
2 oz. spaghetti, broken in pieces
  (or use quick macaroni)
1 small packet frozen peas
grated Parmesan cheese to serve

Early in the day, or the day before, place the shin of beef, bone and beans in a large saucepan. Cover with the water and add the salt. Bring to the boil, skim, cover with a lid and simmer gently for 3 hours. When the stock is almost ready, prepare the vegetables. In the hot olive oil, gently fry the onion and garlic (if liked) for 5–10 minutes, or until softened. Then discard the garlic clove. Remove the bone from the stock and cut off any meat in small pieces. Add the meat to the stock, along with the fried onion, prepared celery, cabbage, carrots and tomatoes. Simmer gently for 20 minutes or until the vegetables are soft.
Draw the pan off the heat and leave until quite cold, possibly overnight in the refrigerator. Skim away any fat from the surface and bring soup slowly to the boil. Add the spaghetti or macaroni and peas and cook in a covered pan for about 10 minutes. Check the seasoning and serve very hot, topped with lots of Parmesan cheese.

Fish chowder

YOU WILL NEED FOR 6 SERVINGS:

¼ lb. belly of pork
3 onions, finely sliced
5 potatoes (approx. 1¾ lb.) pared and sliced or diced
4 level teaspoons salt
pinch of pepper
1 pint boiling water
1½ lb. fresh cod fillet
2 pints milk
¼ pint single cream
1 oz. butter or margarine

Cut the pork into ½ in. cubes and fry in a large saucepan over moderate heat until browned. Remove the pork pieces and reserve them. Add the onions to the pork fat and cook until tender—about 10 minutes. Add the potatoes, salt and pepper and boiling water.

Arrange the fish, cut in neat, medium-size pieces, on top. Cover the pan with a lid and simmer gently for 25–30 minutes or until the potatoes are tender. Draw the pan off the heat and remove any pieces of skin from the fish and flake the flesh. Bring milk to the boil and add immediately with cream, butter or margarine and fried pork pieces. Sprinkle with crushed biscuit crackers and serve.

Vegetable soup with cheese dumplings

YOU WILL NEED FOR 6 SERVINGS:

1½ lb. mixed vegetables—potato, carrot, swede, onion and celery, all neatly diced
2 tablespoons washed lentils, soaked overnight
1 level teaspoon salt
and pinch of pepper
2 pints stock or water
1 level tablespoon flour mixed to a cream with cold water (*see recipe*)
1 tablespoon finely chopped parsley
FOR THE DUMPLINGS:
3 oz. (or 3 rounded tablespoons) self-raising flour
1 oz. (or 3 level tablespoons) shredded suet
salt and pepper
1½ oz. grated cheese
milk to mix

Prepare the vegetables and place in a large saucepan with the soaked lentils, seasoning and stock or water. Bring to the boil, cover with a lid and simmer gently for 1¼ hours.

In a small mixing basin blend the flour with sufficient cold water to make a thin cream. Stir a small quantity of the hot soup into this to blend and pour the creamy mixture into the soup. Stir until boiling and slightly thickened.

To prepare the dumplings, sieve the flour into a mixing basin, add the suet, seasoning to taste and grated cheese. Stir in enough milk to mix to a scone-like dough. With lightly floured hands, roll the mixture into small dumplings, about the size of large marbles. Add the dumplings immediately to the boiling soup, put the lid on the pan again and simmer gently for 20 minutes. Sprinkle with chopped parsley before serving.

Bacon and lentil soup

YOU WILL NEED FOR 4 SERVINGS:

6 oz. lentils, soaked overnight
3–4 pints stock or water
1 small knuckle of bacon
½ oz. butter or margarine
2 onions, peeled and chopped

Soak the lentils overnight in the stock or water. Also soak bacon knuckle overnight separately.

Next day melt the butter or margarine in a large saucepan, and fry the chopped onions for five minutes until soft. Stir in the soaked lentils and stock or water and add the soaked bacon knuckle after scraping the rind well.

Bring to the boil and simmer gently covered with a lid for 1½ hours. When the lentils are quite soft, draw the pan off the heat and lift out the bacon knuckle. Pass the liquid through a sieve and return to the saucepan.

Remove the rind from the bacon and scrape away the meat from the bone. Chop the meat coarsely and add to the soup. Check seasoning, reheat and serve.

Corn and potato chowder

YOU WILL NEED FOR 8 SERVINGS:

¼ lb. streaky bacon rashers, trimmed
2 medium-sized onions, peeled and sliced
2 lb. potatoes, peeled and cut in dice
1 pint water
1 level teaspoon salt
¼ level teaspoon pepper
2 (11 oz.) tins cream style sweetcorn
1 pint milk
1 small packet frozen peas, thawed
¼ pint single cream
FOR THE PARMESAN CROÛTONS:
3–4 slices white bread, crusts removed
1½–2 oz. butter or margarine
1 rounded tablespoon grated Parmesan cheese

Chop the bacon rashers coarsely and place in a large saucepan. Set over a low heat and cook until the bacon fat runs and bacon pieces are crisp. Discard the bacon pieces and add the onion to the hot bacon fat. Cook gently, covered with a lid, until the onion is tender but not browned, takes about 5 minutes. Add the prepared potato, toss and then stir in the water and seasoning. Bring up to the boil and simmer for 20 minutes.

Add the sweetcorn, milk, and peas, reboil and simmer a further 5 minutes. Just before serving, check the seasoning and stir in the cream. Serve the soup sprinkled with Parmesan croûtons prepared as follows while the soup is cooking. Cut the trimmed bread slices into small dice. Add to the melted butter in a frying pan and toss over moderate heat until the bread cubes are browned. Draw the pan off the heat, sprinkle with the Parmesan cheese, toss and serve.

Cream soups

Use good quality fresh vegetables and thicken soup with flour, cornflour, blended egg yolk or cream. Never boil when cream or eggs have been added. Reheat, if necessary, in the top of a double boiler. The consistency may vary according to the cooking. If you cook it too quickly the liquid will evaporate and your soup will be too thick. The remedy is simple—a little more milk or stock. Basic rule: simmer slowly in a lidded pan. Follow this and you won't go far wrong.

Cream of corn

YOU WILL NEED FOR 4 SERVINGS:

2 tins of whole kernel sweetcorn
$1\frac{1}{2}$ pints milk
1 oz. butter or margarine
1 small onion, finely chopped
1 level tablespoon flour
1 level teaspoon salt
$\frac{1}{4}$ pint single cream
chopped parsley to garnish

Empty the sweetcorn into saucepan and add $\frac{1}{2}$ pint of the milk. Simmer the corn 20 minutes or until tender. Reserving one tablespoon for garnish, rub the remaining mixture through a sieve to make a purée. In a saucepan melt the fat over moderate heat and add the onion. Cook gently, covered with a lid, until the onion is tender. Stir in the flour and then the remaining milk, corn purée, and salt.
Bring to the boil and simmer gently for 5 minutes. Draw the pan off the heat and stir in the cream. Serve sprinkled with chopped parsley and reserved sweetcorn.

Cream of cucumber

YOU WILL NEED FOR 4 SERVINGS:

2 young cucumbers
1 oz. butter
pinch of sugar, salt and pepper
$\frac{1}{4}$ pint chicken stock
$\frac{1}{4}$ pint single cream
paprika pepper to garnish
FOR THE WHITE SAUCE:
$\frac{1}{3}$ pint (or 1 teacup) milk
$\frac{1}{2}$ onion
1 bay leaf
$\frac{1}{2}$ oz. butter or margarine
1 level tablespoon flour

First make the white sauce: Put the milk, onion and bay leaf on to boil. Draw the pan off the heat and leave to infuse for 10 minutes. Melt the fat in a small saucepan and stir in the flour. Stir in the strained milk and bring to the boil, stirring well. Cook gently for 2–3 minutes, then set aside to add to the soup. Peel the cucumbers, slice in half lengthways, remove the seeds and slice cucumber thinly. Blanch in boiling water for 2 minutes, then drain.
Reserve a few pieces for garnish. Melt the butter in a heavy pan, add the cucumber, sugar, salt and pepper. Cover with a lid and cook gently until soft. Add the chicken stock and the white sauce, cover and cook gently for a further 15 minutes.
Rub the soup through a fine sieve, return it to the saucepan and reheat. Draw the pan off the heat and stir in the cream. Garnish with reserved cucumber and paprika.

Cream of cauliflower

YOU WILL NEED FOR 4 SERVINGS:

1 small cauliflower
few drops lemon juice
$\frac{1}{4}$ teaspoon salt
1 oz. butter
1 medium-sized onion, chopped
1 stick celery, chopped
1 rounded tablespoon flour
$1\frac{1}{2}$ pints chicken stock
1–2 tablespoons single cream
pinch of nutmeg
extra salt and paprika pepper

Cut the stem off the cauliflower, remove all the outer leaves and soak the head in cold, salted water for a few minutes. Half fill a small saucepan with water and bring to the boil. Slash deep cuts into the stalk of the cauliflower and place, head downwards, in the boiling water. Add lemon juice to the water to keep cauliflower white, salt, and simmer for 10 minutes or until the stalk is just tender. When cooked, drain and reserve the water which can be substituted for half the chicken stock if liked. Cut the cooked cauliflower into florets, reserve a few for garnish, and rub the remainder through a sieve.
Melt the butter in a saucepan, and gently sauté the onion and celery until tender. Stir in the flour, and cook gently for a few minutes.
Add the chicken stock and the cauliflower water if used, stirring all the time. Bring to the boil, strain and then add the cauliflower purée. Reheat. Draw the pan off the stove, stir in the cream, the reserved florets, the nutmeg, salt and paprika pepper.

From the top: Corn, prawn bisque, celery, mushroom and cucumber cream soups

Cream of mushroom

YOU WILL NEED FOR 4 SERVINGS:

½ lb. mushrooms
1 onion
½ pint stock or water
1 oz. butter or margarine
1 oz. (or 1 rounded tablespoon) flour
¾ pint milk
1 level teaspoon salt
good pinch of pepper
1 egg yolk
1 tablespoon cream

Wash and slice the mushroom tops and stalks, and finely chop the onion. Simmer in the stock or water (covered with a lid) for 15 minutes until tender, and then rub through a sieve to make a purée.
In a saucepan melt the fat and stir in the flour. Gradually stir in the milk, beating well to give a smooth consistency, and then add the mushroom and onion purée, and season with salt and pepper. Simmer gently for 5 minutes.
Draw the pan off the heat. Blend the egg yolk and cream together, mix with 2–3 tablespoons of the hot soup, stir into remaining soup and serve.

Cream of spinach soup

YOU WILL NEED FOR 4 SERVINGS:

1–1½ lb. spinach
2 oz. butter
¾ pint milk
1 bay leaf
½ onion, stuck with a clove
1 oz. (or 1 rounded tablespoon) flour
pinch salt and pepper
½ pint chicken stock or water plus stock cube
4 tablespoons evaporated milk or cream
¼ pint double cream for serving (optional)

Wash the spinach and tear out large mid-ribs. Sauté the spinach in 1 oz. of the butter over a gentle heat until quite soft—takes about 6–8 minutes.
Meanwhile bring the milk up to the boil with the bay leaf and onion added. Draw off the heat and infuse for 10 minutes. Melt the remaining butter in a saucepan over low heat and stir in the flour. Cook for a further few moments. Gradually stir in the strained milk beating well all the time to make a smooth sauce. Bring up to the boil and season with salt and pepper. Stir the sauce into the spinach and heat together for about 5 minutes. Draw the pan off the heat and pass the mixture through a sieve to make a purée. Return the purée to the saucepan and thin down to the required consistency with chicken stock.

Check the seasoning and just before serving stir in the cream or evaporated milk. If liked whip the cream with salt and float on top of each serving of soup.

Cream of celery

YOU WILL NEED FOR 4 SERVINGS:

1 head of celery
1 oz. butter or margarine
1 onion, finely chopped
1 pint stock or water
½ oz. (or 1 rounded tablespoon) cornflour
½ pint milk
pepper and salt
2 tablespoons cream
chopped parsley to garnish

Wash the celery thoroughly, shred coarsely and blanch in boiling water for 2 minutes. In a saucepan melt the fat, add the prepared celery and onion and fry gently, covered with a lid for 10 minutes.
Stir in the stock or water and simmer gently, covered with a lid, for 30–60 minutes or until the vegetables are soft. Rub mixture through a sieve and return to the saucepan. Blend the cornflour with the milk and stir into the soup. Bring just up to the boil, simmer 2 minutes, and then draw the pan off the heat. Correct the seasoning, stir in the cream, and serve sprinkled with chopped parsley.

Artichoke soup

YOU WILL NEED FOR 8 SERVINGS:

2 lb. Jerusalem artichokes
2 small onions, peeled and chopped
1 small head of celery, trimmed and shredded
2 oz. butter or margarine
1 level teaspoon salt
¼ level teaspoon pepper
2 level teaspoons castor sugar
2–3 bacon rinds
1 pint stock or water, plus chicken stock cube
2 pints milk
2 oz. (or 2 rounded tablespoons) plain flour
¼ pint single cream

Peel the artichokes under cold water to prevent discolouration and cut up any large ones. Heat the butter in a large saucepan and add the prepared onion, celery and artichokes, seasoning, sugar and bacon rinds and sauté gently, covered with a lid, for 8–10 minutes.
Add the chicken stock, bring up to the boil and continue to simmer covered with a lid until the vegetables are very soft—takes about 25–30 minutes.

Draw the pan off the heat, rub the soup through a fine sieve and then return purée to the saucepan. Add 1 pint of the milk to the soup and pour the second into a mixing basin. Sift the flour over the milk and using a rotary beater whisk thoroughly to mix. Stir this blend into the soup and bring up to the boil, stirring all the time until thickened. Check flavour and seasoning and just before serving stir in the cream.

Cream of onion

YOU WILL NEED FOR 4 SERVINGS:

1 lb. onions
1 oz. butter or margarine
salt and pepper
2 oz. white bread slices
1 pint milk
½ pint water
2–3 tablespoons cream or evaporated milk

Skin the onions and slice very thinly. Melt the fat in a heavy pan and add the sliced onions. Season, cover with a lid and cook very gently for 1 hour. Stir occasionally and take care to keep the heat low enough that the onions *do not brown*.
Trim the crusts from the bread and break up the centre. Add to the onions along with the milk and water. Recover and cook gently for a further hour. Draw the pan off the heat and either rub the soup through a sieve or purée in a liquidizer. Reheat, check seasoning and stir in the cream or evaporated milk.

Prawn bisque

YOU WILL NEED FOR 4 SERVINGS:

2 pints cooked prawns (or 8 oz. frozen prawns)
2 oz. butter or margarine
½ onion, finely chopped
1 level tablespoon flour
1½ pints milk
¼ pint single cream
2 tablespoons sherry
salt, pinch of pepper and nutmeg
paprika

Peel the prawns, reserve a few for garnish, and finely mince the rest. In a saucepan melt the fat, add the onion, cover the pan with a lid and cook gently for 10 minutes or until the onion is tender. Stir in the flour, then the minced prawns and lastly the milk. Bring to the boil and cook for 2 minutes, stirring all the time. Draw the pan off the heat and stir in the cream and sherry. Add seasoning to taste and garnish with reserved prawns and paprika.

Iced soups are fun to serve in summer, and Vichyssoise is a famous chilled French soup. It can be served hot if preferred, but in this case use only ¼ pint cream.

Vichyssoise

YOU WILL NEED FOR 5–6 SERVINGS:

3 leeks
2 small onions
1 lb. potatoes
1½ oz. butter or margarine
1½ pints chicken stock or water
¼ level teaspoon pepper
½ level teaspoon salt
dash of Worcestershire sauce
pinch nutmeg
½ pint single cream
chives to garnish

Wash and finely shred the white part of the leeks, chop the onions finely, peel and slice the potatoes. Melt the fat in a large pan and add the leeks and onions. Cover with a lid and cook gently until tender. Add the stock, sliced potatoes, seasoning, Worcestershire sauce and nutmeg. Bring to the boil, then lower heat and simmer gently for 30 minutes. Pass the soup through a fine sieve. Chill well and stir in the cream. Sprinkle with chopped chives and serve.

Iced avocado

YOU WILL NEED FOR 4 SERVINGS:

2 ripe avocado pears
¼ level teaspoon onion salt
½ pint chicken broth or stock
1 carton of soured cream
1 carton of single cream
juice of half a lemon
¼ teaspoon salt

Scoop out the avocado flesh and rub through a fine hair sieve. Add the onion salt, chicken broth, soured cream and single cream, add lemon juice. Blend until smooth and then chill. Check the seasoning adding extra salt if necessary before serving. Alternatively this soup can be made in an electric blender.

For that extra touch

Let guests help themselves from a bowl of croûtons. To make them, cut bread in tiny cubes, fry in butter until golden and drain. Serve hot.

ALL ABOUT *Fish*

Fish rich in oil

Few foods give as much flavour for so little effort as these rich and succulent fish. Pop them under the grill, into the frying pan or into a savoury poaching liquor—and that's it. Or bake them in their own juices in the oven . . . the variations are endless. They are rich in fats so will need little extra oil or butter unless you are deep frying.

Preparation

These fish are cooked with their skins on and usually whole so they should be prepared carefully. Hold the fish by the tail and remove the scales by scraping with the blade of a knife from the tail to the head. Wash frequently under cold running water to remove any loose scales.

Often the fishmonger will clean out the fish for you. But if you do this yourself, remove the head, make a small incision further down the belly of the fish, and with the fingers draw out the inside. Wash the cavity under cold water. Save roes from herrings and discard everything else.

To bone herrings: remove the scales as above, cut off the head and slit the herring down the under side. Place the fish, under side downwards, on a working surface. Press firmly with the thumb and forefinger all along the backbone to loosen it. Turn over the fish, take hold of the bone at the tail and pull firmly. The small bones come with it. Wash and pat fish dry with a clean cloth or kitchen paper.

Preparing spiced herrings

Grilling

Preheat the grill and grease the rack with melted butter or oil, or remove rack and cover the base of the grill pan with foil. Clean or bone the fish and season the inside. Place at least 3 in. from the heat. It is not necessary to brush any fat over it.

Herring or mackerel: buy one fish per person. Make three slits across the skin on each side. Allow 6–8 minutes for herrings, 15–20 minutes for mackerel, turning once. Serve with a wedge of lemon or a sauce.

Mustard sauce for herrings: To ½ pint white sauce add 1 level tablespoon dry mustard blended with 1 tablespoon vinegar, a teaspoon of sugar and seasoning to taste. Reheat, add a little lemon juice if liked.

Gooseberry sauce for mackerel: top and tail ½ lb. gooseberries and place in a small saucepan with 1 tablespoon water and ½ oz. butter. Cover and cook gently until soft. Sieve and reheat with 1 tablespoon castor sugar. Simmer 1–2 minutes.

Frying

Whitebait: often served as a starter to a meal. Wash and dry thoroughly, then dip in flour and plunge into hot deep fat. Fry for 2–3 minutes until crisp and brown. Serve with a wedge of lemon and some brown bread and butter.

Herrings: whole fish should be cooked gently for 3–6 minutes on each side, then drained and served with melted butter. Otherwise bone fish and dip fillets in flour, breadcrumbs, or oatmeal and then fry them in hot lard or dripping until crisp and golden—takes 10–15 minutes.

Trout: nicest floured and fried in butter. Cook gently 6–8 minutes, turning once. Serve with a wedge of lemon and melted butter. Chopped parsley or toasted almonds may be added to the butter before serving.

Sprats: wash and dry thoroughly. Flour and fry in butter for 3–4 minutes. Allow 1 lb. for 3 people, serve with lemon, brown bread and butter.

Smelts: wash and dry thoroughly, flour lightly then dip in beaten egg and brown breadcrumbs. Fry until golden brown in hot fat or oil, takes about 5 minutes. Serve with butter.

Poaching

Clean and weigh the fish, then cook in a court bouillon liquor—instructions *see below*. Fish should be simmered in just enough liquid to cover. Large pieces of fish or whole fish are best cooked in a special fish kettle with a removable base, as the cooked fish is very fragile.

Salmon: here's how to cook a whole piece of salmon or salmon trout—a 2 lb. piece will serve 6 people. Wipe the fish and place on the tray of the fish kettle or in a large saucepan. Cover with cold water and add the ingredients for a court bouillon. Cover the pan tightly with a lid and bring slowly to the boil. Simmer for 3 minutes, then remove from heat and take off lid. Leave fish in liquid for 10 minutes and serve hot. Or allow to cool in liquid, serve cold.

Salmon cutlets: place the cutlets in a large shallow pan—a frying pan with a lid will do. Cover with cold water and add the ingredients for a court bouillon. Cover with a lid, bring slowly to the boil. Draw the pan off the heat, remove the lid and leave in the cooking liquid for 1 minute. Then drain and serve with a hot parsley sauce, *see page 102*.

Mackerel or trout: prepare the fish and clean out the insides. Place in a large saucepan or fish kettle and cover with cold water and ingredients for court bouillon. Bring slowly to the boil and simmer mackerel gently for 10 minutes, trout for 5–10 minutes. The fish is cooked when the flesh comes away from the bone. Serve mackerel with hot parsley sauce and trout with hot hollandaise sauce, *see page 106*.

Court bouillon

YOU WILL NEED:

½ pint water
rind and juice ½ lemon
1 small bay leaf
2 peppercorns
sprig parsley
½ level teaspoon salt
1 small onion, peeled and sliced

Bring all ingredients for court bouillon to the boil. Cover with a lid, simmer for 10 minutes and then strain liquid over fish to be cooked. Alternatively put the fish in cold water, add the other ingredients and bring to the boil.

Sweet spiced herrings

YOU WILL NEED FOR 4 SERVINGS:

4 fresh herrings
salt and pepper
¼ pint tarragon vinegar
¼ pint water
1 bay leaf
1 oz. (or 1 rounded tablespoon) brown sugar
1 level teaspoon salt
2–3 cloves
few peppercorns
½ onion, sliced in rings

Remove scales, clean and bone the herrings. Cut off the tails and all fins except the back one. Sprinkle the flesh with salt and pepper and roll up from head to tail. Pack in a pie dish.
Meanwhile put vinegar, water, bay leaf, sugar, salt, cloves, peppercorns and onion into a saucepan. Bring to boil and simmer for 5 minutes.
Strain the liquid over the herrings, and cover with a buttered paper. Place in the centre of a moderate oven (355 deg. or Gas No. 4) and bake for 30 minutes. Remove from the heat and allow to cool in the liquor, then drain and serve. This dish is particularly nice if served with crisp, fresh lettuce and potato salad.

Stuffed herrings

YOU WILL NEED FOR 3 SERVINGS:

3 fresh herrings
salt and pepper
squeeze of lemon juice
½ oz. butter
FOR THE STUFFING:
1 oz. (2 heaped tablespoons) fresh breadcrumbs
2 heaped teaspoons parsley, finely chopped
pinch of mixed herbs
little grated lemon rind
1 tablespoon melted butter
little beaten egg to bind

Remove scales and wash the herrings. Cut off the heads and draw out the insides of the fish, including the roes. Then rinse out under cold running water, snip off the tails and fins with scissors.
Mix together the stuffing ingredients with a fork, adding enough egg to make it moist, and then season well; stuff the insides of the herrings, but not tightly because skin is thin.
Place in a buttered fireproof dish, sprinkle with salt and pepper and a squeeze of lemon juice. Dot with butter and cover with buttered grease-proof paper. Place in the centre of a moderate oven (355 deg. or Gas No. 4) and bake for 25–30 minutes. Serve with

boiled new potatoes and grilled tomatoes. Use this method also for cooking mackerel or trout.

Red mullet in a parcel

YOU WILL NEED FOR 3–4 SERVINGS:

1 red mullet (medium size)
salt and pepper
oil
1 tablespoon lemon juice
lemon slices and parsley to garnish

Remove scales and cut off the fins. Take out the eyes, but leave on the head and tail. Slit the fish along the base and remove the inside. Wash inside well and sprinkle it with salt and pepper.
Place fish in well-oiled greaseproof paper or foil, twisting ends securely. Set on a baking tray and place in the centre of a moderately hot oven (355 deg. of Gas No. 4) and bake for 20 minutes. When cooked loosen the paper carefully and arrange the fish on a hot dish. Add the lemon juice to the liquid which has collected on the paper and pour this over the fish. Garnish with lemon and parsley and serve. Red Mullet is delicious served cold with mayonnaise. Use this method of cooking also for mackerel, trout or herrings.

Fresh trout with almonds

YOU WILL NEED FOR 4 SERVINGS:

4 fresh trout
1 oz. (or 1 rounded tablespoon) flour
1 level teaspoon salt
pinch pepper
2–3 oz. butter
1 lemon for serving
1–2 oz. toasted flaked almonds

Ask fishmonger to clean trout and remove heads. Sift flour, salt and pepper on to a plate. Roll trout one at a time in prepared seasoned flour and add to hot butter in a large frying pan.
Cook over moderate heat for about 5 minutes, turning them once. Lift trout out gently onto a hot serving platter. Add juice of half the lemon and the almonds to hot butter in pan; heat for a moment, then pour it over fish.
Serve with sliced remainder of lemon.

White fish

White fish does not have as much flavour as other types, so you must cook it carefully to preserve the maximum taste. To test if it is cooked, press the fish lightly at the thickest part or near the bone, and the flesh should come apart in flakes. Often it is served with a savoury sauce or parsley butter—this is made by beating some chopped parsley and lemon juice into a little butter.

Most white fish has been cleaned and filleted or cut in portions before being sold. When buying plaice or sole ask the fishmonger to fillet it.

Then you will need to skin each fillet of plaice before cooking. To do this, place the fillet, skin side downwards, on a board with the tail towards you. Loosen a piece of skin at the tail end. Dip your fingers in salt (gives a firm grip) and, holding the end of the skin down on the board, scrape the fish away, using a sharp knife held at an angle.

A sole is usually skinned before filleting and the fishmonger will do this for you. However to do it yourself, cut a slit across the tail on the dark side of the flesh. Work the skin up, using the thumb and forefingers, drawing the skin across to the centre of the fish from both left and right edges. Dip the fingers in salt, take hold of the skin at the tail end, and quickly draw it towards the head. Remove the white skin in the same manner. The fillets can be lifted away from the bone, using a sharp knife. Cut through the flesh down the backbone, ease off each fillet carefully.

Poaching

Use fillets cut in pieces, folded in half or curled up; or steaks cut from thicker fish such as cod, turbot or halibut. Prepare and season the fish, place in a buttered dish and add enough milk to cover the base of the dish. Cover with a lid or buttered greaseproof paper and bake in the centre of a moderate oven (355 deg. or Gas No. 4) for 15–20 minutes.

Sole in saffron rice

YOU WILL NEED FOR 4 SERVINGS:

4 fillets of sole
¼ pint milk
pinch of saffron
8 oz. long grain rice
pinch paprika pepper

FOR THE SAUCE:
1 oz. butter
1 oz. (or 1 rounded tablespoon) flour
½ pint mixed fish liquor and milk (see recipe)
salt and pepper
1 egg yolk
juice of 1 lemon
1½ teaspoons sugar

Season the fillets, roll up and place in a buttered pie dish. Pour ¼ pint milk around the fish. Cover with a lid or buttered greaseproof paper and place in the centre of a moderate oven (355 deg. or Gas No. 4) and bake for 15–20 minutes. Drain the fish, reserving the liquid for the sauce, but keep the fish hot.

To make the sauce: melt butter in a saucepan over low heat and stir in flour. Gradually stir in the fish cooking liquid made up to ½ pint with fresh milk, beating well to get a smooth sauce. Bring to the boil and cook for 2–3 minutes.

Draw the pan off the heat, season well with salt and pepper, and stir in the egg yolk, lemon juice and sugar.

Meanwhile, add a pinch of saffron to boiling salted water and cook the rice for 10 minutes. Drain and serve the fish on the hot rice and pour over both the lemon sauce. Sprinkle with a little paprika pepper.

Baking

Prepare the fish, removing the skin from fillets, and snipping off the fins from steaks. Fillets may be spread with stuffing and then rolled up or folded in half. Steaks should have the centre bone snipped out and the hole stuffed. Whole plaice are nice with the fillets lifted on either side of the backbone, to make pockets which are then stuffed. The stuffing in the following recipe can be adapted for any of these.

Whether plain or stuffed, the fish should be placed in a buttered baking dish, seasoned with salt and pepper and dotted with butter. Then cover it with buttered greaseproof paper and bake in a moderate oven (355 deg. or Gas No. 4) for 15–20 minutes.

Serve the fish with a savoury sauce or parsley butter.

Deep-fried fish and sole in saffron rice

Stuffed cod steaks

YOU WILL NEED FOR 3 SERVINGS:

3 tail-end cutlets of cod
salt and pepper
½ pint well-seasoned white sauce
chopped parsley
FOR THE STUFFING:
1 oz. butter
4 oz. button mushrooms
1 heaped tablespoon fresh white breadcrumbs
1 dessertspoon chopped parsley
pinch of mixed herbs

First prepare the stuffing. Melt the butter and add half the button mushrooms, finely chopped, and fry gently for 2–3 minutes.

Mix together the breadcrumbs, parsley, and mixed herbs. Add the cooked mushrooms and the hot butter, and blend with a fork to a moist, crumbly consistency. Rinse the 3 cod cutlets, and snip away the fins. Using a pair of kitchen scissors, snip out the centre bone from each cutlet. Place the fish in a buttered baking tray and pack the cavity in each with the mushroom stuffing. Sprinkle with salt and pepper, dot with butter, and cover with a buttered paper. Bake in the centre of a moderate oven (355 deg. or Gas No. 4) for 15–20 minutes.

Drain on to a hot serving dish and coat with hot, well-seasoned white sauce, to which the rest of the mushrooms, sliced and sautéed, have been added. Sprinkle with chopped parsley and serve.

Grilling

Fish with a delicate flavour such as sole or halibut give good results. Plainer fish are best soaked in a marinade before cooking.

Heat the grill and grease the grid or rack with melted butter or oil. Or remove rack and cover base of grill pan with buttered kitchen foil. Clean and prepare the fish—sole or plaice are usually grilled whole; halibut, cod or turbot in steaks. Sprinkle with salt and pepper and brush with melted butter or oil. Place under the grill at least 3 in. away from the heat.

Grill the fish for 2 minutes under high heat on both sides, then lower to medium heat for remaining time—a total of 10–12 minutes, according to thickness.

Serve immediately with melted or parsley butter, or tartare sauce, *see page 106*.

Marinade for fish

YOU WILL NEED:

6 tablespoons vegetable oil
3 tablespoons vinegar
1 tablespoon chopped parsley
1 level teaspoon salt
½ level teaspoon pepper
juice of 1 lemon
½ onion, finely chopped

Combine the ingredients, pour into a shallow dish and add the fish steaks. Leave to soak for 2–4 hours, turning occasionally. Drain off liquid, cook fish.

Frying

Before frying in shallow fat, white fish should be given a protective coating. This helps to make the cooked fish easier to handle, gives a nicer appearance and crisp outer texture. Fillets of plaice or cod, the latter cut in small pieces, and fish steaks, are suitable. Prepare the fish, if liked soak in a marinade *(see above)* and dip in beaten egg, then drain and coat in browned breadcrumbs. Pat the coating on firmly. Fry in hot fat or lard over moderate heat, turning once, until golden brown. Drain thoroughly and serve with lemon wedges and tomato sauce, *see page 103*, or parsley butter.

Fish to be deep fried is best if cut in pieces not too thick or large. Best are cod or haddock fillets cut into medium-sized portions.

Beaten egg and breadcrumbs can be used but the nicest coating is a batter, particularly a yeast batter which stays light and crisp after cooking. Prepare the fish and then dip first in flour and then in batter *(recipe below)*. Fry until light and golden brown— takes 5–6 minutes. Drain on absorbent paper and serve with a wedge of lemon and tomato or tartare sauce, *see pages 103, 106*.

Fried fish in yeast batter

YOU WILL NEED FOR 4 SERVINGS:

¾ lb. cod or fresh haddock fillets
fat for deep frying
lemon and parsley to garnish
½ pint tomato sauce to serve *(see page 103)*
FOR THE BATTER:
4 oz. (or 4 rounded tablespoons) flour
¼ level teaspoon salt
½ oz. fresh (1 level teaspoon dried) yeast
½ level teaspoon sugar
¼ pint milk

To prepare the batter, sift together the flour and salt into a mixing basin and set in a warm place. Cream fresh yeast with the sugar and stir in the warm milk (or sprinkle dried yeast over warm sugar and milk, leave until dissolved, about 5 minutes). Pour this yeast liquid into the centre of the flour and mix with a wooden spoon until all the flour has been worked in. Beat slightly, then cover with a cloth and leave in a warm place for 30 minutes. Beat slightly again, add a little more warm milk or water if necessary—the batter should be of a thick coating consistency.

Meanwhile wash, wipe and skin the fish fillets. Cut into small, thick pieces, allowing about 2 portions to each person. Coat the fish lightly in flour, then more thickly in batter, and fry in hot, deep fat. Drain, and garnish with parsley and slices of lemon. Serve with a hot tomato sauce.

Baked haddock in cider

YOU WILL NEED FOR 4 SERVINGS:

1 tail end piece of fresh haddock—about 3 lb.
salt and pepper
1 lemon
1 onion, finely chopped
1 clove garlic, crushed and chopped
1 tablespoon olive oil
½ pint water
1 glass dry cider or white wine
1 tablespoon chopped parsley
½ lb. tomatoes, sliced

Place the haddock in a baking dish, sprinkle with salt and pepper and the juice of half the lemon. Fry the onion and garlic in the oil until tender—about 5 minutes—then stir in the water and simmer for 5 minutes. Pour over the fish and add the white wine or cider, remaining lemon cut in slices, chopped parsley and tomatoes.

Place in the centre of a moderate oven (355 deg. or Gas No. 4) and bake for 45 minutes.

Skate with caper sauce

YOU WILL NEED FOR 4 SERVINGS:

about 2 lb. wing of skate
court bouillon—*see page 26*
FOR THE CAPER SAUCE:
2 oz. butter
juice of ½ lemon
1 tablespoon capers
1 tablespoon finely chopped parsley

Rinse the skate, cut into suitable sized pieces, and place in a saucepan. Measure the ingredients for court bouillon into a second saucepan and bring to the boil. Simmer covered with a lid for 10 minutes, then strain over the skate.

Bring slowly to the boil, cover with a lid and poach for 15–20 minutes. Drain from the hot liquid and arrange on a warm serving plate.

Meanwhile melt the butter, draw the pan off the heat and add the lemon juice, capers and parsley. Pour over the fish and serve.

Devilled grill

YOU WILL NEED FOR 4 SERVINGS:

4 cod cutlets
1 oz. margarine
1 level teaspoon chutney (chop any large pieces)
1 level teaspoon curry powder
1 level teaspoon dry mustard
1 teaspoon anchovy essence (optional)
salt and pepper to taste

Snip the bone away from the centre of the cutlets and cut away any fins. Place on a greased grid in the grill pan. Cook one side only for 3 minutes under a hot grill without turning. Meanwhile, cream the margarine and beat in the other ingredients to make a stiff paste. Turn the fish over and spread the uncooked side with the devilled mixture. Return to the grill and cook under medium heat for 7–10 minutes, until the fish is cooked through. Serve at once.

Best times to buy

Bream	July to December
Cod	October to March
Haddock—fresh	October to January
Hake	June to January
Halibut	June to April
Plaice	June to December
Skate	November to April
Sole	November to March
Whiting	October to March

Shellfish

Quick freezing means that shellfish is available all year round. Make sure the pack is solidly frozen and doesn't show signs of shrinking or dehydration. Allow cooked frozen shellfish to thaw out naturally, then use quickly. Otherwise cook as soon as the pieces can be separated. Be guided by the manufacturers' instructions about the length of time your refrigerator will keep deep frozen foods—usually it is overnight in the body of the fridge or between 1 week or 3 months in the frozen food compartment, depending upon the star marking.

Shrimps are sold by the pint. When picked (or shelled) 1 pint yields about $3\frac{1}{2}$–4 oz. edible shrimps. Because of their small size shrimps are usually shelled and eaten with lemon and brown bread and butter—or potted and served on toast. Allow $1\frac{1}{2}$–2 oz. prepared shrimps per person, or $\frac{1}{4}$–$\frac{1}{2}$ pint each in their shells.

Prawns are also sold by the pint. When picked, 1 pint yields about 3 oz. edible prawns. Allow $1\frac{1}{2}$–2 oz. prepared prawns per person in a recipe, or buy 1–$1\frac{1}{2}$ pints fresh prawns for 2–3 servings. Although often served plain, they are excellent in recipes—remove the dark vein from the back before using.

Dublin Bay prawns or scampi: these are usually sold by weight. Scampi are the tail ends of Dublin Bay prawns. To prepare, break the shells open from underneath and remove the flesh in one piece. Allow about 3–4 oz. prepared scampi per person—they are particularly delicious deep fried.

Lobster: best weight is 1–$1\frac{1}{2}$ lb., which gives two servings. They are sold whole or in halves. To serve, remove the claws by giving them a sharp twist, crack open and remove the meat. Lift out the tail flesh from the lobster halves, wash the shells and discard dead men's fingers and stomach found in the head section. Replace the sliced flesh in the cleaned shells and serve with a green salad tossed in a French dressing, and thinly sliced brown bread and butter.

Crab: these come in varying sizes. Cock crabs are the best buy—be guided by the narrow tail flap underneath. For four servings buy a young crab about 2–$2\frac{1}{2}$ lb. With advance notice your fishmonger will dress the crab for you.

Scallops: the fishmonger will open the scallops for you and remove the beard. Ask him to let you have the deep half of the shell—it makes a useful and pretty serving dish. Allow one large or two small scallops per person. Loosen the scallops from the shell with a knife, wash and then poach gently in milk for 15–20 minutes. Serve in a white or cheese sauce, *see pages 100, 102*, in the deep scallop shell.

Mussels: allow 1 quart of mussels for two servings. Discard any with broken shells. If some are open, tap sharply with another mussel, they will close up quickly if alive; discard any that still remain open. Scrub the mussels and, using a knife, pull away the 'beard'. Wash them in several waters—best way is to cover them with water, shake pan vigorously, then pour away and re-cover with fresh water. Repeat until the water remains clear. It's important to clean mussels well to remove all traces of sand or grit.

Oyster: the only shellfish that are eaten raw—so they must be absolutely fresh. Order them specially from fishmonger and ask him to open them for you. Allow about six per person and serve on crushed ice, with lemon wedges, freshly ground black pepper and thinly sliced brown bread and butter.

Crab and rice

YOU WILL NEED FOR 4 SERVINGS:

1 oz. butter
1 small onion, finely chopped
1 small green pepper, shredded
1 (15 oz.) tin tomatoes
1 teaspoon salt
pinch of pepper
1 level teaspoon sugar
$\frac{1}{2}$ level teaspoon Worcestershire sauce
1 bay leaf
8 oz. long grain rice
6–8 oz. white crab meat
2 oz. grated Parmesan cheese

Melt butter in a saucepan over moderate heat, and sauté onion and green pepper 2–3 minutes to soften. Add tomatoes, salt and pepper, sugar, Worcestershire sauce and bay leaf. Add lid and simmer gently for 10 minutes.
Meanwhile, put rice in plenty of boiling water and cook for 10 minutes. Drain well and add to tomato mixture with crab meat and extra seasoning if necessary. Spoon into a casserole or baking dish, and sprinkle with Parmesan cheese. Place near the top of a hot oven (375 deg. or Gas No. 5) and bake for 15–20 minutes or until bubbling and brown.

Lobster mayonnaise

Fried scampi

YOU WILL NEED FOR 4 SERVINGS:

1 lb. prepared scampi
fat for deep frying
FOR THE BATTER:
2 oz. plain flour
pinch of salt
1 dessertspoon oil
4 tablespoons water
1 egg white

Sift flour into a bowl with salt, make a well in the centre, add oil and gradually stir in water, beating well. Beat the egg white stiffly and fold it in. Dip scampi in batter to coat evenly, and fry in deep fat until golden brown, about 3 minutes. Remove from fat and drain.
Serve piled in a serving dish with tartare sauce, *see page 106*, and lemon wedges.

Potted prawns

YOU WILL NEED FOR 8 SERVINGS:

5 oz. butter
¾ lb. peeled prawns
freshly ground black pepper
salt
pinch of cayenne pepper
nutmeg
lettuce leaves and cucumber slices

Heat butter in a small pan, add prawns and seasoning to taste and mix well together. Pour into small pots and leave to set. Turn out on lettuce and garnish with cucumber. Serve brown bread or toast separately.

Scampi Americaine

YOU WILL NEED FOR 4 SERVINGS:

1 lb. prepared scampi
8 oz. long grain rice
1 tablespoon parsley, finely chopped
1 oz. butter

FOR THE SAUCE:
2 oz. butter
1 small onion, finely chopped
1 (15 oz.) tin tomatoes
1 wine glass white wine
pinch of pepper
½ level teaspoon salt
1 rounded tablespoon flour

First prepare the sauce. Melt half the butter in a medium saucepan, and gently sauté onion until soft. Stir in tomatoes, wine and seasoning, then simmer gently, covered with a lid, for 10 minutes. Cream remaining butter and flour and add to the sauce. Bring to the boil, stirring well. Add scampi and simmer until heated.
Meanwhile, cook rice in plenty of boiling salted water for 10 minutes or until soft. Drain and toss with parsley and butter. Press firmly into a buttered ring mould (6–7 in. diameter holds about 1 pint), then turn on to a heated serving dish. Spoon scampi mixture into the centre. Rice may be served loose if preferred.

Lobster mayonnaise

YOU WILL NEED FOR 2 SERVINGS:

1 cooked lobster, cut in two halves
salt and cayenne pepper
lemon juice
½ small head of lettuce
2–3 tablespoons mayonnaise
½ cucumber, sliced
1 hard-boiled egg

Crack open the lobster claws and remove meat from them and the tail. Cut the flesh into small pieces or shred coarsely. Discard the dead men's fingers and stomach found in the head section, wash shells out thoroughly and dry. Toss meat with salt, pepper and lemon juice to taste and set aside to marinate.
Wash lettuce leaves and arrange on a serving platter. Blend lobster meat with the mayonnaise and spoon back into the shell halves. Arrange on the platter and garnish with cucumber slices and hard-boiled egg slices.

Creamed lobster

YOU WILL NEED FOR 3–4 SERVINGS:

8 oz. cooked lobster meat
½ pint thick white sauce
2 tablespoons double cream
1–2 tablespoons sherry
salt, pepper and cayenne pepper

FOR THE TOPPING:
1 oz. butter
2 heaped tablespoons fresh white breadcrumbs

If using fresh lobster, prepare as directed above, add to the white sauce in a small pan and heat gently. Stir in cream and sherry, season to taste and, when thoroughly hot, pour into 3–4 individual buttered ramekin dishes. To make the topping, melt butter in a saucepan, draw off heat and, with a fork, stir in breadcrumbs. Spoon on to lobster and brown under grill.

Moules Marinière

YOU WILL NEED FOR 4 SERVINGS:

2 quarts mussels
1 small onion, peeled and finely chopped
3–4 tablespoons dry white wine or milk
1 oz. butter
1 level teaspoon flour
chopped parsley for garnish

Wash and clean mussels as page 32. With a buttered paper thoroughly grease the inside of a large saucepan. Sprinkle with chopped onion, and add wine or milk. Place all the mussels in the pan at once, and cover with a lid.
Place over a high heat and shake the pan for 3–5 minutes until mussels have opened. Draw off heat and drain mussels from the pan. Discard one shell from each. Place in a serving dish.
Cream butter and flour together and stir into the liquid in the pan. Stir over low heat until thickened and boiling. Add chopped parsley and pour over the mussels.
Serve at once, with pepper and brown bread and butter.

Scallops in the shell

YOU WILL NEED FOR 4 SERVINGS:

4 large scallops
2 oz. mushrooms, trimmed and sliced
½ pint water
1 wine glass dry cider
1 lemon, sliced
1 bay leaf
1 lb. potatoes, boiled and mashed with seasoning
chopped parsley for garnish
FOR THE SAUCE:
1 oz. butter
1 level tablespoon flour
⅓ pint (or 1 teacup) cooking liquid
salt and pepper
2 tablespoons cream

Cut each prepared scallop into six or eight pieces and place in a saucepan along with the mushrooms, water, cider, lemon and bay leaf. Bring to the boil,

lower the heat and simmer gently for 15–20 minutes. Strain and reserve ⅓ pint (or 1 teacup) of the cooking liquid for the sauce. Discard the lemon slices and the bay leaf. For the sauce: melt the butter in a small saucepan over a low heat. Stir in the flour and then cook gently for 1 minute. Gradually stir in the cooking liquid, beating well all the time to get a smooth sauce. Bring to the boil and simmer gently for 2–3 minutes.
Now add the mushrooms and scallops and season well with salt and pepper. Reheat gently then draw off heat and stir in the cream.
Pipe a border of mashed potato round the edges of four scallop shells; pile the hot fish mixture in the shells and sprinkle with chopped parsley to garnish.

Iced prawn curry

YOU WILL NEED FOR 4 SERVINGS:

8 oz. prepared prawns
8 oz. cooked long grain rice for serving
1 hard-boiled egg
parsley
FOR THE SAUCE:
1 small onion, finely chopped
1 oz. butter
1 level teaspoon flour
2 level tablespoons curry powder
1 small (8 oz.) tin peeled tomatoes
½ level teaspoon salt
1 level teaspoon sugar
1 tablespoon sweet mango chutney
¼ pint mayonnaise
dash of tabasco sauce
2 tablespoons single cream
juice of ½ a lemon

Gently sauté onion in butter until soft. Stir in flour and curry powder. Then stir in tomatoes, salt, sugar and chutney and bring to the boil. Cover with a lid and simmer for 30 minutes.
Draw the pan off the heat and pass curry sauce through a sieve. Blend with mayonnaise, add tabasco sauce, cream and lemon juice. Chill until ready to serve then stir in the prepared prawns or shrimps. Spoon it over boiled rice, cooked and tossed in French dressing (¼ teaspoon each salt, pepper, mustard, 1 tablespoon each vinegar and water, 3 tablespoons salad oil—shake in screw-topped jar) and garnish with hard-boiled egg and parsley.
(See illustration on page 37)

Chilled fish dishes

The delicate flavour of white fish and shellfish is emphasised when they are served cold. These fish are usually pale, so add a touch of colour in the garnish and serve with a crisp green salad. Fish in lemon aspic jelly is particularly delicious; you can use the jelly as a glaze or set the fish in it in an attractive mould. The jelly should be used when cold and almost on the point of setting.

Lemon aspic jelly

YOU WILL NEED FOR ½ PINT:

¼ pint cold water
½ oz. (or 1 rounded tablespoon) powdered gelatine
1 tablespoon lemon juice
1 tablespoon vinegar (tarragon or wine)
1 tablespoon sugar
½ level teaspoon salt

Measure water into a saucepan and sprinkle gelatine powder on top. Leave to soak for 5 minutes. Then warm over very low heat and stir until gelatine is dissolved *but do not boil.*
Draw pan off heat, add lemon juice, vinegar, sugar and salt. Cool and use as directed in recipes. If the jelly sets before you can use it, stir over hot water and it will liquefy.

Glazed plaice fillets

YOU WILL NEED FOR 4 SERVINGS:

6–8 plaice fillets
milk
aspic mayonnaise (as for Salmon in aspic)
prawns
chopped parsley
lemon aspic jelly

Skin plaice fillets, season on both sides and roll up. Secure each with a cocktail stick and poach gently in milk in the centre of a moderate oven (355 deg. or gas No. 4) for 15–20 minutes. Drain and cool.
Coat with aspic mayonnaise as for Salmon in aspic. Garnish with prawns and parsley, both dipped in lemon aspic jelly, and leave to set firm. Spoon over remaining jelly.

From the top clockwise: glazed plaice fillets, salmon loaf, crab mousse, iced prawn curry, shellfish cocktails and salmon pâté

Salmon in aspic

YOU WILL NEED FOR 4 SERVINGS:

1½ lb. fresh salmon or 4 salmon cutlets
1 teaspoon salt
lemon slices
peppercorns
1 bay leaf
lemon aspic jelly *(see page 36)*
3–4 tablespoons mayonnaise *(see page 106)*
red pimento
thinly sliced radish
carrot
cucumber or tomato

Place salmon in cold water to cover, add 1 teaspoon salt, slices of lemon, peppercorns and bay leaf. Cover with a lid, bring slowly to the boil, and simmer the large piece for 3 minutes or the cutlets for 1 minute. Draw pan off heat and let fish cool. Drain fish and remove bones and skin (if using a whole piece of salmon divide into 4 equal portions). Arrange the pieces ready for coating on a wire cooling tray—catch drips on a plate.
Blend equal quantities of lemon aspic jelly and mayonnaise. Stir over ice-cold water until mixture begins to thicken. Spoon the mayonnaise over the salmon pieces, coating 2–3 times to get a smooth surface. Leave to set firm. Arrange a decoration of vegetable pieces on each portion of fish, spoon over a little more aspic jelly and allow this also to set firm. Then spoon on top the remaining almost set jelly and leave in a cool place to set.
Serve on lettuce or chopped aspic jelly with potato and green salads.

Jellied salmon loaf

YOU WILL NEED FOR 4–6 SERVINGS:

1 envelope (or 1 rounded tablespoon) powdered gelatine
¼ pint cold water
juice of ½ a lemon
1 (1 lb.) tin red salmon
8 oz. carton cottage cheese
¼ pint mayonnaise
1 green pepper, finely chopped
2 tablespoons finely chopped chives or parsley
1 level teaspoon salt
pinch of cayenne pepper
½ cucumber, sliced, for garnish

Sprinkle gelatine on cold water in a pan and leave for 5 minutes. Warm over very low heat, stirring until melted but do *not* allow mixture to boil. Draw off heat and add lemon juice. Set aside to cool.
Combine together salmon (removing any skin and bones), cottage cheese, and mayonnaise. Add green

pepper, chives or parsley and seasoning. Pour 2–3 tablespoons of the aspic jelly into a wet loaf tin, garnish with slices of cucumber, and chill until set. Blend the remaining jelly mixture with salmon and spoon it into the mould.
Chill for several hours until firm. Then serve sliced with green salad.

Crab mousse

YOU WILL NEED FOR 4 SERVINGS:

8 oz. fresh or tinned crab meat
6 oz. cream cheese
¼ pint mayonnaise
pinch of salt and pepper
½ cucumber peeled and chopped
lemon aspic jelly *(see recipe)*

Flake crab meat, removing any sinews. Set aside about 2 tablespoons.
Blend cream cheese until soft, then gradually beat in mayonnaise. Add salt, pepper, cucumber and crab meat (except that reserved for decoration). Spoon a little of the lemon aspic jelly into the reserved crab meat and blend the remainder with the mayonnaise mixture. Spoon into a china soufflé or serving dish and chill until firm.
Carefully spoon over the reserved crab meat (if this has set, stir over warm water to soften). Chill for several hours until firm. Serve with green salad, sliced tomato and brown bread and butter.

Salmon pâté

YOU WILL NEED FOR 6–8 PORTIONS:

1 lb. fresh or tinned salmon
3 tablespoons dry sherry
1 lb. white fish
2 oz. fresh white breadcrumbs
1 oz. butter, melted
1 level teaspoon salt
¼ level teaspoon pepper
pinch of cayenne pepper
juice of 1 lemon
1 egg yolk

Remove skin and bone and soak salmon in sherry for 2–3 hours, turning the pieces occasionally.
Skin the white fish and mince it and salmon finely then blend the two together. Add the white breadcrumbs, butter, salt, pepper, lemon juice and egg yolk. Beat well to blend and then pack into a buttered baking dish. Cover with foil, and place in the centre of a moderate oven (355 deg. or Gas No. 4) and bake for 1 hour. Remove from heat, weight the top and leave overnight. Serve sliced with toast, lettuce and tomato.

Halibut mayonnaise

YOU WILL NEED FOR 4 SERVINGS:

    4 small cutlets halibut
    aspic mayonnaise (as for Salmon in aspic)
    slices of cucumber
    chopped parsley
    aspic jelly

Poach small cutlets of halibut for 10 minutes as for salmon cutlets, *see page 26*, and leave to cool in the cooking liquor. Remove the skin and coat as before with aspic mayonnaise. Garnish with slices of cucumber and chopped parsley before finally glazing with clear aspic jelly. Cutlets of cod may be prepared in the same manner.

Shellfish cocktails

YOU WILL NEED FOR 4 SERVINGS:

    8 oz. prepared prawns, lobster or crab meat
    1 small lettuce
    cucumber for garnish
    FOR THE COCKTAIL SAUCE:
    2 tablespoons mayonnaise
    2 tablespoons tomato ketchup
    1–2 tablespoons thick cream
    dash of tabasco sauce
    1 teaspoon Worcestershire sauce
    squeeze of lemon juice

Blend all sauce ingredients together and fold in the prepared shellfish. Wash and finely shred lettuce and place in four individual glass dishes.
Pile the cocktail mixture on top and garnish with slices of cucumber (and a prawn if liked) slotted on to the rim of the glass.

Quick summer lunches

Smoked cod's roe

YOU WILL NEED FOR 4 SERVINGS:

    6–8 oz. smoked cod's roe
    1–2 tablespoons cream
    1 tablespoon lemon juice
    salt
    pepper
    hot buttered toast
    lettuce
    tomato

Measure the smoked cod's roe into a bowl—scoop the centre from the outer skin. Add lightly whipped

cream, and lemon juice. Blend well, adjust ingredients if necessary to make a spreadable mixture. Season with salt and pepper and pile on rounds of hot buttered toast. Serve garnished with lettuce and tomato.

Stuffed tomatoes

YOU WILL NEED FOR 3–4 SERVINGS:

    6–8 large tomatoes
    1 (7 oz.) tin crab meat
    2 chopped hard-boiled eggs
    2–3 tablespoons white sauce
    1 tablespoon cream

Wash the tomatoes, cut off the tops and scoop out the insides. Flake the crab meat and mix it with 2 chopped hard-boiled eggs. Add the well-seasoned white sauce and cream. Fill the tomatoes and replace the lids. Serve the tomatoes on rounds of buttered toast.

Eggs stuffed with shrimps

YOU WILL NEED FOR 4 SERVINGS:

    4 eggs
    small tin shrimps
    ¼ pint white sauce
    shredded lettuce

Hard boil eggs and shell when cold. Cut in half lengthwise and remove the yolks. Strain the contents of tin of shrimps and chop coarsely, then add to well-seasoned white sauce. Spoon this filling back into the egg white. Sieve the egg yolk over the filling and serve the eggs on a base of shredded lettuce with French bread and butter.

Poached eggs with mayonnaise

YOU WILL NEED FOR 4 SERVINGS:

    4 eggs
    lettuce leaves
    ¼ pint well-seasoned white sauce
    2–3 tablespoons mayonnaise
    2 oz. chopped shrimps
    mustard and cress

Lightly poach eggs and leave to become quite cold. Place each egg on a large lettuce leaf. Cover with well-seasoned white sauce to which mayonnaise and prepared and chopped shrimps have been added. Garnish with mustard and cress and serve with hot toast fingers.

ALL ABOUT *Meat, Poultry & Game*

Cuts of meat

BEEF

Choosing for quality: Fat should be creamy in colour and the meat a light red. Look for small flecks of fat in the lean part of the meat— this is called marbling and helps bring flavour and tenderness to the cooked meat.

To refrigerate: Remove butchers wrappings. Place unwrapped meat either in the special meat chiller or rewrap loosely in waxed paper or foil and place on a plate under the ice compartment.

Large joints will keep 5 days, steaks 2–3 days, stewing meats, 1–2 days. Minced meat and liver 1 day, but preferably use the day it is bought.

Cuts of meat

Sirloin: Excellent joint for roasting and one of the most expensive because it includes part of the fillet.

Topside: Another good joint for roasting or it can be braised or pot roasted, with plenty of carrots and onions.

Fillet: The choice and most tender cut of beef— usually cut into steaks.

A selection of meat cuts

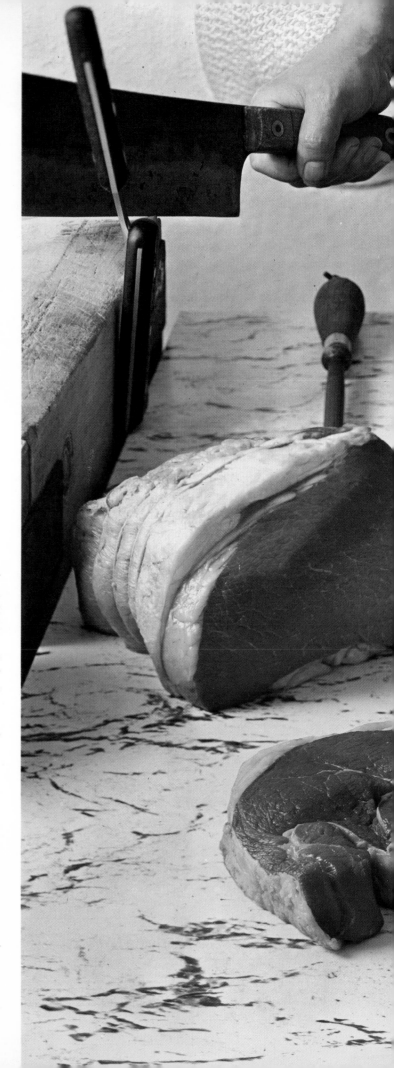

Rump: An excellent cut of meat, makes very good steaks for grilling. A good, but more expensive, choice for galantines, meat loaves or casseroles.

Brisket: A rather fatty joint, but is excellent fresh for braising or can be bought salted and then boiled.

Rib: A good joint for roasting, braising or pot roasts. Can be left on the bone or boned and rolled.

Skirt and flank: Both cheap cuts of meat. Can be used minced or cut up small and used in stews, casseroles and pies or any recipe where slow cooking is required.

Chuck or stewing steak: Both suitable for casseroling or stews, long slow cooking is required.

Shin of beef: A good cheap, lean cut, but has a coarse grain. Needs long slow cooking, good for stews or casseroles and excellent for soups.

Minced beef: Usually cheap cuts of meat minced. Can be fried or used for hamburgers or in meat sauces for pasta or meat loaves.

Cow heel or cheek: Both coarse and very gelatinous. Best used for making beef stock for soups.

Oxtail: Ask butcher to cut the tail into joints, make excellent casseroles or soups—needs long slow cooking. High proportion of bone and so allow about 10 oz. per serving.

Heart: A coarse part of the meat. Can be stuffed and then slowly roasted or braised.

Tongue: Usually salted and boiled then pressed and served cold.

Tripe: The inner lining of the stomach. Very tender and digestible—nicest stewed.

LAMB

Choosing for quality: Lamb is a little darker in colour than beef and the fat almost white in colour. If the meat has been frozen the fat can be rather brittle and crumbles easily.

To refrigerate: Remove butchers wrappings. Place unwrapped meat in the special meat chiller or rewrap loosely with waxed paper or foil and place on a plate under the ice compartment.
Joints will keep for 4 days, chops for 2–3 days, fillet or cuts for casseroling 1–2 days.

Cuts of meat

Leg: An excellent joint for roasting—nice rubbed over with dried rosemary first.

Shoulder: Also a good joint for roasting and can be boned and stuffed before cooking.

Fillet: An inexpensive cut which can be used for casseroles or pies.

Best end: Can be bought as a joint, boned stuffed rolled and roasted. Alternatively the joint cut can be cut up to make chops.

Loin and best end chops: Can be grilled or fried, nice in mixed grill.

Chump chops: Largest chops and slightly more expensive. They are leaner than ordinary chops and are better for frying.

Neck of lamb: Best for stewing, casseroling or hot pots.

PORK

Choosing for quality: Pork is available all year round. The meat should be a light pinky colour with a smooth skin. Fat should be firm and a milky white appearance.

To refrigerate: Remove butchers wrappings. Place unwrapped meat in the special meat chiller or rewrap loosely with waxed paper or foil and place on a plate under the ice compartment.
Large joints may be kept 4 days, pork chops 2–3 days, pork sausage meat and sliced liver 1 day, pork fillet 2–3 days.

Cuts of meat

Shoulder: Excellent joint for roasting, may be purchased with the bone or boned and rolled. Alternatively it can be boned and stuffed with sage and onion stuffing.

Leg: Another excellent joint for roasting. Rind should be well scored before cooking.

Loin: Can be scored and roasted as one joint.

Bladebone: A cheaper cut, nice boned, stuffed and then braised

Fillet: Sometimes called tenderloin. A very lean and delicious cut. Can be rolled and roasted, or sliced, beaten out flat and fried in butter.

Spareribs: Can be roasted with a spicy barbeque sauce or cut into chops and fried, grilled or casseroled.

Hand and spring: Should be boned and rolled and can be roasted or braised. Hand of pork is often salted and then boiled.

Belly: A very fatty cut, sometimes salted and boiled. Or if fresh, sliced and fried or rolled with stuffing and roasted.

VEAL

Choosing for quality: All dairy fed veal should have an external layer of thin creamy white fat. Veal is a young and very lean meat and should be a slight pink colour.

To refrigerate: Remove butchers wrappings. Place unwrapped meat in the special meat chiller or rewrap loosely with waxed paper or foil and place on a plate under the ice compartment.
Large joints may be kept 3–4 days, chops or escalopes 2 days, stewing or pie veal 1–2 days.

Cuts of meat

Fillet: A very expensive but delicious joint for roasting.

Escalopes: Thin slices of veal cut from the fillet, should be floured or egg and breadcrumbed and fried in butter.

Loin· Sold either with the bone or boned and rolled, excellent for roasting. Nice stuffed with herb stuffing.

Shoulder: Makes a good joint for roasting, can be boned, stuffed and rolled. Can also be used for fricassée, casseroles or pies.

Breast: A cheaper cut that is delicious boned, stuffed and roasted. Can also be pot-roasted or cut up and used in casseroles.

Best end of neck: Can be roasted or braised or cut up into cutlets for frying.

Middle and scrag end of neck: Cheaper cuts that are excellent for stews and casseroles.

Knuckle: Can be used for casseroles or for soup or boiled and the meat used for pie fillings.

Stuffings

These are used, not only to add a good flavour to a roast, but in many cases to keep meat moist and to give it a good shape—particularly in the case of poultry.
Always stuff a joint or bird just before cooking. If stuffing is to be prepared ahead, store in a basin covered with foil in a cool place, and stuff the bird when required. Pack stuffing loosely; it expands on cooking and would otherwise split the skin. Any extra stuffing can be baked in a separate pan beside the meat for the last hour of cooking.

Basic crumb stuffing

Into a large mixing basin measure 12 oz. (or 5 teacups) soft white breadcrumbs, 1½ level teaspoons dried thyme (or marjoram or mixed herbs), 3 level tablespoons chopped parsley, 1 teaspoon grated lemon rind, and a good pinch each of salt and pepper. Using a fork, stir in 3 oz. melted butter or margarine and 1 lightly beaten small egg.
Use the stuffing as required for any roast or poultry.

Apple stuffing

Peel, core and chop 2 or 3 mellow cooking or dessert apples and add to the basic crumb stuffing with 2 tablespoons chopped celery and 1 tablespoon seedless raisins.

Bacon stuffing

Trim and lightly fry ¼ lb. bacon rashers. Remove from pan and chop into small pieces. Add to the basic crumb stuffing ingredients with 1 onion, finely chopped.

Chestnut stuffing

YOU WILL NEED FOR 8–10 LB. TURKEY:

1 lb. chestnuts
about ½ pint stock or milk and water
1 oz. shredded beef suet
½ lb. sausage meat
2 oz. (or 4 heaped tablespoons) fresh white breadcrumbs
1 teaspoon chopped parsley
¼ teaspoon thyme, powdered
pepper
salt

Slit chestnuts on the flat side and roast in a hot oven (400 deg. or Gas No. 6) for 15 minutes. Then remove both the skins and place nuts in a saucepan with stock or milk and water.
Simmer the mixture gently until tender and then rub chestnuts through a sieve.
Add remaining ingredients to the sieved nuts and mix well. Use the mixture as needed to stuff the neck of the bird.

Stews and hot-pots

Stewing is one of the easiest and most economical methods of cooking meat. The ingredients are cooked slowly with a small amount of liquid in a pan or casserole, covered with a tight-fitting lid. Cooking can be done in the oven or on top of the stove—either way the meat should simmer gently for several hours, but never boil. Best buys are the coarser, cheaper cuts of meat, and add plenty of flavouring vegetables and herbs. The long, slow cooking makes the meat tender and succulent and draws out the delicious flavours from the ingredients. The new cast-iron and flame-proof casserole dishes are ideal for these recipes since they can be placed over a high heat for browning the meat and vegetables and then put into an oven to finish the cooking.

Best cuts to buy are:

Beef: chuck or buttock steak, skirt or shin, flank or oxtail.
Lamb: scrag end of neck or middle neck.
Pork: not really suitable
Veal: best end of neck, breast of veal, knuckle or pie veal.
Liver: pig's, lamb's or calves' liver.
Rabbit: most economical to buy pieces.

Old fashioned beef stew

YOU WILL NEED FOR 4 SERVINGS:

1½ lb. chuck or stewing steak
1 oz. lard or dripping
2–3 onions, peeled and sliced
1 lb. carrots, scraped and sliced
bouquet garni sprig of thyme, bay leaf and a few parsley
    stalks, tied together
1 rounded tablespoon flour
1 pint stock or water plus stock cube
salt and pepper

Discard extra fat and gristle and cut the meat into cubes. Fry in hot fat, turning until browned evenly on all sides. Remove from pan and place meat in a casserole dish with onions, carrots and bouquet garni. Stir flour into hot fat in the frying pan and cook until browned. Gradually add the hot stock, stirring well to make a smooth gravy; the gravy at this stage should be fairly thin. Season and add a little gravy browning, if liked, to get a good colour.

Draw pan off heat and strain into the casserole dish. Cover with a tight fitting lid and place in the centre of a slow oven (310 deg. or Gas No. 2). Cook for 2½–3 hours until meat and vegetables are quite tender. Remove bouquet garni and serve.

Rabbit stew

Follow previous recipe but use 1½–2 lb. rabbit pieces instead of chuck or stewing steak and cook for only 1½ hours.

Liver casserole with bacon dumplings

YOU WILL NEED FOR 4 SERVINGS:

1 lb. lambs' liver
seasoned flour
2 oz. butter or frying
6–8 carrots
1–2 stalks of celery
2 onions
½ level teaspoon mixed herbs
1 pint stock or water plus stock cube
FOR THE BACON DUMPLINGS:
4 oz. (or 4 rounded tablespoons) self-raising flour
1 level teaspoon grated lemon rind
2 oz. (or 2 rounded tablespoons) shredded suet
2 rashers of bacon, trimmed and chopped
3 tablespoons water
squeeze of lemon juice

Trim liver and remove any skin. Dip the slices in seasoned flour and brown lightly in hot butter. Chop carrots and celery finely, slice onions and add the herbs. Arrange the liver and prepared vegetables in layers in a casserole dish. Begin and end with a layer of vegetables.
Pour on the boiling stock. Cover with a lid and place in the centre of a moderate oven (355 deg. or Gas No. 4) and cook for 1½ hours.
Then prepare bacon dumplings. Sift flour into small basin, and add lemon rind, suet and bacon, and mix to a dough with the water and lemon juice.
Roll into 6–8 small balls. Add dumplings to the liver casserole, placing them on top of the nearly-cooked vegetables and meat. Do not submerge in the liquid. Cover dish again with a lid and continue simmering for the last 30 minutes.
Serve immediately.

Old-fashioned beef stew

Hamburger stew

YOU WILL NEED FOR 4 SERVINGS:

1 oz. butter or margarine
1 level tablespoon flour
½ pint stock or water plus stock cube
1 (15 oz.) tin tomatoes
2 tablespoons chopped parsley
FOR THE MEAT BALLS:
¾ lb. mince
½ onion, finely chopped
1 level teaspoon salt
¼ level teaspoon pepper
½ lightly beaten egg
seasoned flour

Mix the mince, onion, seasoning and beaten egg. Roll into 12 neat balls (if you lightly oil your fingers it makes it easier). Roll each in a little seasoned flour. Heat butter or margarine in a heavy pan and put in the meat balls. Cook gently for a few minutes, turning to brown them evenly. Put them in a casserole dish. Add flour to remaining fat in pan and stir over heat until beginning to brown. Add stock and stir gently until mixture has thickened and is boiling. Add tomatoes plus liquid from the tin. Pour mixture into the casserole. Cover with a lid and place in centre of moderate oven (355 deg. or Gas No. 4) and cook for 45–50 minutes or until bubbling hot. Serve sprinkled with parsley.

Country lamb casserole

YOU WILL NEED FOR 4 SERVINGS:

1½ lb. scrag end of neck of lamb
1 oz. lard or dripping
2 onions, peeled and sliced
1 oz. plain flour
1 pint hot stock or water plus stock cube
salt and pepper
4 potatoes, peeled and sliced
8 small carrots, scraped and cut in 1 in. slices
1 small turnip, peeled and cut in 1 in. slices
1 small packet frozen peas

Cut meat in pieces. Heat fat in saucepan or casserole and brown meat and onions in it. Drain meat and onion and stir in flour. Cook gently for a few moments until brown, then stir in hot stock and bring to boil. Stir well until smooth.
Replace meat and onions in gravy, and add plenty of seasoning. Cover with close-fitting lid and simmer gently for 1 hour, either on top of stove or in moderate oven (355 deg. or Gas No. 4).
Add prepared potatoes, carrots and turnip and cook a further 45 minutes. Add peas 5 minutes before serving.

Lancashire hot pot

YOU WILL NEED FOR 4 SERVINGS:

1 lb. scrag end or neck of lamb
½ lb. chuck or buttock steak
1–2 oz. seasoned flour
2 oz. lard or dripping
½–¾ lb. potatoes
6–8 carrots
1 large onion
1–2 stalks celery
¼ level teaspoon mixed herbs
1 level teaspoon salt
pinch of pepper
¾ pint stock or water plus stock cube
chopped parsley

Discard any excess fat, gristle and bone and cut meat into neat cubes. Roll in seasoned flour and brown lightly in hot fat.
Peel and slice potatoes, reserving about half of the neatest slices for the top. Arrange the remainder in the base of a casserole dish.
Peel and slice carrots, skin and slice onion. Wash, trim and slice celery. Toss these with the herbs and plenty of salt and pepper.
Arrange alternate layers of mixed vegetables and meat over the potato slices in the casserole. Top finally with reserved potatoes arranged neatly in layers. Pour in the stock.
Cover with greased paper then a lid and place in the centre of a moderate oven (355 deg. or Gas No. 4) and cook for 2–2¼ hours. Half an hour before serving, remove the lid and paper from the casserole. Brush potatoes with a little fat, sprinkle lightly with salt and brown in the oven. Sprinkle with chopped parsley.

Beef and lentil stew

YOU WILL NEED FOR 4 SERVINGS:

4 oz. lentils
1½ lb. stewing steak
1 oz. shortening
1 lb. onions. sliced
½ lb. carrots, scraped and sliced
1½ pints stock
3 level teaspoons salt
¼ teaspoon pepper

Soak the lentils overnight in cold water. Trim away any fat or gristle from the meat and cut meat into neat pieces. In the base of a stew pan or pressure cooker, sauté the onions in the hot fat for about 5 minutes until tender. Add the prepared meat and cook quickly to seal on all sides. Add the prepared carrots and the drained lentils, stir in the stock and seasoning. Cover and simmer for 2–2½ hours. If using a pressure cooker cover and place over a high heat. Allow ingredients to come up to the boil and steam until a steady stream of air comes from the centre vent slowly and the air has been removed. Place on weights and bring up to 15 lb. pressure, lower heat sufficient to maintain the pressure and cook for 30 minutes. Reduce pressure rapidly under cold water and open the cooker. Serve with a green vegetable.

Chilli con carne

YOU WILL NEED FOR 4 SERVINGS:

1 lb. lean stewing steak
2 tablespoons oil
1 onion, sliced
1 clove garlic, crushed with salt
1 (15 oz.) tin tomatoes
¼ pint stock or water plus stock cube
1 level teaspoon chilli powder according
   to taste, mixed with 2 tablespoons water
¼ teaspoon salt
1 teaspoon sugar
1 (16 oz.) tin baked beans
8 oz. long grain rice

Trim away any fat or gristle and cut the meat into neat pieces. Heat the oil in a frying pan and fry the onion quickly. Add the chopped garlic and fry for a further few moments, then add the meat and allow to brown. Stir in the tomatoes, plus liquid from the tin, stock, blended chilli powder, salt, sugar and beans. Cover and simmer gently for 2½–3 hours until meat is tender.
About 15 minutes before serving add the rice to a large pan of boiling salted water and cook rapidly for 10 minutes until tender. Drain, and return the rice to the pan, for 2–3 minutes to steam dry. Spoon the rice around the edges of a hot serving dish and pour the chilli con carne into the centre.

Kidney stew

YOU WILL NEED FOR 4 SERVINGS:

6 lambs kidneys
½ lb. chipolata sausages
2 oz. butter or margarine
1 lb. button or small onions, peeled and left whole
1 level tablespoon flour
¾ pint stock or water plus stock cube
¼ pint red wine
1 (2½ oz.) tin tomato purée
salt and pepper
1 bay leaf
½ lb. small carrots, scraped and cut in 1-inch lengths
½ lb. mushrooms, trimmed and sliced
1 small packet frozen peas

Remove the skin from the kidneys, cut in half and snip out the core using scissors. Separate the sausages

and twist the ends in opposite directions to make smaller sausages. Snip in half and fry in the hot butter, along with the kidneys, until browned. Add the onions, and fry gently for a further 5 minutes. Lift all the contents from the pan, transfer to a casserole dish and set aside.
Stir the flour into the hot fat in the frying pan and cook gently stirring occasionally until browned. Stir in the stock, red wine and tomato purée. Season well with salt and pepper and strain over the contents of the casserole dish. Add the bay leaf, carrots and mushrooms, cover with a lid and place in the centre of a moderate oven (355 deg. or Gas No. 4). Cook for 1½ hours, then add the peas and cook for a further 10 minutes before serving.

Pressure cooking

This is an ideal method to use for cooking the less expensive cuts of meat. Cooking time is reduced considerably and results in a tender meat with a delicious, rich gravy. Always follow the instructions given with your cooker, the following are general: According to the recipe chosen, brown the meat in the hot fat in the base of the cooker, then add vegetables and liquid. Or, where the meat is not browned in the first instance, simply arrange it, and any vegetables on the base of the cooker and add the liquid. The amount of liquid required is determined by the length of cooking time, the minimum quantity to be used is ¼ pint of liquid for each ¼ hour of cooking time plus an extra ¼ pint. Take care never to fill more than half full of liquid. Fit the lid on the cooker and secure firmly. Place over a high heat until a steady stream of steam comes from the vent—this takes about 5 minutes.
Place the 15 lb. weight over the vent and continue to heat until the cooker begins to hiss. This shows that enough pressure has been built up.
Lower the heat until a steady pressure is maintained and *start timing*. When the cooking time is completed, according to instructions either cool rapidly by dipping the base of the cooker into cold water or allow to cool slowly. Then remove the lid but *never* before the pressure is back to normal.

Stews	Water or stock	Time at 15 lb. pressure
Beef	¾–1 pint	20 min.—cool rapidly
Veal	½–1 pint	12–20 min. for veal knuckles—cool rapidly
Rabbit	½–¾ pint	15 min.—cool rapidly
Lamb	½–¾ pint	15 min.—cool rapidly
Oxtail	1–1½ pint	45 min.—cool rapidly
Liver	½ pint	8 min.—cool rapidly

Frying and grilling

Grilling

Season the meat, as suggested, and brush all over with oil or melted fat. Light the grill, allow 2 minutes for heating up, then place meat under grill using the lower grill position. Cook each side for 1 minute to seal in the juices, then lower flame and continue to cook first on one side and then on the other. Baste occasionally with a little extra oil or butter or one of the special bastes (*see recipes, page 50*).

Sometimes a tablespoon of oil in the base of the grill pan helps prevent the dripping burning and avoids lots of unpleasant smoke and smell.

Steak: A steak may be cooked 'rare'—that is under-cooked with the meat still very pink in the middle; or 'medium'—just a little pink; or 'well done'—cooked right through. For fillet steak—7–12 minutes according to thickness and individual tastes. A rare steak takes only 3–4 minutes. For rump steak 10–15 minutes according to thickness and taste.

Lamb Chops: 12–14 minutes.
Chicken Joints: 20–25 minutes.
Kidneys: 6–8 minutes
Sausages: 15 minutes.

Frying and grilling are two simple and quick methods of cooking lean, good quality cuts of meat. The meat is cooked first at a high heat to seal it, then the temperature is lowered to allow the meat to cook evenly. The accompaniments are important—serve flavoured butters with any grilled or fried meats (*see recipes below*), horseradish sauce with beef or sausages, mustard baste with chicken, redcurrant jelly with lamb, lemon with veal and apple sauce with pork.

Preparation of suitable meats

Steak: Any good quality steak; choose from rump, fillet or thin minute steaks. Trim the meat, removing any excess fat and cut rump steak into suitably sized portions. Season with salt and freshly ground black pepper.

Lamb: Best end of neck cutlets, loin or chump chops. Trim fat neatly away at the top of the bone. Garnish with a cutlet frill just before serving. Season with salt and pepper or a little dry mustard or a sprinkling of ground cinnamon.

Pork: Loin chops and pork tenderloin, sometimes called fillet. Use a small knife to cut the fat at $\frac{1}{2}$ in. intervals on pork chops—it helps to prevent buckling while cooking. Cut tenderloin halfway through lengthwise, then lay flat and cut into suitably sized portions. Coat with flour, egg and breadcrumbs before cooking. Season with salt and Jamaica pepper or a pinch of sage.

Veal: Loin chops and escalopes—a thin slice cut from the fillet. Trim chops (as for lamb) and flatten escalopes, using a rolling pin with the meat placed between two sheets of wetted grease-poof paper. Season with salt or seasoning salt, and pepper.

Chicken: Small joints or halved spring chickens. It is not necessary to remove the skin from chicken joints before cooking, simply trim away any loose pieces. Season with salt, pepper and a pinch of thyme, rosemary or ground ginger.

Lambs kidneys, either calves or lambs liver and sausages: Kidneys should be cut in half, skinned and cored. Snip away any tubes from liver slices and remove the skin from the edges. Do not prick the sausages—this only allows juice to escape. Sprinkle kidneys with salt; sausages need no extra seasoning.

Hamburger mixed grill

YOU WILL NEED FOR 4 SERVINGS:

1 lb. minced beef
1 level teaspoon salt
$\frac{1}{2}$ level teaspoon pepper
pinch of sage or thyme, optional
1 onion coarsely grated
1 heaped tablespoon fresh white breadcrumbs
1 small lightly mixed egg
2–3 tablespoons oil or dripping for frying
FOR THE MIXED GRILL:
4 chipolata sausages
4 mushrooms
4 bacon rashers, trimmed

Place mince, seasoning, herbs, if used, onion and breadcrumbs in a large mixing bowl. Add egg and mix ingredients together using a fork. Mixture should be soft but not sticky and should cling together when lightly pressed into shape. Divide mixture into 8 equal portions and shape into a flat patty about $\frac{1}{2}$ in. deep.

Arrange them on grid with sausages. Brush with oil and place under a hot grill about 3 inches from heat. Grill for 10–12 minutes, turning once. After 6–8 minutes, add mushrooms, bacon rashers and complete grilling time.

Ingredients for a superb steak grill

Frying

Season meat and add to hot fat in frying pan. Vegetable oils, lard, dripping, butter or margarine may be used. Oil or lard will reach a high temperature necessary to seal meat very quickly. Butter gives a better flavour but burns easily—the addition of a tablespoon of oil helps prevent burning.

Seal meat quickly over high heat, on both sides, then lower heat and cook gently until meat is tender.

Steak: 8–12 minutes, turning once according to thickness and taste.

Kidneys: 6–8 minutes.

Chicken joints: 20–25 minutes.

Sausages: 15 minutes.

Liver: 6–8 minutes.

When cooked remove the meat and drain, if liked, for a moment on absorbent kitchen paper.

Coating for fried meat

Meat such as liver or veal escalopes should be dipped in seasoned flour before frying.

Pork chops, tenderloin, or veal escalopes may be coated with egg and breadcrumbs before cooking. For this, first dip the seasoned, prepared meat in a little beaten egg or egg marinade, drain and then coat with fresh white or browned breadcrumbs and pat on firmly to make a coating.

Marinades

Good cooks discovered that meat soaked in a marinade before cooking was deliciously tender and had more flavour. Marinades consist of oil and vinegar or lemon juice, with additional flavourings. Spoon over chicken joints, steaks, chops or hamburgers 15 minutes to 1 hour before cooking and leave to soak, turning the meat over occasionally.

All purpose

Mix 3 tablespoons salad oil, 3 tablespoons vinegar (or dry wine or lemon juice) a seasoning of salt and freshly ground pepper. Add a little chopped onion or crushed clove of garlic—or parsley stalks, if liked to give extra flavour.

Egg

Ideal to use in any recipe where the meat is to be coated with breadcrumbs before cooking. Blend together 1 egg, 1 teaspoon chopped parsley, a little finely grated lemon rind, 1 teaspoon melted butter or oil and seasoning of salt and pepper. Beat lightly together with a fork.

Bastes

To give extra flavour to grilled meat use special bastes—brush them over chops, chicken joints, hamburgers or sausages before grilling and when turning meat.

Barbecue

Lightly fry 1 small finely chopped onion in 2 oz. of butter until tender—takes about 5 minutes. Draw the pan off the heat and add 1 tablespoon Worcestershire sauce, 2 tablespoons brown sugar, ½ level teaspoon salt, juice of ½ a lemon, and 4 tablespoons tomato ketchup. Brush over hamburgers, chicken joints or sausages.

Mustard

Blend together 1 tablespoon vinegar, 1 tablespoon prepared mustard, and 2 oz. brown sugar. Brush over chicken joints, sausages, pork chops and steak.

Butter

Melt 4 oz. butter and stir in 4 tablespoons bottled meat sauce and 3 tablespoons tomato ketchup. Brush over hamburgers, steak and lamb chops before grilling.

Butters

Grilled or fried foods are rarely served with a gravy. Instead they are topped with delicious flavoured butters. Prepare the butter several hours ahead, then spoon it on to a square of kitchen foil. Shape into a roll—twist the ends like a cracker—and chill in the refrigerator until quite firm. Slice butter just before serving and place on top of each piece of cooked meat. These recipes make enough for 6–8 portions—any butter not used will store in the refrigerator for some time.

Parsley

Blend a squeeze of lemon juice and 1 tablespoon finely chopped parsley with 2 oz. butter.

Lemon

Blend together the finely grated rind and juice of ½ a lemon and 1 level dessertspoon castor sugar with 2 oz. butter.

Sharp

Blend 1 level teaspoon dried mustard, dash of onion or celery salt, ½ level teaspoon curry powder, a little ground pepper, with 2 oz. butter.

Stuffed pork chops

YOU WILL NEED FOR 4 SERVINGS:

4 pork chops, cut at least ½ in. thick
1 egg, lightly mixed
white breadcrumbs
1 oz. vegetable fat or lard
FOR THE STUFFING:
1 large cooking apple, peeled, cored and chopped
2 oz. seedless raisins
2½ oz. (1 teacupful) fresh white breadcrumbs
1 teaspoon salt
1 oz. (or 1 rounded tablespoon) castor sugar
1 oz. butter or margarine
1 small onion, finely chopped
1 tablespoon water

First prepare the stuffing. In a mixing basin combine together apple, seedless raisins, breadcrumbs, salt and sugar. Heat butter or margarine and lightly fry onions until soft—it takes about 5 minutes. Add this to the contents of the mixing basin together with the water; mix lightly with a fork.

Using a sharp knife, slit each pork chop from the outside edges into the bone and make a pocket. Sprinkle with salt and pepper both inside and out, then stuff the pocket loosely and press down lightly to reshape the chop. Dip each one first in mixed egg and then breadcrumbs, pat the crumbs on firmly to make a good coating, and fry quickly in the hot fat to brown both sides. Cover the pan with a lid and cook the chops, turning occasionally for 45 minutes. Remove pan lid 15 minutes before the end of the cooking time to crisp the outside of the chops.

Veal cordon bleu

YOU WILL NEED FOR 4 SERVINGS:

4 veal escalopes
seasoning
egg marinade—*see page 50*
3 oz. thinly sliced Gruyère cheese
3–4 oz. thinly sliced ham
2½ oz. (1 teacupful) fresh white breadcrumbs
2–3 tablespoons oil for frying

Before flattening veal escalopes, cut a small pocket in the side of each, the length of the piece. Place each escalope between two sheets of wetted greaseproof paper and, using a rolling pin, beat them out flat. In the pocket of each one tuck small slices of both ham and cheese. Pat firmly to flatten, season and place in a shallow plate. Pour marinade over them and leave to soak for 15 minutes to 1 hour.

Drain escalopes from the marinade and coat with fresh white breadcrumbs, patting firmly to make a good coating. Fry in hot oil, allowing about 3–5 minutes cooking on each side, turning to brown evenly. Drain and serve with wedges of lemon, green peas and sauté potatoes.

Veal chops with Marsala

YOU WILL NEED FOR 4 SERVINGS:

4 thick veal chops
seasoned flour
2–3 oz. butter
¼ pint Marsala wine
½ pint stock or water plus stock cube
salt and pepper

Trim the veal chops and coat both sides in seasoned flour. Add to the hot butter in the pan and brown quickly on both sides, takes about 10 minutes. Drain from the pan and place in a casserole dish.

Add about 1 level tablespoon of the seasoned flour to the fat in the frying pan and cook gently stirring until browned. Stir in the Marsala and stock or water plus stock cube. Season with salt and pepper and bring up to the boil, stirring well all the time to make an evenly thickened sauce.

Draw the pan off the heat and strain over the veal chops. Place the chops in the centre of a moderate oven (355 deg. or Gas No. 4) and allow to cook for a further 30 minutes.

Beef strogonoff

YOU WILL NEED FOR 4 SERVINGS:

1 lb. fillet steak
2 oz. butter
1 onion, finely chopped
½ lb. button mushrooms, trimmed and sliced
salt and pepper
1 carton soured cream
½ lb. ¼-inch wide noodles, for serving
½ oz. butter, for serving

Trim the meat and cut into thin strips about 2 × ½-inch and set aside. Heat half the butter in a frying pan, add the onion and mushrooms and sauté gently for 5 minutes. Drain the vegetables from the pan and keep warm. Add rest of butter and steak to the hot butter in the pan and fry quickly 3–4 minutes to seal the meat. Add the onion, mushrooms and a good seasoning of salt and pepper, lower the heat and stir in the soured cream. Reheat thoroughly, *but do not allow to boil* otherwise the cream will separate.

Meanwhile add the noodles to a pan of boiling salted water. Re-boil and cook for 10 minutes. Drain and return the noodles to the hot pan, add the butter and toss. Serve the noodles with the beef strogonoff.

Roasting a joint

A roast with all the trimmings is a favourite with most families. It's economical, too, because any left overs make a satisfying meal served cold with salad or pickles.

Roasting cuts

Beef: sirloin and wing-rib on the bone, or boned and rolled; top rump and topside are the choice, favoured in that order. The flesh should be firm and red and the fat soft and creamy. Meat lightly marbled with fat or edged with fat has the best flavour. Best buying times for home produce are autumn and early winter.

Lamb: loin, best end of neck, leg and shoulder; breast when boned, stuffed and rolled. The flesh should be firm and pink, fat white and firm, not excessive. Best buying time for Welsh produce May – June, Lowland March – April and for New Zealand and Australian February – March.

Veal: top of the leg or fillet, loin and the best end of neck. The shoulder can be roasted and so can the breast. The flesh should be palest pink, and any fat should be white. As veal is deficient in fat it is usually cooked with bacon. Best buying times for home produce, December and June.

Pork: leg, shoulder (bladebone), loin and spare rib. The meat should be pink and fat white. Best buying times for home produce; the peak is at Christmas but quality is good all the year round.

Oven roasting

Wipe meat, and if frozen allow to thaw before cooking. Weigh and calculate the cooking time — *see chart*. If your joint is less than 3 lb. or less than 3 in. in depth, reduce cooking time by 5 minutes per lb.

Rub the meat well with seasoning before cooking, then dredge a little flour over the fatty part and rub well in to get a crisp golden finish. Alternatively brush the joint with salad oil and rub it liberally with dry mustard, then sprinkle with pepper, salt and flour. A crushed clove of garlic rubbed over lamb adds flavour.

For best results the meat should be kept out of the hot fat while roasting, so stand it on a trivet or a bed of flavouring vegetables. Use carrots or onion, cut into large pieces (during the cooking, the vegetables will go slightly caramel at the edges, giving a delicious flavour and colour to the gravy). Add a tablespoon of dripping and a bay leaf and if the meat is very lean spread a little dripping on top. Protect veal with a covering of streaky bacon rashers.

Place in the centre of a hot oven (425 deg. or Gas No. 7) and when the fat begins to spit, reduce the heat to moderate (355 deg. or Gas No. 4) until the fat spits gently, for the rest of the cooking time. If you use an open tin, the meat should be basted every 20–30 minutes to help keep it moist. (It is not necessary to baste at all if a covered tin is used). About 20 minutes before the roasting time is completed turn the joint and baste again. Serve on a hot platter and keep hot while making gravy.

Pot roasting

A joint of meat cooked in a heavy, lidded pot on top of the stove is as tender and juicy as any oven roast, and less expensive joints of meat may be used. Topside or fresh brisket are excellent. Prepare the meat as for oven roasting, then brown all over in hot fat in the pan, add a cup or two of water, cover and cook *very gently* allowing the same time as for roasting— *see chart, page 54.*

Slow roasting

Meat cooked slowly at a low temperature has many advantages. It is more tender and moist, retains more flavour and has less weight loss than meat cooked quickly. A joint cooked at low temperatures will require one third longer cooking time than one cooked at a high temperature by the oil method. The meat is cooked at (335 deg. or Gas No. 3) for the whole of the cooking time— *see chart, page 54.* Even lower temperature may be used but the time must be increased accordingly.

At this temperature the fat is cooler, and doesn't spit as much so your oven won't get so greasy. Yorkshire pudding or fruit pies needing a higher temperature can quite easily be cooked with the roast. Set the oven at the higher temperature, place the pie or Yorkshire on the top shelf and the roast on the floor of the oven where it will cook quite slowly.

Important —this method is not suitable for pork.

The perfect roast

Foil roasting

Kitchen foil reduces meat shrinkage, saves basting and retains all the delicious meat juices. For the best results roast at a *high* temperature since this avoids any chance of undercooking.

Before starting preheat your oven to very hot (425 deg. or Gas No. 7). Prepare and season the meat as for oven roasting. Stand it on a piece of foil large enough to cover it completely—you may need the extra wide foil, 18 in. width. Wrap completely and seal edges with a tight fold to make a neat package. Place in the roasting tin, in the centre of the oven and following cooking times—*see chart*. To brown the meat, open the top of the foil for the last 20 minutes of cooking time. Then use the juices that collect in the foil to make a rich gravy to serve with it.

Beef is nicest slightly underdone, lamb should be well done but not too dry and both veal and pork should be well done. Here are approximate guides.

Meat	*Oven Roast*	*Pot Roast*	*Slow Roast*	*Foil Roast*
Beef	20 min. per lb. plus 20 min.	20 min. per lb. plus 20 min.	40 min. per lb. plus 45 min.	30–40 min. per lb. to taste
Lamb	25 min. per lb. plus 25 min.	25 min. per lb. plus 25 min.	45 min. per lb. plus 45 min.	35–40 min. per lb.
Pork	35 min. per lb. plus 35 min.	35 min. per lb. plus 35 min.	not suitable	35–40 min. per lb.
Veal	30 min. per lb. plus 30 min.	30 min. per lb. plus 30 min.	50 min. per lb. plus 50 min.	40–45 min. per lb.

ACCOMPANIMENTS are all important—Yorkshire pudding and mustard or horseradish sauce go with beef, mint sauce with lamb, and apple sauce or baked apples with pork and veal.

Yorkshire pudding

YOU WILL NEED FOR 4 SERVINGS:

2 oz. (or 2 rounded tablespoons) plain flour
pinch of salt
1 egg
¼ pint liquid (about 3 parts milk and 1 part water)

Sift flour and salt into a mixing basin. Add egg and about half the mixing liquid. Using a wooden spoon, beat egg and milk gradually drawing in flour from around the edges—work from centre of the basin to sides and mix to a smooth batter.

Add remainder of the liquid gradually, stirring all the time. Beat well for a few minutes until thoroughly aerated, then cover the bowl with a cloth and leave to stand for 1 hour, or until required. Stir again before using because the starch grains tend to settle at the bottom.

Yorkshire pudding may be cooked in a sheet of tartlet or bun tins, a Yorkshire pudding tin, small roasting tin or Pyrex dish. If a large container is to be used, put a heaped teaspoon dripping or fat in the dish and heat thoroughly at the top of the oven for a few minutes. Pour in the stirred batter and replace on the top shelf of a hot oven (425 deg. or Gas No. 7) and cook until well risen and golden—about 30 minutes. For small tartlet or individual bun tins, heavily grease about eight and heat thoroughly in the oven, then pour the batter into each using a jug, and filling each fairly full. Bake as before until crisp and golden, about 12–15 minutes. Serve at once.

Toad-in-the-hole

Put 6–8 small sausages in tin with 1 oz. fat in a fairly hot oven (400 deg. or Gas No. 6) until fat is very hot. Quickly pour in the batter and bake just above centre of oven for 25–30 minutes. For steak or chops allow 40–45 minutes.

To make the gravy

Remove cooked meat from roasting tin and pour away the hot fat very slowly so that all the sediment and meat juices are retained in the tin. Place over low heat on cooker top.

Thin gravy: add a dash of salt and pepper and stir in about 1 pint stock or vegetable cooking water. Stir and boil briskly till gravy is reduced by about half. Taste and correct seasoning; strain into a hot gravy boat.

Thick gravy leave a tablespoon of fat in the tin and stir in a tablespoon flour. Cook for 1 minute until bubbling and frothy, then draw the tin off the heat and stir in about ½ pint stock or vegetable cooking water. Put tin on the heat again and bring to the boil, stirring well, and cook 2–3 minutes. Taste and check seasoning, add a little gravy browning if liked, then strain into a hot gravy boat.

Carving the joint

After taking the roast out of the oven, leave it to stand for 5–10 minutes; it will be easier to carve. Slice across grain of meat towards the bone, using a very sharp carving knife, and remember beef should be carved in the thinnest of slices; lamb, pork and veal a little thicker.

Roast chicken

YOU WILL NEED FOR 6 SERVINGS:

> 3–4 lb. chicken
> salt
> ½ lemon
> corn stuffing, *see right*
> 2 oz. butter or dripping
> few streaky bacon rashers
> bread sauce

Have the chicken drawn and cleaned by the butcher. If it is a frozen oven-ready bird allow 6–8 hours to thaw out. Check the weight and prepare stuffing a few hours before required.

Rinse chicken out and pat dry with a clean cloth. Rub inside with a little salt and outside with a cut lemon. If you do not intend to stuff the chicken, place a 2 oz. pat of butter inside the bird to keep it moist while roasting. Otherwise stuff the neck cavity of the bird not too tightly with a little corn stuffing. Pull neck skin down over the stuffing, underneath the bird, twisting the wing tips forward and under, and secure both with a skewer. Place remaining stuffing in the body cavity (any stuffing left over can be put in a buttered ovenproof dish, covered with foil and baked in the oven with the bird for the last hour of cooking).

Place chicken in a roasting tin. Smear with a little butter or dripping and place remainder in the tin. Cover breast with trimmed bacon rashers, and a piece of kitchen foil.

Place in the centre of a moderately hot oven (380 deg. or Gas No. 5) and roast for the required time (20 minutes per lb. plus 20 minutes), basting frequently. About ¼ hour before cooking time is complete remove foil and bacon rashers, dredge breast with a little flour and return chicken to oven to brown. Serve with giblet gravy (prepare as previous recipe, using chicken giblets) and bread sauce.

Bread sauce: Put ½ pint milk and 1 onion, peeled and stuck with 2 cloves, into a saucepan.

Simmer the mixture gently for about 30 minutes and then strain milk; return milk to the saucepan and add 2 oz. (1 level teacup) fresh white breadcrumbs, and ¼ level teaspoon salt.

Continue to simmer mixture gently, stirring occasionally, until sauce thickens to a creamy consistency. Add 1 oz. of butter or margarine and 1 tablespoon cream or top of the milk, reheat and serve.

Corn stuffing

YOU WILL NEED FOR 3–4 LB. CHICKEN:

> 6 oz. (or 2 rounded teacups) fresh white
>   breadcrumbs
> 1 level teaspoon salt and a pinch of pepper
> ¼ level teaspoon thyme
> 1 tablespoon chopped parsley
> 1 tin (12 oz.) whole kernel sweetcorn
> 4 oz. butter or margarine
> 1 onion, finely chopped

Combine together breadcrumbs, seasoning, thyme, parsley and sweetcorn. Melt butter and gently sauté onion until soft—takes about 5 minutes. Then, using a fork to mix, stir the cooked onion into the breadcrumb mixture. Use as required.

Roast goose

YOU WILL NEED FOR 6–8 SERVINGS:

> 1 roasting goose
> veal forcemeat stuffing, *see page 58*
> salt
> 1 oz. lard
> apple sauce to serve

Ask butcher to draw, clean and truss bird. Check weight and prepare stuffing a few hours before required.

Wipe goose with a clean, damp cloth and stuff body cavity from the tail end. Stitch with coarse thread or skewer the tail end closed to keep in the stuffing. Sprinkle goose with salt and place in a roasting tin. Add lard and place bird in the centre of a moderately hot oven (380 deg. or Gas No. 5) and roast, allowing 20 minutes for every lb. Baste frequently; goose is very fatty and needs no protective bacon rashers, but should the body brown too quickly protect with a piece of foil towards the end of cooking time.

Serve with giblet gravy (prepare as for turkey), and apple sauce.

Roasts fit for a King

Magnificent roast poultry or joints, cooked with delicious stuffings and served with regal accompaniments. They are ideal for dinner parties and while they are cooking slowly in the oven, you'll have time to prepare the table and yourself.

Traditional roast turkey

YOU WILL NEED FOR 12–14 SERVINGS:

1 turkey, weighing about 10–12 lb.
chestnut stuffing—*see page 43*
veal forcemeat—*see page 58*
coarse salt
2–3 oz. butter or dripping
¼ lb. streaky bacon rashers
½ lb. bacon rashers for rolls
cranberry jelly, chipolata sausages
and bunch of watercress to serve

Have the turkey drawn and cleaned by the butcher, and check the weight for calculating cooking time. Prepare all the necessary stuffings about 2–3 hours beforehand. If you have a frozen oven-ready turkey, allow at least 24 hours for it to thaw out before cooking and don't remove it from its vacuum-sealed bag until you are ready to stuff and roast it. Rinse the inside of the turkey with cold water and pat dry with a clean cloth. Stuff neck cavity with prepared chestnut stuffing. Don't pack too tightly—the stuffing will swell a little during cooking. Pull neck skin tight under the front of the bird and fix underneath with the wings by twisting them forwards and under. Secure with a skewer. Stuff the body of the bird with veal forcemeat.
If necessary fasten the legs into position with string or a skewer.
Add about 2 lb. to the weight of the bird to allow for stuffing and calculate cooking time:

7–10 lb. bird needs 3–3½ hours
10–14 lb. bird needs 3½–4 hours
14–20 lb. bird needs 4½–5 hours

Preheat the oven at a low temperature (335 deg. or Gas No. 3). At this heat the bird will slow roast and will be tender and juicy when it is finished. Rub turkey skin with coarse salt and smear with dripping or soft butter; cover breast with rashers of streaky bacon and loosely cover whole bird with kitchen foil. Place in a large roasting tin with a little extra fat. Set tin on a low shelf in the oven and

Left to right: roast turkey, duckling with orange sauce, grouse, crown of lamb and breast of veal

leave to cook for the required time. Baste occasionally with hot fat in the tin.

Towards the end of the cooking time, remove foil and bacon. Dredge the breast with a little flour and put back in the oven. Raise oven temperature to 375 deg. or Gas No. 5, and brown the bird.

Serve with giblet gravy and cranberry jelly. Garnish with watercress, sausages and bacon rolls (roll bacon rashers, skewer and grill).

Giblet gravy:

Place turkey giblets in a saucepan, and cover with cold water. Bring to the boil and simmer for half an hour. Meanwhile, in a small basin mix 1 rounded teaspoon gravy thickening powder and 2 rounded teaspoons flour with enough cold water to make a thin paste. Stir in ½ pint of hot stock strained from the giblets. Return gravy to the saucepan and stir over the heat until it thickens and boils.

Veal forcemeat

YOU WILL NEED FOR A 10 LB. TURKEY:

9 oz. (or 3 rounded teacups) fresh white
  breadcrumbs
3 oz. shredded beef suet
2 tablespoons chopped parsley
salt
pepper
1 teaspoon dried thyme
finely grated rind of ½ lemon
2 rashers of bacon, trimmed and chopped
beaten egg to bind

Prepare and mix together all the ingredients except egg; using a fork, stir in enough beaten egg to make the mixture bind together. Use to stuff the body cavity of the turkey.

Any extra stuffing may be shaped into balls, coated with a little beaten egg, and then with brown breadcrumbs, and fried. It is a good idea to prepare these the day after cooking the turkey, when a renewed supply of stuffing would be very welcome with the cold meat.

Crown roast of lamb

YOU WILL NEED FOR 6–8 SERVINGS:

2 sections best end of neck of lamb, 6–7 chops
  on each, shaped into a crown, the butcher will do this
  for you if you ask
seasoning
cooking oil
1 small tin apricot halves
mint jelly

1 oz. dried apricots, soaked overnight
2½ oz. (or 1 teacup) fresh white breadcrumbs
½ cooking apple, peeled, cored and chopped
1 tablespoon chopped walnuts
finely grated rind of ½ lemon
1 oz. butter, melted

Place joint in a large roasting tin. Season with salt and pepper and wrap a small piece of foil round the top of each rib to prevent it from scorching during cooking. Brush whole of the crown with a little cooking oil.

Prepare stuffing. Using a pair of scissors, snip fruit into fairly small pieces. Put in a small mixing basin and combine with breadcrumbs, apple, nuts and grated lemon rind. Then, using a fork, mix in the melted butter.

Pack stuffing into the middle of the crown, having first removed the fatty pieces placed there by the butcher. Place in a large roasting tin, with a little oil, and then put in the centre of a moderately hot oven (380 deg. or Gas No. 5) and roast for 1¼–1½ hours.

When cooked, remove pieces of foil, top each rib with a cutlet frill and garnish with apricot halves filled with mint jelly. To carve simply cut down between rib bones.

Roast breast of veal

YOU WILL NEED FOR 8 SERVINGS:

1 breast of veal—about 4 lb. in weight
salt and pepper
1 tablespoon dried mixed herbs
1–2 tablespoons oil
½ pint stock or water plus stock cube
FOR THE STUFFING:
4 oz. (2 level teacups) fresh white breadcrumbs
1 tablespoon chopped parsley
salt and pepper
1 tablespoon cream or top of the milk
juice of ½ lemon
½ small onion, finely chopped
½ oz. butter
1 egg

Ask the butcher to bone joint, then rub the skin with salt and pepper and set the meat aside while preparing the stuffing.

In a mixing basin, combine breadcrumbs with chopped parsley, and seasoning, cream and lemon juice. Stir in the onion, which should be sautéed in the butter until soft, and lightly mixed egg.

Lightly pack stuffing over joint, roll up and tie in several places with string, then sprinkle with dried herbs. Set prepared joint into a roasting tin with the oil, and place in the centre of a hot oven (425 deg.

or Gas No. 7). Brown the joint—it takes about 10 minutes—then lower heat to moderate (355 deg. or Gas No. 4), add stock and cook, allowing 30 minutes per lb. plus 30 minutes added to the total.

Remove the string, allow the joint to stand for 5 minutes, then slice for serving.

Roast duckling with orange sauce

YOU WILL NEED FOR 6 SERVINGS:

4 lb. oven-ready duckling
2 oranges for the body cavity
watercress
FOR THE ORANGE SAUCE:
5 tablespoons granulated sugar
2 tablespoons water
2 tablespoons vinegar
2 oranges
1 tablespoon orange marmalade
¼ pint stock from giblets—*see recipe*
2 level teaspoons cornflour blended with 1 tablespoon water

Wipe duckling and rub a little salt into the skin. Stuff the body cavity with the oranges, cut in chunks. Place in a roasting tin and add 2 tablespoons water. Duck is very fatty and there is no need to add any dripping. Place in the centre of a preheated, moderately hot oven (375 deg. or Gas No. 5) then, after 30 minutes, lower the heat to 355 deg. or Gas No. 4 and complete roasting time, allowing 20 minutes for every lb. in weight. It is not necessary to baste the bird.

Place giblets in a saucepan, cover with cold water and bring to the boil. Simmer gently for 30 minutes. In the meantime begin preparing the orange sauce.

Measure sugar and water into a small saucepan and stir over moderate heat until the sugar has dissolved and the mixture becomes a caramel colour. Add vinegar—take care as the mixture will hiss furiously at this stage. Reboil, stirring to dissolve the caramel. Add juice and pieces of flesh from 1 orange, marmalade and ¼ pint of stock strained from the giblets. Cover with a lid and simmer gently for about 30 minutes.

Strain liquid and return it to the saucepan. Stir in cornflour blend and cook over moderate heat, stirring all the time until it thickens and boils. Add segments of remaining orange, cut in half lengthwise, and half the rind which has been cut in small slivers and cooked in boiling water until soft—for about 20 minutes.

Remove duckling from roasting tin on to a hot serving platter, pour orange sauce over it, garnish with watercress and serve.

Unusual roasts

Game has the perfect accompaniment in buttered breadcrumbs which counteract any slightly dry flavour in the meat. Simply melt 4–6 oz. butter in a frying pan and add lots of freshly made white breadcrumbs. Use day-old bread and grate or rub through a coarse sieve. Stir over moderate heat until golden and crisp.

Roast pheasant

Available October 1—February 1

One pheasant serves 4–5. Place a large nut of butter inside the bird, cover the breast with bacon rashers, tie on with string and place either on a trivet or bed of prepared vegetables in a roasting tin. Cover tin with lid or sheets of kitchen foil, and place in centre of a very hot oven (425 deg. or Gas No. 7). After 10 minutes reduce oven heat to hot (400 deg. or Gas No. 6).

If the bird is cooked in an open tin baste frequently to keep moist. Roast a young bird for 30–40 minutes and an older bird for 40–60 minutes. About 10 minutes before cooking time is completed remove lid or foil and bacon rashers and dredge breast of the bird with flour. Return to the oven near the top, and cook until browned.

Serve with watercress, potato crisps, fried breadcrumbs and gravy.

Roast grouse

Available August 12—December 10

One bird will serve 1 or 2 portions according to size and taste. Place a knob of butter inside each trussed bird and tie a rasher of fatty bacon over the breast of each. Place birds, breast side up, in a baking tin with a little lard or butter and cook for 30–45 minutes in a hot oven (400 deg. or Gas No. 6), basting frequently.

Remove bacon from the birds about 10 minutes before the cooking time is completed, dredge the breasts with flour and return to hot oven to brown. Place each bird on a circle of toast, garnished with bacon rolls and watercress.

Serve gravy, fried breadcrumbs and potato crisps separately.

Casseroles and braising

Braising is a cooking method that combines roasting with stewing, and may be carried out in a casserole dish in the oven or a saucepan covered with a lid. In either case the meat is cooked on a bed of vegetables with sufficient stock to keep it moist and make a good gravy. Braised meat has a delicious flavour and the method is particularly suitable for lean pieces that are not quite tender enough to roast. Prepare as recipe directs, weigh the meat and cook for 30–40 minutes per pound, adding another 30 minutes to the total.

Braised steak with onion rice

YOU WILL NEED FOR 4 SERVINGS:

1½ lb. braising steak
seasoned flour
1 oz. butter or margarine
2 onions, finely chopped
4 oz. mushrooms, washed and sliced
2 rashers of bacon
¾ pint stock or water plus stock cube
1 rounded teaspoon cornflour
FOR THE RICE:
1 oz. butter or margarine
1 onion, finely chopped
8 oz. long grain rice
1 pint stock or water plus stock cube

Trim away the fat and gristle from the meat and cut into four neat pieces. Dip in seasoned flour. Heat the butter or margarine in a pan, add the meat and brown on both sides.
Lift the meat from the pan and add the onions to the hot fat. Cook gently until onions are soft and beginning to brown—takes about 10 minutes. Then add the mushrooms, trimmed and chopped bacon rashers and put the meat on top. Add the stock, cover with a tight-fitting lid and simmer gently for 1½–2 hours.
About 30 minutes before cooking time is finished, prepare the rice; melt the butter or margarine in a heavy pan. Add the onion and rice.
Stir over low heat for 2–3 minutes, then stir in the hot stock. Bring up to the boil, cover with a lid and simmer very gently for 20 minutes or until the rice is tender and stock is absorbed.

Spoon the cooked rice onto a hot serving platter and place the meat on top. To make the gravy—blend the cornflour with a little water to make a thin paste and stir into the vegetables and stock in the pan. Stir until boiling, simmer for 1 minute, then spoon over the meat and rice.

Beef olives

YOU WILL NEED FOR 4 SERVINGS:

4 thin slices of buttock steak, about 3–4 oz. each
seasoned flour
1 oz. dripping or lard
2 carrots, scraped and sliced
2 onions
bouquet garni (*see Braised beef*)
¼ pint stock or water plus stock cube
1 tablespoon sherry
1 level tablespoon cornflour blended to a smooth paste with water
FOR THE STUFFING:
1 oz. butter or margarine
4 oz. mushrooms, chopped
2½ oz. (or 1 teacupful) fresh white breadcrumbs
1 tablespoon chopped parsley
pinch of mixed dried herbs
½ level teaspoon salt and a pinch of pepper

Trim the meat, wrap between sheets of greaseproof paper and beat until thin with a rolling pin. Prepare the stuffing as follows:
Melt the butter or margarine and lightly fry mushrooms for 2–3 minutes. Mix together in a small basin breadcrumbs, parsley and mixed herbs. Add mushrooms and butter from the pan and, using a fork, blend the ingredients and season well.
Divide the stuffing into four portions and roll a portion inside each piece of meat. Tie neatly with fine string or strong thread, like a parcel, and roll in seasoned flour. Fry in hot fat to seal on all sides. Drain, add the prepared vegetables to the hot fat and brown lightly.
Put the stuffed beef olives on top of the vegetables, add the bouquet garni and stock which should not quite cover the vegetables. Cover with a lid; simmer gently for 1½–2 hours.
Lift out the olives, remove the string, and keep warm. Strain the cooking liquor into a saucepan and stir in the sherry and the cornflour blend and stir until boiling.
Check the seasonings, and then pour over the meat and serve with creamed potatoes and braised celery.

From top left: beef olives, veal paprika, chicken hunter style and beef goulash.

Chicken hunter style

YOU WILL NEED FOR 4 SERVINGS:

4 chicken joints
seasoned flour
2 oz. butter for frying
1 onion, finely chopped
1 (15 oz.) tin tomatoes
¼ pint white wine
salt and pepper
small bay leaf
1 level teaspoon castor sugar
¼ lb. button mushrooms

Lightly coat chicken joints with seasoned flour and brown quickly in hot butter. Place joints in a large saucepan or flame-proof casserole and add onion to the hot butter, frying it gently until softened and brown. Add to the contents of the saucepan or casserole dish with tomatoes, and liquid from the tin, white wine, seasoning, bay leaf, and sugar. Cover with a lid and simmer gently for 1½ hours or until the chicken is tender.

Fry mushrooms in a little butter and, about 5 minutes before cooking time is completed, remove bay leaf from casserole; add mushrooms.

Top with freshly chopped parsley and serve with boiled rice and crusty French bread.

Beef goulash

YOU WILL NEED FOR 4 SERVINGS:

1–1½ lb. best stewing steak
seasoned flour
1 oz. dripping
1 onion, peeled and sliced
1 (15 oz.) tin tomatoes
1 small clove of garlic, crushed with a little salt
bay leaf
salt and pepper
1 level tablespoon paprika pepper or goulash seasoning
½ pint stock or water plus stock cube
1 carton soured cream, optional

Wipe the meat and trim away any fat or gristle. Cut the meat into neat pieces and roll in seasoned flour. Heat the dripping in a large pan, add the onions and fry gently until soft and browned—takes about 5 minutes. Add the meat and fry quickly to brown. Add the tomatoes plus liquid from the tin to the meat, along with the finely chopped garlic, bay leaf, a seasoning of salt and pepper and the paprika or goulash seasoning. Stir in the stock and bring up to the boil. Lower the heat and simmer gently for 2½–3 hours. Stir in the soured cream just before serving.

Braised beef

YOU WILL NEED FOR 6 SERVINGS:

2 lb. brisket of beef, boned and rolled
seasoned flour
1 oz. dripping
2 onions, sliced
2 carrots, scraped and sliced
½ turnip, peeled and sliced
½ pint stock or water plus stock cube
salt and pepper
bouquet garni (tie together few stalks parsley, a bay leaf, sprig of thyme)
1 level tablespoon cornflour, blended with water to a smooth paste

Wipe meat and roll it in seasoned flour. Place in a large saucepan, brown on all sides in the hot dripping and then remove from the pan. Add prepared onions, carrots and turnip to the hot fat and brown them lightly. Put meat on top, add stock (it should just cover the vegetables), seasonings, and bouquet garni. Cover with a lid and simmer gently, allowing 30–40 minutes to the lb. and 30 minutes over (i.e. 1 hour 30 minutes to 1 hour 50 minutes).

To serve, remove meat from pan and put in dish surrounded by cooked vegetables. Make a gravy by stirring cornflour blend into the strained stock from the saucepan and bring to the boil, stirring all the time until thickened.

Serve with parsley potatoes (toss boiled potatoes in chopped parsley and butter) and a green vegetable.

Veal paprika

YOU WILL NEED FOR 4 SERVINGS:

1 oz. butter or margarine
4 veal escalopes
1 small onion, finely chopped
1 clove garlic, finely chopped (optional)
1½ level tablespoons paprika pepper
1 level teaspoon salt
¾ pint stock or water plus stock cube
¼ pint single cream
1 rounded tablespoon flour
1 carton soured cream
8 oz. long grain rice for serving
little chopped parsley

Melt fat in a heavy saucepan, and brown veal. Remove from the pan and add onion and garlic to the fat. Sauté gently until golden brown. Add paprika pepper and salt, then gradually stir in the stock. Bring to the boil, cover with a lid and simmer for 10 minutes. Add browned veal, replace lid and simmer gently for about 20–30 minutes more.

Measure single cream into a small basin, sift flour on top and whisk quickly and thoroughly until blended. Stir in a little of the boiling stock, blend well and then return to the pan. Cook, stirring until ingredients thicken and boil. Draw the pan off the heat and stir in soured cream.

Serve with parsley rice. Plunge the rice into boiling salted water, cook for 10 minutes, drain, toss in butter and add the chopped parsley.

Oxtail casserole

YOU WILL NEED FOR 4 SERVINGS:

1½–2 lb. oxtail, cut at the joints
bouquet garni (2 parsley stalks, small bay
    leaf, sprig of thyme tied together)
½ lb. onion, peeled and sliced
1 lb. carrots, scraped and sliced
½ oz. dripping or lard
1 level tablespoon flour
1 pint cooking liquid (*see recipe*)
salt and pepper
1 teaspoon tomato purée
juice of ½ lemon

Wash and dry the oxtail and finish cutting through at the joints. Place in a saucepan, cover with cold water, add bouquet garni and bring to the boil. Cover with a lid and simmer for 2 hours. Strain off liquid and, when cool, skim off and discard heavy layer of fat; reserve liquid. Sauté onions and carrots in hot fat until browned; place in a large casserole dish with the oxtail. Stir flour into the hot fat and cook slowly, stirring until browned. Gradually stir in the 1 pint of reserved cooking liquid, and bring to the boil. Season well and add tomato purée.

Strain over the contents of the casserole, cover with a lid, and either simmer on top of the stove for a further 1½–2 hours, or place in the centre of a slow oven (335 deg. or Gas No. 3) and cook for 2–3 hours until the meat is tender. Add lemon juice and serve.

Braised lamb chops

YOU WILL NEED FOR 4 SERVINGS:

4 lamb chops
seasoned flour
2 oz. butter or margarine
1 large onion, sliced
pinch of dried rosemary
¼ pint white wine (or use water plus stock cube)
1 lb. potatoes
¼ lb. button mushrooms, trimmed and sliced
1 level teaspoon salt
1 large packet frozen peas

Trim and wipe the lamb chops and coat well in the seasoned flour. Heat the butter in a frying pan until hot, then brown the chops on both sides—takes about 10 minutes. Remove from the pan and place in the base of a large casserole dish. Peel and slice the onion and fry gently in the hot fat for about 5 minutes, then add the rosemary and the wine or stock and stir well to mix in the sediment in the base of the pan. Pour this sauce over the chops in the casserole dish, cover with a lid and place in the centre of a moderate oven (355 deg. or Gas No. 4) and cook for 1 hour.

Meanwhile scrape or peel the potatoes and cut up small. Bring a pan of salted water to the boil, add the potatoes and boil gently for 15 minutes, until barely tender. Drain and set aside. Add the mushrooms, salt, peas and potatoes to the lamb chops. Stir well to mix and replace in the oven for a further 20 minutes, until the vegetables are well heated and cooked through.

Braised steak in tomato sauce

YOU WILL NEED FOR 4 SERVINGS:

1½ lb. braising steak
2 oz. (or 2 rounded tablespoons) plain flour mixed with 1 level
    teaspoon salt and
    pinch pepper
2 oz. lard or dripping
1 medium onion, peeled and sliced
1 clove garlic, crushed and chopped with a little
    salt
1 (15 oz.) tin tomatoes
2 level teaspoons tomato purée
¾ pint stock
1 level teaspoon oregano
2 tablespoons white wine or stock (optional)

Trim away all fat and gristle from the meat and cut into neat pieces. Then coat thoroughly in the seasoned flour.

Heat the lard or dripping in a medium-sized saucepan and then gently fry the onion and garlic until soft, takes about 5 minutes. Add the meat and brown quickly on all sides, then sprinkle remainder of the flour over the meat and stir well, cooking gently for a few minutes. Add the tomatoes plus liquid from the tin, 1 teaspoon of tomato purée, the stock and oregano and stir well to mix, then bring to the boil, stirring all the time. Reduce the heat and simmer for 1½ hours very gently, stirring occasionally, then add the second spoonful of tomato purée and stir in the white wine or stock if used, simmer for a further 30 minutes, or until the meat is tender then serve.

63

ALL ABOUT
Cold Meats

Economical cold joints

One salted or cured joint can make several meals; serve with pickles, salad and crusty fresh bread and butter, or potatoes and a hot vegetable.

In most cases the joints should be soaked overnight in cold water to rid meat of excess salt. If time is short, however, cover joint with cold water, bring to the boil, drain and cover with fresh water, then proceed with the cooking as directed in the particular recipe chosen.

Simmer very gently to avoid over-cooking and breaking up the meat. Allow all meats except pork to cool in the cooking liquor to keep it moist.

All these joints keep excellently. If stored in the refrigerator, wrap well in greaseproof paper or foil to prevent the meat from drying out.

Boiling bacon joints

All cuts of bacon provide excellent boiling joints, the most common are collar, forehock, and cuts of gammon. Streaky and back bacon, usually cut into rashers, may also be treated in this way. Ask your grocer the weight of the joint you have purchased so that you may calculate the cooking time correctly.

Soak bacon joint for several hours, or overnight, in clear, cold water. Remove bacon and rinse under the cold tap. Place skinned side down in a large pan and cover completely with fresh cold water. Bring slowly to the boil, and remove any scum that arises. As soon as it comes to the boil turn down the heat and let it simmer very gently, covered with a lid, allowing 20 minutes for each lb., plus 20 minutes extra.

Top up the pan with extra boiling water whenever necessary, always keep the joint covered with water. Allow cooked joint to cool in the cooking liquor, then strip off the rind with a knife. Sprinkle fat with freshly toasted breadcrumbs.

Cold bacon is delicious served sliced with green or potato salad, sliced tomato, beetroot and cucumber. Or it may be served with new boiled potatoes and a hot vegetable.

Any left-over bacon can be made into appetising open sandwiches. Arrange sliced bacon on buttered slices of brown bread, and top with an attractive arrangement of cooked vegetables, sliced tomato or cucumber and mayonnaise.

Ham joints

A ham is the hind leg of a bacon pig cut and cured separately. The curing can vary considerably, but the method of cooking remains the same and is similar to bacon joints.

Weigh joint to calculate the cooking time needed. Soak ham for 24 hours in cold water. Then rinse in cold water and scrape surface to remove any bloom. Place in a large pan and cover with fresh cold water. Skim and simmer gently; allow 20 minutes per lb., plus 20 minutes extra for up to a 12 lb. ham; 15 minutes per lb., plus 15 minutes extra for a joint over 12 lb.

Allow to cool in the water in which it was cooked. Remove and place on a board for a few hours to 'set'. Remove skin, and coat with toasted breadcrumbs and brown sugar mixed in equal portions.

Succulent baked ham

Stuffed streaky bacon

YOU WILL NEED FOR 8 SERVINGS:

  2 unsliced pieces streaky bacon each weighing about 1½ lb.
  2 oz. toasted breadcrumbs
  1 oz. lard
  FOR THE STUFFING:
  1 onion, chopped
  1 oz. butter
  1 heaped teaspoon chopped parsley
  6 oz. white breadcrumbs
  1 heaped teaspoon thyme
  1 teaspoon grated lemon rind
  1 level teaspoon salt
  ¼ level teaspoon pepper
  1 large egg

Remove any small bones and soak joints in cold water overnight. Fry chopped onion in butter until soft, then add it to the parsley, white breadcrumbs, thyme, lemon rind, and seasoning. Bind with beaten egg to make a moist, crumbly consistency.

Sandwich two joints together with stuffing, and tie them firmly together with string. Place in a baking tin with lard, cover with greaseproof paper or foil, and bake in centre of a moderate oven (355 deg. or Gas No. 4) for 1½ hours.

When joints are cooked, place them between two plates and press with a weight until cold. Then remove string and rinds. Cover fat well with toasted breadcrumbs.

Baking ham or bacon joints in a flour and water crust

This is an ideal method for ham joints and lean bacon cuts. All the flavour and juices are retained and the meat is deliciously moist. It's advisable to soak the joint for 24 hours before baking to ensure that it is not too salty.

Sieve about 1 lb. flour into a mixing basin, stir in about ½ pint water and mix to an elastic dough—use double quantities for a large joint. On a lightly floured working surface, roll out evenly to a piece large enough to enclose the meat.

Place joint on dough and wrap firmly around to enclose completely. Moisten edges and press to seal. Place in a greased roasting tin and bake in centre of a moderately hot oven (400 deg. or Gas No. 6) for first 15 minutes, then lower heat to moderate (355 deg. or Gas No. 4) and bake for remaining time, allowing 30 minutes per lb.

When ready, remove from the oven, break away crust and lift out bacon. Strip off rind, score fat and sprinkle with freshly toasted breadcrumbs.

Glazed salt beef

YOU WILL NEED FOR 6–8 SERVINGS:

  2 lb. boned and rolled salt brisket of beef
  3 onions, sliced
  few crushed peppercorns
  bouquet garni—tie together a few parsley stalks,
    a bay leaf and a sprig of thyme

Wipe meat and soak in a bowl of cold water for 2 hours. Drain and place into a large saucepan with onions and peppercorns. Cover with fresh cold water and a lid and bring slowly to the boil. Skim well and add bouquet garni.

Cover with a lid and simmer gently, allowing 25 minutes per lb. plus 25 minutes extra. When cooked, draw pan off the heat and leave meat in the cooking liquor until cool enough to handle. Then take the meat out, cover with a plate and a weight and press until cold.

Brush joint with meat glaze, *see recipe below*. Serve salt beef sliced with sweet and sour cucumber pickles.

Meat glaze for cold joints

  ¼ pint stock or water
  ¼ oz. (or 1 level tablespoon) powdered gelatine
  1 level teaspoon meat extract

Measure the water into a saucepan, sprinkle over the gelatine and allow to soak for 5 minutes. Then stir over low heat until gelatine has dissolved but do not boil.

Draw the pan off the heat and stir in the meat extract. Allow to cool and use when beginning to thicken.

Pressed spiced beef

YOU WILL NEED FOR 6–8 SERVINGS:

  one (2 lb.) piece of fresh brisket of beef, rolled
  cooking salt
  3–4 cloves
  12 peppercorns
  blade of mace
  4 tablespoons vinegar
  water—*see recipe*
  toasted breadcrumbs to coat

Rub the meat over with coarse salt. Place in a deep bowl with the cloves, peppercorns, mace, vinegar and just enough water to cover. Leave to marinate for 24 hours, turning several times.

Drain and place the meat in a large casserole, cover with enough of the marinade to come about half way up the joint, then add the peppercorns but discard the cloves and mace. Cover with a lid and cook in the centre of a slow oven (335 deg. or Gas No. 3) for 2½–3 hours.

Allow the cooked meat to cool in the liquid, then drain and place on a plate, cover with a second plate and a heavy weight and leave until quite cold. Sprinkle with browned breadcrumbs and serve sliced.

Pressed ox tongue

YOU WILL NEED FOR 8–10 SERVINGS:

1 salted or pickled ox tongue, weighing about 4 lb.
1 onion
2 cloves
2 carrots
piece of turnip
1 bay leaf

Wash tongue and soak it overnight in cold water. Place in a large pan, cover with fresh cold water and bring to the boil. Remove from heat, drain off water and cover again with more cold water. Add peeled vegetables and bay leaf, sticking cloves into the onion. Bring to the boil, and simmer gently for 3–4½ hours until tender. Remove any scum from the water when it rises, and add extra boiling water, if necessary, to keep the tongue covered.

To test when it is ready, run a sharp skewer into the tip of the tongue; if it feels tender, then the tongue is cooked. Drain from the pan, and plunge immediately into cold water. Remove skin, ducts and gristle and any bones from back of the tongue. Curl tongue round and fit tightly into a deep, round cake tin, casserole or baking dish, about 6 in. in diameter.

Cover with a large plate and press down with a heavy weight. Leave for 24 hours, then turn out of the dish. There will be sufficient jelly round edge of the tongue, so no extra aspic jelly is required. Serve sliced with mustard pickles.

Jellied lambs' tongues

YOU WILL NEED FOR 4 SERVINGS:

4 lambs' tongues
1 pint stock, or water plus stock cube

Wash tongues and place in a deep saucepan. Cover with stock and bring to the boil. Cover with a lid and simmer for 1½–2 hours until tender—test with a knife point at the tips of the tongues. Alternatively, tongues may be cooked in a pressure cooker. Place in the base of the cooker, cover with stock and bring to the boil. Cover cooker with lid and cook at 15 lb. pressure for 30 minutes. Allow cooker to cool slowly before removing lid.

While cooked tongues are still hot, peel off skins and remove any gristle at the back. Select a small, round cake tin or baking dish, and press in tongues quite tightly with the widest parts to the centre and the tips round outside edge.

Cover with a square of kitchen foil or greaseproof paper and a heavy weight, and leave overnight. It's not necessary to add stock—there is sufficient jelly in the tongues.

Serve sliced with pickled onions or mixed pickle.

Cold pickled pork

Belly and hand of pork are the two cuts of pork usually salted. Belly is usually cooked flat and hand of pork can be left either with the bones in or boned and rolled.

Check weight to calculate cooking time, then wash joint thoroughly in cold water. Place it in a large pan and cover with fresh cold water. Bring slowly to the boil, skim and then simmer gently for 30 minutes per lb.

When cooked, remove joint from hot liquor and strip off rind. Cool belly of pork and press under a plate and a heavy weight. It is not necessary to press hand of pork. Leave until quite cold—then serve sliced with plum or apple chutney.

Potted pork

YOU WILL NEED:

8 oz. cold cooked pork, minced
½ small onion
¼ lb. bacon rashers, fried until crisp
2 oz. butter
salt and pepper and a pinch of mace
2 teaspoons tomato sauce

Pass pork through mincer a second time with onion and bacon. Add butter, seasoning, spice and sauce, beat well. Pack into a small jar and run a little melted butter over the top. Store in the refrigerator.

Jellied and spiced meats

These traditional recipes are unbeatable for flavour. It's important to press cooked meats thoroughly to ensure a close texture in the finished recipe; they are easier to slice and taste better, too. Cover the meat with a square of kitchen foil or greaseproof paper and top with a plate, saucer or any flat object making sure when you are using a basin or mould that the two are approximately the same shape and diameter. On top of this place a heavy object—scale weights or a tin of fruit—and leave meat until quite cold and set firm. Use a sharp knife for slicing and cut fairly thick slices to prevent meat from breaking.

Tomato pork brawn

YOU WILL NEED FOR 4–6 SERVINGS:

½ large pig's head
1 trotter
1 level teaspoon dried basil
1 level teaspoon dried thyme
2 bay leaves
2 onions, peeled and sliced
6 peppercorns
6 cloves
2 tablespoons tomato purée
½ oz. (or 1 rounded tablespoon) powdered gelatine, soaked in 1 tablespoon water
salt and pepper

Put well-cleaned head and trotter into pan with cold water to cover. Bring to the boil, skim, then add herbs, onion and seasonings and simmer gently for about 2 hours.
Turn off heat, remove all meat and cut into small pieces. Return bones to cooking liquid and boil rapidly to reduce to just over 1 pint. Strain, then into hot liquid stir tomato purée and soaked gelatine. Stir until gelatine has dissolved, season and set aside to cool.
Set about ½ in. of jelly in base of 1½ pint mould. (If liked, a little decoration of cooked sliced carrot or olives can be added at this point. Arrange over jelly layer and add a little more jelly).
Mix cut-up meat with about ¾ pint cool jelly, stir well and pour into mould.
Set aside in a cool place—preferably overnight until set firm, then serve sliced.

Old-fashioned spiced pork

YOU WILL NEED FOR 4–6 SERVINGS:

1 lb. pork fillet
¼ level teaspoon ground ginger
¾ level teaspoon ground cinnamon
1 level teaspoon paprika pepper
6 crushed black peppercorns
½ level teaspoon salt
FOR THE STOCK:
1 pork bone
1 large onion, sliced
1 bay leaf
½ pint of water

First make the stock. Ask your butcher to chop the bone in half. Place this in a saucepan along with sliced onion, bay leaf and water. Bring to the boil, cover with a lid and simmer gently for 30 minutes. Cut pork meat into fairly small pieces and mix with spices, peppercorns and salt. Meanwhile strain cooked stock and return to the saucepan. Add meat and spices. Bring to the boil, cover with a lid and simmer gently until meat is tender—takes about 1½–2 hours. Turn into a 1½–2 pint pudding basin and when cool put a plate over the top of the meat. Add heavy weights and leave until quite cold and set firm. Serve sliced with mustard, pickles or plum sauce.

Minced beef loaf

YOU WILL NEED FOR 6 SERVINGS:

1 oz. dripping or vegetable shortening
1 onion, finely sliced
1½ lb. minced beef
2 level tablespoons flour
½ pint stock or water plus stock cube
1 (2½ oz.) tin tomato purée
1 level teaspoon salt
pinch pepper

Heat the fat in a large saucepan, add the onion and fry until soft—about 5 minutes. Stir in the minced beef and brown quickly. Add the flour, stir in the stock, tomato purée and seasoning. Cover with a lid and simmer for 30 minutes.
Draw the pan off the heat and while still hot, pour the mince mixture into a greased 1½ pint pudding basin. Cover with a buttered paper and set aside in a cool place until set firm.
To unmould, loosen sides, turn out on to a platter and serve sliced.

Old-fashioned spiced pork

Pressed veal

YOU WILL NEED FOR 8 SERVINGS:

1 breast of veal (about 3–4 lb.)
salt and pepper
¼ lb. bacon rashers
finely grated rind of half a lemon
pinch of thyme
2 onions
few stalks of celery
1 carrot
½ turnip
bouquet garni—tie together a few stalks of parsley,
   bay leaf and sprig of thyme
10 peppercorns
1 level teaspoon salt.

Ask the butcher to bone joint and give you the bones for stock. Wipe meat and season well. Arrange trimmed bacon rashers lengthways, add lemon rind and pinch of thyme, roll up tightly and tie with string. Slice onions, celery, carrot and turnip and place in a saucepan with the bones, any meat trimmings, bouquet garni, peppercorns and one level teaspoon salt. Place meat on top and add water up to the depth of the vegetables. Cover meat with a buttered paper, cover saucepan with a lid and cook gently for three hours, basting occasionally. When meat is tender drain and place between two plates with weights on top until quite cold. Strain and reserve the stock. The following day boil stock rapidly until reduced to a glaze, add a little gravy browning if liked. Trim meat and brush over with glaze.
Serve sliced with tomato chutney.

Chicken and asparagus

YOU WILL NEED FOR 4–6 SERVINGS:

4 chicken joints
2 carrots, sliced
2 onions, sliced
1 bay leaf
few peppercorns
1 level teaspoon salt
1 level teaspoon dried savory
few parsley stalks
1 pint water
½ oz. (or 1 rounded tablespoon) powdered gelatine
1 tin asparagus spears

Wipe chicken joints and place in a large roasting or baking tin. Add prepared vegetables, bay leaf, peppercorns, salt, savoury, parsley stalks and water. Cover with a buttered paper or kitchen foil and

place in the centre of a moderate oven (355 deg. or Gas No. 4); bake for 1½ hours until joints are tender. Sprinkle gelatine over two tablespoons water and leave to soak.

Drain joints from cooking broth and allow to cool. Strain liquid into a saucepan and add soaked gelatine and stir over low heat until dissolved. Draw pan off the heat and season to taste with salt if necessary. Over base of a loaf tin or pie dish arrange a few of the trimmed asparagus spears. Pour over a little of the broth and leave to chill until set firm. Carefully lift chicken flesh off the bones and cut meat into chunky slices. Arrange these over the asparagus base placing the nicest pieces in first and filling in with smaller bits. Add any remaining asparagus pieces cut small, and fill, just to cover meat, with more chicken broth. When cold, cover with a square of foil, a plate and a heavy weight. Leave in a cool place overnight until set firm. Serve sliced.

Cold stuffed breasts of lamb

YOU WILL NEED FOR 6 SERVINGS:

2 boned breasts of lamb
3 onions, cut into quarters
2–3 carrots, sliced thickly
FOR THE APRICOT STUFFING:
4 oz. dried apricots
4 oz. seedless raisins
10 oz. (or 4 teacups) fresh white breadcrumbs
1 level teaspoon salt
1 large green pepper, deseeded and chopped
3 oz. butter

Wipe meat and trim away any surplus fat. Season and lay flat, skin side down, on a clean working surface. Meanwhile prepare stuffing. Place apricots and raisins in a saucepan, cover with cold water, bring to the boil and then strain. Snip apricots into small pieces, add raisins, breadcrumbs, salt and green pepper. Melt butter and pour on to the ingredients, mixing with a fork until blended.

Divide stuffing equally between breasts of lamb and spread evenly over to within about ½ inch of the edges. Roll up from one end and tie securely with string. Wrap each joint in a square of kitchen foil, like a parcel—this is not essential but helps to keep stuffing intact while cooking.

Place prepared vegetables in base of a large saucepan and arrange the joints on top. Add sufficient water just to cover vegetables, cover pan with a lid and bring slowly to the boil. Lower heat and simmer gently for 1½ hours.

Remove meat from the pan and discard silver foil wrappings. Place joints on a plate, cover with a second plate and heavy weight. Leave overnight in a cool place until set firm.

Next day, remove string, trim ends evenly and then slice for serving.

Veal pâté stuffing

YOU WILL NEED:

½ lb. pie veal
¼ lb. fresh or (3 oz. packet frozen)
    chicken livers
1 onion, cut into quarters
½ lb. sausagemeat
2½ oz. (or 1 teacup) fresh white breadcrumbs
½ level teaspoon salt

Trim away any excess fat and chop veal coarsely. Slice livers and remove any core.

Pass veal and livers with the onion, through mincer into a mixing basin. Use coarse blade on the mincer and if necessary mince twice.

Add sausagemeat and mix well, then stir in breadcrumbs and salt. This stuffing makes a good alternative for the apricot stuffing in previous recipe. Use in the same way.

Aspic meat moulds

Nowadays commercial aspic jelly crystals replace the old-fashioned method of obtaining aspic jelly from bones. These crystals are simple to use — follow directions for use given on the packet — and have a pleasant beefy flavour. Cooked meat and vegetables used with the jelly can make very appetising moulds. After preparing the jelly it should be allowed to cool. It's important to use it when almost setting and the mould should be prepared in stages so that each layer has time to set before the next is added.

When beginning remember that the base of the mould will be the top, and the nicest part of the decoration should be there. All moulds should be lined with a layer of aspic jelly before filling. Spoon a little of the cooled jelly into the mould — either chill the mould before using, or have at hand a mixing basin with ice cubes and cold water and dip the base of the mould in the iced water. Either way, run the aspic jelly round the inside of the mould covering the base and sides until the jelly sets and covers it completely. Keep the jelly moving until it sets, to ensure only a thin coating.

Next the decoration: Pour a little jelly into a saucer and dip slices of hardboiled egg or cooked vegetables into it and then arrange them over base and sides of the mould. When design is completed put to chill until set firm before adding the filling.

Place meat and remaining cooked vegetables into a mixing basin, add enough aspic jelly to moisten and spoon into the centre of the decorated mould to fill it. Chill until set firm and then when ready to serve, run a knife tip round the top edge, dip base and sides into warm water to loosen and invert meat mould on to a plate.

Lamb cutlets in aspic

YOU WILL NEED FOR 4–6 SERVINGS:

1 piece best end of neck of lamb
1 lb. carrots, peeled and cut into ½ in. lengths
1–2 level teaspoons salt
French dressing, *see page 91*
1 tablespoon chopped parsley
½ pint aspic jelly
skinned tomato flesh and hard-boiled egg
    white for decoration

Ask the butcher to chine only the base of the joint *not* to crack the rib bones.

Place in a large saucepan with prepared carrots, enough water to cover them, and add salt. Bring to the boil and simmer for 45 minutes. Drain meat and carrots and allow to cool.

Using a sharp knife cut meat into cutlets — making four or six according to the number of bones, and cut them away from bone at the base. Trim cutlets neatly and with a knife blade scrape the tips of each cutlet bone clean. Arrange on rack or wire cooling tray ready to decorate.

Place carrots in a mixing basin, add enough French dressing to bind, and add chopped parsley. Leave to marinate, turning occasionally while preparing cutlets. Prepare aspic jelly crystals to normal strength following directions on the packet. Cool until almost setting and spoon a first coating over the cutlets and leave to set firm. Meanwhile trim pieces of skinned tomato flesh and hard-boiled egg white into neat petal shapes. When first aspic coating has set firm, dip decoration in remaining jelly and place on the cutlets. Spoon final coating of aspic jelly over the cutlets and leave to set firm.

Garnish each cutlet bone with a paper frill and serve with the marinated carrots.

Galantines and meat loaves

Make the recipe fit the occasion; a galantine can be left plain or coated with toasted breadcrumbs for a family supper—garnished with chaudfroid sauce and aspic jelly when there's company. If you don't have a mincer, your butcher might find time to mince the mixture for you.

Basic cooking methods

A galantine is cooked either by steaming or simmering in stock. Steaming is the easiest method; the ingredients are packed in a greased pudding basin, straight-sided stone jar or loaf tin, covered with double thickness greased papers, pleated and tied firmly. Use a steamer set over a pan of boiling water, or large saucepan with tight-fitting lid and false bottom or two skewers for the basin or mould to rest on. (Fill saucepan with water to come one-third up the side of the basin and bring to the boil). Set the basin or mould in the pan and add lid. Steam gently, topping up with boiling water when it is necessary. The traditional method is to simmer the galantine gently in a light stock. *See page 12.*

Old-fashioned meat roll

YOU WILL NEED FOR 3–4 SERVINGS:

    10 oz. rump steak or lean stewing steak
    4 oz. lean bacon
    2½ oz. fresh white breadcrumbs
    ½ level teaspoon salt
    pinch of pepper
    1 small egg
    brown breadcrumbs for finishing

Grease a stone 1-lb. jar and a paper to cover. Mince meat and bacon twice if possible. Add white breadcrumbs, salt and pepper and beaten egg. Mix well together until evenly blended and moist. Pack mixture into greased jar and cover with pleated paper tied firmly with string. Steam gently for 2–2½ hours.
Cover with fresh papers and leave a weight on top overnight. Approximately 15 minutes before serving carefully remove meat roll from jar (warm base gently if necessary). Coat with browned breadcrumbs and slice for serving.

Left to right: galantine of beef, stuffed pork, old-fashioned meat roll, chaudfroid of chicken and lamb cutlets in aspic

Galantine of beef

YOU WILL NEED FOR 6–8 SERVINGS:

1 lb. lean rump or chuck steak
4 oz. lean ham or gammon
8 oz. sausagemeat
4 oz. (or 2 level teacups) fresh white breadcrumbs
1 heaped tablespoon chopped parsley
1 level teaspoon mixed herbs
1 level teaspoon salt
freshly ground pepper
2 small eggs
toasted breadcrumbs or chaudfroid sauce
    for coating

Wipe meat and trim away any fat or gristle. Trim rinds and fat from ham or gammon, mince steak and ham finely twice then add other ingredients and mix thoroughly.

To cook in a jar or tin
Pack mixture tightly into a greased loaf tin or straight-sided stone jar. Cover with double layers of greased, greaseproof paper with a pleat across the centre and tie securely. Steam for 2½–3 hours then cover again, with fresh papers. Alternatively, bake galantine in the loaf tin in a warm oven (335 deg. or Gas No. 3) for 2 hours. Set on a plate to catch the juices and press under a weight until quite cold. Turn out and coat with toasted breadcrumbs or with chaudfroid sauce—*see recipe on page 75.*

To cook in a cloth
With lightly floured hands, shape mixture into a thick, firm roll. Dust a scalded cloth with flour and wrap up the roll in the cloth, tying the ends firmly like a cracker.
Simmer gently in stock for 1½–2 hours. Lift out and drain. Untie and re-wrap the roll, then press between weighted boards or plates until cold.
Coat with toasted breadcrumbs or chaudfroid sauce.

Stuffed pork

YOU WILL NEED FOR 10–12 SERVINGS:

1 boned piece of neck end of pork with a
    pocket cut the length of the joint from where
    the bone has been removed
seasoning
chaudfroid sauce—*see page 75*
strips of leek, thinly sliced carrot for decoration
½ pint aspic jelly

FOR THE STUFFING:
1 lb. pork fillet
½ lb. calves' liver
1 onion, peeled and quartered
1 clove garlic, crushed with a little salt
1½ level teaspoons dried basil
2 tablespoons chopped parsley
2½ oz. (or 1 teacup) fresh white breadcrumbs
1 level teaspoon salt
½ level teaspoon pepper
1 tablespoon brandy or stock

Wipe meat and season inside and out. Set meat aside while preparing the stuffing.
Trim away any fat or gristle from pork and liver. Pass twice through mincer, with onion and garlic. Add basil, parsley, breadcrumbs and seasoning, Stir in enough brandy or stock to make a moist stuffing and pack, not too tightly, into the pocket in the pork joint.
Tie in several places with string to make a neat shape.
Wrap the joint completely in foil (use double sheets if foil is not wide enough) and close ends like a parcel. Place meat in a roasting tin and put above centre in a very hot oven (425 deg. or Gas No. 7) and cook, allowing 40 minutes per lb. The foil protects the meat in the high temperature which ensures it is thoroughly cooked.
Remove cooked joint from the foil wrapping, cut away any string and strip off the rind. Top with a plate and heavy weight and leave until quite cold.
Trim joint neatly and wipe surface with clean muslin (dip muslin in boiling water, leave a few minutes to cool slightly, wring out) to remove any grease. Prepare chaudfroid sauce and coat joint as directed—*see recipe and instructions.* Prepare a decoration, using thinly sliced carrot for flower heads and strips of outside green leaves of leek for flower stalks and leaves. Dip decoration in aspic jelly and arrange on the joint—*see directions on page 75.* Finish with a final coat of aspic jelly.

Glazed cold meats

These joints are a boon when entertaining. Prepare them well in advance and take time over the decoration to make a really pretty finish. Make sure you remove any joint from the refrigerator at least 1 hour before serving; they should be served cold but not chilled.
An ideal accompaniment is cold cooked vegetables marinated in French dressing. Leave to marinate for 1 hour, turning occasionally, then serve as a garnish on the meat platter.

Chaudfroid sauce

YOU WILL NEED FOR 1 PINT SAUCE:

½ pint water
aspic jelly crystals — *see recipe*
½ pint milk
½ onion stuck with a clove
1 bay leaf
few parsley stalks
1 oz. butter or margarine
1 rounded tablespoon flour

Heat ½ pint of water almost to boiling, then draw pan off the heat and stir into it sufficient aspic jelly crystals to set 1 pint of normal strength jelly. *(See packet directions.)* Set aside to cool while preparing the rest of the sauce.

Measure milk into a saucepan and add onion, bay leaf and parsley stalks. Heat till almost boiling, then draw pan off the heat and set aside to infuse for 10–15 minutes. Strain and discard flavouring ingredients. Melt butter or margarine in a saucepan and stir in flour. Cook over very low heat for 1 minute then gradually stir in strained milk, beating well all the time to get a really smooth sauce. Bring to the boil and simmer gently for 2 minutes. Draw pan off the heat and allow sauce to cool — stirring occasionally to prevent a skin forming.

When both aspic jelly and sauce are tepid, whisk jelly into the sauce, then pass through a very fine sieve or squeeze through a scalded linen cloth into a clean bowl. Leave until sauce is just beginning to set, stirring occasionally, then use at once.

To coat with chaudfroid sauce or aspic jelly

Whether you are preparing a galantine or cooked joint, it should be well chilled in advance. Stand the food to be coated ready on a rack (use a wire cooling tray) set over a large plate or tray to catch the drips. For a beginner these coatings can be a little difficult to handle at first. It's most important that the jelly or sauce should be just on setting point when spooned over the meat. If it is too thin it will quickly run off and if too thick a rough, uneven surface will result as the mixture will set too quickly. Ideally the sauce or jelly should flow over the food so that the surface is smooth, but thick enough to mask the food completely.

The easiest method is to have one basin of ice cubes and cold water and a second one of hot water. If the sauce becomes too cool while working, warm the basin of sauce in the bowl of hot water.

Alternatively, if the mixture is too warm, cool the basin in the bowl of iced water.

Use a metal spoon to pour sauce quickly over small portions of meat and if a large joint or whole chicken is to be masked, pour the sauce from the basin. The sauce running on to the plate or basin below may be melted and used for further coating.

The decoration

Prepare pieces of decoration from vegetables, selecting food with colours that will show up.

Plan the decoration and have all the pieces prepared before beginning work.

Dissolve 1 level teaspoon aspic jelly crystals in 2 tablespoons boiling water and pour on to a plate. Dip the prepared pieces of decoration first in the jelly and then arrange on a set base of chaudfroid sauce. Use two sewing needles or skewers to handle the decoration. When the decoration is finished and set firm — the aspic jelly will hold it in position — prepare a further ¼ pint of normal strength aspic jelly according to packet directions. When this has cooled and is beginning to thicken, spoon gently over the decoration and leave to set firm.

Chaudfroid of chicken

YOU WILL NEED FOR 6 SERVINGS:

6 chicken joints
2 onions, peeled and halved
1 bay leaf
1–2 level teaspoons salt
chaudfroid sauce — *see recipe*
½ pint aspic jelly
thinly sliced cucumber skin and small pieces of
   pimento for decoration

Trim joints, if legs, tie with string into a neat shape. Place with onions and bay leaf in a roasting or baking tin, just cover with cold water and add salt. Place above centre shelf in a hot oven (400 deg. or Gas No. 6) and cook for 1½–2 hours or until joints are tender. Drain and allow to cool, then chill until ready to finish. Remove any skin and protruding pieces of bone. Wipe joints with a clean piece of muslin (dip in boiling water, allow to cool slightly, then wring out) to remove any grease, then arrange the pieces on a rack or wire cooling tray.

Prepare the chaudfroid sauce and coat joints as directed.

Prepare a decoration using neatly cut squares of cucumber skin and pieces of pimento skin. Dip in aspic jelly and arrange neatly on the portions of chicken and then finish with a final coating of aspic jelly. Arrange on a bed of chopped aspic jelly before serving.

Pâtés and pastes

A pâté is a smooth, well seasoned, mixture of meat—usually liver or game, temptingly spiced. When mincing fresh meat or liver use the coarse blade and mince twice if necessary to get a smooth texture. Meat passed through a fine blade takes twice as long to prepare. Pâté should be served with fresh unbuttered toast. Trim away crusts and slice into triangles. As pâté has a rich flavour, portions are best kept small. It makes a delicious first course. Store pâté in the refrigerator and use it within a week.

Pâté maison

YOU WILL NEED FOR 8–10 SERVINGS:

6 oz. bacon rashers
1 clove of garlic, crushed with a little salt
2 lb. calves' liver, cut in slices
2 eggs
1 level teaspoon salt
little freshly ground pepper
2 tablespoons thick cream
1 tablespoon brandy

Trim bacon rashers, discard any gristle and stretch them out thinly, then use them to line a medium to large pâté mould or 7 in. round baking dish; allow ends of rashers to overlap top edge.
Rub crushed clove of garlic round inside of a mixing basin to give a little flavour, then discard the clove. For a stronger flavour reserve and use in recipe.
With a pair of scissors, snip away any core from the liver, and pass through mincer, using the coarse blade. Add the crushed garlic if liked. Beat in eggs, salt and a seasoning of pepper. Then stir in the cream and the brandy.
Spoon mixture into centre of prepared dish and fold top edges of bacon rashers into the centre. Cover with a buttered paper and square of kitchen foil or greaseproof paper and place dish in a roasting tin or baking tin with 1 in. cold water. Set in centre of a slow oven (335 deg. or Gas No. 3) and bake for 2 hours.
Remove from heat, pour away any liquid fat and cover with fresh papers, a plate and a heavy weight, and leave overnight in a cool place until pâté is quite firm.
Then turn out of mould and slice pâté for serving.

Easy liver pâté 1

YOU WILL NEED FOR 6 SERVINGS:

5 rashers streaky bacon
1 lb. pig's liver cut in slices
1 egg, blended
1 tablespoon instant potato powder
1 level teaspoon mixed herbs
2 level teaspoons salt
¼ teaspoon black pepper
1 large clove garlic, finely chopped
2 tablespoons sherry
½ lb. pork dripping, warmed

Well grease 1 lb. loaf tin and line with the trimmed bacon rashers. Mince liver finely (or put in electric liquidiser with all other ingredients except dripping, which should be blended in at the end). Blend all ingredients together with a wooden spoon and turn into the prepared tin. Cover with a buttered paper and set in a shallow roasting or baking tin with 1 in. water. Place in the centre of a slow oven (335 deg. or Gas No. 3) and bake for 1 hour. Allow to cool. Turn out and serve sliced.

Easy liver pâté 2

YOU WILL NEED FOR 4–6 SERVINGS:

½ lb. lamb's liver cut in slices
1 small onion, cut in quarters
½ lb. pork or beef sausagemeat
1 level teaspoon salt and pinch of black pepper
2 teaspoons chopped parsley
1 clove garlic, crushed and chopped
1 egg
6–8 streaky bacon rashers
2 bay leaves

Mince the liver and onion together into a mixing basin. Add the sausagemeat, the seasoning of salt and pepper, parsley, garlic and egg. Mix together thoroughly, using a fork.
Line a 1 pint baking or pie dish with the trimmed and stretched bacon rashers. Pack in the pâté mixture and fold the rasher inwards to cover the top. Top with the bay leaves, cover with a buttered paper and place the pâté in a large roasting or baking tin filled with 1 in. of cold water. Place in the centre of a moderately hot oven (380 deg. or Gas No. 5) for 1½–1¾ hours. Remove from the oven, cover with a clean square of kitchen foil and press with a heavy weight overnight.

Pâté maison and potted chicken

Easy liver pâté 3

YOU WILL NEED FOR 3–4 SERVINGS:

3 oz. butter
½ lb. lambs' or chicken's liver, cut in slices
salt and pepper
1 tablespoon brandy

Melt 1 oz. of butter in a saucepan and add liver. Brown on both sides then cover with a lid and cook gently for 5 minutes.
Draw pan off heat and pass liver mixture through coarse blade of mincer into a mixing basin. Add remaining butter, plenty of seasoning and tablespoon brandy. Beat well with a wooden spoon until smooth, then pack into a small pâté dish, cover with a little extra melted butter or a lid and store in refrigerator.

Chicken liver pâté with anchovy

YOU WILL NEED FOR 6–8 SERVINGS:

¾ lb. (or four 3 oz. packets of frozen) chicken livers
¼ lb. streaky bacon rashers
5 anchovy fillets
2 oz. melted butter for the top
FOR THE SAUCE:
½ pint milk
1 bay leaf
1 onion, sliced
few peppercorns
1 oz. butter
1 oz. (or 1 rounded tablespoon) flour
salt and pepper

Slice chicken livers and snip away any cores. Trim and chop bacon rashers. Mince these and anchovy fillets, using coarse blade.
Meanwhile measure milk, bay leaf, onion and peppercorns into a saucepan. Bring slowly to the boil, then draw pan off heat and leave to infuse for 15 minutes. Melt butter over low heat and stir in flour. Gradually add strained milk, beating well all the time to get a smooth sauce. Bring to the boil and season with salt and pepper. Draw pan off heat and stir in minced ingredients.
Pour mixture into a buttered pâté mould or 6 in. baking dish, cover with a buttered paper, square of foil or greaseproof paper. Set in a roasting or baking tin with 1 in. cold water and place in centre of a slow oven (335 deg. or Gas No. 3). Bake for 1 hour. Leave overnight until quite cold, then run a little melted butter over surface to keep pâté moist and store in a refrigerator.

Pork pâté

YOU WILL NEED FOR 8 SERVINGS:

1 lb. pigs' liver, cut in slices
¼ lb. streaky bacon rashers
¼ lb. belly of pork
2 oz. butter
1 onion, sliced
1 tablespoon tomato purée
pinch of mixed herbs
½ level teaspoon salt
little freshly ground pepper
¼ pint red wine or stock
1 tablespoon brandy
little grated lemon rind
1 clove garlic, crushed with a little salt
1 bay leaf
1–2 oz. melted butter, for the top

Snip away any skin and gristle from the liver. Cut away rinds and chop bacon. Trim and chop pork. Melt butter in a saucepan, add onion, and fry gently until golden brown. Then add liver, bacon and pork. Stir in tomato purée, herbs, seasoning and wine or stock. Cover with a lid and cook gently for 1 hour.
Pass cooked mixture through coarse blade on a mincer into a mixing basin. Add brandy and lemon rind and mix well. Rub crushed garlic round inside of a large pâté mould or 1½-pint baking dish, then discard clove. Press the pâté mixture, spread level and top with bay leaf. Cover with a lid and cook in centre of a slow oven (335 deg. or Gas No. 3) for 30 minutes.
Remove from heat, discard bay leaf, cover with a buttered paper, a plate and a heavy weight. Leave overnight in a cool place until set firm. Run melted butter over top of the pâté to keep it moist, and store in the refrigerator until required.

Bacon and corned beef loaf

YOU WILL NEED FOR 6 SERVINGS:

1 vacuum packed bacon joint — about 2 lb.
1 (12 oz.) tin corned beef
1 onion, peeled and quartered
2½ oz. (or 1 teacup) fresh white breadcrumbs
1 tablespoon finely chopped parsley
1 teaspoon prepared mustard
salt and pepper
2 eggs
FOR THE DECORATION:
½ cucumber
2 tomatoes
1 egg, hardboiled
chopped parsley

Place bacon in its vacuum-sealed bag in a saucepan and cover with cold water. Bring slowly to the boil and simmer for time directed—about 2 hours. Lift out of pan, remove from sealed bag and mince bacon with corned beef and onion into a mixing basin. Add breadcrumbs, parsley, mustard and seasoning. Stir in eggs to bind mixture together.

Pack mixture in a large greased loaf tin or 1½–2 pint baking dish. Place in centre of a moderate oven (355 deg. or Gas No. 4) and bake for 30 minutes. Remove from heat and allow to become quite cold, then loosen sides and unmould meat loaf on to a serving platter. Garnish with slices of cucumber, tomato, hardboiled egg and chopped parsley. Serve sliced.

Potted meats and meat pastes are ideal for using up left-over poultry or meat from a joint. The cooked meat is minced finely, then smoothly blended with butter and spices to make a delicious spread for sandwiches and toast.

Potted turkey or chicken

YOU WILL NEED:

2–3 bacon rashers
8–10 oz. cooked turkey or chicken meat
pinch of ground mace
dash of Worcestershire sauce
2–3 oz. butter
2–3 tablespoons fresh cream
salt and pepper

Fry trimmed bacon rashers in a saucepan until quite crisp. Pass these, with chicken or turkey meat, through mincer into a mixing basin. Add ground mace, Worcestershire sauce and beat in butter and cream. Taste and season with salt and pepper, as necessary. Pack into small pots and cover with extra melted butter or a lid and store in the refrigerator.

Potted veal

YOU WILL NEED:

1 lb. pie veal
1 bay leaf
1 level teaspoon salt
few peppercorns
¼ lb. ham or cooked bacon
finely grated rind and juice of ½ lemon
4 oz. butter
salt and pepper

Trim away any excess fat and gristle from pie veal and place meat in a saucepan. Add bay leaf, salt and peppercorns and just cover with cold water. Cover with a lid and bring slowly to the boil. Lower heat and simmer gently for 1½ hours.

When tender, strain meat from cooking liquor. Pass meat with ham or cooked bacon through the coarse blade on a mincer. Mince twice to get a smooth texture, then add lemon rind and juice, butter, and beat well. Add any extra salt and pepper to taste, then press into small pots. Cover with a little extra melted butter or a lid and store in the refrigerator.

Giblet paste

YOU WILL NEED:

2 sets chicken or 1 set turkey giblets
¼ lb. ham or cooked bacon
4 oz. butter
pepper and salt
cayenne pepper
powdered mace

Wash the neck, liver and heart and place in a saucepan and cover with cold water. Bring to boil and simmer gently for 1 hour. Drain, slice heart and liver, and remove meat from neck, discarding bones. Pass meat mixture through mincer with the ham or bacon cut into small pieces.

Gradually beat into the soft butter, season well and add a pinch of cayenne pepper and powdered mace. Pack into small pots, pour a little salted, melted butter over paste and store in the refrigerator.

Potted beef

YOU WILL NEED:

8 oz. cooked left-over beef, minced
¼ lb. bacon rashers, fried until crisp
2 oz. butter
salt and pepper
pinch of mace
2 teaspoons Worcestershire sauce

Pass the beef through the mincer a second time along with the bacon rashers. Add the butter, seasoning, spice and sauce and beat well together. Pack into a small jar and run a little melted butter over the top. Store in the refrigerator for not more than 2–3 days. It makes a delicious filling for sandwiches.

ALL ABOUT
Vegetables & Salads

Root vegetables and onions

Cooking guide

Vegetable	Method	Time
Artichokes (Jerusalem)	boiled	20–30 min.
Beetroot	boiled	30–60 min.
	baked	1–1½ hrs.
	roasted	1–2 hrs.
Carrots	boiled	15–30 min.
	braised	30 min.
Leeks	boiled	15–20 min.
Onions	boiled	15–30 min.
	braised	30–40 min.
	fried	15–20 min.
	roasted	45–60 min.
Parsnips	boiled	30–40 min.
	braised	30–40 min.
Potatoes		
new	boiled	10–12 min.
old	boiled	15–20 min.
	baked in jacket	45–60 min.
	roasted	45–60 min.
	chips	15–20 min.
sweet	boiled	20–25 min.
Swedes and	boiled	20–40 min.
Turnips	braised	30–40 min.

Prepare properly

In general when peeling root vegetables use a parer that doesn't take off too much skin as this contains much of the nutriment. Exceptions are turnips and swedes which must be peeled thickly.

New carrots and potatoes are best scraped or scrubbed since the young skins are very thin. Sweet potatoes should be scrubbed and cooked with their skins on.

Beetroot should be washed and cooked whole; trim off all but 1 in. of the leaves, don't cut the tap root.

Don't prepare vegetables until you are ready to cook them; if they are left standing too long in water many of the soluble minerals will be lost.

Useful tips for those who weep when peeling onions— hold them under cold water as you work, or pour boiling water over them, leave until cold and then slip off the skins.

Cook with care

Root vegetables are usually boiled but they can then be garnished.

To boil: place prepared vegetables in a pan and just cover with cold water, add 1 level teaspoon salt for every pint of water.

A selection of root vegetables and onions

Bring to the boil, cover pan with a lid and simmer for the required cooking time (*see chart page 80*).

The length of time is counted from the moment the water boils. New potatoes, which cook more quickly, are best plunged into boiling water.

Cooked vegetables should keep their shape and feel tender when tested with a pointed knife. Don't over-cook or they will be soggy.

Drain off the water and toss vegetables over a gentle heat to dry them.

Tasty garnishes

New potatoes: toss in butter, with chopped mint or grated lemon rind.

Old potatoes: mash with salt, pepper and a nut of butter. Add 1–2 tablespoons milk and beat until smooth. Fork into a mound in a hot dish and top with parsley; or spoon into a cotton or nylon piping bag fitted with a large rosette tube and pipe a border round the serving dish.

Sweet potatoes: peel off skin and serve with butter and a sprinkling of paprika pepper or parsley.

Carrots: serve with onion butter. To make this melt 2 tablespoons butter and add $\frac{1}{2}$ small onion, finely chopped. Cook gently until the onion is soft then add cooked carrots.

Or serve *Candied carrots*—drain cooked carrots, dry and roll in granulated sugar. Fry lightly in hot butter stirring often until golden brown and glazed.

Onions: serve in a well-seasoned white sauce.

Parsnips: add salt and pepper and serve in a white sauce seasoned with nutmeg. Or make *parsnip fritters*—mash cooked, seasoned parsnip and shape into small flat cakes, roll in flour and fry in butter.

Turnip: season with salt and pepper, and toss in butter. For a special occasion fold in a little cream and lemon juice or sherry.

Beetroot: stand cooked beetroot in cold water for 1 minute, then slip off the skin. Leave whole if small (otherwise slice it) and serve hot, dotted with butter.

Jerusalem artichokes: toss in butter or in a well-seasoned white sauce.

New ways

Braise or casserole: prepare vegetables and cut in neat pieces. Put in a casserole dish with 1 oz. butter or dripping and 3 tablespoons water to every 1 lb. of vegetables. Cover with a lid and cook in a moderate oven until tender, $\frac{1}{2}$–1 hour. When tender remove the lid, sprinkle with salt and serve. This method is suitable for all except potatoes and beetroot.

Roasting: cover the vegetables with boiling salted water, bring to the boil again and simmer for 3–5 minutes, drain and dry (this is called par-boiling). Heat sufficient dripping in a roasting tin to give $\frac{1}{4}$ in. depth and when hot put in the vegetables and baste with the dripping.

Place fairly high up in a hot oven (400 deg. or Gas No. 6) and cook for $\frac{3}{4}$–1 hour, turning and basting often to brown evenly.

Vegetables may be roasted round a joint. If they haven't been par-boiled more time should be allowed. Most suitable vegetables are beetroot, onion and potatoes or parsnips.

Deep frying: prepare the vegetables (any thickly cut vegetables must first be par-boiled as for roasting). Drain fried foods on absorbent paper, then season with salt before serving.

Potato chips or French fried potatoes: cut the prepared potato into slices about $\frac{1}{4}$ in. thick, then into strips. Dry in a clean cloth and pile into a frying basket—half filling it only. Lower into hot, deep fat and fry gently, shaking to move them freely until cooked but not brown—takes about 5–10 minutes. Drain and allow the fat to reheat until very hot. Fry a second time quickly until brown and crisp. This gives a soft centre and a crisp outside—the chips may be partly cooked early in the day.

Deep fried onion rings: peel and slice the onion across. Separate out the rings, dip them first in milk and then in flour. Fry in hot fat until crisp and golden.

Shallow frying: try delicious sauté potatoes. Prepare the potatoes and boil until almost tender. Drain and slice. Fry very quickly in butter until golden brown on both sides. This is an excellent way of using up left-over boiled potatoes—but not over-boiled ones which tend to break up. These can be mashed, shaped into potato cakes and fried on both sides in butter (add a little chopped onion or chives for flavour).

Sauté onions: peel and slice onions, or cut them into rings. Fry in hot dripping or lard, turning to brown evenly. If liked, add a little bottled meat sauce, soy sauce or curry powder before serving.

Baking: select large potatoes, scrub clean and prick the skins. Stand on the centre shelf of a fairly hot oven (375 deg. or Gas No. 5) and cook for 1–1$\frac{1}{2}$ hours according to size. When cooked they should feel soft when squeezed gently.

To serve, cut a cross in the centre, squeeze the potato gently and fluff up the centre with a fork. Serve with butter or spoon soured cream and chopped chives into the opening and top with more chives. Or top with grated cheese and crumbled bacon.

Bacon-fried carrots

YOU WILL NEED FOR 4 SERVINGS:

3–4 bacon rashers, trimmed
1 onion, sliced
1 lb. new carrots, scraped and diced
salt and pepper
pinch of sugar
1 oz. butter

In a large, shallow pan, gently fry the bacon rashers until crisp. Drain rashers and set aside. Add the onion and carrots to the hot bacon fat, season well and add a good pinch of sugar (new carrots should taste sweet). Cover the pan with a lid and cook over low heat for 10–15 minutes until the carrots are just tender. Remove the pan lid, add the butter and continue cooking, stirring occasionally, until the carrots are lightly browned, then add the crumbled bacon rashers and serve.

Baked stuffed onions

YOU WILL NEED FOR 6 SERVINGS:

3 Spanish onions
3 tablespoons stock or water
FOR THE STUFFING:
6 oz. sausagemeat
salt and pepper
2 oz. mushrooms, fried and chopped
2 heaped tablespoons breadcrumbs
1 oz. butter, melted

Peel and boil the onions until just tender, then drain and cool. Remove the onion centres to make stuffing and separate the outer layers to make about 6 shells.
In a small bowl, mix together the coarsely chopped onion centres, sausagemeat, salt, pepper, mushrooms, breadcrumbs and melted butter. Carefully spoon into the onion shells.
Place the stuffed onions in a baking dish and add the stock. Cover with a lid and bake in a moderate oven

(355 deg. or Gas No. 4) for a further 30 minutes, removing the lid for the last 10 minutes.

Potato cheese

YOU WILL NEED FOR 4 SERVINGS:

1½–2 lb. potatoes
1 large onion, chopped
salt and pepper
butter or margarine
½ pint cheese sauce, see page 102
2 oz. grated Cheddar cheese

Peel and slice potatoes ¼ in. thick. Cook in boiling water 4–5 minutes then drain. Put alternate layers of potato and chopped onion into a well-buttered baking dish. Season each layer well and add a few dots of butter or margarine.
Pour the sauce over the potatoes, cover with well-buttered greaseproof paper, and a lid, and bake in centre of a slow oven (310 deg. or Gas No. 2) for about 2 hours. When cooked remove lid and paper, top with grated cheese and brown under the grill before serving.

Baked onions in white sauce

YOU WILL NEED FOR 4 SERVINGS:

1 lb. medium onions, peeled and left whole
½ oz. butter
1 tablespoon water
FOR THE SAUCE:
1 oz. butter or margarine
1 level tablespoon flour
⅓ pint (or 1 teacupful) milk
salt and pepper

Peel the onions leaving them whole. Place in a saucepan, cover with cold water and bring up to the boil, simmer for 1 minute then drain and place in a casserole dish, along with the butter or margarine and water. Cover with a lid and place above centre in a moderate oven (355 deg. or Gas No. 4) and bake for 45 minutes—1 hour or until tender.
Meanwhile melt the butter or margarine in a saucepan over low heat. Stir in the flour and cook gently for 1 minute. Gradually stir in the milk beating well to get a smooth sauce. Bring up to the boil, season with salt and pepper and simmer for 2–3 minutes.
When the onions are cooked and ready to serve, remove lid from the casserole, drain away any liquid, pour over the sauce and serve.

Green vegetables

Cooking guide

Vegetable	Method	Time
Beans		
broad	boiling	10–15 min.
French	boiling	10–20 min.
runner	boiling	10–20 min.
Broccoli		
purple	boiling	10–15 min.
white	boiling	10–20 min.
		(20–30 min. if whole)
Brussels		
sprouts	boiling	7–15 min.
tops	boiling	5–10 min.
Cabbage		
green	boiling	10–15 min.
red	boiling	30–60 min.
spring	boiling	7–10 min.
Cauliflower		
whole	boiling	10–15 min.
sprigs	boiling	10–12 min.
Peas	boiling	10–15 min.
Seakale	boiling	20–30 min.
Spinach	boiling	10–15 min.
Celery	boiling	15–20 min.
	braising	45–60 min.
Chicory	boiling	15–20 min.
	braising	40–45 min.

Preparing

Wash and prepare green vegetables, then soak them in cold, salted water for a few minutes. The salt water draws out grubs which are sometimes found in the outer leaves.

Remove only the discoloured leaves from cabbage and Brussels sprouts—use the darker outer leaves, they are richer in food value than the pale inner ones. Cabbage should be halved, quartered, the hard stem removed and the leaves shredded. Brussels sprouts are left whole and a small gash made in the base so that they cook evenly. Red cabbage should be treated as ordinary cabbage; and sauerkraut, which is white cabbage preserved by salting, is usually bought ready-prepared from a delicatessen. Wash spinach very carefully in plenty of water as the leaves tend to be gritty. Leave whole, but nip out the coarse centre vein. Discard any discoloured leaves.

French and runner beans can be left whole if small, or shredded if larger. Remove strings from sides. Vegetables with white stems—such as celery—should have any discoloured parts and green stems removed, since these are bitter. Very pale green stem may be used, however, as the slight bitterness is removed by cooking. Scrub well.

Break up cauliflower into sprigs, unless it is to be used whole. If using it whole, leave a few of the tiny green leaves around the base to give a little colour, slit the base to help to cook evenly.

Cut off tough parts of stalks and remove coarse leaves from broccoli. Peel stalks and slit the larger ones lengthwise for an inch or two to ensure even cooking. Remove any bruised outer leaves from chicory. Wash quickly, and with a pointed knife remove the hard core at the base. When boiling chicory it's advisable to add a little lemon juice to bleach it. Otherwise it may discolour. If you find chicory bitter, add one or two lumps of sugar.

Cooking

Braising: blanched stems such as chicory and celery are the only vegetables suitable (other than root) for this method. The inner parts of the celery, or celery hearts, are best, but the outer stalks may be cut up into 2 in. lengths and braised also. Fry the celery in a little hot dripping until lightly brown. Add salt and pepper and half cover with stock. Cook gently with the lid on the pan until tender (*see chart*). Serve in a hot dish with the juice.

To braise chicory—prepare as directed, then for each lb. melt 2 oz. butter in a saucepan or fireproof dish. Add the chicory, sprinkle with salt and a few drops of lemon juice. Cover with a lid and cook slowly until tender (*see chart*).

Boiling: the basic method of cooking green vegetables is by boiling. The water should be boiling rapidly before you add the vegetables. Use 1 level teaspoon salt for every pint of water. Don't use too much water—and remember that some greens, such as cabbage and spinach, reduce quite considerably during cooking. Cook vegetables rapidly for the required time (*see chart*). Cooking time starts from the moment the water containing the vegetables starts to boil.

It is very important not to over-cook green vegetables—they should be boiled until tender and crisp—or they lose their flavour and food value and

From the top clockwise: cauliflower—in white sauce, French fried, polonaise, au gratin, with melted butter and chopped parsley

become very soft and easily broken. Boil cauliflower less rapidly then the other greens, as it breaks up easily. Cauliflower should be boiled with the head downwards in the water.

Never add soda to preserve the colour of green vegetables—it immediately destroys any vitamins. Rather cook the vegetables carefully as described above. By cooking rapidly the cooking time is shortened and maximum colour preserved.

Serving

Cabbage: coarsely chop and toss with salt, pepper and a little butter. Spring greens and Brussels tops should be treated in the same way.

Brussels sprouts: leave whole and toss with butter. Or serve in parsley butter or parsley sauce. When in season, some cooked and coarsely chopped chestnuts are nice served with Brussels sprouts or sliced sautéed mushrooms.

Cauliflower: cook whole and serve with a well-seasoned white sauce—garnish with paprika pepper. Or cook in sprigs and serve with melted butter and chopped parsley. For a change try it as the Continentals like it: 'au gratin'—coated with a white sauce, topped with grated cheese and browned under the grill; 'polonaise'—topped with fresh white breadcrumbs which have been fried in hot butter until golden brown and then mixed with coarsely chopped hard-boiled egg.

Peas, French, runner and broad beans: serve tossed in butter with a little parsley. To young peas add a little chopped mint, and to French or runner beans add sliced sautéed mushrooms or toasted flaked almonds. Broad beans are popular served in a well-seasoned white or parsley sauce.

Celery: may be served in melted butter, or in a well-seasoned white sauce. Alternatively it may be boiled in stock and served in a tomato sauce, or mashed and seasoned with salt, pepper and grated nutmeg.

Chicory: although it is often served in salad it also makes an excellent hot vegetable. Serve with melted butter and chopped parsley, or with a well-seasoned white sauce, topped with cheese and grilled until brown. Or top the chicory with a mixture of cheese and buttered breadcrumbs and brown under the grill.

Broccoli and seakale: serve with seasoning and melted butter. Or coat with hollandaise sauce or a well-seasoned white sauce. Broccoli can be served with white sauce, grated cheese and browned under the grill.

Spinach: chop or finely cut it and season with butter, salt and pepper. It is often served 'en branche' (whole leaves) and served with melted butter or hollandaise sauce. Alternatively add a little white sauce and a tablespoon of cream to chopped spinach. Reheat gently, season and serve.

Green beans Lyonnaise

YOU WILL NEED FOR 4 SERVINGS:

1 lb. French or runner beans
4 rashers bacon, diced
½ small onion, finely chopped or grated
½ level teaspoon salt
1 teaspoon vinegar
pinch of pepper

Prepare beans and boil (*see directions*). Meanwhile, in a saucepan fry bacon pieces until crisp. Remove the bacon bits and reserve. To the hot bacon fat add onion and sauté until tender. Add salt, vinegar, pepper, bacon bits and drained, cooked beans. Toss and serve.

Braised celery and tomato

YOU WILL NEED FOR 4 SERVINGS:

1 oz. butter or margarine
1 head of celery prepared and cut into 1-inch pieces
salt and pepper
1 (15 oz.) tin tomatoes

Melt butter or margarine in a saucepan, add celery, season well, cover with a lid and simmer for 40 minutes or until tender. Add tomatoes and cook covered for 5 minutes or until tomatoes are hot.

French fried cauliflower

YOU WILL NEED FOR 4 SERVINGS:

1 cauliflower
1 egg
1 tablespoon cooking oil
salt and pepper
brown breadcrumbs for coating
fat for deep frying

Remove any green leaves and break cauliflower into sprigs, keeping them fairly large. Place in a saucepan, cover with boiling water, add a pinch of salt, and cook gently with a lid on until just tender (*see chart*), then drain. Lightly mix egg, oil and plenty of seasoning. Dip cooked sprigs of cauliflower first into egg mixture, then in breadcrumbs. Fry in deep, hot fat until golden—about 5 minutes. Drain. Sprinkle with salt and serve.

Green peas French style

YOU WILL NEED FOR 4 SERVINGS:

1½–2 lb. fresh garden peas
¼ cos lettuce
12 spring onions
¼ pint water
1 oz. butter or margarine
1 level teaspoon salt
2 level teaspoons sugar
1 level teaspoon arrowroot blended with 2 tablespoons water

Shell peas, wash and shred lettuce and peel and shred onions. Place lettuce and onions in a saucepan with water and butter or margarine. Add peas, seasoning and sugar, cover with a lid and simmer gently until peas are tender (*see chart*). Stir in arrowroot and cook 2–3 minutes longer.

Cauliflower and bacon savoury

YOU WILL NEED FOR 4 SERVINGS:

1 large cauliflower
1 onion, peeled and chopped
4 streaky bacon rashers
½ oz. butter or margarine
2 oz. mushrooms, trimmed and sliced
FOR THE CHEESE SAUCE:
2 oz. butter or margarine
1½ oz. plain flour
¾ pint milk
salt and pepper
4 oz. grated Cheddar cheese

Trim cauliflower and break into sprigs. Wash well, then cook in boiling salted water until tender — takes about 10 minutes.
Drain and arrange sprigs in an oven-proof dish. Fry onion and trimmed, chopped rashers in fat until soft. Sprinkle over cauliflower.
For the sauce, melt the butter or margarine in a pan over low heat, and stir in flour; beat in milk, stirring to get a smooth sauce. Bring to the boil, add salt and pepper and simmer for 2–3 minutes. Stir in half the cheese and, when blended, draw the pan off the heat and pour over the cauliflower sprigs. Sprinkle with remaining cheese, and place near the top of a hot oven (400 deg. or Gas No. 6) until heated through and browned. Garnish with fried mushrooms.

Spinach with eggs and cheese

YOU WILL NEED FOR 4 SERVINGS:

4 eggs
1½ lb. fresh spinach (or 1 large packet frozen)
FOR THE CHEESE SAUCE:
1 oz. butter or margarine
1 oz. (1 rounded tablespoon) plain flour
½ pint milk
salt and pepper to taste
4 oz. cheddar cheese, grated

Soft boil eggs, then plunge them into cold water and remove shells. Wash fresh spinach very thoroughly, remove coarse veins and stalks. Place in large saucepan, add no water there will be sufficient clinging to the leaves, cover with a lid and bring up to the boil. Cook 10–15 minutes. Strain, then chop coarsely. Alternatively prepare frozen spinach according to packet directions and leave to heat through while preparing sauce.
Melt butter or margarine over low heat and stir in flour. Cook gently for 1 minute. Gradually stir in milk and bring to the boil, stirring until thick and smooth. Simmer gently for 2–3 minutes, then season with salt and pepper, stir in half grated cheese, and remove pan from heat.
Spoon spinach into base of a heatproof serving dish. Make four hollows in it with the back of a spoon and place a shelled egg in each hollow. Pour the cheese sauce on top. Sprinkle with remaining cheese, grill until hot and brown.

Coleslaw

YOU WILL NEED FOR 4 SERVINGS:

½ cabbage heart
½ lb. new carrots, grated
1–2 dessert apples, peeled and chopped
2–3 tablespoons French dressing, *see page 91*
4 tablespoons mayonnaise
little cream or top of the milk
chopped parsley to decorate

Wash the cabbage and shred it very finely. Leave to soak in cold, salted water for 2–3 hours, or until crisp. Drain cabbage and combine it with carrots, apples and French dressing. Toss the salad well and chill for 15–20 minutes.
Add the mayonnaise, thinned with a little cream or top of the milk. Toss well to mix.
Serve in a salad bowl, sprinkled with chopped parsley. *(See illustration on page 88)*

Salads

As well as the usual green vegetables, a savoury salad can include tomatoes, melon, citrus fruits and so on, tossed together in a French dressing. It can be served on its own or with meat or fish, instead of a vegetable. Serve a salad in winter as well as summer. It makes a delicious contrast to a hot main dish.

Preparation

Lettuce and curly endive: select crisp fresh heads and wash in plenty of cold water. Best way is to dunk the head up and down in cold water to draw out all the dirt. Break apart and separate the leaves, tear lettuce into smaller pieces if liked but never cut with a knife. Shake the leaves in a colander or salad basket, or pat dry in a clean tea towel.
Choose from round lettuces or the long, crisper cos variety.

Tomatoes: wash and cut into slices or quarters. Or cut into attractive tomato lilies. For these make zigzag cuts round the middle of each tomato with a sharp knife. Separate into two neat halves. Sliced tomatoes topped with spring onions or chives are delicious in French dressing, *see page 91.*

Radishes: wash thoroughly and trim off tops and tails. Add to a salad sliced or whole, or make these pretty radish roses: using a small sharp knife slit the radish down from the tail end, 4–6 times to form petals. Take care not to cut right through. Leave in iced water to open out.

Cucumber: wash thoroughly and peel thinly, or flute the skin by running the prongs of a fork down the length. Slice thinly across.

Cress, chives and watercress: wash very thoroughly under running cold water. Use the tops only, snipped off with scissors.

Garlic: only the merest suspicion should be used in salads. Best way is to crush the clove and rub round the inside of the salad bowl or dish. Then discard clove.

Celery: cut off the green tops and the hard base. Separate the stalks and scrub well to remove dirt. Cut away any discoloured parts, and remove any stringy pieces. Slice and use raw.

Left to right-back: avocado and fruit, potato, green salad. Front: devilled eggs, tomato and chives, French sweetcorn, salad niçoise, coleslaw

Carrots: scrub to remove any dirt. Always use new, young carrots cut into thin matchsticks; or pare off very thin layers lengthwise to make carrot curls. Leave them in iced water to go crisp.

Beetroots: buy them already cooked, slide off the skins using forefinger and thumb and slice or dice the flesh. If you are not serving it separately add it last as the colour quickly stains lettuce.

Mushrooms: select small button mushrooms. Wash in cold water and trim the ends of the stalks. Slice thinly downwards and use raw.

Onions: ordinary onions should be peeled and sliced into rings. Cover with vinegar for several hours before using—this way they soften slightly. Spring onions should be well washed, then you should trim off roots and top parts of the green.

Green peppers: slice in half lengthwise. Remove seeds and core, then shred flesh and use it raw.

Side salads

These attractive smaller salads are served instead of vegetables with cold meat, poultry or shellfish.

Potato

YOU WILL NEED FOR 4 SERVINGS:

   1 lb. cooked potatoes
   1 tablespoon finely chopped or grated onion
   salt and pepper
   4 tablespoons mayonnaise
   little cream or top of the milk
   chopped parsley or chives to decorate

Dice potatoes—new ones are delicious—don't overcook them or they may break up when mixed. Add the onion and season with salt and pepper. Thin the mayonnaise with a little cream or top of the milk and add to the potato mixture. With a fork toss the mixture until the potatoes are well coated with the mayonnaise. Serve in a salad bowl, garnished with a little chopped parsley or chives.

Avocado and fruit

YOU WILL NEED FOR 3 SERVINGS:

   1 grapefruit
   2 oranges
   1 avocado pear
   French dressing, *see page 91*
   few sprigs curly endive

Using a sharp knife, and cutting in a downwards direction, slice away skin from grapefruit and oranges. Be sure to remove all the bitter white pith. Separate grapefruit into segments and cut the oranges in slices crosswise.

Using a vegetable baller, scoop out the flesh from the avocado pear. Toss it with the fruit in French dressing and arrange the mixture in a salad dish. Tuck small pieces of curly endive round the edges for an attractive garnish.

Devilled eggs

YOU WILL NEED FOR 4 SERVINGS:

   6 hard-boiled eggs
   4 level tablespoons mayonnaise
   salt and pepper
   ½ teaspoon made mustard
   ¼ small onion, finely chopped
   ¼ teaspoon curry powder
   cress for decoration

Slice shelled eggs in half lengthwise. Remove the yolks with a teaspoon and place them in a small bowl. Set the whites aside. Mash yolks with a fork and blend in mayonnaise. Season well and add remaining ingredients except cress.
Fill the whites with heaped teaspoons of the mixture or pipe it in. Garnish with a little of the cress and arrange in a serving platter on a base of shredded lettuce.

Salad Niçoise

YOU WILL NEED FOR 4 SERVINGS:

   ½ lb. French beans
   ½ cucumber
   salt
   ½ lb. tomatoes
   2–3 tablespoons flaked tuna fish
   French dressing, *see page 91*
   anchovy fillets
   2 oz. black olives
   chopped parsley

Cook the sliced French beans in boiling salted water until tender, drain and rinse under cold water. Peel and cut the cucumber into chunks and sprinkle lightly with salt. Skin the tomatoes, cut into quarters and remove the pips (or the tomatoes may be sliced). Arrange the beans, tomatoes, flaked tuna fish and cucumber in a salad dish, pour over the French dressing, and garnish with anchovy fillets, black olives and chopped parsley.

French sweetcorn

YOU WILL NEED FOR 4 SERVINGS:

1 (12 oz.) tin of whole kernel sweetcorn, drained
½ green pepper, chopped
½ cucumber, peeled and chopped
½ small onion, finely chopped
French dressing, *see opposite*
chopped parsley to decorate

Combine all dry ingredients except parsley in a mixing bowl. Add the French dressing and mix well. Heap on to a salad dish and sprinkle the mixture with chopped parsley before serving.

Tossed green salad

This is the most popular type of all. Basically it consists of a variety of fresh green vegetables but many extra ingredients may be added to give colour and taste.

Basic recipe

YOU WILL NEED FOR 4 SERVINGS:

½ head lettuce
¼ bunch curly endive
½ bunch watercress
2 tomatoes, cut in wedges
½ cucumber, sliced
½ green pepper, sliced
few spring onions
French dressing, *see opposite*

Prepare the salad ingredients. Break the lettuce into a salad bowl, tear the endive in small pieces, removing the stalks. Snip off the watercress tops and wash thoroughly. Arrange these in the base of the dish with the lettuce, and top with the remaining ingredients. Pour the dressing over and toss lightly—this means turning the salad ingredients in the dressing.
Don't add the dressing until just before serving or the vinegar will make the lettuce go limp.
A basic green salad can be varied in many ways. Try small individual salads served in separate bowls. Garnish to make them attractive and finally toss in a salad dressing (*see opposite*). Add any of these:

Apple wedges: use rosy apples, cut fairly thinly.

Avocado slivers: halve avocado pears, remove the stones, peel and slice the flesh. Toss in lemon juice to keep the colour.

Cauliflower sprigs: break the cauliflower head into very small sprigs and use raw.

Cheese: use any kind, but nicest are grated Cheddar, crumbled Danish blue, or slivers of processed cheese.

Chicken, ham, luncheon meat or turkey: cut into dice or in slivers before adding.

Salami: buy thinly sliced salami and remove the outer rind before using.

Egg: hard boil and thinly slice before adding—an egg slicer is neater.

Grapefruit or oranges: cut away the peel and break fruit into sections. Remove pips and white pith.

Olives: drain from jar and use whole or sliced.

Tuna fish, sardines, salmon, crab meat or shrimps: remove any skin and bone and break up large pieces. Leave sardines and shrimps whole.

Walnuts: use whole or coarsely chopped, add at the last minute.

Savoury dressings

Basic dressing is the French oil and vinegar and there are many variations on it. Easiest way to make the dressing is to measure all the ingredients into a screw-topped jar, fasten lid and shake well to mix. Store the dressing in the jar and use only as much as is required—any over will keep perfectly in a cool place.

Basic French dressing: in a screw-topped jar mix ¼ teaspoon salt, ¼ teaspoon pepper, ¼ teaspoon dry mustard, 1 tablespoon vinegar, 3 tablespoons salad oil, and 1 tablespoon water. Place the cap on the jar and shake well before serving.

Lemon dressing: omit the mustard and pepper from the basic dressing and substitute lemon juice for the vinegar. Add ¼ teaspoon paprika pepper and ½ teaspoon grated lemon rind.

Roquefort dressing: prepare as for the basic dressing but add to the made mixture one tablespoon Roquefort or blue cheese, crumbled, and one teaspoon finely chopped onion.

Creamy dressing: prepare dressing as in basic recipe, then add one tablespoon cream, a dash of Worcester sauce, a dash of tabasco sauce and the unbeaten white of a small egg. Shake very well before using.

Chive dressing: use basic dressing ingredients plus ½ small carton of soured cream, 1 tablespoon chopped chives. Combine them together and shake well before using.

Foreign and luxury vegetables

These more exotic vegetables give you plenty of scope for fancy cooking. Many of these recipes—particularly for stuffed vegetables—make delicious dishes on their own. I include in this section tomatoes, corn on the cob, aubergines, mushrooms and cucumbers which—though not vegetables—are usually served as such.

Asparagus

Fresh asparagus should feel crisp and moist and the tips should be firm.
Prepare for cooking by cutting the stalks into even lengths, removing the tough lower parts. Scrape the stalks lightly, dipping in water occasionally. Tie into bundles with tape.
Simmer for 15–20 minutes in boiling salted water. Stand the bundle upright so that the heads are above the water and cook in the steam. Drain, remove the tapes, and serve hot with melted butter or hollandaise sauce—or cold with vinaigrette sauce.

Aubergines

Before using, wipe the skins and remove the green stalk at the end. Aubergines are most popular stuffed—in this case they should be carefully sliced in half lengthwise. The centre pulp must be scooped out, chopped up and added to the stuffing (*see recipe*). They may also be peeled, thinly sliced and fried in shallow fat; or more thickly sliced, coated with beaten egg and breadcrumbs and fried in deep fat.

Corn on the cob

When selecting, open green outer leaves and check that corn is ripe to the end of the stalk. The kernels should feel firm and contain plenty of 'milk'.
Remove the green outer husks and silks from the cob. Cook just enough for one helping per person and make second helpings freshly.

To cook, drop the corn into 1 in. of boiling water, cover with a lid and simmer until tender, this can be anything from 5–15 minutes according to the corn. Add a pinch of salt to the water towards the end of the cooking time. Salt tends to toughen corn and so should not be added too soon. A pinch of sugar, too, helps the flavour of corn that is not very young.
With forks or tongs remove the cooked corn from the water and place on a hot platter covered with a napkin, (now start cooking any second helpings).
Serve with butter or salt, or butter in which a crushed clove of garlic or snipped chives have been standing.

Courgettes

These are really baby marrows and range in length from 3–6 in. They need not be peeled or de-seeded before cooking—just topped and tailed. Sometimes they have a slightly bitter taste so blanch them before using. To do this, plunge them into boiling water for 2 minutes, drain and use. Courgettes are best braised in butter—blanch, then slice and arrange in a buttered fireproof dish. Sprinkle with salt and pepper, add a squeeze of lemon juice, cover and cook in a moderate oven (355 deg. or Gas No. 4) for 30 minutes.

Cucumber

Although most often served raw in salad, cucumber can also make a delicious hot vegetable.
Discard the outer green skin and slice into 1½ in. pieces. Sprinkle with salt, and steam for 20–30 minutes until tender. Or try thinly sliced cucumber simmered gently in stock or water in a covered pan about 5–10 minutes. Season and serve with butter or a sauce.

Green peppers

Cut peppers in half, or if they are to be stuffed, slice off the top and stalk. Either way discard the hot, peppery seeds from the inside. The flesh may now be shredded and added to stews, casseroles or salads as a garnish. If they are to be stuffed, blanch to remove any bitter taste—plunge peppers into boiling water for 3–5 minutes then drain.

Aubergine provençale

Globe artichokes

Leaves should be fairly tightly closed, they should not be dusty or dried up at the tips, and they should have about 6 in. of stem attached.

To prepare for cooking cut off the stalk, trim away any brown leaves and snip off the leaf tips with scissors. Plunge into boiling water, add salt, and cook for 30–40 minutes. Serve hot with melted butter or hollandaise sauce, or cold with vinaigrette sauce.

Marrow

Peel thickly to remove all the hard skin, and discard the seeds from inside. Sprinkle flesh with salt, steam for 20–30 minutes and serve, coated with white sauce, and with extra cheese or tomato sauce. Or it may be cut into rings, partly boiled in salted water and stuffed.

Mushrooms

You have a choice of three types. Buttons are tightly closed and usually used for garnishes or whole in recipes. Cups are slightly open and are often sliced and used in casseroles or soups, or left whole and stuffed with a savoury filling. Opens are wide open and flat, served as a separate side vegetable.

It's not necessary to peel cultivated mushrooms, just wash and trim stalks level—don't discard stalks, they can be used in a casserole or stuffing.

Ratatouille Niçoise

YOU WILL NEED FOR 4 SERVINGS:

2–3 tablespoons olive oil
2 onions
1–2 green peppers, de-seeded
1 aubergine, skinned and cubed
3–4 courgettes, skinned and cubed
1 lb. tomatoes
chopped parsley to garnish

Heat oil in a large saucepan and sauté sliced onions and peppers gently for 15 minutes, covered with a lid. Add the aubergine and courgettes, cover pan, and simmer gently for a further 30 minutes. Add skinned and chopped tomatoes and simmer for 15 minutes. Sprinkle with parsley. Cooking time for Ratatouille should not exceed 1 hour.

Aubergine Provençale

YOU WILL NEED FOR 4 SERVINGS:

2 large (or 3 small) aubergines
FOR THE STUFFING:
2 oz. patna rice
¼ pint water
salt
3 tablespoons olive oil
1 large onion, finely chopped
1 clove garlic, finely chopped
4 oz. minced beef
3 large tomatoes, skinned and de-seeded
2 tablespoons water
pepper, salt and nutmeg
juice of 1 lemon

Prepare aubergines and cut in half lengthwise. Remove some of the pulp from the centre and chop finely. Sprinkle the shell with salt.

To make the stuffing put rice, water and salt into a saucepan. Cover with a lid and bring slowly to the boil. Reduce heat and simmer without stirring until cooked, takes about 10 minutes. Set aside until required.

Melt one tablespoon of olive oil in a saucepan and sauté onion and garlic until golden brown. Add minced beef and brown quickly. Chop two of the tomatoes and add to the saucepan with chopped aubergine pulp and water. Simmer for a few minutes, remove from heat, add rice and season with salt, pepper and nutmeg.

Heat the remaining oil in a heavy frying pan. Dry the aubergines and sauté them on all sides in the oil for a few minutes.

Arrange in a fireproof dish and pack with stuffing. Slice the remaining tomato and arrange on top. Sprinkle with lemon juice, cover with a tightly fitting lid and cook in a moderate oven (355 deg. or Gas No. 4) for 20 minutes or until tender.

Stuffed green peppers

YOU WILL NEED FOR 3–4 SERVINGS:

6–8 medium green peppers
buttered breadcrumbs
little grated cheese
FOR THE FILLING:
4 oz. patna rice
1 oz. butter or margarine
1 medium onion, sliced
½ lb. mince
1 (15 oz.) tin tomatoes
1 level teaspoon castor sugar
½ level teaspoon salt

Cook the rice for 10 minutes in boiling salted water. While the rice is cooking prepare the other ingredients. In a large saucepan melt the butter or margarine. Add the onion and mince, and cook until lightly brown.

Stir in the tomatoes, salt and sugar. Bring to the boil and simmer gently for 5 minutes. Add cooked drained rice and continue to simmer gently, covered with a lid, for 30 minutes. Slice tops off peppers, scoop out the seeds and discard—tops may be reserved for decoration. Put the green peppers into rapidly boiling salted water and cook for 5 minutes until tender. Drain and fill with the hot rice mixture. Top with buttered breadcrumbs and sprinkle with grated cheese. Arrange close together in a baking dish. Place in the centre of a moderate oven (355 deg. or Gas No. 4) for 20–25 minutes or until thoroughly heated and browned.

Marrow and tomato casserole

YOU WILL NEED FOR 4 SERVINGS:

1 small marrow
4 tomatoes
1 large onion
2–3 stalks celery
1 level teaspoon salt
pinch pepper
1 level teaspoon sugar
1 oz. butter
chopped parsley for serving

Wipe and peel the marrow. Halve and scoop out the seeds, then cut the marrow into small cubes.
Plunge the tomatoes into boiling water for 1 minute, then drain and peel away the skins and slice them. Peel the onion, scrub and remove strings from celery and slice both thinly. Mix together the salt, pepper and sugar.
In a buttered casserole dish, arrange alternate layers of vegetables, sprinkling the mixed seasoning over. Finish with a layer of marrow and dot with butter. Cover with a tight fitting lid and place in the centre of the oven and bake for 40–45 minutes. Sprinkle with chopped parsley and serve.

Baked marrow

YOU WILL NEED FOR 4 SERVINGS:

1 medium sized marrow
1 oz. butter
salt and pepper
2 oz. Cheddar cheese, grated

Peel and remove seeds from the marrow. Cut the flesh into chunks and place in a saucepan. Cover with cold water add plenty of salt and bring to the boil. Draw the pan off the heat and drain. Place the marrow flesh into a casserole dish along with the melted butter and plenty of salt and pepper. Cover with a lid, place in the centre of a moderate oven (355 deg. or Gas No. 4) and bake for 25–30 minutes until tender. Sprinkle with grated cheese and serve.

Corn fritters

YOU WILL NEED FOR 4 SERVINGS:

2 eggs separated
salt and pepper
1 level tablespoon plain flour
1 (11 oz.) can whole kernal sweetcorn
2 oz. butter or margarine for frying

Crack the egg yolks into a mixing basin, season with salt and pepper, and add the flour and drained sweetcorn. Mix well. Lightly whisk the egg whites and fold into the mixture.
Heat the butter or margarine in a frying pan and when hot add tablespoons of the fritter mixture into the pan. Brown lightly on one side, then flip over and brown on the second side. Continue until all the mixture is used up—makes about 12 fritters. Serve at once—delicious with fried chicken, grilled bacon or gammon steaks.

These important and more unusual vegetables are more seasonable than any others. The seasons can vary considerably from year to year according to weather conditions. This is a rough guide to when you can expect to see and buy some of them.

Asparagus	April – July
Aubergines	Spring to Autumn—best in Autumn
Corn on the cob	August – October
Courgettes	May – October
Cucumber	All year round—including imported ones
Green peppers	Almost all year—best in Autumn
Globe artichokes	June – July
Marrow	August – October
Mushrooms	All year round

ALL ABOUT
Eggs &
Omelettes

Eggs are a versatile food; they can be prepared and used in many ways. Being rich in food value they can take the place of fish or meat in a menu.

Because the egg shell is porous, ideally eggs should be stored in a covered container to avoid loss of moisture. The low temperature in a refrigerator will help keep evaporation to a minimum. Eggs taken straight from the refrigerator should never be used in recipes; they should always be allowed to come up to room temperature first. Eggs that are too cold some times curdle cake mixtures and never beat up to good volume for soufflé or other light desserts. Left-over egg yolk may be stored in your refrigerator if covered with a little cold water. Put left-over egg whites in a small container, cover and then refrigerate. Mark on the container how many whites are inside, if you forget, pour the contents slowly out of the basin, and you will find that the egg whites fall out one at a time, allowing you to recount them.

To boil an egg

Method 1

Heat enough water to cover the egg in a small pan. Lower the egg into the steadily boiling water, too rapid boiling may crack the egg shell, and set your timer for $3\frac{1}{2}$–4 minutes. If the egg does crack, add salt to the water to congeal the escaping white.

Method 2

Place the eggs in a saucepan, cover with cold water and bring up to the boil. Lower heat and boil gently for 1–2 minutes.

Sweet omelette

Method 3

Heat enough water to cover the eggs to boiling point. Add the eggs gently, cover the pan with a lid and draw off the heat. Leave for 8 minutes and then serve.

To poach an egg

Bring 1 in. of salted water to the boil either in a saucepan for 1 or 2 eggs or in a frying pan for more. Add 1 teaspoon vinegar or lemon juice, this helps to congeal the white quickly and keep a good shape. Crack the eggs one at a time into a teacup, then add to the simmering water very close to the surface. Simmer gently until the yolk just begins to set (takes 1–2 minutes). Loosen with a fish slice and lift out gently. To keep the eggs in a neat round shape, try placing a buttered round pastry cutter in the pan of boiling water and crack the egg into this.

To scramble eggs

Allowing 1–2 eggs per person, crack as many as required into a mixing basin. Season well with salt and pepper and add 1 tablespoon of milk for each egg. Beat well to mix thoroughly and then allow to stand until ready to cook. In a saucepan melt ½–1 oz. butter, then strain in the egg mixture. Cook over gentle heat, stirring occasionally until the mixture has thickened but is still moist. Draw the pan off the heat, the heat in the saucepan will finish the cooking, and serve on hot buttered toast.

Baked eggs

Crack the eggs into buttered ramikin dishes (a small individual baking dish). Season with salt and pepper, add a small piece of butter and 1 tablespoon cream. Set the dishes on a baking tray or in a shallow baking tin. Set in the centre of a slow oven (335 deg. or Gas No. 3) and bake for 12–15 minutes.

To fry an egg

Break the eggs to be fried one at a time into a cup or saucer. Heat sufficient fat for frying, allow about 1 tablespoon per egg (use bacon fat or vegetable shortening) in a frying pan. Add the eggs; it is important that the fat should not be too hot. Cook gently, basting with the hot fat until the egg is set (takes 2–3 minutes). Loosen carefully with a fish slice or palette knife and lift out on to a hot serving plate.

Basic recipe for savoury omelettes

YOU WILL NEED FOR 1 SERVING:

2 large eggs
salt and pepper
2 teaspoons water
knob of butter for frying

Break the eggs into a mixing basin. Season with salt and pepper and add the water. Mix the eggs thoroughly with a fork and either use straight away or leave to stand until ready to use.

Heat the butter in a 6–7 in. omelette or frying pan over moderate heat until bubbling hot. Add all the egg mixture and stir gently until the mixture begins to thicken. Then stop stirring and allow the omelette to brown on the under side. When almost set but still moist and creamy, loosen the edges with a palette knife, tip the pan away from you and jerk slightly until the edge of the omelette extends over the far side of the pan. If you are making a filled omelette add half of any filling at this stage, *see recipes.* Fold both edges of the omelette into the centre and push into the far side of the pan ready to turn out. Holding the pan over a warm serving plate, tip towards you and allow the omelette to fall out gently. Spoon any remaining filling on top and serve at once. For variety, add one of these ingredients to the basic egg mixture:

Cheese: Grate 2 oz. Cheddar or Parmesan cheese. Add most of it to the basic mixture, but save a little for the topping. Serve with grilled tomatoes and green salad.

Herb: Chop up a little fresh parsley and a few chives. Stir into the egg mixture. If you have no fresh herbs, use 1 level teaspoon of dried mixed herbs. Serve this omelette with crisp green salad tossed in French dressing, *see page 91,* and with fingers of hot buttered toast.

Bacon and onion: Chop up 2 rashers of bacon and one small onion. Sauté gently in a knob of butter until tender. Do not brown. Drain both from fat and add to basic mixture. Serve the omelette with extra grilled bacon rashers and sauté potatoes

The following alternative fillings can be spooned on to the cooked omelettes:

Tomato: quickly dip 3 tomatoes into boiling water. Remove skins and halve, taking out seed. Chop the tomato flesh and add 1 level teaspoon mixed dried herbs. Sauté this gently in 1 dessertspoon of hot oil for 5 minutes. Spoon over the cooked omelette and serve with cooked buttered brocoli and chipped potatoes.

Mushroom: wash and chop 2 oz. mushrooms, and sauté gently in a little butter for 2–3 minutes. Drain from the fat and spoon over the cooked omelette. Serve with grilled bacon and chipped potatoes.

Prawn: stir a thawed 2 oz. packet of frozen prawns into 2–3 tablespoons of white sauce or cream. Heat thoroughly and spoon over the cooked omelette. Serve with grilled mushrooms and a crisp salad of lettuce, cucumber and watercress tossed in French dressing.

Omelettes for more than one

The nicest omelettes are made one at a time and are eaten at once. But often it is necessary to make them for two people. It will save you time and trouble to make a large omelette and divide it into portions. The following details may help you to remember quantities:
For one person cook a 2–egg omelette in a 6–7 in. omelette pan. For two people cook a 4–egg omelette in an 8 in. pan. Increase filling accordingly.

Spanish omelette

YOU WILL NEED FOR 1–2 SERVINGS:

3 eggs
3 teaspoons water
salt and pepper
pinch of cayenne pepper
1 dessertspoon olive oil
1 onion, sliced
2 tomatoes, sliced
1 teaspoon tarragon vinegar or lemon juice

Crack the eggs into a mixing basin, add water, salt, pepper and cayenne pepper and set aside.
Heat the olive oil in a 7 in. omelette or frying pan, add the onion and cook gently until tender, about 5 minutes. Then add the tomatoes and cook a further few moments. Stir in the vinegar or lemon juice and the egg mixture. Cook, stirring over moderate heat until the egg is beginning to thicken. Allow to brown on the underside, then using a palette knife turn over and brown on the second side.

Because the omelette is bulky, it is served flat instead of folded, as is customary.

Soufflé omelettes

Soufflé omelettes vary from the usual method. They are specialities, fun to make and should be served as a dessert.

Jam soufflé omelette

YOU WILL NEED FOR 1–2 SERVINGS:

2 egg yolks
2 level teaspoons castor sugar
2 egg whites
knob of butter for cooking
FOR THE FILLING:
1–2 tablespoons red jam, warmed

Preheat the oven to moderate heat (355 deg. or Gas No. 4). Lightly whisk together the egg yolks and sugar in a basin until light and creamy. Whisk the egg whites until stiff and, using a metal spoon, fold into the egg mixture. Heat the butter in the 6–7 in. omelette pan until bubbling hot, add all the omelette mixture. Spread evenly over the pan and allow to cook gently over the heat for 1–2 minutes. Then place in the centre of the preheated oven and cook for 8–10 minutes or until risen and firm to the touch. Remove from the heat and either turn out immediately on to a sugared paper and spread with the warmed jam, or spread the omelette in the pan with jam. Either way fold the omelette in half, dust with icing sugar and serve immediately.

Orange soufflé omelette

Follow the recipe as above but fill with the following filling:
Melt together the juice of ½ orange and 2 tablespoons chunky orange marmalade. Keep them hot while preparing the omelette.

Rum soufflé omelette

Follow the recipe above, adding 1 good tablespoon best quality rum to the egg yolks. Put the cooked omelette on a hot dish and pour 3–4 tablespoons of warmed rum around. Light the rum and serve immediately.

ALL ABOUT
Sauces & Soufflés

Simple sauces

There are two success secrets for a really good sauce. First, prepare it over a gentle heat, taking care not to scorch it: a burnt flavour will ruin any recipe. Second, stir in the liquid a little at a time, beating well between each addition to avoid lumps. A well-made sauce is smooth and glossy and has a good flavour

Basic white

(using the roux method)

YOU WILL NEED FOR ½ PINT SAVOURY SAUCE:

½ pint milk
½ onion, stuck with a clove
1 oz. butter or margarine
1 oz. (or 1 rounded tablespoon) flour
salt and pepper

Measure the milk into a saucepan, add the onion and clove, and bring slowly to the boil. Draw the pan off the heat, cover with a lid and leave to infuse for 5–10 minutes.
In a saucepan, melt the fat over a low heat and stir in the flour to make a smooth paste. This is called a roux. Cook the roux gently for a further minute or so, until it lightens in colour and has a grainy texture.

Gradually stir in the warm, flavoured milk a little at a time. Cold milk may be used if time is short, but warm infused milk makes blending easier and adds extra flavour. Each addition of milk should be thoroughly beaten in. Bring the sauce up to the boil and allow to simmer for 2–3 minutes to ensure thorough cooking of the flour.
Season with salt and pepper and then add any flavouring required (*see suggested variations following*). When preparing this sauce, you may like to use a mixture of liquids—perhaps hot stock or vegetable water plus milk—to give extra flavour.

Basic white

(using the blending method)

MAKES ½ PINT

Omitting the initial stage of infusing the milk, but using the ingredients given above (except onion and clove), first blend together the flour and cold milk, as follows. Measure the liquid into a mixing basin, and sift the flour into it. Using a whisk, mix the two quickly and very thoroughly.
Melt the fat in a saucepan, pour in the blend and cook, stirring until the mixture is boiling.
Simmer gently for a further 2–3 minutes, then season and stir in flavouring.

Variations on basic white

To the well-seasoned basic white sauce add any of the following:-

Cheese: Stir in ½ level teaspoon made mustard and 3 oz. grated Cheddar or Parmesan cheese. *Serve with* fish, egg, vegetable or pasta dishes.

Parsley: Add 1 tablespoon freshly chopped parsley. *Serve with* fish (add squeeze of lemon juice to sauce), vegetable dishes and boiled ham.

Egg: Gently fold in 1–2 coarsely chopped hard-boiled eggs. *Serve with* fish and vegetable dishes.

Shrimp: Add 4 oz. prepared shrimps, squeeze of lemon juice and ¼ level teaspoon anchovy essence or 1 tablespoon tomato ketchup. *Serve with* fish dishes.

Caper: Prepare the sauce, using half liquid from boiled meat and half milk. Stir in 2–3 tablespoons capers, chopped or whole. *Serve with* boiled mutton.

White sauce can be used for tasty supper and vegetable dishes.

With vegetables: particulary cauliflower and leeks. Prepare white sauce, using half milk and half vegetable cooking water.

Dish up the hot, cooked and drained vegetables. Pour on top the well-seasoned white sauce and decorate with a pinch of paprika or parsley

If using a cheese sauce, top the finished dish with grated cheese and grill until bubbling hot and brown.

For fish: cook the fish in the oven, in milk with seasoning and a nut of butter. Prepare the sauce, using strained milk from the fish made up to ½ pint with fresh milk.

When cooked, add seasoning, a squeeze of lemon juice, pinch of parsley and a chopped hard-boiled egg or shrimps. Pour sauce over fish and serve.

In cheese dishes: for macaroni cheese, prepare a cheese sauce, stir in 4 oz. cooked macaroni and 1–2 skinned, seeded and chopped tomatoes and pour into a buttered pie dish.

Top with extra grated cheese and grill.
This quantity serves 4.

Basic brown

(using the roux method)

YOU WILL NEED FOR ½ PINT:

- 1 onion
- 1 carrot
- 1 oz. butter or margarine
- 2 bacon rashers
- 1 oz. (or 1 rounded tablespoon) flour
- 1 teaspoon concentrated tomato purée, or ¼ lb. fresh skinned seeded tomatoes

¾ pint stock or water plus stock cube
salt and pepper
few mushroom stalks or trimmings

Prepare and finely dice the onion and carrot. In a saucepan melt the fat and add the trimmed and chopped bacon and prepared vegetables. Fry gently until the vegetables become a golden brown. Stir in the flour and continue to cook gently, stirring from time to time until the flour is a rich nutty brown colour. Add the tomato purée (or fresh tomatoes), and gradually stir in the hot stock. Bring to the boil stirring constantly. Season with salt and pepper and add the mushroom stalks. Cover with a lid and simmer gently for 30 minutes, then strain through a fine sieve.

Variations on basic brown

To the prepared, well-seasoned brown sauce add any of the following:-

Mushroom: Add 2–3 oz. sliced mushrooms which have first been sautéed in hot butter. *Serve with* fried liver, savoury flans and pasties.

Madeira: Add 3 tablespoons Madeira wine to the finished brown sauce. *Serve with* grilled or fried steaks or try it with chops and ham.

Barbecue: Add 1 level teaspoon made mustard, 1 tablespoon redcurrant jelly, 1 tablespoon vinegar and ½ level teaspoon paprika pepper. *Serve with* sausages and hamburgers.

Piquante: Add 1 dessertspoon brown table sauce, ketchup or Worcester sauce and 1 tablespoon vinegar. *Serve with* meat patties, croquettes and cutlets made from cooked meat.

Orange: Add the juice of one orange and one lemon, a little finely-grated orange rind if liked, and a glass of port wine. *Serve with* roast duck.

Demi-glaze: Boil the basic sauce for a further 20 minutes to reduce, then add 1 tablespoon sherry and use for glazing cold meat, game or galantines.

For cooks who prepare a lot of sauces—here's a handy time saver. Prepare the basic roux mixture ahead, it can be stored covered in a refrigerator for several weeks and used to make sauces in half the time.

To make the basic white roux

Put 8 oz. butter or margarine in a heavy saucepan and heat gently until melted. Stir in 8 oz. (or 8 heaped tablespoons) plain flour and continue to cook very gently over a low heat for about 15 minutes. Stir occasionally to prevent the roux from browning. When ready the mixture will have a granular appearance and be light in colour.

To make a brown roux

Cook the basic mixture for a longer time, stirring occasionally until the mixture is a nutty brown colour,—takes about 40 minutes.

Draw the pan off the heat and leave to stand for about 10 minutes to allow the fat to rise to the top. Either pour the fat away or gently stir in extra flour to absorb the fat. When quite cold place the roux in a screw topped jar and store in a cool place.

To use the roux

For a white sauce—bring a quantity of milk up to the boil. Draw the pan off the heat, break the white roux into the hot liquid. Quantities are about 1 tablespoon for each ¼ pint liquid. When the roux is melted replace the pan over the heat and bring to the boil stirring briskly until thickened.

The brown roux can be used for brown sauces made as above using stock or for thickening stews and gravies.

Three tasty sauces

A velouté sauce is rich and well flavoured, used for fricassées or blanquettes of chicken, veal or rabbit. The ingredients for the fricassée are always boiled first and the flavoured stock used to make the sauce. For fish dishes the sauce is often made with part fish stock and part white wine. The sauce must be varied according to the ingredients that are to be served in it. It should be thin in consistency if it is to be served with boiled rice.

Velouté sauce

YOU WILL NEED FOR ABOUT ¾ PINT:

2 oz. butter or margarine
1½ oz. (or 2 level tablespoons) flour
1 pint hot stock
6–8 button mushrooms
few parsley stalks
1 egg yolk with ½ gill (⅛ pint) cream
salt and pepper
juice of half a lemon

Prepare a sauce following the directions for basic white sauce, roux method, using hot stock. Bring to the boil and add the chopped mushrooms and parsley stalks. Simmer gently for 20 minutes, stirring and skimming frequently. Strain the sauce and reheat, then draw the pan off the heat and stir in the blended egg yolk and cream. Season to taste with salt and pepper and add the lemon juice. Reheat if necessary but *do not allow to boil*. Stir in the cooked ingredients and serve.

Fresh tomato sauce

YOU WILL NEED FOR ½ PINT:

1 oz. butter or margarine
1 rasher of bacon
1 small onion, sliced
1 small carrot, scraped and sliced
½ lb. tomatoes
1 rounded teaspoon flour, blended with a little water
½ pint stock or water plus stock cube
pepper and salt
1 teaspoon sugar
1 teaspoon vinegar or lemon juice

Melt the fat in a saucepan, trim and chop the bacon rasher and fry lightly in the hot fat. Add the sliced onion and carrot, and fry gently a further 5 minutes. Wash and quarter the tomatoes and add to the ingredients in the saucepan, cover with a lid and cook for a few minutes until softened.

Stir in the flour, stock, seasoning, sugar and vinegar or lemon juice. Bring to the boil, stirring well and allow to simmer, covered with a lid, for 30 minutes. Rub the sauce through a fine sieve. Discard the skin and pips and reboil the sauce, correct the seasoning and serve. Delicious with fried fish.

To make Bolognese sauce for pasta or spaghetti, fry ½ lb. minced beef in the hot fat, then add the remaining ingredients, taking care to skin and remove seeds from tomatoes first.

Curry sauce

YOU WILL NEED FOR ½ PINT:

1 onion, finely chopped
1 oz. butter or margarine
½ cooking apple, chopped
2 level tablespoons curry powder
1 level teaspoon flour
½ pint stock or water plus stock cube
1 tablespoon gooseberry jam or sweet mango chutney
1 tablespoon soft brown sugar
juice of half a lemon
½ level teaspoon salt
1 oz. sultanas

Add the onion to the hot fat, cover with a lid and fry gently until soft—about 5 minutes. Add the apple and fry a further few minutes. Stir in the curry powder and flour and gradually stir in the stock, jam or chutney, sugar, lemon juice, salt and sultanas. Bring up to the boil, cover with a lid and simmer gently stirring occasionally for 20–30 minutes. Use as it is or strain if preferred.

A curry sauce should be fairly thin so that it is easily absorbed by the rice it is served with. Add cooked meat, fish or hard-boiled eggs to the hot sauce and simmer for 3–4 minutes to heat through.

From French sauces to soufflés

If you can make a successful egg sauce you've a basis for several Continental varieties that will turn ordinary meat and fish into dishes fit for the gods. You can make real egg custard, mayonnaise and tartare sauces. Then take it just one step further and create a perfect, melt-in-the-mouth soufflé and any number of sweet and savoury variations.

Hot sauces

These aren't difficult to make but do need care and attention. The egg mixture is cooked over a gentle heat until thick—but be sure not to overcook it. Serve as directed.

Béarnaise sauce

YOU WILL NEED FOR ¼ PINT:

little chopped fresh tarragon
10 turns of the pepper mill
1 shallot, finely chopped
1 tablespoon white malt vinegar
2 tablespoons water
2 egg yolks
1 oz. butter, melted
pinch of salt
juice of ½ lemon
little chopped fresh parsley

Place the tarragon, pepper, shallot and vinegar in a small enamel pan. Heat gently until the vinegar has boiled away, but take care not to burn the shallot. To the hot pan add the water and egg yolks and whisk over gentle heat until thick and frothy. Draw the pan off the heat and gradually whisk in the melted butter. Season with salt and stir in the lemon juice and chopped parsley.
This sauce is particularly good served with grilled steak and chops.

Take care not to prepare the whisked hollandaise or béarnaise sauces in an aluminium saucepan. The action of a metal whisk against the base of the pan could turn the sauce green.

Cheese soufflé, with savoury sauces left to right, béarnaise, mayonnaise, cocktail, tartare and hollandaise

Hollandaise sauce

YOU WILL NEED FOR ¼ PINT:

2 egg yolks
2 tablespoons water
1 oz. butter, melted
salt and pepper
juice of ¼ lemon

Measure the egg yolks and water into a small enamel pan and whisk over very gentle heat until frothy and thick. For beginners it's often a safer method to whisk the mixture in a small basin set over a pan of boiling water. Either way, remove the sauce from the heat when it is thick, and gradually whisk in the melted butter. Season with salt and pepper and stir in the lemon juice.
Nicest served with poached fish, particularly salmon.

Custard sauce

YOU WILL NEED FOR ⅓ PINT:

1 large egg
1 teacup (⅓ pint) milk
2 teaspoons castor sugar
little vanilla essence

Lightly beat the egg to mix thoroughly. Heat the milk almost to boiling point and pour on to the beaten egg gradually, stirring well all the time. Strain the sauce back into a small saucepan or, for preference, a double boiler or mixing basin set over a pan of simmering water. In each case cook gently until the custard has thickened slightly and the egg is cooked. Be careful not to boil it or the egg will curdle.
Remove from the heat and add the sugar and vanilla essence.

Coffee sauce

Use the custard recipe, but omit vanilla essence, add 1–2 teaspoons coffee essence to taste.

Chocolate sauce

To the above custard sauce add 2–3 oz. plain chocolate broken into small pieces, stir well to blend.

Brandy sauce

Use the above custard sauce, but omit vanilla essence, add 1–2 tablespoons brandy to taste.

Cold sauces

These are made by beating the ingredients gradually into the egg yolk. Don't add them too quickly or the mixture will curdle. Follow the instructions carefully and you won't go wrong.

Mayonnaise

YOU WILL NEED FOR ¼ PINT:

1 egg yolk
¼ level teaspoon each salt, pepper and dry mustard
1 level teaspoon castor sugar
1 tablespoon wine vinegar
¼ pint olive oil
1 tablespoon cream (*see recipe before adding*)

Place the egg yolk in a deep mixing basin. Add the seasonings, sugar, and 1 teaspoon of the vinegar and whisk thoroughly to mix—it's easier if you place the basin on a folded damp cloth or sponge square to steady it while mixing.
Add the oil *drop by drop*, whisking all the time. A handy method is to measure the oil into a narrow bottle, place your thumb over the open top, tip the bottle up and allow the oil to drip out. After about half the oil has been added, pour in the remainder in a thin stream. Stir in the remaining vinegar, and if using immediately, the cream or top of the milk. Without the cream this mayonnaise will keep for one or two weeks in a cool place. To keep longer, place the basin containing the newly made mayonnaise over a pan of hot water and whisk well for about 5 minutes. Then store in a screw-top jar, no longer than 4–5 weeks. Add cream just before using.

Tartare sauce

Prepare the mayonnaise as above. Add 1 rounded teaspoon each of chopped gherkins, caper and parsley to the finished sauce.
Serve with fried fish.

Cocktail sauce for shellfish

Prepare the mayonnaise as above. Mix together 3 tablespoons each mayonnaise, tomato ketchup and cream. Stir in 1 teaspoon Worcester sauce, squeeze of lemon juice, dash of tabasco sauce and a pinch of paprika pepper. Serve as a dressing blended with about 8 oz. prepared prawns, shrimps, lobster or crabmeat.

Points worth noting

Should your mayonnaise curdle because you've added the oil too quickly, don't despair. Put a fresh egg yolk in another basin and add the curdled mayonnaise drop by drop. Whisk well all the time, using a mechanical rotary whisk, if possible.

It is not a complete disaster if your custard sauce should curdle. Strain it immediately into a cool basin and whisk it well. Do not reheat.

To keep a prepared sauce hot while waiting to use it, stand the base of the pan in another deep pan or baking tin with a couple of inches of gently simmering water. The sauce will then keep hot without scorching.

If you know you'll have to keep a custard sauce standing, here's how to prevent a skin forming. Make the sauce, using all but 1–2 tablespoons of the milk. Warm this milk and pour it over the cooked, thickened sauce—and don't stir it in. When ready to serve the custard, stir in the milk.

Mayonnaise can be made very successfully with an electric blender. Set it to a low speed, and blend the egg yolk with the seasonings and vinegar. Then turn it to a high speed and gradually add the oil, drop by drop, through the hole in the top of the blender. Use double the basic recipe.

Cheese soufflé

YOU WILL NEED FOR 4 SERVINGS:

1 oz. butter or margarine
1 oz. (or 1 rounded tablespoon) flour
¼ pint plus 2 tablespoons milk
seasoning
¼ level teaspoon prepared mustard
4 oz. grated cheese
4 eggs

In a large saucepan melt the fat and stir in the flour. Cook gently for 1 minute, do not allow to brown. Gradually stir in all the milk, beating well to make a smooth sauce.

Bring to the boil—the mixture at this stage will be very thick. Season with salt and pepper and stir in the mustard and cheese. When the cheese has melted and is blended draw the pan off the heat. Cool until the hand can be held comfortably against the sides before adding the eggs. Beat in the egg yolks one at a time, then whisk the whites until stiff and gently fold into the mixture.

Pour into a 6–7 in. buttered soufflé dish, place in the centre of a moderate oven (355 deg. or Gas No. 4) and bake for 35–40 minutes.

Don't peep while the soufflé is baking—a sudden draught of cold air might cause it to collapse. Serve as soon as it is cooked.

Dark chocolate soufflé

SERVES 4:

Proceed as for cheese recipe but omit the salt, pepper, mustard and cheese. Add instead 2 oz. (or 2 rounded tablespoons) castor sugar, 2 teaspoons vanilla essence and 4 oz. plain chocolate melted in 2 tablespoons cold water over low heat. Blend well to mix and allow to cool as in the basic recipe. Beat in the egg yolks and then the stiffly-whisked whites.

Pour the mixture into a well-buttered 7 in. soufflé dish. Place in the centre of a moderate oven (355 deg. or Gas No. 4) and bake for 40–45 minutes.

Serve immediately, sprinkled with sifted icing sugar and with single cream or rum sauce. For the sauce mix together in a small saucepan 2 oz. butter and 2 oz. (or 2 rounded tablespoons) castor sugar until creamy. Place over low heat and stir until the mixture has just come to the boil. Draw off the heat and stir in 3 tablespoons rum. Serve hot.

Little ginger soufflés

SERVES 6:

Prepare as for cheese recipe but omit salt, pepper, mustard and cheese. Add instead 1 oz. (or 1 rounded tablespoon) castor sugar, 2 level teaspoons ground ginger, 2 tablespoons finely chopped stem ginger and 3 tablespoons ginger syrup from the jar.

Blend all ingredients well to mix and allow to cool as in the basic recipe. Beat in the egg yolks and then the beaten whites. Spoon the mixture into six individual buttered baking dishes. Place in the centre of a moderate oven (355 deg. or Gas No. 4) and bake for 20–30 minutes. Alternatively the soufflé may be baked in a 6–7 in. buttered soufflé dish and baked, following directions in basic cheese recipe.

Serve soufflés immediately with chocolate sauce. To make this measure into a small saucepan 3 tablespoons milk and a nut of butter. Bring just up to the boil and then draw the pan off the heat. Add 4 oz. chocolate chips or plain chocolate until melted and blended.

On the Continent a savoury soufflé is often served as a starter to a meal—cheese soufflé being the most popular for this.

All these soufflé mixtures can be prepared ahead, but don't add the egg white. This should be beaten and folded in just before baking.

ALL ABOUT
Rice & Pasta

Types and methods

There are many different types of rice and pasta so it is essential to learn the basic cooking methods for each before you attempt more complicated recipes. They can be used plain in meat dishes, or are delicious topped with a savoury sauce or tossed in butter and sprinkled with grated Parmesan cheese.

Rice

There are many types of rice to choose from, and recipes usually specify which you should use. Cooking methods vary in each case.

Long grain: often referred to as savoury rice. It's a long, thin, white rice ideal for savoury recipes. The grains cook up light and fluffy and stay separate. It is good with curries, risotto or similar dishes.

Short grain: often called pudding rice. It is easily recognisable by the short fat shape of the grain. Use it in dessert recipes, as the cooked grains stick together and give a delicious creamy base.

Brown rice: the whole unpolished grain, or rice with only the outer hull and a small amount of bran removed. It has a nutty taste and slightly chewy texture. It is very nutritious as all the vitamins are retained, and is particularly good in vegetable dishes or used as a stuffing.

Parboiled rice: specially processed rice which comes from America. It takes a little longer to cook but the grains stay beautifully fluffy and separate and have a delightful nutty flavour. Follow directions on the packet.

Precooked rice: needs only to be soaked in boiling water to make it ready. It is useful for cooks in a hurry; add plenty of seasoning.

Light, fluffy, savoury rice is easy to cook and is good with most dishes, particularly those with a rich sauce. These are two cooking methods, try both then stick to the one you find most successful.

Method 1

YOU WILL NEED FOR 4 SERVINGS:

    8 oz. long grain rice
    3—4 pints boiling water
    1—2 level teaspoons salt

Put rice into a sieve or colander, wash lightly under cold running water and remove any dark or discoloured bits. Drain and sprinkle into boiling salted water, add slowly so that the water never comes off the boil. Boil rapidly for 8 minutes, stirring occasionally to make sure no grains stick to the base of the pan.
To test if it is cooked, pinch a grain between thumb and forefinger, there should be no hard core. Draw pan off heat, strain the rice into a colander and hold under running *hot water* for about 1 minute, just enough to rinse off the starchy cooking water. Fluff up with a fork, add a knob of butter or an additional flavouring before serving. Some cooks like to return rice to the hot saucepan, cover with a lid and allow to steam dry for a few minutes before serving.

Method 2

YOU WILL NEED FOR 3–4 SERVINGS:

> 1 cup long grain rice
> 1 level teaspoon salt
> 2 cups water

This is ideal for all types of American rice, you must use the same size cup for measuring both rice and water. A teacup holds about 6 oz. rice and a breakfast cup about 8 oz. Select a saucepan with a tight-fitting lid and lightly butter the inside. Measure rice, salt and water into a pan and bring to the boil. Stir once then lower the heat. Cover with lid and simmer for 15 minutes without removing the lid or stirring. Test if it is cooked—see previous method. When soft, draw the pan off the heat, fluff up the rice with a fork and serve straight from the pan.

Add any of the following to rice cooked by either of the two methods and serve with a main savoury dish.

Cheese: 2 oz. grated cheese, Cheddar or Parmesan, and 1 oz. butter. Tasty with stews or casseroles.

Onion: chop 1 small onion and lightly sauté with a little butter until tender. Fold it into the cooked rice with an extra $\frac{1}{2}$ oz. of butter and fluff with a fork. Serve with steak or chops.

Saffron rice: add a pinch of powdered saffron to the water while cooking rice. Stir occasionally and when cooked add 1 oz. butter and fluff up with fork. Serve with fish and shellfish.

Orange rice: cook the rice by method 2, using tinned orange juice instead of water. Delicious with veal.

Mint rice: with a fork stir in 1 oz. butter and 3 tablespoons mint jelly. Serve with lamb.

Herb rice: to cooked rice add 2 oz. butter, 1 tablespoon chopped parsley and a good pinch of dried mixed herbs. Serve with stews, casseroles.

To cook brown rice

Add required quantity of brown rice to plenty of boiling salted water. Allow at least 4–5 pints for every 4–8 oz. rice. Sprinkle rice slowly on to water so that it does not come off the boil. Boil briskly for 50–60 minutes until tender. Stir occasionally with fork to prevent sticking. Test by rubbing a grain between forefinger and thumb—there should be no hard core. When tender, drain through strainer and rinse under hot water. Return cooked rice to pan and place over very low heat or in slow oven to dry out.

Cooking time can be cut in half if rice is soaked in tepid water for an hour before cooking.

Tomato rice stuffing

YOU WILL NEED FOR 4 SERVINGS:

> 4 oz. long grain rice
> 1 oz. butter
> 1 small onion, finely chopped
> 4 oz. minced beef
> 1 teaspoon chopped parsley
> 1 (8 oz.) tin peeled tomatoes
> salt and pepper

Cook rice as basic directions using whichever method you prefer. Meanwhile melt butter in a small pan and add onion. Fry gently until soft, then stir in the minced beef and brown it lightly. Draw pan off heat and stir in the cooked rice, parsley, tomatoes and seasoning.
Use to stuff blanched green pepper shells, or scooped out tomato shells and bake on centre shelf of moderate oven (Gas No. 4 or 355 deg.), tomatoes will be ready in 8–10 minutes, peppers, 20–30 minutes.

Rice and egg stuffing

YOU WILL NEED FOR 4 SERVINGS:

> 4 oz. long grain rice
> chicken consommé or stock
> 1 small onion
> 1 green pepper
> 1 oz. butter
> 2 hard-boiled eggs, chopped
> 1 tablespoon chopped parsley
> $\frac{1}{2}$ level teaspoon salt
> pinch of pepper
> 2 tablespoons cream

Cook rice as basic directions using consommé or stock instead of water. Chop onion and pepper finely and sauté in butter until tender. Draw pan off heat and stir in cooked rice, chopped hard-boiled eggs, parsley, seasoning and cream. Use to stuff fish cutlets or ham rolls.

Nutty rice stuffing

YOU WILL NEED FOR 4 SERVINGS:

> 2 rashers streaky bacon, chopped
> 1 small onion, chopped
> 4 oz. long grain rice
> 1 ($10\frac{1}{2}$ oz.) tin condensed beef consommé
> 1 tablespoon Worcestershire sauce
> $\frac{1}{2}$ level teaspoon salt
> 1 tablespoon finely chopped walnuts

In a small saucepan heat bacon very slowly until the fat runs and the bacon is crisp.

Discard the bacon pieces and add onion to the fat with the rice. Fry until both are golden brown. Stir in the consommé, Worcestershire sauce, salt and bring to the boil. Cover lightly with a lid and simmer for 15–20 minutes until the rice is tender and liquid absorbed. Draw pan off heat, add nuts and fluff up with fork. Use with poultry and game.

Pineapple rice stuffing

YOU WILL NEED FOR 4 SERVINGS:

1 oz. butter
½ small onion, finely chopped
3–4 stalks celery, sliced
1 tablespoon chopped parsley
4 oz. long grain rice, cooked
1 (8 oz.) tin pineapple pieces, drained
2 oz. chopped walnuts

Melt butter and lightly sauté onion until tender. Add remaining ingredients and blend with fork. Use as stuffing for pork chops (cut a small pocket from edge into lean) or ham rolls.

Pasta

Cook in plenty of boiling salted water in a large pan, use about 1 level teaspoon salt for each pint of water. When it is at a full rolling boil, add pasta all at once (an exception is spaghetti which should be added gradually). Boil rapidly—the cooking times vary with the type of pasta, see below. Lift a strand out and press with the fingers or bite it—when cooked it is quite tender but still a little chewy. Drain into a colander and rinse under the hot water tap to wash away the starchy water. Use in a recipe as required or melt a little butter in pan, toss pasta in it and serve with grated Parmesan cheese.

Cannelloni: small sheets of pasta, cooked and then rolled up with a stuffing, served usually with a hot tomato sauce, *see page 119.* Boil for 15–20 minutes.

Lasagna: ribbons of pasta about 1½ in. wide. Most often used in baked pasta dishes. Add 1 tablespoon oil to the cooking water and boil lasagna for 15–20 minutes.

Macaroni: covers a wide variety of larger pasta. Generally tubular shaped, but also comes in elbows or shells. Quick cooking macaroni takes 7 minutes, standard varieties take 7–12 minutes and thicker types 15–20 minutes.

Ravioli: stuffed squares of pasta served in a tomato sauce. Boil for 15–20 minutes.

Spaghetti: long thin pasta, served often with main dishes or a Bolognese sauce, *see page 103.* Cook for 12–15 minutes.

Tagliatelle: or noodles, rather flat-shaped ribbons of pasta. Cook for 12–15 minutes.

Vermicelli: long thin curly pasta used in soups such as chicken noodle. Takes 2–3 minutes, boiling gently.

Nouilli paste

YOU WILL NEED:

6 oz. (or 6 rounded tablespoons) plain flour
pinch of salt
1 standard egg, lightly mixed
3 tablespoons water
1 tablespoon olive oil

Sift flour and salt on to a wooden board, or working surface. Make a well in the centre and add egg water and oil. Using your fingers, mix ingredients together thoroughly and then gradually knead to a smooth dough. Set aside to rest for 15 minutes before using.

To make ravioli

YOU WILL NEED FOR 4 SERVINGS:

nouilli paste (*see recipe above*)
½ pint tomato sauce (*see page 119*)
2–3 oz. grated cheese
FOR THE STUFFING:
8 oz. cooked meat, minced
1 level tablespoon flour
½ small onion, chopped
1 teaspoon chopped parsley
salt and pepper
1 small egg, lightly mixed

Make up the nouilli paste according to recipe above and set aside to rest while preparing the filling. Mix the minced meat, flour, onion and parsley together. Season well with salt and pepper and add enough egg to bind the mixture together.

Roll out paste to a wide oblong about 18 by 12 in. Mark the centre line and dot the stuffing in neat rows over half of the pasta, allowing a little space between each mound of filling. Brush the other half with a little beaten egg and carefully fold it over the filling. Seal carefully between heaps of filling, working from the centre of each mound to exclude as much air as possible. Cut the ravioli into squares using a pastry wheel or sharp knife, and spread out to dry until required for cooking. Cook in boiling salted water for 15–20 minutes and serve with tomato sauce *see page 119* and grated Parmesan cheese.

111

Rice, tapioca, macaroni puddings

What could be nicer than a hot, creamy rice pudding with a rich brown skin? Or a sweet, smooth semolina? Too often these puddings are thought of as nourishing but not very appetising—lukewarm, lumpy stodge cast aside with school dinners. In fact, properly cooked, these and similar puddings—tapioca, sago, macaroni—are delicious plain or dressed up with lemon, chocolate or almond flavourings, meringue, caramel or cream toppings. On a warm day they are equally tasty served cold.

Whole grain puddings

YOU WILL NEED FOR 4 SERVINGS:

    1½ oz. (or 3 level tablespoons) short grain rice
    1 oz. (or 1 rounded tablespoon) castor sugar
    1 pint milk
    vanilla essence or grated nutmeg
    ½ oz. butter
    1 tablespoon cream or evaporated milk

Wash rice in cold water, drain and sprinkle over the base of a buttered 1½ pint pie dish. Add sugar and milk and stir well—at this stage a few drops of vanilla essence may be added for flavour. Add butter in small pieces, top with grated nutmeg (omit if vanilla essence has been added) and place in the centre of a slow oven (310 deg. or Gas No. 2) and bake for 2 hours.

To get a really creamy rice pudding stir in the first three skins as they form. After stirring in the third skin add a tablespoon of evaporated milk or cream, stir and leave to brown.

Serve hot with top of the milk, cream or jam sauce.

Variations

Rice pudding with egg: when the pudding has cooked for 1¾ hours remove it from the oven, allow to cool for 10 minutes, and stir in a lightly-beaten egg. Return to the oven and cook a further 15 minutes, then serve as above.

Lemon pudding: add a little finely grated lemon rind to the mixture instead of vanilla essence.

Tapioca pudding: substitute 1½ oz. tapioca for the rice and cook as basic recipe above.

Macaroni pudding: substitute 1½ oz. macaroni for the rice, break it into ½ inch lengths and cook as above.

Crushed grain puddings

YOU WILL NEED FOR 4 SERVINGS:

    1 pint milk
    1½ oz. (or 2 rounded tablespoons) sago or semolina
    1 oz. (or 1 level tablespoon) castor sugar
    a little grated nutmeg

Heat milk gently in a rinsed saucepan and when hot sprinkle the grain over it, stirring all the time. Bring to the boil and add sugar, then lower heat and cook gently for about 5 minutes, stirring occasionally. Draw pan off the heat, pour the mixture into a buttered 1½ pint pie dish and sprinkle with nutmeg. Place in the centre of a moderately slow oven (310 deg. or Gas No. 2) and bake for a further 30 minutes. Serve with a little warmed raspberry jam, top of the milk or cream. Make egg or lemon versions as for whole grain puddings.

Raisin rice meringue

YOU WILL NEED FOR 4 SERVINGS:

    1 pint milk
    2 oz. (or 5 level tablespoons) short grain rice
    2 oz. (or 2 rounded tablespoons) castor sugar
    2 egg yolks
    ½ teaspoon vanilla essence
    2 oz. seedless raisins
    FOR THE TOPPING:
    2 egg whites
    1½ oz. (or 2 level tablespoons) castor sugar

Rinse saucepan with cold water and bring milk to the boil. Sprinkle in the washed rice. Stir until the milk reboils, then lower the heat and simmer mixture very gently, covered with a lid, until thick and creamy—takes about 30–35 minutes.

Draw pan off heat and stir in sugar, egg yolks, vanilla essence and raisins. Pour into a buttered 1½ pint pie dish and top with a meringue mixture.

To make this beat egg whites until stiff and fluffy, then gradually whisk in sugar. Spoon over the hot pudding base and place in the centre of a hot oven (400 deg. or Gas No. 6) and bake for 3–5 minutes until golden brown. Serve at once with cream.

Rice pudding

Lemon rice meringue

Bake as for Raisin rice meringue but substitute finely grated rind and juice of half a lemon for vanilla essence and seedless raisins.

Chocolate rice meringue

Bake as for Raisin rice meringue but omit the seedless raisins. Add instead 4 oz. plain chocolate broken in pieces, with the vanilla essence to the hot mixture. Stir until melted and then top with meringue.

Soufflé rice pudding

Bake as for Raisin rice meringue, but omit seedless raisins. Instead of topping with a meringue, whisk the egg whites until stiff and fold into the creamy rice mixture. Pour into a buttered pie dish and place in the centre of a moderate oven (355 deg. or Gas No. 4). Bake for 30 minutes or until the pudding has risen, and is puffy. Serve hot with a jam or marmalade sauce.

Caramel rice toppers

YOU WILL NEED FOR 6 SERVINGS:

    4 oz. (or 4 rounded tablespoons) granulated sugar
    1 tablespoon water
    1 pint milk
    2 oz. (or 5 level tablespoons) short grain rice
    2 oz. (or 2 rounded tablespoons) castor sugar
    juice of half a lemon
    FOR THE TOPPING:
    ¼ pint double cream
    chopped walnuts

Measure granulated sugar into a heavy saucepan and stir over moderate heat until melted and a golden caramel. Draw pan off the heat and add water—take care as the mixture hisses furiously at this stage. Add milk, put pan on the heat again and stir until caramel has dissolved and milk comes to the boil. Sprinkle in the washed rice, lower the heat and simmer gently, covered with a lid, until the mixture is thick and creamy—takes about 30 minutes. Draw pan off heat, stir in castor sugar and lemon juice and spoon the mixture, while still warm, into individual serving glasses. Serve warm or cold, topped with a spoonful of the whipped cream and sprinkled with the finely chopped walnuts.

Rice and cream ring

YOU WILL NEED FOR 4 SERVINGS:

    1 pint milk
    2 oz. (or 5 level tablespoons) short grain rice
    2 oz. (or 2 rounded tablespoons) castor sugar
    1 teaspoon vanilla essence
    ½ pint double cream
    FOR THE TOPPING:
    ½ lb. fresh or frozen strawberries
    1–2 oz. (or 1–2 rounded tablespoons) castor sugar

Slice the strawberries for the topping, sprinkle with sugar and set aside for at least 30 minutes while preparing the rice base.
Bring milk to the boil in a rinsed saucepan, and sprinkle in the washed rice. Stir until milk boils, covered with a lid, until mixture is thick and creamy—takes about 30 minutes.
Draw pan off heat and stir in sugar and vanilla essence. Leave the mixture until quite cold, stirring occasionally to prevent a skin forming. Whip the cream until thick and fold into the rice mixture. Spoon it into a wet ring mould, or into serving glasses. Chill for several hours, turn out the ring mould, if used, and top with the strawberries just before serving.

Pineapple rice pudding

YOU WILL NEED FOR 4 SERVINGS:

    1 pint milk
    2 oz. (or 5 level tablespoons) short grain rice
    2 oz. (or 2 rounded tablespoons) castor sugar
    1 egg
    1 (8 oz.) tin pineapple pieces
    juice of half a lemon
    ¼ pint double cream
    FOR THE TOPPING:
    2 oz. plain chocolate

Bring milk to the boil in a rinsed saucepan and sprinkle over it the washed rice. Stir until the milk comes to the boil, then lower heat and simmer gently, covered with a lid, until the mixture is thick and creamy—takes about 30 minutes.
Draw pan off heat and stir in sugar, egg yolk, pineapple pieces (drained from tin) and lemon juice. Set aside to cool, stirring occasionally to prevent a skin forming. Whip cream until thick and egg white until stiff and fold gently into the pineapple mixture. Pour into a pretty glass serving dish and top with coarsely grated chocolate. Chill for several hours until ready to serve.

Caramel rice pudding

YOU WILL NEED FOR 4 SERVINGS:

1 pint milk
1½ oz. round grain rice
2 oz. (or 2 rounded tablespoons) castor sugar
2 eggs
few drops vanilla essence
FOR THE CARAMEL:
2 oz. (or 2 rounded tablespoons) granulated sugar
2–3 tablespoons water

Bring milk to boil in fairly large saucepan and add rice. Stir well and re-boil. Cover with lid, lower heat and simmer gently for 30 minutes or until rice is soft. Stir occasionally to prevent rice sticking.

Meanwhile prepare caramel. Measure sugar and water into small saucepan and place over low heat to dissolve, then raise heat and bring to boil. Cook rapidly until whole mixture turns caramel colour. Remove from heat immediately and allow bubbles to subside. Pour caramel into fireproof dish, and holding dish with teacloth—it is very hot—run caramel over base and round sides.

Remove pan of cooked rice from heat and stir in sugar, eggs and vanilla essence. Pour into caramel-lined dish and bake in centre of oven (400 deg. or Gas No. 6) until pudding is set—about 20–30 minutes. Serve either from baking dish, or allow to cool 5 minutes and then turn out. Accompany with cream or top of the milk.

Chocolate rice creams

YOU WILL NEED FOR 4 SERVINGS:

1 pint milk
2 oz. round grain rice
4 oz. plain chocolate, broken into pieces
¼ teaspoon vanilla essence
2 tablespoons castor sugar
FOR THE TOPPING:
¼ pint double cream
1 level tablespoon castor sugar
1 tablespoon sherry
extra grated chocolate for decoration

Bring milk to boil, add rice and cover with lid. Cook gently stirring occasionally, for 30 minutes until soft. Remove from heat and add chocolate. Stir until melted, then add vanilla and castor sugar. Set aside, stirring occasionally until cool. Spoon into individual serving glasses.

Whip cream until just beginning to thicken, then fold in sugar and sherry. Spoon over chocolate mixture and decorate with extra grated chocolate.

Hot almond fruit cream

YOU WILL NEED FOR 4 SERVINGS:

1 pint milk
finely grated rind of 1 orange
1 oz. (or 1 rounded tablespoon) castor sugar
2 oz. (or 3 heaped tablespoons) fine semolina
2 oz. (or 2 rounded tablespoons) ground almonds
1 tablespoon chopped peel
2 oz. chopped dates
1 egg

Measure milk, orange rind and sugar into a saucepan. Heat until almost boiling, then sprinkle in semolina and stir until mixture is boiling and has thickened.

Draw pan off the heat and stir in ground almonds chopped peel, dates and lightly-whisked egg. Pour into a buttered 1½ pint pie dish and bake in a moderate oven (355 deg. or Gas No. 4) for 30 minutes or until soft and lightly browned.

Semolina apricot ring

YOU WILL NEED FOR 4 SERVINGS:

1 pint milk
1½ oz. semolina
2 level tablespoons castor sugar
1 (15 oz.) tin apricot halves
¼ oz. (or 2 level teaspoons) powdered gelatine

Bring the milk almost to the boil and sprinkle in the semolina. Boil, and cook gently stirring all the time until thick and creamy. Add the sugar and when this has dissolved draw the pan off the heat and leave to cool stirring occasionally. Strain the apricots and make the juice up to ½ pint with water, if necessary. Measure the gelatine into a small saucepan and add 2 tablespoons of the juice. Leave to soak for 5 minutes then add remaining juice and stir over low heat until the gelatine has dissolved. Pour a little of the juice into the base of a 1½ pint ring mould and allow to set firm.

Arrange the apricot halves on the jelly and pour over a little more of the juice. Allow this to set firm and then pour over remaining juice and leave to set. Pour over the cooled semolina mixture and leave for several hours until quite cold. Loosen sides and turn out onto a plate.

Savoury rice and pasta

Rice and pasta are economical, easy to cook, and make perfect foils for savoury sauces and cheese. If cooking them with other ingredients in a recipe—as for risotto—use a good, well-seasoned stock. If cooking them separately—as for curries, or blanquette of veal—the sauce should be well-flavoured but quite thin so that it can be absorbed.

Mushroom and cheese risotto

YOU WILL NEED FOR 4 SERVINGS:

8 oz. long grain rice
2 tablespoons cooking oil
4 rashers of bacon, trimmed and chopped
1 small onion, finely chopped
1 pint stock or water plus stock cube
4 oz. mushrooms
½ oz. butter
3 oz. grated Cheddar or Parmesan cheese

Wash rice and remove any dark grains. Heat oil in a shallow pan with chopped bacon, onion and rice. Sauté gently for 2–3 minutes, stirring to blend the ingredients. Stir in hot stock and bring to the boil. Lower heat, cover with a lid and simmer for 20–30 minutes until rice is tender and all liquid absorbed. Meanwhile sauté mushrooms gently in butter until tender—takes about 5 minutes. When rice is cooked, fold in mushrooms and half the grated cheese. Turn the risotto into a hot serving dish, sprinkle with the remaining cheese and serve.

Macaroni cheese and tomato

YOU WILL NEED FOR 4 SERVINGS:

3–4 oz. quick cooking macaroni
FOR THE SAUCE:
1 oz. butter or margarine
1 rounded tablespoon flour
½ pint milk
½ level teaspoon salt and a good pinch of pepper
¼ level teaspoon made mustard
4 oz. grated Cheddar cheese
½ lb. tomatoes

Cook the macaroni in plenty of boiling, salted water for 7 minutes. Drain and rinse under hot water. Meanwhile prepare the cheese sauce. Melt the butter or margarine in a saucepan over moderate heat, stir in flour and cook gently for 1 minute. Gradually stir in milk, beating well all the time to get a really smooth sauce.
Bring the mixture to the boil and season well, then add mustard and half the grated cheese. Stir over the heat until cheese has melted.
Dip tomatoes into boiling water for 1 minute, then peel off the skins. Slice half the tomatoes and set aside. Remove seeds and coarsely chop the remainder and add to the sauce with the cooked macaroni.
Pour into a hot, buttered dish, and top with alternate rows of the reserved tomato slices and cheese. Place the dish under a hot grill and cook until the cheese has melted and is a bubbling brown. Serve it with hot buttered toast or a green salad.

Rice curry salad

YOU WILL NEED FOR 4 SERVINGS:

6 oz. cooked long grain rice
1 small packet frozen peas
1 green pepper, deseeded and chopped
4 oz. prepared prawns
2 tablespoons chutney
½ level teaspoon salt
1 level teaspoon curry powder
1 tablespoon vinegar
2 tablespoons salad oil

Measure rice into mixing basin, then add cooked peas, chopped pepper, prawns, chutney, salt and curry powder. Blend together vinegar and oil and add to the other ingredients, tossing to blend thoroughly. Serve cold with cold sliced ham or tongue. Garnish with lettuce if liked.

Pineapple rice salad

YOU WILL NEED FOR 4 SERVINGS:

6 oz. cooked long grain rice
1 small (4 oz.) tin pineapple, chopped
2–3 tablespoons seedless raisins
1 small onion, chopped
FOR THE DRESSING:
pinch each salt, pepper and sugar
2 tablespoons vinegar
4 tablespoons salad oil
½ onion, finely chopped
1 tablespoon finely chopped parsley

Mix together rice, pineapple, raisins, and onion. Blend together salt, pepper, sugar and vinegar and add oil, onion and parsley. Shake well and toss rice mixture in it. Serve with cold meat, poultry or game.

Rice curry salad, cannelloni and blanquette of veal

Blanquette of veal

YOU WILL NEED FOR 4 SERVINGS:

1½ lb. boneless stewing veal
1 onion, finely chopped
1–2 carrots, thinly sliced
¾ pint stock or water plus stock cube
salt and pepper
1 small bay leaf
4 oz. button mushrooms, lightly fried
2–3 bacon rashers
8 oz. long grain rice
pinch of saffron
FOR THE SAUCE:
1 oz. butter
1 oz. (or 1 rounded tablespoon) flour
½ pint cooking liquor *(see instructions)*
2 egg yolks mixed with 2 tablespoons cream

Discard any skin or fat and cut meat into neat cubes. Blanch by plunging into boiling water for 2 minutes and then drain. Place the vegetables in the base of a large stew pan or flame-proof casserole dish and add meat and stock.

Bring to the boil and skim if necessary. Lower the heat and add seasoning and bay leaf, cover with a lid and simmer gently for 1½ hours, until meat is tender. Draw the pan off heat, remove bay leaf, and strain the liquor, reserving it for the sauce. Keep meat and vegetables hot.

Now make the sauce. Melt butter in a saucepan stir in flour and cook gently for 1 minute. Gradually stir in ½ pint of the hot cooking liquor, and bring up to the boil. Add more stock if necessary to make a fairly thin sauce. Check seasoning and add meat and vegetables. Draw pan off heat and stir in blended egg yolks and cream. Add mushrooms and serve garnished with bacon rolls (roll up trimmed rashers and grill), on rice.

Sprinkle the rice into plenty of boiling, salted water, add a pinch of saffron and cook rapidly for 8 minutes, strain and serve.

Cannelloni

YOU WILL NEED FOR 4 SERVINGS:

cannelloni shells, allow 2–3 per person
½ pint tomato sauce, *see page 119*
2–3 oz. grated Parmesan cheese
FOR THE STUFFING:
½ pint well-seasoned white sauce *(see instructions)*
salt and pepper
12 oz. cooked minced chicken

Plunge cannelloni into boiling salted water and cook for 15–20 minutes, drain and set aside.

Meanwhile prepare the stuffing. First make white sauce using 1 oz. butter and 2 level tablespoons flour, blended with ½ pint milk. Season well with salt and pepper. Add chicken with extra seasoning if necessary.

Stuff the cannelloni with the filling and arrange in a warm serving dish.

Pour over the prepared tomato sauce, sprinkle with grated cheese and brown in the top of a hot oven (400 deg. or Gas No. 6). Serve sprinkled with extra grated Parmesan cheese.

Buffet rice

For a party, give your guests a choice of three different types of rice salad. Cook 8 oz. brown rice and 1 lb. long, then mix as follows:

Bacon pepper rice

Toss half the cooked long rice with 4–6 bacon rashers, fried until crisp and then crumbled in pieces, and 1 coarsely chopped green pepper. Toss with basic French dressing, *see page 91.*

Pineapple rice

Add remainder of cooked long grain rice to 1 oz. hot melted butter, then add 1 small tin pineapple drained and chopped, with 2 tablespoons of the juice and 1 tablespoon chopped toasted almonds.

Nutty brown rice

Toss cooked brown rice with 4 oz. sliced sautéd mushrooms and 2 oz. finely chopped walnuts. Toss with basic dressing.

Heap the three kinds of rice side by side on a spacious serving platter or tray, with rows of tomato and cucumber slices in between—having tossed them in French dressing, *see page 91.* There will be enough for 16–18 servings.

Sauces

Pasta can be served plain, tossed in melted butter and topped with grated cheese, but a sauce adds extra flavour. It should be well-seasoned and tasty as pasta itself has very little flavour.

Tomato sauce

YOU WILL NEED FOR ½ PINT:

1 tablespoon cooking oil
1 small onion, finely chopped
1 clove garlic (optional)
1 (14 oz.) tin tomatoes
½ level teaspoon salt
½ level teaspoon oregano or basil
½ level teaspoon castor sugar
1 rounded teaspoon cornflour blended with
1 tablespoon water

Heat oil in a small saucepan, and add onion. Cover with a lid and sauté gently for about 5 minutes until tender. Add finely chopped garlic, if liked, and sauté for a further minute. Stir in tomatoes, salt, herbs and sugar and simmer, covered with a lid, for 20–25 minutes, stirring occasionally.
Strain sauce and return to the saucepan. Stir in the cornflour blend and bring to the boil, stirring well.

With mushrooms

Sauté onion as for tomato sauce then add 4–5 oz. sliced button mushrooms and sauté a further 5 minutes. Then continue with tomato sauce recipe but do not strain.

With minced beef

Sauté onion as for tomato sauce then add 4 oz. minced beef and stir over moderate heat until brown. Continue with tomato sauce recipe, simmering it for 30 minutes, then thicken if necessary, but do not strain.

Mushroom sauce

YOU WILL NEED FOR 4 SERVINGS:

1 large onion
1 small head celery, scrubbed and shredded
3 oz. butter
1 lb. button mushrooms, trimmed and sliced
3 level teaspoons salt
½ teaspoon dried mixed herbs
2 level tablespoons flour
1 pint water plus chicken stock cube
juice 1 lemon
chopped parsley, for serving

Add the chopped onion and celery to the hot butter in a large saucepan. Cover and cook gently until softened—takes about 10 minutes. Add the mushrooms and cook a further 5 minutes. Sprinkle with the salt, mixed herbs and flour and mix well. Stir in the stock and lemon juice, bring up to the boil and cook gently until sauce has thickened. Check seasoning, sprinkle with chopped parsley and serve with cooked spaghetti.

Tomato and ham sauce

YOU WILL NEED FOR 4 SERVINGS:

1 oz. butter or margarine
1 rasher of bacon, trimmed and chopped
1 small onion, sliced
1 small carrot, sliced
1 level tablespoon flour
1 (1 lb. 3 oz.) tin tomatoes
½ pint stock
pepper and salt
1 tablespoon tomato purée
1 level teaspoon castor sugar
1 teaspoon lemon juice or vinegar
½ lb. fresh tomatoes
½ lb. cooked ham, cut in one piece

Melt butter or margarine in a saucepan. Add chopped bacon and fry lightly. Add sliced onion and carrot and fry gently without browning. Stir in the flour, tomatoes, stock, seasoning, tomato purée, sugar and lemon juice or vinegar. Bring to the boil, cover with a lid, and simmer for 30 minutes over low heat.
Draw pan off heat. Rub sauce through a sieve and return to pan. Check seasoning and reheat.
Meanwhile, nick the skins on the tomatoes and plunge into boiling water for 1 minute. Drain, peel off the skin and cut the tomato in quarters, removing pips. Add the flesh to the sauce along with the cooked ham cut in dice. Heat through.

Shellfish sauce

YOU WILL NEED FOR 4 SERVINGS:

2 oz. butter or margarine
1 onion, peeled and finely chopped
1 green pepper, deseeded and chopped
2 level tablespoons flour
½ pint stock or water plus stock cube
1 small (2½ oz.) tin tomato purée
4 oz. grated cheese
pinch of pepper
8 oz. prepared prawns

Heat the butter in a saucepan, add the onion and green pepper and fry gently covered with a lid for about 5 minutes to soften. Stir in the flour and cook a further few moments. Gradually stir in the stock and bring up to the boil stirring all the time, to get a really smooth sauce. Add the tomato purée, grated cheese and pepper and cook stirring until cheese has melted. Add the prawns, heat through.

Party dishes

Entertaining is made easy with rice and pasta because they are easy to prepare, look impressive and taste delicious. They are economical, too. The first recipes are ideal for supper parties for four people, reduce the ingredients for serving two.

Apricot rice salad

YOU WILL NEED FOR 4 SERVINGS:

6 oz. cooked long grain rice
1 small (4 oz.) tin apricots, chopped
2–3 tablespoons seedless raisins
1 small onion, chopped
FOR THE DRESSING:
pinch each salt, pepper and sugar
2 tablespoons vinegar
4 tablespoons salad oil
½ onion, finely chopped
1 tablespoon finely chopped parsley

Mix together rice, apricots, raisins and onion. Blend together salt, pepper, sugar and vinegar and add oil, onion and parsley. Shake well and toss rice mixture in it. Serve with cold meat, poultry or game.

Prawns in rice ring

YOU WILL NEED FOR 4 SERVINGS:

2 oz. butter
1 small onion, finely chopped
1 (14 oz.) tin tomatoes
1 wine glass red wine
½ level teaspoon salt and a pinch of pepper
1 oz. (or 1 rounded tablespoon) flour
2 tablespoons tomato ketchup
8–10 oz. prepared prawns

Melt half butter in a medium-sized saucepan, and gently sauté onion until soft. Stir in tomatoes, wine and seasoning. Cover with a lid and simmer gently for 10 minutes. Cream the remaining butter and flour, add to the sauce ingredients with tomato ketchup and bring to the boil, stirring well. Add the prepared prawns, and simmer gently until heated through. Spoon into rice ring (made as for Chicken in rice ring, *see page 122*). Sprinkle with chopped parsley and serve or garnish the outside of the rice ring with a few reserved prawns.

Left to right: lasagna, gnocchi parmigiani, prawns in rice ring, kedgeree and herb bread

Chicken in rice ring

YOU WILL NEED FOR 4 SERVINGS:

4 chicken joints
salt and pepper
3 oz. butter
1 onion, finely chopped
½ pint single cream
squeeze of lemon juice
little chopped parsley to decorate
FOR THE RICE RING:
8 oz. long grain rice

Season chicken joints with salt and pepper. Heat butter in a heavy frying pan and add the chicken, skin-side down, and onion. Fry the joints over low heat until tender and browned, turning occasionally—takes about 25–30 minutes.

Meanwhile cook rice in plenty of boiling salted water for 10 minutes until tender. Pack firmly into a buttered ring mould, then turn out on to a serving plate. Cover with a buttered paper to keep warm. Rice can be served loose if preferred. Drain cooked chicken from pan, gently lift the flesh from the bones and spoon into the rice ring. Pour off all but 1 tablespoon of the hot butter in the pan, removing most of the onion. Reheat until boiling, draw pan off heat and quickly stir in cream and lemon juice. Spoon the cream sauce over the cooked chicken and rice, top with parsley.

Gnocchi parmigiani

YOU WILL NEED FOR 6 SERVINGS:

2 pints milk
4 oz. butter or margarine
1 level teaspoon salt
freshly milled pepper
little grated nutmeg
1 lb. fine semolina
2 egg yolks, lightly mixed
4 oz. grated Parmesan cheese
¼ pint single cream
bunch of watercress for garnish

In a large saucepan bring milk to the boil with butter, seasoning and grated nutmeg. When on boiling point, sprinkle in semolina and stir vigorously with a wooden spoon or whisk to prevent lumps forming. Bring to the boil, stirring well until thickened, and then draw pan off heat. Beat in the egg yolks and 2 oz. of the grated cheese. Pour the mixture out into buttered shallow baking or roasting tin. The mixture should be about ½ in. thick. Leave in a cool place to set firm for several hours, then using a 1½–2 in. round cutter

make small rounds of gnocchi, or cut it into squares. Arrange these overlapping in a well-buttered oven-proof dish. Pour the cream over the gnocchi.

Sprinkle with rest of cheese. Place just above centre of hot oven (400 deg. or Gas No. 6) and bake until hot and golden — about 25 minutes. Garnished with watercress.

Kebabs and rice

YOU WILL NEED FOR 4 SERVINGS:

4 rashers back bacon
8 oz. calves liver, not sliced
8 mushrooms
4 tomatoes
oil, salt and pepper
FOR THE ONION RICE:
¾ pint water
½ level teaspoon salt
knob of butter
½ onion, chopped
2 teaspoons Worcestershire sauce
1 teaspoon lemon juice
8 oz. long grain rice

Trim bacon. Cut rashers in half and roll up. Cut liver into cubes, prepare mushroom caps, halve tomatoes. Thread 4 skewers with alternate liver cubes, bacon rolls, mushroom caps and halved tomatoes. Brush with oil, sprinkle with salt and pepper. Grill under a medium heat turning occasionally, for 10–15 minutes. Serve on bed of onion rice.

Meanwhile melt butter and fry onion, in a saucepan, draw pan off heat, then add water, salt, Worcestershire sauce and lemon juice. Bring to the boil and stir in rice. Lower heat, cover with a tight-fitting lid and simmer gently for about 15 minutes, until rice is cooked and liquid absorbed. Fluff rice with a fork in a warm dish.

Flavoured bread

Hot, flavoured bread and rolls make the perfect party accompaniment to rice and pasta. Slit a French loaf into oblique slices, leaving the bottom crust whole. Spread both sides of each slice with flavoured butter, wrap in aluminium foil and place in a hot oven (400 deg. or Gas No. 6) for 20 minutes or until heated through. Serve in the foil.

Herb: cream together 4 oz. butter, 1 tablespoon lemon juice, 1 tablespoon chopped parsley, and 1 level teaspoon dried herbs.

Garlic: cream together 4 oz. butter, and 1 tablespoon chopped parsley. Crush 1 clove garlic and finely chop with a little salt. Beat this into the butter.

Barbecue: cream together 4 oz. butter, 2 heaped tablespoons grated cheese, ½ teaspoon Worcestershire sauce, 1 tablespoon prepared mustard, 1 tablespoon chopped onion or parsley.

French onion bread: Slit loaf in chunky 1 in. thick slices. Cream the butter until soft, add chopped parsley if liked and spread generously beween the slices. Cut an onion in thin slices and slip between the bread slices. Sprinkle with salt and pepper and place on a baking tray. Bake in a hot oven (400 deg. or Gas No. 6) 10–12 minutes until warm, serve at once.

Hot seeded rolls: cut bridge rolls into lengthwise quarters. Brush all over with melted butter and roll in poppy seeds (or try Parmesan cheese for a change). Bake in a hot oven (400 deg. or Gas No. 6) for 7–10 minutes until crisp and beginning to brown.

Pasta and rice are ideal for serving hot at a large party—your guests will wonder how you ever managed it! In fact it's all done by advance preparation. All these recipes are started earlier in the day, finished off up to an hour before serving. Decrease the ingredients for a smaller number of people. Remember that rice increases in bulk so you will need to use a very large pan. Easy check is to add up liquid in recipe, add two pints and measure pan with water.

Lasagna

YOU WILL NEED FOR 16 SERVINGS:

1 (2 lb. 3 oz.) tin tomatoes
1 pint tomato sauce *see page 119* (or use about 2 tins
 condensed tomato soup made up to 1 pint with water)
3 level teaspoons salt
¼ level teaspoon pepper
4 tablespoons cooking oil
2 large onions, finely chopped
2 lb. minced beef
1 lb. medium or wide lasagna
3 (8 oz.) cartons cottage cheese
2 eggs
4 oz. Parmesan cheese, grated

Early in the day: in a large saucepan combine tinned tomatoes, tomato sauce or the soup, 1 teaspoon of salt, and pepper. Bring slowly to the boil, stirring occasionally.

Meanwhile heat oil in a frying pan, add onions and cook gently until soft and golden brown. Stir in minced beef and remaining salt. Fry for 5–6 minutes or until browned, add to the sauce mixture.

Simmer gently, uncovered for 2½ hours until meat is cooked and sauce thickened.

Towards the end of the cooking time for the sauce, cook the lasagna in boiling salted water (add 1 tablespoon oil to prevent pieces from sticking together) for 15–20 minutes. Drain and separate the pieces. Mix the cottage cheese and eggs.

Put some sauce into two very large or 3 smaller ovenproof baking dishes. Top with a layer of over-lapping lasagna, then with half the mixed cottage cheese and egg and half the Parmesan cheese. Repeat the layers finishing with grated cheese. Set aside.

About 50 minutes before serving time: put lasagna in the centre of a moderately hot oven (355 deg. or Gas No. 4) and bake for 30–40 minutes or until bubbling hot and browned. Cool slightly before serving.

Kedgeree

YOU WILL NEED FOR 16 SERVINGS:

4 medium-sized smoked haddock or 2–2½ lb. smoked cod
few stalks of parsley
2 bay leaves
3 lemons
few peppercorns
6 hard-boiled eggs, sliced
2–2 tablespoons chopped parsley
6 oz. butter or margarine
2 onions, finely chopped
2 lb. long grain rice
4 pints boiling fish liquor—*see instructions*
pepper and salt

Early in the day: rinse and cut up the haddock or smoked cod, do not remove skin or bones. Place in a large pan with about 5 pints water, parsley stalks, bay leaves, one lemon, sliced, and peppercorns. Bring to the boil, then simmer very gently until fish is tender. Strain off the liquor, measure and keep for cooking the rice. Discard skin and bone from the fish and break flesh into flakes, slice the hard-boiled eggs and chop the parsley. Set all aside in a cool place until later.

About 50 minutes before serving time: melt **4 oz.** of the butter or margarine in the largest saucepan you have—make sure it holds at least 5–6 pints. Add the finely-chopped onion and rice and fry gently for about 5 minutes. Stir in the boiling fish liquor. Cover with a lid and simmer very gently, stirring occasionally for 30–40 minutes or until the rice is tender and the liquid absorbed. Season if necessary, then fold in the flaked fish, hard-boiled eggs (reserve a few slices for garnish), chopped parsley, juice of remaining lemons and remaining butter. Heat for about 5 minutes, then pile into a serving dish and garnish with reserved egg slices.

ALL ABOUT *Cold Sweets*

Summer puddings and jellies

Milk and cereal puddings

Moulded desserts are stiffened either with starchy cereal or with gelatine. The starches are usually ground or powdered grains such as ground rice or cornflour, but occasionally whole grains like rice, semolina or tapioca are used. Cornflour, arrowroot or ground rice should be blended with a little milk from the recipe to make a smooth paste, before being added to the remaining liquid. This makes it blend smoothly without any lumps.

Whole grain cereals should be sprinkled over the hot liquid (to avoid making lumps) and stirred until reboiling. Cook the mixture gently until thickened.

Use a fairly thick heavy saucepan (thin pans burn milk mixtures very quickly and this may completely spoil the dessert). Rinse the pan out with cold water before heating the milk or any milky mixture—this helps to prevent sticking and burning.

Using powdered grains

YOU WILL NEED FOR 4 SERVINGS:

> 1½ oz. cornflour, arrowroot or ground rice
> 1 pint milk
> 1–2 oz. castor sugar
> flavouring *(see recipe)*
> ½ oz. butter, if liked

Blend the cereal smoothly in a basin with some of the cold milk from recipe, and stir in sugar. Bring remaining milk to the boil, add a strip of lemon rind or a vanilla pod or one of the variations below. Or flavouring can be added to cooked cereal. Strain boiling milk over blended ingredients, stirring well with wooden spoon. Rinse pan, pour back mixture, and heat gently, stirring all the time. Bring to the boil and simmer for about 4–5 minutes to cook the starch very thoroughly.

If no flavouring has yet been used add now a few drops of lemon, vanilla or other essence, a few drops of colouring if wanted, and butter.

Pour the hot mixture into a wet mould and leave to set firm. Turn out and serve with stewed or tinned fruit, or hot jam sauce.

Chocolate cornflour pudding

YOU WILL NEED FOR 4 SERVINGS:

> 2 oz. (or 6 level tablespoons) cornflour
> 1 oz. (or 3 level tablespoons) cocoa powder
> 2 oz. (or 2 rounded tablespoons) castor sugar
> 1 pint milk
> few drops vanilla essence
> finely chopped walnuts for decoration

Sift the cornflour and cocoa powder into a mixing basin and add the castor sugar. Mix to a smooth paste with a little milk taken from the pint.

Heat the remaining milk in a saucepan and when hot stir into the cornflour blend. Mix well and return to the milk saucepan. Stir constantly over moderate heat until the mixture has thickened and is boiling. Draw the pan off the heat and stir in a few drops vanilla essence. Pour the mixture into a serving dish, sprinkle with chopped walnuts and serve warm with cream or top of the milk.

Coffee: add 1–2 tablespoons coffee essence to the mixture after it has been cooked.

Orange: add finely grated rind of an orange to the boiling milk, then add orange colouring to the cooked cereal.

Using whole grains

YOU WILL NEED FOR 4 SERVINGS:

1 pint milk
2 oz. semolina, round grain or pudding rice, or tapioca
1–2 oz. castor sugar
flavouring (*see variations below*)
1 egg (optional)

Heat milk gently just to the boil.
Sprinkle in the grains and slowly reboil, stirring all the time. Lower the heat and simmer gently, stirring occasionally to prevent sticking, until the mixture has thickened. Semolina will take about 20–25 minutes, rice 45 minutes, and tapioca 1 hour.
When cooked, draw the pan off the heat, stir in the sugar and flavouring and the whole egg or egg yolk. The egg is not necessary but does add richness and flavour to the pudding. The egg white may be stiffly whipped and folded in to give extra lightness.
Pour the hot mixture into a wet mould and leave to set firm. Serve with custard, jam sauce or fruit.

Variations

These are most suited to rice.

Chocolate: stir 3–4 oz. plain chocolate pieces, into the hot cooked mixture. Add a few drops vanilla essence.

Tutti-frutti: stir some chopped glacé fruits into the hot cooked mixture.

Jellies

Correct proportions for gelatine are ½ oz. (1 rounded tablespoon) powdered gelatine to 1 pint of thin liquids such as milk, syrups or tinned fruit purées: ¼ oz. (or 1 level tablespoon) powdered gelatine to 1 pint thicker liquids like custards or thicker fruit purées.

Powdered gelatine should be soaked in a small quantity of cold liquid from the recipe—this helps it to soften. Then it should be dissolved carefully, according to recipe instructions, *over very low heat.* On no account should the mixture be allowed to boil or the gelatine will lose its setting properties.
Leaf gelatine should be soaked in cold water then added to a hot mixture and stirred until dissolved. Pineapple has an acidity which can cause the gelatine to lose its setting properties. To avoid this, cook fresh pineapples thoroughly and bring tinned pineapple to the boil for a few minutes before making jelly.

Simple orange jelly

YOU WILL NEED FOR 4 SERVINGS:

½ oz. (or 1 rounded tablespoon) powdered gelatine
2 tablespoons castor sugar
¼ pint cold water
½ pint fresh or tinned orange juice
juice of 1 lemon

Measure gelatine, sugar and water into a saucepan. Leave to soak for 5 minutes, then place over very gentle heat and stir until gelatine is quite dissolved. Draw pan off heat and stir in orange juice (you can also use orange squash diluted with water to make ½ pint) and the lemon juice. Stir to blend and cool until warm, then pour into a wet mould or pretty glass serving dish and leave in a cool place until set firm. Turn out of mould or serve straight from dish with cream or fruit.

Lemon: increase the sugar to 3 tablespoons and substitute lemon squash, diluted with water, for orange squash and add juice of 2 lemons.

Wine: follow orange jelly recipe but instead of orange juice stir in 1 teacup red or port wine and make up to 1 pint with cold water. This jelly is delicious with pears.

Fruit jelly

To make a more attractive dessert, prepared fruit can be set in the jelly. It must be added when the jelly is partly set or it will rise and float on top. There are two methods.
First is to cool the jelly until almost on setting point. Easiest way to do this is to pour the jelly into a small mixing basin and place this in a large bowl of cold water, preferably with a few ice-cubes. Stir gently and as soon as the jelly begins to thicken, remove from the cold water, and stir in the prepared fruit. Pour into a wet mould and leave to set firm. The

fruit and the mould should be ready before jelly is made as it sets very quickly.

Second way is in layers. This is more successful but takes longer. Pour a little of the jelly into the base of a mould and allow to set firm. Over this arrange a little fruit in a pretty decoration which will show up nicely when jelly is turned out. Spoon over a little more of the jelly and allow to set firm.

The jelly you are working with will probably start to set but it can be melted over the heat.

Pour in a third of the remaining jelly and a third of the prepared fruit. Allow this to set firm and then add remaining jelly and fruit in thirds, allowing each layer to set before adding the next.

Then leave the finished jelly to set completely before turning it out on to a serving dish.

Mandarin oranges and black or green grapes are delicious in orange jelly. Green grapes and pears, or sliced peaches and black cherries, or strawberries, or raspberries are perfect in wine or lemon jelly.

Milk and fruit jelly

Many attractive desserts are made by lining the mould with jelly and then filling the centre with a contrasting creamy milk jelly mixture. Pour the fruit jelly into the mould and tilt mould on its side in a small basin filled with cold water (preferably with ice-cubes). Slowly turn the mould round so that the jelly runs over the sides and gradually sets, covering the mould completely on the inside. Stand the mould upright and fill the centre with contrasting milk jelly mixture, *see recipe below.*

Milk jelly

YOU WILL NEED FOR 4 SERVINGS:

½ oz. (or 1 rounded tablespoon) powdered gelatine
3 oz. (or 3 rounded tablespoons) castor sugar
¼ pint water
¾ pint milk
few drops vanilla essence

Measure gelatine, sugar and water into a saucepan and leave to soak for 5 minutes. Then stir over very gentle heat until dissolved. Draw pan off heat and cool until just warm, then stir in the milk (which should be at room temperature—not cold from the refrigerator). Flavour to taste and pour into a wet mould or serving dish, and leave to set firm.

Fruit flavoured: dissolve gelatine and sugar in ¼ pint unsweetened fruit juice. Then proceed with the recipe as above.

Honeycomb mould

YOU WILL NEED FOR 4–6 SERVINGS:

½ oz. (or 1 level tablespoon) powdered gelatine
2 tablespoons water
3 eggs, separated
2 oz. (or 2 rounded tablespoons) castor sugar
1 pint milk
1 teaspoon vanilla essence

Measure the gelatine into a teacup, and add the water, and leave to soak. Blend together the egg yolks and sugar together in a small basin and gradually stir in ¼ pint milk. Heat the remaining milk in a saucepan and when almost boiling, stir into the egg custard blend. Strain back into the milk saucepan, and stirring all the time, cook until the custard has thickened slightly—take care not to allow the mixture to boil.

Draw the pan off the heat and add the vanilla essence and soaked gelatine. Stir well until the gelatine has thoroughly dissolved. Then set aside and allow to cool until beginning to thicken. Beat the egg whites stiffly and fold them into the custard mixture. Pour into a wet 1½ pint mould and leave in a cool place until set firm.

Size of mould

To find what size of mould you need add up very roughly the liquid quantities in the recipe, allow extra for any solid ingredients, and then measure mould with water.

The best moulds are the old fashioned earthenware type but tin, aluminium or copper are also good. Examine the bases—they should have level bases so that they don't tip over when filled with liquid.

Loaf tins, sandwich cake tins and ring tins make satisfactory moulds if no others are available. Make sure any mould is scrupulously clean, and always rinse it out with cold water before using—this makes it easier to remove the finished jelly.

To remove from mould

Run the point of a knife round the jelly, then dip the mould up to the edges in warm (not too hot), water until the jelly is slightly loose; don't let it melt. Place a serving plate over the mould; turn it upside down and shake it gently.

Here's a handy tip—wet the plate slightly, then if the mould is not in the centre it can be moved a little one way or the other.

Fruits and custards

Fresh fruit

In warm summer weather, fresh fruit desserts provide the most refreshing flavours and are often the simplest and least expensive to prepare.

Fruit salad

YOU WILL NEED FOR 4 SERVINGS:

2 dessert pears, peeled and sliced
2 dessert apples, diced
2–3 bananas, peeled and sliced
1 orange, peeled and cut in segments
¼ lb. black or green grapes, halved and deseeded
FOR THE SYRUP:
4 oz. castor sugar
¼ pint water
1 tablespoon kirsch, brandy or sweet sherry

Make the syrup by dissolving sugar in water, bringing to the boil and simmering for 2 minutes (or use Honey Syrup below). Draw pan off heat and cool before adding liqueur.
Add prepared fruit to syrup (dip apples and bananas in lemon juice first). Chill until ready to serve.

Honey syrup

Heat gently until blended 3–4 tablespoons thin honey, finely grated rind and juice of 1 lemon, 2 tablespoons fresh orange juice and 2 tablespoons dry sherry. Draw off the heat. Strain and chill before adding fruit.

Sliced oranges in caramel syrup

YOU WILL NEED FOR 4 SERVINGS:

5 oranges
4 oz. (or 4 rounded tablespoons) castor sugar
water, *see recipe*

Slice the ends off 4 of the oranges, then standing the fruit upright slice down the sides to cut away the skin and leave the orange flesh only. Slice orange flesh across thinly and removing any pips, place in a pretty glass serving dish.

Measure the sugar into a small heavy pan. Place over moderate heat and stir all the time until the sugar has melted and turned a caramel colour. Draw the pan off the heat and add about ½ teacup of water. Take care as the mixture will boil furiously at this stage. Return the pan to the heat and stir gently until the caramel has dissolved.
Draw the pan off the heat and add the strained juice of the remaining orange. Allow the caramel to cool, stirring in a little more water if necessary so that a thin syrup is obtained. Pour over the sliced oranges and chill until ready to serve.

Stewed fruit

Allow 4 oz. (or 4 rounded tablespoons) castor sugar to each lb. of fresh fruit; and ¼ pint water per lb. of soft fruit or ½ pint per lb. of medium, hard or stone fruit.
Dissolve sugar in water and bring to the boil. Add flavouring (piece of stick cinnamon, lemon rind or a clove). Add fruit and simmer gently, covered with a lid, until tender.
Except for apples or pears fruit may be cooked in the oven. To do this place the prepared fruit in a casserole dish, pour over the syrup and cover with a lid. Place in the centre of a slow oven (335 deg. or Gas No. 3) and cook until tender.

Gooseberry fool

YOU WILL NEED FOR 4 SERVINGS:

4 oz. sugar
¼ pint water
1 lb. gooseberries
a little green colouring
½ pint double cream or ¼ pint each double cream
   and egg custard
chopped nuts
sponge or shortbread fingers

Dissolve sugar in water and bring to the boil. Add the prepared gooseberries and stew gently, covered with a lid, until soft. Draw pan off heat and pass fruit through a sieve to make a purée. Add green colouring if liked, and allow to cool.
Blend the cooled purée with the lightly whipped cream or custard and cream (*see Cup custard, page 130, for custard*). Pour into individual glasses and decorate with a few chopped nuts. Serve chilled with sponge fingers or shortbread biscuits.
Try this recipe using rhubarb, raspberries, apples, black currants or ripe bananas (bananas do not need stewing, rub them straight through sieve).

Crème caramel and fresh fruit salad

Baked apples

YOU WILL NEED FOR 4 SERVINGS:

4 large sharp flavoured apples
soft brown sugar—*see recipe*
1 tablespoon sultanas
1 oz. butter
3–4 tablespoons water
¼ pint single cream for serving

Wash the apples and remove the cores keeping the apples whole. Using the tip of a sharp knife run the blade around the centre of the apple just to pierce the skin. Place the apples in a large roasting or baking tin. Fill the centre of each with soft brown sugar and a few sultanas and top each apple with a piece of butter. Add the water to the tin and place in the centre of a moderate oven (355 deg. or Gas No. 4) and bake for 40–45 minutes.

When baked, the apples will puff up and become quite soft—serve with the syrup from the tin and the cream.

Egg custards

These must be cooked with great care in a slow, gentle heat—too much heat makes them curdle. In an oven the dish containing the custard should stand in a larger shallow tin containing about 1 in. of cold water. This is often called 'au bain marie'. For cooking on top of the stove use a double boiler or small pan placed inside a larger pan of simmering water.

Baked custard

YOU WILL NEED FOR 4 SERVINGS:

4–6 eggs
1 oz. (or 1 rounded tablespoon) castor sugar
1 pint milk
vanilla essence and nutmeg if liked

Beat eggs and sugar together and stir in the slightly warmed milk and vanilla essence if used. Strain into a buttered 1½ pint pie dish. Place the dish in a larger baking tin containing about 1 in. of cold water, and place in the centre of a slow oven (335 deg. or Gas No. 3). Bake for 1 hour, or until custard is firm, test by touching the centre lightly. For deeper custards run the point of a sharp knife into the centre—it should come out cleanly. Top with nutmeg and serve warm or cold, nice with stewed fruit.

Cup custard

YOU WILL NEED FOR ½ PINT:

1 egg and 2 egg yolks
1 oz. (or 1 rounded tablespoon) castor sugar
½ pint milk
flavourings *(see recipe)*

Beat eggs and sugar together and pour on the lightly heated milk. Flavouring ingredients such as vanilla pod or lemon rind may be heated with the milk if liked. Stir the mixture thoroughly and strain back into the milk saucepan. Stand the pan inside another containing gently simmering water and cook, stirring all the time. When mixture has thickened slightly and feels quite hot to the little finger, remove pan from heat and allow to cool, stirring occasionally to prevent skin forming.

Pour into custard glasses or use as required in a recipe.

Steamed custard

YOU WILL NEED FOR 4 SERVINGS:

2–3 eggs
1 oz. (or 1 rounded tablespoon) castor sugar
½ pint milk
vanilla essence

Beat together eggs, sugar, milk and essence. Strain into a buttered 1 pint mould, cover with greased papers and place in the top section of a steamer. Cook over *simmering* water for 30–40 minutes, until set firm. Remove from heat and cool at least 5 minutes before turning out. If no steamer is available the mould may be cooked in a pan of water to reach half-way up the sides of the mould.

All sorts of delicious recipes can be made up by adding pieces of sponge cake and chopped glacé fruits to the custard before steaming. Chill, turn out and serve with cream.

Crème caramel

YOU WILL NEED FOR 4 SERVINGS:

3 large eggs
1 oz. (or 1 rounded tablespoon) castor sugar
½ pint milk
few drops vanilla essence
FOR THE CARAMEL:
2 tablespoons granulated sugar
2 tablespoons water

First prepare the caramel. Put sugar in a thick, heavy pan and place over moderate heat. Stir with a wooden spoon until dissolved and a caramel colour. Draw pan off heat and add the water all at once—

take care as the mixture will hiss furiously. Return the pan to the heat, and stir until water is boiling and caramel dissolved. Pour it into the base of a buttered 1 pint baking dish or plain mould or 6–8 individual dariole or castle moulds.

Whisk eggs and sugar together and stir in warmed milk. Flavour with vanilla and strain over caramel. Place in a large baking tin containing about 1 in. of water in the centre of a slow oven (335 deg. or Gas No. 3). Bake small ones for 30–35 minutes, larger ones for 1 hour.

When cooked remove from the heat and allow to become quite cold before turning out. Run the tip of a knife blade round the top of the mould, and invert on to a serving plate. Serve with fresh cream.

Pots de crème

YOU WILL NEED FOR 6 SERVINGS:

6 oz. plain chocolate
4 egg yolks
1 oz. (or 1 rounded tablespoon) castor sugar
1 tablespoon rum
¾ pint milk
¼ pint whipped cream
grated chocolate for decoration

Break chocolate into a mixing basin and set over a pan of hot water until softened and smooth. Remove the basin from heat and add egg yolks, sugar and rum. Blend well and stir in the lightly heated milk. Strain the custard mixture and pour into 6 buttered individual baking or ramekin dishes. Place in a baking tin containing ½ in. water in the centre of a slow oven (335 deg. or Gas No. 3) and bake for 20–30 minutes or until firm. Remove from heat, and leave to cool. Decorate with whipped cream and grated chocolate.

Bread and butter pudding

YOU WILL NEED FOR 4 SERVINGS:

2–3 slices of buttered bread, cut into cubes
1½ oz. sultanas
1 large egg
½ pint milk
1 oz. (or 1 rounded tablespoon) castor sugar
½ oz. butter

Grease a 1½ pint pie dish or baking dish. Place bread cubes over the base and sprinkle with sultanas. In a mixing basin beat together the egg, milk and sugar and strain over the bread. Add the butter in small pieces.

Place the pie dish in a baking tin of water to the depth of 1 in. and place in the centre of a moderate oven (355 deg. or Gas No. 4) and bake for 30 minutes or until puffy and set firm. Serve warm or cold with cream or soft ice cream.

Bread and butter meringue

As an alternative, reserve the white from the egg and whisk into a meringue with 1½ oz. (or 2 level tablespoons) castor sugar. Top baked pudding with a little red jam and then over the prepared meringue. Return to the oven until golden brown.

Ice pudding

YOU WILL NEED FOR 6 SERVINGS:

2 oz. (or 2 rounded tablespoons) plain flour
½ oz. (or 1 rounded tablespoon) cornflour
2 oz. butter or margarine
2 oz. (or 2 rounded tablespoons) castor sugar
½ teaspon vanilla essence
2 egg yolks
1 pint milk
FOR THE MERINGUE:
2 egg whites
3 oz. (or 3 rounded tablespoons) castor sugar

Sift the plain flour and cornflour onto a square of paper and set aside. Cream the butter or margarine, sugar and vanilla essence until light. Add the egg yolks and the sieved flour and mix thoroughly. Bring the milk up to the boil, draw the pan off the heat and gradually stir into the egg mixture whisking well all the time. Strain back into the milk saucepan and bring up to the boil, stirring constantly. Simmer for 1–2 minutes then draw the pan off the heat and pour into a 1½ pint baking or pie dish.

Whisk the egg whites until fluffy, add half the sugar and whisk again until stiff. Using a metal spoon fold in remaining sugar, and spoon the meringue over the custard base. Spread evenly then rough the surface slightly.

Place the pudding just above centre in a moderate oven (355 deg. or Gas No. 4) and bake for 10 minutes. Remove from the heat, cool and then chill until ready to serve — delicious with cream or top of the milk.

Cream and fruit whips

Gelatine must be handled with care. There are several methods of using it but the easiest and most successful is to soak it in cold water, then add it to the hot fruit or custard mixture. When this has cooled almost to setting point it can be whisked or blended with egg whites or cream and set in a pretty dish. Quickest way to do this is to stand the basin containing gelatine mixture inside a bowl of iced water; stir all the time until it begins to thicken and set. Gelatine has a habit of setting as soon as you take your eyes off it. Should this happen, stir it over warm water and it will quickly liquefy. It doesn't matter how many times the gelatine mixture is melted down provided the egg whites and cream have not been added.

Bavarois

YOU WILL NEED FOR 4 SERVINGS:

    1 level tablespoon powdered gelatine
    2 tablespoons water
    2 egg yolks
    1 oz. (or 1 rounded tablespoon) castor sugar
    ½ pint milk
    1 teaspoon vanilla essence
    ¼ pint double cream

Sprinkle gelatine over water and leave to soak. Blend together egg yolks and sugar until thick, creamy and light, then stir in the lightly warmed milk. Blend well and strain back into the milk saucepan. Stand the pan in a larger pan containing simmering water and cook gently until thickened, stirring all the time.
Remove pan from heat and add the soaked gelatine and vanilla essence. Stir until the gelatine has dissolved and then set aside until beginning to set. Fold in the whipped cream and pour into a wet 1 pint mould and leave to set firm. Turn out and serve with stewed fruit.

Coffee: omit the vanilla essence and add 1 level tablespoon instant coffee powder with the milk. When set serve with a chocolate sauce or single cream.

Chocolate: stir in 2–3 oz. plain chocolate, broken in pieces, when adding the soaked gelatine. Leave to set firm.

The bavarois mixture is delicious when used as a filling in a sponge-lined mould. Use plain bavarois or one of the flavoured versions.
To make the mould you will need a box of 8 trifle sponge cakes. Slice them in half lengthwise and use the 8 bottom halves to line the base of a deep, round cake tin—cut them to fit the tin. Line the sides with the top halves, the uncut sides facing outwards.
Sprinkle the sponge cake with fruit juice, sherry or any flavouring that would combine nicely with the chosen filling. Prepare the bavarois as above and when ready to mould, pour into the prepared tin. Leave to set, then trim sponge cakes and turn out.

Banana wedges

YOU WILL NEED FOR 6 SERVINGS:

    biscuit base, *see recipe*
    1 level tablespoon powdered gelatine
    2 tablespoons cold water
    4 oz. (or 4 rounded tablespoons) castor sugar
    grated rind and juice of 2 lemons
    ½ pint hot water
    4 bananas
    ½ pint double cream

Cover the base of a 7–8 in. shallow square or round cake tin with greaseproof paper, leaving ends overhanging. Line with biscuit crumb mixture, given in the following recipe.
Sprinkle powdered gelatine over cold water and leave to soak. Measure sugar and grated lemon rind and juice into a saucepan, add hot water and bring to the boil, stirring until the sugar has dissolved. Simmer gently for 5 minutes, then draw pan off heat. Add soaked gelatine and stir until it has dissolved. Set aside to cool until it is beginning to thicken.
Mash two of the bananas and slice the remaining two for decoration, then whisk the cream until thick, fold in the mashed banana and half the lemon jelly mixture. Pour into the prepared cake tin.
Leave to set firm, then arrange banana slices over the top. Spoon on top the remaining jelly (melt gently first), and chill until set firm.
When ready lift it out of the tin (use paper edges) and cut into wedges. Serve with cream.

Chocolate chiffon

YOU WILL NEED FOR 6 SERVINGS:

    3–4 digestive biscuits
    melted butter
    1 level tablespoon powdered gelatine
    4 oz. (or 4 rounded tablespoons) castor sugar

Lemon whip and shortcake chiffon

1 level tablespoon instant coffee
1 level tablespoon cocoa powder
pinch of salt
½ pint water
½ teaspoon vanilla essence
2 egg whites
grated chocolate for decoration

Line the base of a 7–8 in. shallow square or round tin with a strip of greaseproof paper, leaving ends overhanging (makes it easier to remove mixture when set).

Crush the digestive biscuits with a rolling pin and blend with just enough melted butter—about ½ oz.—to give a moist crumbly consistency. Press over the base of the prepared tin and leave until set firm.

Measure powdered gelatine, sugar, instant coffee, cocoa powder and salt into a saucepan. Add water and soak for 5 minutes, then stir over very low heat until the gelatine has dissolved and the mixture blended. Draw pan off the heat, add vanilla essence and allow to cool until mixture is beginning to thicken. Add the unbeaten egg whites and whisk the whole mixture until light and fluffy. Pour into the prepared tin and chill until set.

To serve, sprinkle with extra grated chocolate, lift out of the tin (use the paper edges) cut into six portions and serve with cream.

Pineapple snow

YOU WILL NEED FOR 6 SERVINGS:

½ oz. (or 1 rounded tablespoon) powdered
  gelatine
3 tablespoons cold water
1 (12 oz.) tin pineapple pieces
  (about ½ pint with juice)
2 oz. (or 2 rounded tablespoons) castor sugar
pinch of salt
1 tablespoon lemon juice
1 small tin evaporated milk

Sprinkle gelatine on to water and leave to soak. Pour pineapple (chop a little if pieces are very large), and juice into a saucepan, add sugar and salt and bring to the boil slowly.

Draw pan off heat and add soaked gelatine and lemon juice. Stir until dissolved. Set aside until beginning to set. Whisk the evaporated milk until thick and, when the gelatine mixture is slightly thickening, whisk it gradually into the milk. Pour into a wet 1½ pint mould and leave in a cool place to set.

Turn out on to a plate and serve with cream or extra pineapple pieces.

Raspberry and vanilla mould

YOU WILL NEED FOR 8 SERVINGS:

1 packet (8) trifle sponge cakes
FOR THE FILLING:
½ oz. (1 rounded tablespoon) powdered gelatine
3 oz. (3 rounded tablespoons) castor sugar
¼ pint water
½ pint milk
1 teaspoon vanilla essence
½ pint double cream
1 (12 oz.) packet frozen raspberries, thawed

Slice the sponge cakes in half and use to line the base and sides of a large loaf tin. Set aside while preparing the filling.

Measure the gelatine, sugar and water into a small saucepan, and allow to soak for 5 minutes. Then stir over very low heat until dissolved but do not allow to come to the boil. Draw the pan off the heat and allow to cool until just warm then stir in the milk which should be at room temperature, and the vanilla essence. Chill until beginning to set then beat until frothy, fold in the cream and raspberries and pour into the prepared tin. Chill for several hours, then trim the sponge cakes level with filling if necessary, loosen sides and turn out. Slice and serve.

Shortcake chiffon

YOU WILL NEED FOR 6 SERVINGS:

4 oz. sweet shortcrust pastry, see page 188
FOR THE FILLING:
1 lb. stewed or canned fruit, or ¼ pint
  fruit purée
1 level tablespoon powdered gelatine
3 tablespoons fruit juice or water
1 level tablespoon custard powder
¼ pint milk
1 oz. (or 1 rounded tablespoon) castor sugar
1 tablespoon lemon juice
colouring if liked
¼ pint double cream

On a lightly floured surface roll out pastry and, using a 6–7 in. flan ring or cake tin with removable base as a guide, cut out two circles. Place on a baking tray, prick well and bake above centre in a hot oven (400 deg. or Gas No. 6) for 8–10 minutes or until lightly browned. Remove from the heat and allow to cool.

Meanwhile prepare the flan ring or tin. Line the sides with a strip of kitchen foil or greaseproof paper standing at least 2 in. high around the edge. Place one of the pastry circles inside as a base.

Reserving a little for decoration, sieve fruit to make a purée. Sprinkle gelatine over the water or fruit juice and leave to soak. In a saucepan blend custard powder with a little of the milk until smooth, then add the remaining milk along with the sugar. Stir over moderate heat until thickened and boiling. Draw pan off heat and add soaked gelatine. Stir until dissolved, add the lemon juice, a little colouring if liked, and more sugar to sweeten if necessary. Add the fruit purée and set aside to cool until beginning to thicken. Then fold in the whipped cream.

Pour into the prepared mould and leave to set firm. Remove the band of paper and remove the ring or tin. Cut the second circle of pastry into 6 portions, dust three alternate ones with icing sugar and place all 6 on top of the fruit cream. Decorate with whorls of cream and the reserved fruit.

Lemon whip

YOU WILL NEED FOR 4 SERVINGS:

½ oz. (or 1 rounded tablespoon) powdered gelatine
¼ pint cold water
4 oz. (or 4 rounded tablespoons) castor sugar
finely grated rind and juice of 2 lemons
2 egg whites
chopped walnuts to decorate

Measure gelatine, cold water and sugar into a small pan and leave to soak for 5 minutes. Stir over a very low heat until gelatine and sugar have dissolved, but do not bring to the boil.

Draw pan off heat and stir in lemon juice and rind. Allow to cool until beginning to thicken, then whisk until light and frothy.

Fold in the stiffly beaten egg whites and pour into pretty glass serving dishes. Leave to set, then decorate the top with finely chopped walnuts. Serve with cream.

Orange whip

YOU WILL NEED FOR 4–6 SERVINGS:

4 tablespoons cold water
½ oz. (or 1 level tablespoon) powdered gelatine
3 eggs
2 tablespoons hot water
3 oz. (or 3 rounded tablespoons) castor sugar
2 oranges

Measure the cold water into a saucepan, sprinkle over the gelatine and allow to soak for 5 minutes. Then stir over a very low heat until dissolved, remove from the heat and set aside to cool.

Separate the egg yolks and whites into two basins. Add the hot water to the yolks, and whisk until frothy, then add 2 oz. of the sugar and whisk until thick. Halve the oranges, and squeeze out the juice, add this along with any pieces of orange flesh and the gelatine, to the egg mixture. Mix thoroughly and put to chill stirring occasionally until beginning to thicken.

Whisk the egg whites until frothy, add remaining sugar and beat until thick. Fold into the orange mixture and pour into a pretty glass serving dish. Chill until firm before serving.

Iced lemon whip

YOU WILL NEED FOR 8 SERVINGS:

4 oz. cornflakes
2 oz. (2 rounded tablespoons) castor sugar
2½ oz. butter
FOR THE ICE CREAM:
2 eggs, separated
juice and grated rind of 1 lemon
4 oz. (4 rounded tablespoons) castor sugar
1 small tin evaporated milk
¼ pint double cream*

Crush the cornflakes to fine crumbs with a rolling pin. Add the sugar and then rub in the butter. Place a 9-inch flan ring on a baking tray or use a 9-inch shallow sponge cake tin with a loose base, or baking tin 11 × 7-inch. Spoon the crumbs into the base of the ring or tin and press over evenly. Place in the centre of a moderate oven (355 deg. or Gas No. 4) and bake for 10 minutes. Remove from the heat and allow to cool while preparing the topping.

Crack the egg yolks into a mixing basin, add the grated rind, lemon juice and sugar and mix well. Whisk the evaporated milk until thick and fold into the lemon mixture. Whisk the egg whites until stiff and fold into the mixture with the stiffly whipped cream. Pour into the ring or tin over the crumb base and place in the freezer or frozen food section of the refrigerator until set like ice cream. Remove from the tin and serve cut in wedges.

* To make it more delicious increase cream to ½ pint and pipe whipped whorls on the top when set and put back in the freezer.

Mousses, creamy ices and sorbets

Mousses

A mousse has a very light, open texture. Usually it is made with gelatine but it can be set with chocolate or by freezing. Allow to thaw slightly before serving—it should be fairly soft, not frozen hard.

Quick chocolate mousse

YOU WILL NEED FOR 4 SERVINGS:

4 oz. plain chocolate
½ oz. butter
3 eggs

Break chocolate into a mixing basin and set over a pan of hot water. Stir until melted and smooth, then add butter and egg yolks. Stir until blended then remove basin from heat. Stiffly whisk the egg whites and fold them carefully into the chocolate mixture.
Spoon into glasses and chill until set firm and ready to serve.

Marshmallow mousse

YOU WILL NEED FOR 4 SERVINGS:

1 tea-cup fruit juice, fresh or tinned
20 marshmallows
juice of ½ a lemon
½ pint double cream

Strain the fruit juice and add marshmallows, first cutting them in pieces with wet scissors. Cook in a double boiler (or basin over pan of simmering water) until marshmallows melt.
Cool. Add lemon juice, and fold in stiffly beaten cream. Freeze in the ice-making compartment of refrigerator at regular temperature.

Coffee marshmallow mousse

Use strong coffee instead of fruit juice, omit lemon juice and flavour with vanilla essence or brandy.

Peach sundaes, pineapple mousse with ginger-snaps, orange cups, chocolate cups and lemon soufflé

Pineapple mousse

YOU WILL NEED FOR 6 SERVINGS:

2 level teaspoons gelatine
1 tablespoon water
1 tin (1 lb. 13 oz.) pineapple chunks
juice of 1 lemon
3 oz. (or 3 rounded tablespoons) castor sugar
¼ pint single cream
¼ pint double cream

Sprinkle gelatine over water and set aside to soak. Drain juice from tin of pineapple chunks and measure ½ pint into a saucepan. Add lemon juice and sugar. Bring to the boil over moderate heat, stirring to dissolve sugar. Simmer for 5 minutes, then draw off the heat and add the soaked gelatine. Stir until it has dissolved.
Cool until beginning to thicken then whisk until frothy. Whip the single cream and double cream together and fold into the pineapple mixture with half of the pineapple chunks, coarsely chopped.
Pour into two large freezer trays and freeze, stirring occasionally during the first hour only. This mousse has a softer consistency and will be ready in 1–2 hours. If frozen very hard, allow to thaw a little before serving, topped with remaining pineapple chunks.

Pineapple mousse with gingersnaps

Serves 6–8

Reserving 6 gingernut biscuits from a ½ lb. packet, crush the remainder with a rolling pin inside double sheets of greaseproof paper. Add 2 oz. melted butter or margarine and 2 oz. (or 2 rounded tablespoons) castor sugar. Blend together with a fork until crumbly and spoon into an 8 in. shallow curved pie plate. Press over the base and round the sides to form a crust. Leave in the refrigerator to set firm before adding the filling. Spoon the frozen pineapple mousse *(see previous recipe)* into the pie shell, top with chopped pineapple chunks. Break reserved ginger biscuits in half and arrange round the edge of the pie dish for decoration. Leave to stand for about 10 minutes before serving in wedges.

Cold soufflés

Traditionally these are set above the edge of the mould, to look as if they have risen like a hot soufflé. However, there's no need to rush this one to the table, it can sit happily in the refrigerator until ready to serve. Use a 6 in. straight sided china, earthenware or Pyrex soufflé or baking dish. Pin a high collar of double thickness greaseproof or waxed paper around the outside, tie with a length of string and secure the top edges with a pin. Place on a larger serving plate for easier handling.

Lemon soufflé

YOU WILL NEED FOR 4 SERVINGS:

½ oz. (or 1 rounded tablespoon) powdered gelatine
2 tablespoons water
juice and grated rind of 2 lemons
3 large eggs
4 oz. (or 4 rounded tablespoons) castor sugar
¼ pint double cream
¼ pint single cream
chopped walnuts and whipped cream

Prepare a 6–7 in. soufflé dish as described above. Sprinkle gelatine over water in a saucepan and leave to soak for 5 minutes. Add the lemon juice and stir over very low heat until gelatine has dissolved. Draw pan off the heat and allow to cool while preparing the rest of the recipe.
Measure egg yolks, sugar and grated lemon rind into a large mixing basin. Set this over a pan of hot water and whisk till very thick and light in colour. Remove from the heat and whisk a further 5 minutes. Strain gelatine into the whisked mixture and continue to whisk until it begins to thicken. Whip the double and single creams together lightly and fold them into the mixture with the stiffly beaten egg whites. Pour into the prepared soufflé dish and leave to set. Dip a knife blade in warm water and run it around the inside edge of the paper collar. Detach the edge and gently peel paper away from the soufflé. Coat sides with chopped walnuts and pipe whorls of cream on top. Alternatively decorate with whorls of cream and mimosa balls.

Cream ices

Use the ice-making tray of your refrigerator or, if you have a large freezer compartment, use a plastic refrigerator box (these are particularly good because ice cream can be stored with the lid on). Chilled evaporated milk may be used instead of cream for a more economical recipe. For a smooth and creamy texture watch for the mixture to solidify round the edges, then transfer it to a mixing basin and beat until smooth. Return to freezer tray and freeze until firm—usually takes about 2 hours.

Vanilla cream ice

YOU WILL NEED FOR 4 SERVINGS:

> ¼ pint double cream
> 1½ oz. (or 4 level tablespoons) icing sugar
> vanilla essence to taste
> 2 egg whites

Lightly whip cream, then whisk in the sifted icing sugar and a few drops of vanilla essence. Whisk egg whites stiffly and fold in.
Pour into ice-making tray and freeze until firm, whisking at least once during that time.
Peach sundae: pile scoops of ice cream into tall glasses with peach slices for a delicious sundae. Raspberries, strawberries, mandarin oranges can also be used.
Crème de menthe: add ½ teaspoon peppermint essence and a few drops of green colouring to basic mixture.
Raisin and rum: soak 2 oz. seedless raisins in lemon juice and 2 tablespoons rum for 1 hour and then add to ice cream after whisking during freezing.
Coffee: add 1 teaspoon coffee essence to the basic mixture.

Chocolate cups

Melt 4–6 oz. plain chocolate in a small mixing basin over a pan of warm water and add a nut of white vegetable fat. Using the tip of a knife or the rounded side of a teaspoon, coat the insides of about 8 thick paper baking cases. Turn upside down and leave to set firm. Carefully peel away the paper and fill the cups with Lemon frost ice cream. Top with grated chocolate.

Lemon frost

YOU WILL NEED FOR 4 SERVINGS:

> 2 eggs whites
> 2 oz. (or 2 rounded tablespoons) castor sugar
> 2 egg yolks
> rind and juice of 1 lemon
> ¼ pint double cream, lightly whipped

Beat egg whites until stiff and then gradually beat in sugar. Lightly mix egg yolks, finely grated lemon rind and juice until light in colour.
Fold this into the beaten egg whites, with the whipped cream.
Pour into one large or two small ice-making trays and freeze, stirring occasionally until firm.

Water ices or sorbets

Prepare a basic syrup and make up your own recipes for simple water ices. Any fruit juice and/or purée can be mixed with the syrup (equal quantities of each). Add colouring, and remember that when the mixture is frozen the colouring and flavour will be weaker.

Basic sugar syrup

YOU WILL NEED:

> ½ lb. granulated sugar
> 1 pint water
> grated rind and juice of 1 lemon

Put sugar, water, lemon rind and juice into a pan and stir over low heat until sugar has completely dissolved. Bring to boiling point and, without stirring, boil briskly for 10 minutes. Remove any scum as it rises to the surface. Draw pan off heat, strain syrup through muslin and leave until cold.

Orange water ice

YOU WILL NEED FOR 4–5 SERVINGS:

> 3 large oranges
> 8 oz. (or 8 rounded tablespoons) castor sugar
> 1 pint water
> half a lemon
> a little orange colouring

Place finely grated rind from oranges with sugar and water in a large saucepan. Stir over low heat to dissolve the sugar. Bring to the boil and cook rapidly for 10 minutes. Draw pan off heat and allow to cool. Stir in the juice from oranges and lemon half, add a few drops of orange colouring.
Strain into one large or two small freezer trays, and freeze until firm, stirring occasionally to make a smooth consistency.

Orange cups

Slice the tops off the oranges to be used for serving cups—recipe fills about 4. Using a teaspoon, scoop out some of the orange flesh from the inside of the peel. By working evenly round the inside of the orange you will then be able to pull away the flesh and leave the shell quite clean.
Remove the flesh from the lid and strip edges to points with a pair of scissors *(see colour picture)*. Spoon frozen water ice into the prepared orange cups, replace the lids and freeze until quite firm. They will go delightfully frosty.

ALL ABOUT
Sponges & Meringues

Victoria sponges, simple meringues and hot puddings

Sponge sandwiches

A Victoria sponge is a creamed mixture and is more moist than a true whisked sponge. It should have a very light texture and a rich, golden crumb. Butter and sugar must be creamed very thoroughly and eggs should not be straight from the refrigerator. Line tin with well-buttered greaseproof paper—if you haven't done this a useful tip is to stand the hot, newly-baked cake on a damp cloth for a few minutes; this causes it to shrink away from the sides of the tin and a sharp tap should then loosen it.

Basic Victoria sponge

YOU WILL NEED FOR TWO LAYERS:

> 4 oz. (or 4 rounded tablespoons) self-raising
>   flour
> pinch of salt
> 4 oz. butter or margarine
> 4 oz. (or 4 rounded tablespoons) castor sugar
> 2 eggs
> $\frac{1}{4}$ teaspoon vanilla essence
> 1–2 tablespoons milk or water to mix

Pre-heat oven to 380 deg. or Gas No. 5. Grease two 6–7 in. sponge sandwich tins and line with circles of greaseproof paper.

Sift flour and salt on to a piece of paper and set aside. Measure butter or margarine and sugar into a warmed mixing basin and beat well until pale and fluffy—takes about 8–10 minutes. Gradually add the lightly mixed eggs and vanilla essence. Beat well between each new addition—if the egg is added too quickly the mixture may curdle.

Using a metal spoon, fold in half the flour. Then fold in the rest with milk or water to give a medium-soft dropping consistency.

Divide mixture equally between prepared tins, and spread evenly. Place in the centre of a moderately hot oven (380 deg. or Gas No. 5) and bake for 20–25 minutes. Remove cakes from oven and cool for five minutes in tins before turning out on to a wire tray. When cool, fill and ice.

Cream sandwich

Make cakes to basic recipe and when cool spread each layer with raspberry or strawberry jam. Fill with $\frac{1}{4}$ pint whipped cream. Or use a vanilla cream. To make this, cream together 2 oz. butter or margarine and 2 oz. (or 2 rounded tablespoons) castor sugar until light and fluffy. Gradually beat in 4 teaspoons hot water, then 6 teaspoons cold milk. Add a few drops of vanilla essence.

Chocolate gâteau

Make as basic recipe, but use 1 tablespoon of cocoa powder instead of 1 tablespoon of the flour; sift it with flour. When baked and cool split and frost top and sides with a seven-minute frosting. To make this, measure into a mixing basin 6 oz. (or 6 rounded tablespoons) castor sugar, 2 tablespoons water, a pinch of cream of tartar and 1 egg white. Place the bowl over a pan of simmering water and, using a rotary or hand beater, whisk until the mixture stands up in peaks—about 7 minutes. Remove from heat and continue beating until peaks are stiff. Use as required.

Lemon or orange sponge

Use finely grated rind of 1 lemon or 1 orange instead of vanilla essence and make as basic recipe. Cool the baked sponges, sandwich with lemon curd and top with lemon or orange glacé icing. Decorate with crystallised orange or lemon slices.

To make icing: sift 4 oz. (or 4 rounded tablespoons) icing sugar into a small mixing basin. Blend to a smooth coating consistency with the strained juice of orange or lemon, whichever was used in the recipe. Pour over the cake and leave to set.

Spice cake

Follow basic recipe but sift ½ level teaspoon each ground nutmeg, ground cinnamon and ground ginger with the flour, and omit the vanilla essence. Sandwich together and frost top and sides with chocolate fudge frosting.

To make this, break 4 oz. plain chocolate into a small saucepan, add 2 tablespoons water and ½ oz. butter. Stir over very low heat until the chocolate has melted and mixture is smooth—do not allow to boil. Draw pan off heat and gradually beat in 2–3 oz. (or 2–3 heaped tablespoons) sifted icing sugar. Beat well until mixture is smooth, set aside for 5–10 minutes until slightly thickened.

Coffee walnut

Follow basic recipe omitting vanilla essence, instead after creaming the butter and sugar beat in 1 tablespoon coffee essence. Fold in 2 oz. finely chopped walnuts with the flour. When baked and cooled, sandwich and top with coffee buttercream made as follows. Cream 4 oz. butter or margarine and gradually beat in 4 oz. (or 4 heaped tablespoons) sieved icing sugar. Add 1 teaspoon coffee essence.

Steamed puddings

Use the basic Victoria sponge recipe to make deliciously light steamed puddings. Well butter a pudding basin, add sponge mixture and cover with double thickness greased greaseproof paper—fold in a pleat to allow pudding to expand, then tie tightly with string. Steam briskly for the required time and don't let pan boil dry. Top up often with boiling water. *See instructions for steaming puddings in suet crust pastry section, page 192.*

Jam or syrup pudding

Serves 4–6:

Butter a 1½–2 pint pudding basin and put a tablespoon jam or syrup in the base of the dish.

Spoon in the basic sponge mixture, cover with buttered greaseproof papers and steam gently for 1½ hours. Turn out and serve with extra jam or syrup sauce made by heating 2–3 tablespoons jam or syrup with lemon juice.

Fruit sponge pudding

YOU WILL NEED FOR 4–6 SERVINGS:

1 (16 oz.) tin dark plums
6 oz. (or 6 rounded tablespoons) self-raising
    flour
pinch salt
4 oz. butter or margarine
4 oz. (or 4 rounded tablespoons) castor sugar
2 eggs
finely grated rind ½ lemon
milk to mix
FOR THE SAUCE:
½ pint juice from can
    (made up with water if necessary)
1 level tablespoon cornflour

Drain plums from tin and reserve juice for sauce. Well butter inside of 1½ pint pudding basin and arrange 6–8 plums over base of basin. Set aside while preparing sponge mixture.

Sift together flour and salt and set aside. Cream together butter and sugar until light, then gradually beat in lightly mixed eggs and lemon rind. Add a little of the sifted flour along with last few additions of egg. Fold in remaining flour and enough milk to mix to a medium-soft consistency.

Spoon the mixture into prepared basin. Cover and steam for 2 hours. Turn out and serve hot.

To make sauce. Measure juice into saucepan. Stir in cornflour, blended to thin paste with water, and bring to the boil. Stir until thickened, add sugar if necessary and serve hot.

Pineapple castles

YOU WILL NEED FOR 4 SERVINGS:

    1 (8 oz.) tin pineapple chunks
    1 oz. butter
    1 oz. (or 1 rounded tablespoon) soft brown sugar
    FOR THE SPONGE MIXTURE:
    3 oz. (or 3 rounded tablespoons) self-raising flour
    pinch of salt
    2 oz. butter
    2 oz. (or 2 rounded tablespoons) castor sugar
    1 egg
    milk to mix
    FOR THE SAUCE:
    ½ pint juice from tin
        (made up with water if necessary)
    1 level tablespoon cornflour

Drain fruit from tin, reserving juice for sauce. Well butter insides of 8 dariole or castle moulds and coat with brown sugar. Place 2 pineapple chunks in base of each. Set aside while making sponge. Sift together flour and salt and set aside. Cream butter and sugar until soft and light, then gradually beat in lightly mixed egg. Fold in the flour and enough milk to make medium-soft mixture. Divide mixture equally between moulds, filling them two-thirds full. Cover with greased squares of kitchen foil, securing with elastic bands. Steam for 1 hour, refilling pan with boiling water when necessary. Turn out and serve with pineapple sauce. Measure juice into saucepan and stir in cornflour, blended to thin paste with cold water. Bring to the boil, stirring all the time, add sugar if necessary and any remaining pineapple chunks, chopped small. Turn out and serve hot.

Chocolate pudding

YOU WILL NEED FOR 4–6 SERVINGS:

    6 oz. (or 6 rounded tablespoons) self-raising
        flour
    1 oz. (or 3 level tablespoons) cocoa powder
    pinch salt
    4 oz. butter or margarine
    4 oz. (or 4 rounded tablespoons) castor sugar
    4 eggs
    ½ teaspoon vanilla essence
    milk to mix

Sift together flour, cocoa powder and salt and set aside. Cream together butter and sugar until light, then gradually beat in lightly mixed eggs and vanilla essence. Add a little of the sifted flour mixture with last few additions of egg. Fold in remaining flour mixture and enough milk to make a medium-soft consistency.

Spoon into well-buttered 1½–2 pint pudding basin. Cover and steam for 2 hours. Serve with chocolate sauce.

Baked puddings

Any mixture of sweetened fresh fruit may be used as a base in these. Try surprise puddings with a sauce that bakes underneath the mixture. In summer hot fruit puddings go wonderfully with ice cream!

Eve's pudding

Serves 4:

Half-fill a buttered 1½ pint pie dish with 2 medium-sized cooking apples, pared and sliced, 1 tablespoon sugar and 1 tablespoon water. Alternatively use tinned or bottled fruit but make sure the liquid in the pie dish is not more than 2 tablespoons.

Spread evenly the basic sponge mixture on top. Place just above centre in a moderately hot oven (380 deg. or Gas No. 5) and bake for 35 minutes or until risen and brown. Dust top with icing sugar and serve hot with single cream or ice cream.

Meringue shells

YOU WILL NEED FOR 12 SMALL SHELLS:

    3 large egg whites
    pinch of salt
    6 oz. (or 6 rounded tablespoons) castor sugar

Carefully separate the egg whites from the yolks—it is important not to have any trace of yolk left. Add salt, and, using a balloon whisk or a rotary beater, whisk egg white until light and fluffy. Gradually whisk in about two-thirds of the castor sugar and beat again until the meringue is smooth, glossy and stands up in peaks. Don't overbeat or it may go soft and become difficult to shape. Using a metal spoon, gently fold in the remaining sugar.

Pipe out shells using a forcing bag fitted with ½ in. tube, or use two dessertspoons, dipped in water. With one spoon take a heaped spoonful of the mixture and, using the second spoon, scoop it out. Place about 1 in. apart on a baking tray, lined with silicone paper. Dredge the tops of the unbaked meringues with sugar. Place in the centre of a very cool oven (240 deg. or Gas No. ¼) with oven door very slightly open. Cook for about 2 hours. Then lift shells out carefully—they should feel firm—and turn them upside-down. Dry out in oven for another 1–2 hours. Sandwich in pairs with whipped cream, or serve with ice cream and fresh fruit.

Whisked sponges

A true sponge has no fat in the recipe. It is made by whisking eggs and sugar until very light—mixture is thick enough when whisk leaves a trail across the surface. Then the flour is sifted over the mixture and folded in gently with a hand whisk or metal spoon—don't use a rotary beater for folding in.

Basic whisked sponge

YOU WILL NEED:

    3 oz. (or 3 rounded tablespoons) self-raising flour
    2 eggs
    3 oz. (or 3 rounded tablespoons) castor sugar
    1 full tablespoon hot water

Preheat the oven to 355 deg. or Gas No. 4 and prepare one 8 in. or two 6–7 in. sponge tins as follows. Brush the base and sides of each tin with melted butter. Sprinkle with a mixture of equal quantities flour and castor sugar (not taken from ingredients), shake to cover the entire surface and knock out any surplus. You can, if you like, line the base first with grease-proof paper.
Sift flour for cake and set in a warm place. Measure eggs and sugar into a medium-sized mixing basin and set over a smaller pan, half filled with hot water (pan should have been removed from heat). The bottom of the basin should not touch the water.
With a whisk, beat eggs and sugar until the mixture is thick and light in colour—this may take about 10–15 minutes. Remove basin from pan and beat a further 5 minutes (stand it on a damp cloth to hold it still). Sift warmed flour over the mixture and add the hot water. Using the whisk (if a hand one) or a metal spoon, very gently fold in the flour, just enough to mix. Pour into the prepared tins and spread evenly.
Place just above centre of a moderate oven (355 deg. or Gas No. 4) and bake the 8 in. layer for 30–35 minutes, the two 6–7 in. layers for 20–30 minutes. When baked the cake will shrink away from the sides of the tin a little and feel quite springy. Run a knife tip round the sides, tap the base sharply and turn out on to a wire cooling tray.

Chocolate sponge

Prepare and bake as basic recipe, but substitute 1 level tablespoon cocoa powder for 1 of flour.

Raspberry layer

Make two layers to basic sponge recipe, split each in half and fill with sweetened, crushed raspberries. Serve in wedges with single cream.

Coffee frost

Make two chocolate sponge layers to basic recipe, and sprinkle each with a little sweetened black coffee. Sandwich together with soft coffee ice cream. Serve at once with hot chocolate sauce.

Banana cream

Sprinkle two sponge layers (basic recipe) with a little sherry or fruit juice. Fill with sliced bananas and whipped cream. Sprinkle with coconut and serve.

Tutti-frutti

Sprinkle two sponge layers (basic recipe) with the juice drained from 1 tin of fruit cocktail. Spoon fruit pieces over the base and add top. Leave to stand 30 minutes then pour over some single cream and serve immediately.

Fruit gâteau

SERVES 6:

Bake 2 sponge layers to basic recipe. Leave to cool and then top each with an arrangement of fresh or tinned fruit. Spoon over a fruit glaze.
To make this measure $\frac{1}{2}$ pint water (or half water and fruit juice) into a saucepan and add 1–2 tablespoons castor sugar according to sweetness required. Stir in 2 level teaspoons arrowroot, blended to a smooth paste first with a little cold water. Stir the contents of the pan over moderate heat until thickened and boiling. Draw pan off heat, cool and spoon glaze over the fruit. Allow to set before serving in wedges with cream.

Baked Alaska and open fruit flan

Baked Alaska

YOU WILL NEED FOR 4–6 SERVINGS:

- 1 sponge layer *(see basic recipe)*
- 2–3 tablespoons sherry or fruit juice
- 2 tablespoons red jam
- 1 family brick ice cream—any flavour
- FOR THE MERINGUE:
- 3 egg whites
- pinch of salt
- 6 oz. (or 6 rounded tablespoons) castor sugar

Prepare a plain or chocolate sponge cake as basic recipe and bake in an 8 in. tin. Remove cooked cake from tin and allow to cool before finishing recipe. Raise oven to hot (400 deg. or Gas No. 6) and leave for at least 10 minutes before putting in the finished cake immediately prior to serving.

Sprinkle cake base liberally with sherry or fruit juice and place on a baking tray or ovenproof serving platter. Spread with a little jam and top with a block of ice cream (spoon over some glacé cherries which have been soaked in a little sherry if you like—as in the colour picture). Ice cream should be as cold and hard as possible, cake and ice cream put in the ice-making compartment of a refrigerator or the coldest place you can find while whisking the meringue.

Crack egg whites into a deep basin, add salt. Whisk until light and fluffy and standing in peaks. Sprinkle in half the sugar and whisk again until stiff and glossy—take care not to overbeat. Remove the whisk and with a metal spoon fold in remaining sugar, just enough to mix, and then spoon the meringue all over the ice cream and sponge base. Take care to cover the dessert completely, as the meringue insulates the ice cream from the heat of the oven and prevents it from melting.

Place the Alaska above centre in hot oven (400 deg. or Gas No. 6) and bake for 2–3 minutes or until just beginning to brown. Serve at once.

Banana cream cake

YOU WILL NEED FOR 4–6 SERVINGS:

- 1 chocolate sponge layer *(see recipe)*
- icing sugar for decoration
- FOR THE FILLING:
- 1 pint packet jelly
- ½ pint hot water
- 3 bananas
- 1 tablespoon lemon juice
- ¼ pint double cream

Prepare the sponge cake according to the basic recipe and bake in one 8 in. sponge layer tin. Remove from the tin and allow to cool while preparing the filling.

Clean the cake tin and set aside to use as a mould for the filling. Dissolve the jelly in the hot water and set aside to cool until beginning to set. Mash two of the bananas with the lemon juice and fold in the lightly whipped cream. Whisk in the almost set jelly and pour the filling into the wetted sponge cake tin. Leave in a cool place until set quite firm.

To finish the cake, slice the chocolate sponge layer in half across, and unmould the banana mousse onto the base. Cover with the top of the cake and dredge with icing sugar. Decorate with remaining sliced banana and serve cut in wedges with extra single cream.

Boston cream pie

YOU WILL NEED FOR 4–6 SERVINGS:

- 1 sponge layer *(see recipe)*
- FOR THE FILLING:
- 3 egg yolks
- 3 oz. (or 3 rounded tablespoons) castor sugar
- 1½ oz. (or 1 heaped tablespoon) flour
- scant ½ pint milk
- FOR THE CHOCOLATE GLAZE:
- 2 oz. plain chocolate
- 1 tablespoon water
- 3–4 oz. (or 3–4 heaped tablespoons) sieved icing sugar
- vanilla essence

Prepare the plain sponge cake as directed in the basic recipe and bake in one 8 in. layer. Remove from the oven and cool.

Meanwhile prepare the filling. Beat together the egg yolks and sugar until light and stir in the sieved flour. Gradually beat in the milk and pour the custard into a saucepan. Cook, stirring continuously over a moderate heat until thickened and boiling. Draw the pan off the heat and cool, stirring occasionally.

Split the sponge layer in half and sandwich with the cooled custard filling. Top with the following chocolate glaze.

Melt the chocolate in the water in a small pan over a very low heat. Draw the pan off the heat and beat in the icing sugar, enough to make a smooth coating consistency. Add a few drops of vanilla essence, and cool just enough to thicken a little, then pour over the cake and leave to set firm. Serve the cake cut in wedges with single cream.

Open fruit flan

YOU WILL NEED FOR 4–6 SERVINGS:

> sponge mixture *(see basic recipe)*
> FOR THE FILLING:
> 1 lb. (approx.) fresh or tinned fruit
> 1 pint packet jelly, choose a suitable flavour
> hot water for mixing

Butter and flour an 8 in. flan tin and pour in sponge mixture. Bake in centre of moderate oven (355 deg. or Gas No. 4) for 30 minutes. Remove from the heat and cool for 5 minutes, turn out and leave until cold before finishing the recipe.
If using fresh fruit wash and slice it; or drain tinned fruit. Arrange attractively in flan case. Make up the jelly with water as directed on the packet and allow to cool, stirring occasionally, until beginning to set and thicken. Then spoon it over fruit. Jelly should be just on setting point otherwise it will soak through the sponge base.
Leave in a cool place for several hours, until firm.
The glaze used for the Fruit gâteau may be used instead of jelly, *see page 144.*

Strawberry shortcake

YOU WILL NEED FOR 6 SERVINGS:

> 2 sponge layers *(see basic recipe)*
> FOR THE FILLING:
> ½–1 lb. fresh strawberries
> 2 tablespoons castor sugar
> ¼ pint double cream
> ¼ pint single cream
> few drops vanilla essence or 1 tablespoon sherry

Remove baked sponges from tins and allow to cool before filling.
Wash and slice strawberries, sprinkle with half the sugar and set aside for 30 minutes to chill. Whisk double and single cream together, when partly beaten add remaining sugar and vanilla essence or sherry and continue beating until light and fluffy. You can use all double cream, but with mixed single and double there's less chance of overbeating.
Spoon half the cream on to one sponge layer, and top with half the sliced strawberries. Top with second sponge layer and decorate with remaining cream and strawberries.

Meringues

Meringue cases can form the base for many fruit and cream desserts. The mixture should be prepared exactly as described on page 155 (use 2 oz. castor sugar for each egg white, whisk egg white, and then gradually whisk in sugar.)

Fruit meringues

Prepare a basic meringue mixture, using 2 egg whites and 4 oz. (or 4 rounded tablespoons) castor sugar. Line a baking tray with silicone paper and spoon on the meringue in tablespoons, not too close together—makes about 6 heaps. Using the back of a teaspoon, hollow each into a nest shape. Alternatively pipe meringue from a forcing bag fitted with a ½ in. tube.
Sprinkle with castor sugar and bake on lowest shelf of a slow oven (240 deg. or Gas No. ¼) for about 2 hours until dry but not browned.
Fill with fresh fruit and cream or ice cream *just before serving.*

Meringue circles

Prepare a meringue mixture, using 3 egg whites and 6 oz. (or 6 rounded tablespoons) castor sugar. Draw an outline of two 8–9 in. circles or three 6–7 in. circles on silicone paper—not too close since the meringue mixture may spread a little. Spoon the prepared meringue into each circle, dividing it equally and spreading with a spoon to the edges.
Place on the lowest shelf of a slow oven (240 deg. or Gas No. ¼) and bake slowly for 3–4 hours or until the circles are dry. After 2½–3 hours turn over to dry the bases.
Sandwich together with cream, or ice cream and fruit and leave for an hour before serving, this softens meringue and makes cutting easier. If filled with ice cream leave in the freezer until required.

Coconut kisses

Makes 16:

To the basic meringue mixture, stir in 4 oz. desiccated coconut. Drop mixture, dessertspoonfuls at a time onto baking trays lined with rice paper—you should get about 16 cookies. Top each one with a glacé cherry. Place in the centre of a moderate oven (355 deg. or Gas No. 4) and bake for 20 minutes. Allow to cool, then peel away excess rice paper.

Genoese sponge and meringue nests

A Genoese—often called a butter sponge—is ideal for small fancy or layer cakes because it is close textured and cuts without crumbling or breaking. Keep decorations simple; they are then much more effective.

Basic Genoese sponge

YOU WILL NEED:

2½ oz. (or 2 well-rounded tablespoons) plain flour
2 large eggs
2 oz. (or 2 rounded tablespoons) castor sugar
colouring and flavouring
1 oz. melted butter

Preheat oven to 400 deg. or Gas No. 6. Grease sponge tin and line base with greased greaseproof paper. Recipe will make one 8 in. or two 6 in. round sponges, or one 7–8 in. shallow square.
Sift flour and set in a warm place. Measure eggs and sugar into a mixing basin and set over a pan of hot water. The pan should be removed from heat and the base of the bowl should not touch the water. Whisk eggs and sugar until very light and thick enough for the mixture to leave a trail over its own surface—takes about 8–10 minutes.
Remove basin from pan and whisk for a further 5 minutes. At this stage any colouring or flavouring may be added—for small fancy cakes or Battenberg cake the mixture may be tinted pink, yellow or green.
Sift flour over the mixture and begin to fold in very gently, using a hand whisk or metal spoon. When it is half mixed in, add the melted butter, it should not be too hot. Add rest of flour.
Pour the mixture into the prepared cake tins. Place in the centre of a hot oven (400 deg. or Gas No. 6) and bake larger cake for 20 minutes, smaller cakes for 15 minutes, until risen and springy to the touch. Cool in the tin for 5 minutes before turning out.

Coloured sponges

Chocolate: substitute 1 oz. cocoa powder for 1 rounded tablespoon flour. Add 2–3 drops vanilla essence.

Pink: add ½ teaspoon vanilla, raspberry, or strawberry essence and some pink colouring.

White: add ½ teaspoon vanilla, almond or lemon essence.

Yellow: add ½ teaspoon lemon essence and lemon colouring.

Green: add ½ teaspoon vanilla or almond essence and green colouring.

Small fancies

Prepare and bake Genoese as basic recipe in either a round or square tin. Trim sides and cut the cooled sponge into small fancy shapes.
Each small cake must be dipped into hot apricot glaze (*see page 150*) and when this has set, coated with white or coloured icing. The hot glaze helps to hold down any loose crumbs which might spoil the surface. When coating the cakes stand them on a wire tray set over a larger tray or sheet of greaseproof paper and surplus glaze or icing will drip through to be used again. The cakes may be decorated as below, they are shown in colour on the page opposite.

Feather ice circles: bake cake in one 8 in. tin and when cooked stamp out small rounds, using a 2 in. cutter. Dip each in hot apricot glaze. Make up glacé icing a little thicker than in recipe. Take a good teaspoon of it and colour this a deeper colour—chocolate is a good choice. Spoon this into a small paper piping bag and have handy a very fine skewer. Thin down the remaining icing to a coating consistency and pour quickly over the cakes. Snip a tiny piece off the end of the piping bag and quickly pipe circular lines of darker icing on top. Using the skewer point, make a feather design as in picture.

Lemon triangles: prepare and bake sponge in a 7–8 in. square tin and cut into strips. Then cut each strip into triangles. Coat with lemon-coloured icing, reserving a little. When this has set, use reserved icing to pipe a triangular shape in the centre and pipe into this a little sieved red jam.

Chocolate and walnut squares: prepare and bake the sponge in a 7–8 in. square tin and cut into neat squares. Dip in hot apricot glaze and coat with green or chocolate glacé icing. Top the green ones with a piped square of green buttercream, see page 142, omit coffee essence, add few drops green colouring, and a walnut half, and the chocolate ones with finely grated or flaked chocolate.

From the top: feather ice circles, lemon triangles, walnut squares, sugar diamonds, chocolate squares, buttercream fingers and dominoes

Sugar diamonds: prepare and bake sponge in a 7–8 in. square tin. Cut into strips and then slice each strip at an angle to make neat diamond shapes. Coat with pink glacé icing, reserving a little. When icing has just set, pipe on a pretty wavy line and decorate with sugared rose or violet petals.

Dominoes and buttercream fingers: bake sponge in a 7–8 in. square tin. Cut the cooled cake into strips. Then cut each into neat oblong or finger shapes. Coat with chocolate or green glacé icing. To finish, pipe chocolate cakes with dots and lines to resemble dominoes, and green ones with green buttercream topped with angelica.

Sponge layer cakes

Bake two round sponges in contrasting colours *(as basic recipe)*. Slice each across and sandwich the layers together in alternating colours.

Or bake a square sponge, and slice in three strips, each 7–8 in. long. Sandwich together vertically. Cover the outside with hot apricot glaze and coat with glacé icing. It may be decorated as small fancy cakes, or the sides can be coated with chopped nuts or coarse coconut (brown this in the oven first if you like).

Apricot glaze

Dissolve ½ lb. granulated sugar in ¼ pint water. Add 1 lb. sieved apricot jam and stir over gentle heat until well mixed. Bring to the boil, and boil steadily until the glaze hangs in heavy drops from a wooden spoon (takes about 5–8 minutes). Makes enough to glaze several small cakes or one large layer cake—any surplus should be cooled and stored in a glass jar. Heat and use as wanted.

Icing syrup

YOU WILL NEED:

    ½ pint water
    1 lb. granulated sugar

Bring water to the boil, and stir in the sugar gradually. Allow it to dissolve thoroughly, then bring to the boil and simmer for one minute.

Strain through muslin and store in a covered jar or bottle. Use instead of water for glacé icing.

Before use the syrup must be gently heated until warm but *not hot*. It makes an icing that sets quickly and firmly.

Glacé icing

YOU WILL NEED:

    USING WATER TO MIX:
    6–8 oz. icing sugar
    about 2 tablespoons *hot* water
    colouring or flavouring
    USING SYRUP TO MIX:
    6–8 oz. icing sugar
    4–5 tablespoons *warm* syrup
    colouring or flavouring

Sift icing sugar into a bowl, add liquid and mix to make a fairly smooth paste. Add flavouring and colouring as required and thin down to a good coating consistency.

To prevent icing setting too quickly when coating small fancy cakes, stand the basin in a pan of warm water.

Chocolate icing: substitute 1 oz. cocoa for 1 oz. icing sugar. Add a few drops vanilla essence.

Chocolate truffle cakes

YOU WILL NEED FOR 12 CAKES:

    4 oz. stale sponge cake crumbs (use left-overs from
      fancies)
    4 oz. (or 4 rounded tablespoons) castor sugar
    4 oz. (or 4 heaped tablespoons) ground almonds
    2 tablespoons hot apricot jam
    FOR THE CHOCOLATE ICING:
    2 oz. plain chocolate
    3 tablespoons water
    4 oz. (or 4 rounded tablespoons) sifted icing
      sugar
    vanilla essence
    chopped walnuts or chocolate vermicelli for
      decoration

Rub cake pieces through a coarse sieve. Add sugar and ground almonds and enough hot apricot jam to bind the mixture together. Divide into 12 round balls each about the size of a walnut. Leave until quite cold and set firm.

Melt plain chocolate in water over gentle heat. Draw the pan off heat and stir in icing sugar. Add vanilla essence and stir until smooth. Dip cakes in icing and roll in walnuts or vermicelli. Place in paper cases and leave to set.

Baked in a pie dish, a fairly soft meringue makes an ideal shell for cold, sweet fillings. The recipes following give a crisp brown crust and soft centre; for a crisper shell bake at a lower temperature for a longer time.

Coffee mallow pie

YOU WILL NEED FOR 6 SERVINGS:

    2 egg whites
    pinch of salt
    3 oz. (or 3 rounded tablespoons) castor sugar
    FOR THE FILLING:
    ¼ pint water
    2 level tablespoons instant coffee
    8 oz. marshmallows
    ¼ pint double cream, whipped
    grated chocolate

Whisk together egg whites and salt until fluffy and thick. Add half the sugar and whisk again until stiff and glossy. Using a metal spoon, gently fold in remaining sugar. Spoon it into an 8 in. lightly-buttered pie plate. Hollow out middle and place in centre of cool oven (300 deg. or Gas No. 2). Bake for 1 hour. Remove from oven and cool.

Measure water, coffee and marshmallows (preferably all white) into a small saucepan. Stir over low heat until marshmallows have melted and mixture has blended. Draw pan off heat and cool mixture until thick, then whip until fluffy and gently fold in cream. Spoon into meringue shell, top with chocolate, and chill until firm.

Chocolate angel pie

SERVES 4–6

Prepare meringue crust as above, but make this chocolate filling. Melt 4 oz. plain chocolate in 3 tablespoons water over low heat. Draw the pan off the heat, stir in 1 teaspoon vanilla essence and allow to cool. Then fold in ½ pint whipped double cream, spoon into meringue and chill until firm.

Apricot pavlova cake

YOU WILL NEED FOR 4–6 SERVINGS:

    3 egg whites
    6 oz. (or 6 rounded tablespoons) castor sugar
    ½ level teaspoon each vanilla essence, cornflour and vinegar
       or lemon juice
    FOR THE FILLING:
    ¼ pint double cream
    1 small tin apricot halves

Whisk egg whites until stiff and gradually whisk in sugar. Continue beating until the mixture is very stiff then fold in vanilla essence, cornflour and vinegar or lemon juice.

Spoon the meringue into a buttered 8–9 in. pie plate, in a nest shape. Place below centre in a slow oven (355 deg. or Gas No. 3) and bake for 1 hour.

When cold fill with whipped cream and place drained apricots on top. Serve it in wedges with extra single cream.

A popular cake made in America is similar in texture to our Genoese or butter sponge, but it is made using oil. Known as Chiffon cake, it is quick and easy to prepare and can be baked either in a tube or angel tin, or deep square cake tin, *see recipe.*

Butterscotch chiffon cake

YOU WILL NEED:

    4 oz. (or 4 rounded tablespoons) self-raising flour
    ½ level teaspoon salt
    7 oz. (or 7 rounded tablespoons) soft brown sugar
    4 tablespoons vegetable or corn oil
    3 eggs
    6 tablespoons water
    1 teaspoon vanilla essence
    FOR THE FROSTING:
    4 oz. (or 4 rounded tablespoons) soft brown sugar
    2 oz. white vegetable fat
    ¼ pint, less 2 tablespoons, milk
    pinch of salt
    walnuts to decorate

Preheat the oven to 335 deg. or Gas No. 3. Sieve the flour, salt and sugar into a large mixing basin and make a well in the centre. Add the oil, egg yolks, water and vanilla and beat until very smooth. Whisk the egg whites until very stiff and using a metal spoon, gently fold into the mixture.

Pour into an *ungreased* 8 in. tube or angel tin or a 7 in. deep square tin. Place in the centre of a slow oven (335 deg. or Gas No. 3) and bake for 1¼–1½ hours. When baked, invert the cake in the tin, over a wire cooling rack and leave until quite cold. Loosen the sides and remove from the tin.

Meanwhile prepare the frosting. Measure the sugar, fat and milk into a saucepan. Stir over low heat to dissolve the sugar and then bring up to the boil. Simmer gently for about 5 minutes, then draw the pan off the heat and beat until lukewarm and of spreading consistency. Pour over the cake and while still soft coat and decorate the top with chopped walnuts.

Luxury gâteaux

The method for making these is the same as an ordinary whisked sponge but the mixture is piped into shape or baked and rolled up. With cream and fruit decorations the results are fabulous. Important points: don't over-mix once the flour has been added, and when the mixture has been prepared, get it into the oven very quickly.

Swiss roll

YOU WILL NEED:

2 oz. (or 2 rounded tablespoons) plain flour
2 large eggs
2½ oz. (or 2 rounded and 1 level tablespoons) castor sugar
FOR THE FILLING:
2–3 tablespoons warmed jam

Preheat oven to 425 deg. or Gas No. 7. Lightly grease a swiss roll tin and line lengthways with a strip of greased greaseproof paper letting ends overhang. Sift the flour several times and set aside in a warm place. Whisk the eggs and sugar together in a mixing basin, set over a pan of hot (not boiling) water, until thick and light. Remove the basin from the heat and beat a further 2–3 minutes. Sift the flour over the mixture and very gently fold in, using a hand whisk or metal spoon.
Pour the mixture immediately into the prepared tin, spreading evenly to the corners.
Place fairly high up in a very hot oven (425 deg. or Gas No. 7) and bake for 7–8 minutes, until brown and springy to the touch.
Remove it from the oven and loosen sides, turn tin on to a clean tea-cloth or sheet of greaseproof paper liberally sprinkled with castor sugar. Lift tin off the cake and peel away the lining paper.
Spread the swiss roll with the warmed jam, trim the sides with a sharp knife and roll up.
Leave to cool wrapped in a cloth or paper and when ready to serve, trim the ends and sprinkle cake with castor or icing sugar.

Chocolate: make swiss roll as above but replace 1 level tablespoon flour with one of cocoa powder and fill cake with cream as below.

With a plain swiss roll try: sweetened whipped cream and fresh raspberries—*see colour picture*—or strawberries; or perhaps raspberry jam and whipped

152   *Left to right: raspberry swiss roll, fruit basket, cherry russe, angel food cake and chantilly heart*

cream, vanilla or a flavoured ice cream. Top with extra whipped cream and fruit.

Sponge fingers and drops

YOU WILL NEED FOR 30 DROPS OR 24 FINGERS:

2 oz. (or 2 rounded tablespoons) plain flour
1 level tablespoon cornflour
2 large eggs
2½ oz. (or 2 rounded and 1 level tablespoon)
    castor sugar

Preheat the oven to very hot (425 deg. or Gas No. 7). Sift the flour and cornflour several times and set aside in a warm place. Whisk the eggs and sugar in a mixing basin set over a pan of hot (not boiling) water until thick and light. Remove the basin from the heat and whisk a further 2–3 minutes. Sift the flour over the surface of the mixture and then very gently fold in using a hand or balloon whisk or metal spoon. Take care not to over-mix.

Spoon the mixture into a cotton or nylon piping bag, fitted with ½ in. plain tube. Pipe it out on ungreased paper placed on a baking tray, in finger shapes about 2½–3 in. long or round drops about the size of half a crown. Sprinkle with a little castor sugar if liked, then place fairly high up—second shelf from top—in a very hot oven (425 deg. or Gas No. 7) and bake for 8–10 minutes. When baked turn the sponge fingers or drops, still on the paper, over on to the table top and cover with a damp cloth until they are all loose.

The drops may be sandwiched in pairs with whipped cream.

Unfilled these will keep perfectly in an airtight tin for a few days.

Cherry russe

YOU WILL NEED FOR 6 SERVINGS:

sponge fingers *(see above)*
1 (1 pint) packet red jelly
1 (14 oz.) tin red cherries
½ pint single cream
½ pint double cream

Prepare and bake the sponge fingers following the basic directions, and allow to cool.

Make up the jelly to ½ pint with hot water. Pour a little over the base of a charlotte russe tin or 6 in. cake tin and allow to set. Remove the stones and halve all the cherries. Arrange a few of them in a pattern over the set jelly base, spoon in a little more jelly and allow this to set firm before finishing the recipe.

Arrange the sponge fingers around the sides of the mould, with the base touching the jelly and each close together with the flat sides inwards *(see colour picture)*.

Cool remaining jelly until beginning to thicken. Whisk the creams together until thick and whisk in the setting jelly. Fold in the remaining pieces of cherry and pour in the centre of the prepared mould. Set aside in a cool place until set firm.

Trim the sponge fingers level and turn the cherry russe out on to a pretty serving plate.

Angel food cake

YOU WILL NEED:

1½ oz. (or 1 heaped tablespoon) plain flour
1 level tablespoon cornflour
4 oz. (or 4 rounded tablespoons) castor sugar
5 egg whites
pinch of salt
1 teaspoon vanilla essence

Preheat the oven to 380 deg. or Gas No. 5. Sift flour, cornflour and half the sugar several times. Whisk the egg whites and salt in a large mixing basin until foamy and gradually whisk in the remaining sugar. Using a hand-whisk or a metal spoon, gently fold in sifted ingredients and vanilla essence, then spoon into a clean, ungreased 8 in. tube or angel cake tin, spreading evenly. Place *just below* the centre of oven 380 deg. or Gas No. 5) and bake for 25–30 minutes until risen and brown. Remove the tin from the oven and turn it upside down to cool, preferably over a narrow bottle neck—the cake should hang upside down without the top or base touching anything if possible.

When cold remove from the tin and top with crushed fruit or the following glaze.

Chocolate glaze

YOU WILL NEED:

4 oz. plain chocolate
2 tablespoons water
½ oz. butter
2 oz. (or 2 heaped tablespoons) sifted icing sugar

Melt chocolate pieces in water over low heat, add the butter and stir until very smooth. Draw the pan off the heat and gradually beat in the icing sugar. Beat well until smooth. Set aside for 5–10 minutes or until thickened slightly, then pour over the cake top and sides.

Piped meringues

To hold its shape when piped a meringue mixture must be really stiff—whisking takes about ten minutes in all, less with an electric mixer.

Basic meringue mixture

YOU WILL NEED:

> 4 egg whites
> pinch of salt
> 8 oz. (or 8 rounded tablespoons) castor sugar
> 1 tablespoon lemon juice

Put the egg whites into a large mixing basin and add the salt. Don't use eggs that are straight out of the refrigerator—eggs at room temperature whisk up to a greater volume. Using a hand or rotary whisk, beat the egg whites until light and fluffy and continue to beat while adding the sugar gradually. Easiest way to do this is to shake in the sugar from a piece of paper or ask a friend to add while you whisk.
Once all the sugar is added, whisk in the lemon juice and beat until the mixture is very thick and will hold its shape.
Spoon into a cotton or nylon piping bag fitted with a rosette tube and use as required in the recipes.

Chantilly heart

YOU WILL NEED FOR 6 SERVINGS:

> basic meringue mixture *(see above)*
> FOR THE FILLING:
> ½ pint double cream
> 1 tin mandarin oranges

On two separate sheets of silicone or greaseproof paper, draw a heart approximately 7½ in. deep and 8 in. across. Place each sheet of paper, pencilled side down, on a baking sheet. (If greaseproof paper has been used brush over with a little olive oil.) Prepare the meringue mixture according to the basic recipe and spoon into a nylon or cotton piping bag, fitted with a rosette tube.
Pipe meringue in stars inside the traced outline of the heart shapes, filling in completely and taking care to keep a neat shape.
Place the baking sheets in the centre and on the bottom shelf of a very cool oven (240 deg. or Gas No. ¼), leave door slightly open and bake for several

hours. When the meringues have dried out, allow them to cool and then carefully peel off the paper. Whip the cream until thick and spread over the base of one of the meringue hearts. Sprinkle with the drained mandarin segments—reserve a few for decoration. Put the second heart on top, and decorate in one corner with a few mandarin orange segments as shown in colour picture on page 153.

Fruit basket

YOU WILL NEED FOR 6 SERVINGS:

> basic meringue recipe *(see opposite)*
> FOR THE FILLING:
> ¼ lb. grapes, halved and deseeded
> 2–3 bananas, sliced
> 1 large tin pineapple chunks
> 2–3 apples, peeled and sliced
> ½ lb. fresh strawberries

Using a round cake tin or plate as a guide, outline two 8 in. circles on separate sheets of silicone or greaseproof paper. Turn over on to baking trays, pencilled side down, (brush greaseproof paper over with olive oil).
Spoon the basic meringue mixture into a large nylon or cotton piping bag, fitted with a rosette tube. Pipe the mixture on to the pencilled shapes. Fill in one circle completely, piping in a circular movement from the centre out to the edge to make the base. The second needs only a ring of meringue piped round the pencilled line—this makes the sides. Using the remaining meringue, pipe out at least 10–12 small whorls for the top edge of the basket, use the same baking trays.
Place in the centre and on the bottom shelf of a cool oven (240 deg. or Gas No. ¼) and leave overnight with the door of the oven slightly open. When crisp and dry peel off the paper.
To assemble the basket—Place the base on a serving platter and, using the following sugar syrup, stick the ring on top of the base to make the basket and arrange the smaller meringues round the very top to form a decorative edge.
Measure 2 tablespoons castor sugar and 1 tablespoon water into a small saucepan, dissolve over low heat and then bring liquid to the boil. Simmer until a sticky syrup has been formed—it will take about 2–3 minutes. Draw the pan off the heat and with the blade of a knife moisten the base of each meringue piece with the hot syrup as directed.
Fill the basket with the prepared fruit, moistened with the pineapple juice and serve with fresh cream.

ALL ABOUT
Teacakes & Cookies

Scones and teacakes

Rubbed in mixtures are the simplest beginnings of a tempting range of scones, cookies and teacakes. Rubbing in means adding small knobs of fat to the flour, lifting and rubbing fat and flour together lightly between thumbs and forefingers, and letting it fall back into the mixing basin. As well as blending the fat and flour this incorporates plenty of air. Work quickly and use a pre-heated oven.

Afternoon tea scones

YOU WILL NEED FOR 12 SCONES:

- 8 oz. (or 8 rounded tablespoons plain flour)
- $\frac{1}{2}$ level teaspoon salt
- 1 level teaspoon bicarbonate of soda
- 2 level teaspoons cream of tartar
- $1\frac{1}{2}$ oz. butter or margarine
- $1\frac{1}{2}$ oz. (or 2 level tablespoons) castor sugar
- 1 egg made up to $\frac{1}{4}$ pint with milk (measure if possible, if not add approximately 4 tablespoons)

Into a large mixing basin sift flour, salt and raising agent (bicarbonate of soda and cream of tartar) or 4 level teaspoons baking powder may be used as a raising agent instead. Rub in the fat and stir in the sugar. Lightly mix the egg and milk and pour all at once into the centre of the dry ingredients.
Using the blade of a knife, or a fork, mix quickly to a dough. It should be soft but not wet. Turn out on to a lightly-floured working surface and pat or roll out to a thickness no less than $\frac{1}{2}$ in.

Cut into squares with a floured sharp knife, or stamp out rounds with a 2 in. cutter, flouring the cutter each time you use it.
You should get about 12 scones. Place not too closely on a floured baking tray, sprinkle with flour and place near the top of a hot oven (425 deg. or Gas No. 7). Bake for 10 minutes or until risen and brown; the sides should feel springy.

Fruit scones

Add 2 oz. cleaned currants or sultanas after rubbing in the fat. Brush the scones before baking with a little beaten egg and milk.

Wholemeal scones

Use half wholemeal and half white flour in the recipe. But sift the salt and raising agent with the white flour and then add the wholemeal flour to this.
Proceed as for the basic recipe, adding sultanas if liked.

Cheese scones

Follow the basic recipe omitting the sugar. After rubbing in the fat add 3 oz. finely-grated cheese—use Parmesan or Cheddar—and a pinch of cayenne pepper.

Girdle scones

Follow the basic recipe and turn the dough out on to a lightly floured working surface. Pat or roll out to about ½ in. in depth and using a 2 in. plain round cutter stamp out about 12 scones.

Rub a buttered paper over the surface of a heavy frying pan, or old fashioned girdle. Place over gentle even heat and when hot place the scones over the surface of the pan not too close together. Cook for about 7 minutes until risen and browned on the under side. Turn over and cook on the second side for about 5 minutes. Serve at once while still hot.

Banana tea bread

YOU WILL NEED FOR 1 LARGE LOAF:

8 oz. self-raising flour
½ level teaspoon salt
pinch mixed ground spice
4 oz. butter or margarine
6 oz. (or 6 rounded tablespoons) castor sugar
2 oz. chopped mixed peel
2 oz. walnuts, coarsely chopped
2 oz. glacé cherries, rinsed and quartered
1 lb. ripe bananas, mashed
2 standard eggs

Sift the flour, salt and spice into a large mixing basin, rub in the butter or margarine and then add the other ingredients. Beat well with a wooden spoon until thoroughly mixed.

Spoon into a greased and lined large loaf tin and place in the centre of a moderate oven (355 deg. or Gas No. 4) and bake for 1 hour, then reduce the temperature to slow (335 deg. or Gas No. 3) and bake for a further ½–¾ hour, or until the loaf is well risen and browned and springy to the touch.

Date and walnut loaf

YOU WILL NEED FOR 1 LARGE LOAF:

1 lb. plain flour
1 level teaspoon salt
2 level teaspoons baking powder
4 oz. butter or margarine
4 oz. (or 4 rounded tablespoons) soft brown sugar
6 oz. cooking dates, coarsely chopped
2 oz. walnuts, coarsely chopped
1 egg
¼ pint milk

Using a large mixing basin, sift in flour, salt and baking powder. Rub in the fat and stir in the sugar, dates and walnuts. Make a well in the centre and add

the egg and enough milk to mix to a soft dough consistency. Using a fork, mix quickly to a rough dough then turn out on to a floured surface and knead lightly.

Shape the mixture into a roll and place in a greased large loaf tin, about 9 by 5 by 2 in. Brush the top with a little milk and place in the centre of a fairly hot oven (375 deg. or Gas No. 5) and bake for 50–60 minutes. Allow to cool before slicing and buttering.

Cherry loaf

YOU WILL NEED FOR 1 LARGE LOAF:

12 oz. (or 12 rounded tablespoons) plain flour
3 level teaspoons baking powder
6 oz. butter or margarine
6 oz. (or 6 rounded tablespoons) castor sugar
6 oz. glacé cherries, rinsed, dried and halved
3 eggs
1 teaspoon vanilla essence
milk to mix

Into a large mixing basin sift the flour and baking powder. Rub in the fat and add the sugar and prepared cherries. Lightly mix the eggs and vanilla essence and stir into the centre of the dry ingredients. Mix with a fork to a medium-soft consistency, adding a little milk to the mixture if necessary. Spoon the mixture into a greased and lined large loaf tin, spreading it evenly and hollowing centre slightly.

Place in the centre of a moderate oven (355 deg. or Gas No. 4) and bake for 1½ hours.

When baked, a warmed skewer pushed into the centre of the loaf should come out quite clean. Cool before slicing. This loaf should keep very well for a week or more if stored in an airtight tin.

Apple cake

YOU WILL NEED:

10 oz. (or 10 rounded tablespoons) plain flour
3 level teaspoons baking powder
½ level teaspoon salt
4 oz. butter or margarine
1 oz. (or 2 heaped tablespoons) finely-grated
    Cheddar cheese
1 oz. (or 1 rounded tablespoon) castor sugar
¼ pint milk
4 medium-sized eating apples
FOR THE TOPPING:
2 oz. (or 2 rounded tablespoons) demerara sugar
½ level teaspoon ground cinnamon

Into a large mixing basin sift the flour, baking powder and salt. Rub in the fat and stir in the grated cheese and sugar. Make a well in the centre and add the milk all at once. Using a fork, mix a rough scone-like dough. Turn out on to a lightly-floured working surface and knead lightly. Pat the dough into a greased, shallow baking tin—medium-sized; the dough should be about $\frac{1}{2}$ in. thick.

Peel, quarter and core the apples. Slice thinly and arrange neatly on top in rows, slightly overlapping. Sprinkle with the topping, made by mixing together the demerara sugar and cinnamon. Place just above the centre in a hot oven (400 deg. or Gas No. 6) and bake for 25 minutes until golden brown. Serve hot with cream or cold cut in slices.

Rock cakes

8 oz. (or 8 rounded tablespoons) self-raising flour
$\frac{1}{4}$ level teaspoon salt
pinch of mixed spice
3 oz. butter or margarine
3 oz. (or 3 rounded tablespoons) castor sugar
3–4 oz. mixed dried fruit
1 egg
2 tablespoons milk
demerara sugar for topping

Using a large mixing basin, sift in flour, salt and mixed spice. Rub in the fat and add the castor sugar and dried fruit. Lightly mix the egg and milk and pour into the centre of the dry ingredients. With a fork, mix quickly to a rough dough, the mixture should be fairly stiff.

Pile the mixture in rough heaps, not too close together, on a greased baking tray. Sprinkle a pinch of demerara sugar on top of each and place in the centre of a hot oven (400 deg. or Gas No. 6) and bake for 10–15 minutes or until lightly browned.

Raspberry buns

Prepare the rock cake mixture as above omitting the mixed spice, fruit and demerara sugar from the recipe. Instead turn the mixture out onto a lightly floured working surface and roll into a sausage about 12 in. long. Cut into 16 pieces and shape each one into a ball. Place on a greased baking tray not too close together and make a small indent with a floured thumb in the centre of each one. Fill with raspberry jam and then pinch the sides of each to help keep the jam in the centre while baking. Brush with milk or water and sprinkle with crushed lump sugar. Place just above centre in a hot oven (400 deg. or Gas No. 6) and bake for 20–30 minutes.

Shortbread

YOU WILL NEED FOR 8–10 PIECES:

8 oz. (or 8 rounded tablespoons) plain flour
4 oz. (or 5 rounded tablespoons) cornflour
4 oz. (or 4 rounded tablespoons) icing sugar
8 oz. butter

Sift together the flour, cornflour and icing sugar into a large basin. Add the butter, cut in lumps, and rub into the cornflour.

First, the mixture will become crumbly, but continue rubbing in with the fingers until it clings together in heavy lumps. Turn on to a lightly floured board and knead lightly.

Press into a buttered 8–9 in. shallow round cake tin. Nip the edges with lightly floured fingers to make a pattern and prick all over with prongs of a fork. Place in the centre of a moderately hot oven (355 deg. or Gas No. 4) and bake for 1 hour. Five minutes before the cooking time is up, mark into sections with a knife, then return shortbread to oven for remaining cooking time. When baked remove from the oven and allow to cool in the tin.

Raisin spice cookies

YOU WILL NEED FOR 12–18 COOKIES:

8 oz. (or 8 rounded tablespoons) plain flour
pinch of salt
2 oz. butter or margarine
2 oz. (or 2 rounded tablespoons) castor sugar
milk to mix
FOR THE FILLING:
2 oz. seedless raisins, chopped
$\frac{1}{4}$ level teaspoon mixed spice

Into a large mixing basin sift the flour and salt. Rub in the fat and add the sugar. Using a fork, mix to a stiff dough with a little milk.

Turn the dough out on to a lightly-floured working surface and roll out to an oblong about $\frac{1}{8}$ in. thick. Cut across in half.

Mix together the raisins and spice to make the filling, and sprinkle over one half of the dough. Carefully put the remaining dough on top of the fruit. Roll out the double mixture, keeping the sides straight, until it's about $\frac{1}{8}$ in. thick and the fruit begins to show. Using a sharp knife, cut the dough into squares, triangles or fingers and place on a greased baking tray.

Put above centre in moderate oven (355 deg. or Gas No. 4) and bake for 10–15 minutes or until golden brown.

Rich creamed biscuits and cakes

Most of these recipes can be made up into a variety of fancy cakes and there's lots of scope for pretty decorations. Butter gives a better flavour, so use it whenever you can. Always use castor sugar—granulated may make your cakes speckly. When it's at the right consistency for baking, the mixture should drop off the spoon at a slight flick. Pre-heat the oven for at least 20 minutes and store the cooked cakes in an airtight tin lined with greaseproof paper.

Madeleines

YOU WILL NEED FOR 8–10 MADELEINES:

> 4 oz. (or 4 rounded tablespoons) self-raising flour
> pinch of salt
> 4 oz. butter or margarine
> 4 oz. (or 4 rounded tablespoons) castor sugar
> 2 eggs
> 1–2 tablespoons milk to mix
> FOR THE DECORATION:
> hot, sieved jam
> desiccated coconut
> small pieces of glacé cherry

First sift the flour and salt and set aside. Cream the butter or margarine and sugar together until soft and light. Gradually beat in the lightly-mixed eggs, adding a little of the sifted flour with the last few additions. Using a metal spoon, fold in rest of flour and enough milk to mix to a medium-soft consistency.

Spoon the mixture into 8–10 well-buttered castle moulds—it's a good idea to line the bases with small discs of greaseproof paper. Fill each mould about half full.

Arrange the filled moulds on a baking tray and place just above centre in a moderately hot oven (375 deg. or Gas No. 5) and bake for 15–20 minutes or until risen and brown. Allow to cool for 5 minutes, then gently remove the cakes from the tins—loosen the sides with a knife first.

Cut the tops of the cakes level and holding each on the end of a fork, dip into hot jam (apricot or strawberry are particularly delicious). Then roll immediately in the desiccated coconut. Place each in a paper case and decorate the top with a small piece of glacé cherry.

Butterfly cakes

MAKES 14–16

Prepare the mixture exactly as for the madeleines. Spoon it into 14–16 paper baking cases previously arranged in bun tins or on a baking tray. Place in the centre of a moderately hot oven (375 deg. or Gas No. 5) and bake for 15 minutes or until well risen and brown.

When the cakes are cold, cut a circle from the top of each, using a sharp knife and holding it sloping slightly inwards. Cut each of the small circles in half and set aside. Place a small teaspoon of buttercream (made by creaming together 2 oz. butter and 4 oz. sifted icing sugar with a few drops vanilla essence) in the centre of each cake. Press two semi-circular pieces into the buttercream so that they stand up to look like butterfly wings.

If you like, use a small piping bag and rosette tube to make small rosettes of buttercream around the replaced butterfly wings.

Queen cakes

YOU WILL NEED FOR 9 CAKES:

> 3 oz. (or 3 rounded tablespoons) self-raising flour
> pinch of salt
> 2 oz. butter or margarine
> 2 oz. (or 2 rounded tablespoons) castor sugar
> 1 egg
> few drops lemon essence
> 2 oz. currants
> about 1 tablespoon milk to mix

Sift together the flour and salt and set aside. Cream the butter or margarine and sugar until soft and light. Gradually beat in the lightly-mixed egg and lemon essence, adding a little of the sifted flour with last few additions. Fold in remaining flour with currants and enough milk to mix to a medium-soft consistency.

Spoon mixture into paper baking cases (set them in bun tins or on a baking tray) or into well-greased queen cake moulds. Place just above centre in a moderately hot oven (375 deg. or Gas No. 5) and bake for 15–20 minutes, until risen and brown. Tap the base of each mould sharply to loosen the baked cakes.

Clockwise from top right: Shrewsbury biscuits, butterfly cakes, Vienna shortcakes, madeleines, bourbons, chocolate oatmeal cookies and queen cakes

Madeira cake

YOU WILL NEED:

8 oz. (or 8 rounded tablespoons) self-raising
   flour
¼ level teaspoon salt
4 oz. butter or margarine
5 oz. (or 5 rounded tablespoons) castor sugar
2 eggs
few drops vanilla or lemon essence
2 tablespoons milk to mix
one thin slice of citron peel

Sift together the flour and salt and set aside. Cream
the butter or margarine and sugar until soft and light.
Gradually beat in the lightly-mixed eggs and essence,
adding a little flour with the last few additions. Using
a metal spoon, fold in the remaining flour and enough
milk to mix to a medium-soft consistency.

Spoon the mixture into a greased and lined 6 in.
round deep cake tin. Place in the centre of a
moderate oven (355 deg. or Gas No. 4) and bake for
1 hour. After 40 minutes, gently open the oven door
and place the slice of peel on the top of the partly-
baked cake, just where the crack appears. Leave to
bake for remaining time. When baked the cake
should feel firm to the touch and a warmed skewer
pushed into the centre should come out cleanly.
Allow the baked cake to cool for 5 minutes in the
tin before taking it out. Leave on a wire tray to go
cold.

Almond cake

YOU WILL NEED FOR 6 SERVINGS:

5 oz. (or 5 rounded tablespoons) self-raising
   flour
pinch of salt
3 oz. ground almonds
8 oz. butter or margarine
8 oz. (or 8 rounded tablespoons) castor sugar
4 eggs, lightly beaten
6 drops of almond essence
icing sugar for dusting

Sieve the flour and salt on to a piece of paper, add
the ground almonds and set aside. Cream the butter
or margarine and then add the sugar, beating well
together until light and fluffy. Gradually add the
eggs lightly mixed with the almond essence, beating
well after each addition, and add a little of the
sieved flour along with the last few additions to
prevent the mixture curdling.

Fold in the remaining flour, then pour the mixture
into a well greased 8–9 in. (or 3½ pint) fluted ring
tin. Bake just above centre in a moderate oven (355

deg. or Gas No. 4) for 55 minutes—1 hour or until
well risen and firm to the touch. Allow to cool then
dust with sieved icing sugar and serve plain.

Vienna shortcakes

YOU WILL NEED FOR 6 SHORTCAKES:

3 oz. (or 3 rounded tablespoons) plain flour
1 oz. (or 3 level tablespoons) cornflour
4 oz. butter or margarine
1½ oz. (or 2 rounded tablespoons) sifted
   icing sugar
few drops almond essence
FOR THE TOPPING:
extra sifted icing sugar
raspberry jam

Sift together the flour and cornflour and set aside.
Cream the butter or margarine very thoroughly until
soft. Avoid using fat straight from the refrigerator; if the fat is not creamed and softened sufficiently, the resulting mixture will be very difficult
to pipe.

Add the icing sugar and flavouring and cream in
thoroughly. Gradually work in the flour and cornflour
until smooth and blended. Spoon the mixture into a
large nylon or cotton piping bag, which has been
fitted with rosette piping tube (large size to fit
the bag). Pipe the mixture into paper baking cases
arranged in bun tins or on a baking tray. Pipe twice
round the outer edge so there is a hollow in the
centre.

Place the cakes in the centre of a moderate oven
(355 deg. or Gas No. 4) and bake for about 20 minutes
or until risen but still very pale in colour. Cool
the cakes thoroughly before dusting each liberally
with sifted icing sugar. Finish with a little
raspberry jam in the centre of each cake.

Bourbon biscuits

YOU WILL NEED FOR 18 BISCUITS:

4 oz. (or 4 rounded tablespoons) plain flour
½ level teaspoon baking powder
½ oz. (or 2 level tablespoons) cocoa powder
2 oz. butter or margarine
2 oz. (or 2 rounded tablespoons) castor sugar
1 level tablespoon syrup
FOR THE CHOCOLATE FILLING:
1 oz. plain chocolate
1½ tablespoons water
2 oz. (or 2 heaped tablespoons) sifted icing
   sugar
few drops vanilla essence

Sift together the flour, baking powder and cocoa powder and set aside. Cream the butter or margarine and sugar until soft and light and then beat in the syrup. Stir in half the flour mixture and mix until smooth. Turn the dough on to a working surface and knead in rest of flour.

Roll the dough out thinly to $\frac{1}{4}$ in. thick on a sheet of greaseproof paper or kitchen foil. Scatter a little granulated sugar over the top and lightly roll the pin over to fix it. Cut the dough into neat fingers about 1 in. wide, and $2\frac{1}{2}$ in. long. Lift carefully on a palette knife and place on a greased baking tray.

Prick each biscuit two or three times with a fork. Place in the centre of a slow oven (335 deg. or Gas No. 3) and bake for 15–20 minutes. Cool before adding the chocolate filling.

To prepare the filling: Melt chocolate in water over a very gentle heat. Draw the pan off the heat, stir in the sifted icing sugar and beat till glossy. Add the vanilla essence and cool until the mixture is of a soft, spreading consistency.

Sandwich the biscuits in pairs while the filling is still warm.

Shrewsbury biscuits

YOU WILL NEED FOR 12 BISCUITS:

4 oz. (or 4 rounded tablespoons) plain flour
$\frac{1}{4}$ level teaspoon baking powder
2 oz. butter or margarine
$1\frac{1}{2}$ oz. (or 2 level tablespoons) castor sugar
1 tablespoon lightly-mixed egg
3–4 drops lemon essence
icing sugar for dusting
lemon curd for filling

Start by sifting together the flour and baking powder and set mixture aside. Cream the butter or margarine and sugar until soft and light. Gradually beat in the mixed egg and lemon essence. Add half the sifted flour mixture and mix to a smooth paste, then turn the dough on to a working surface and knead in remaining flour. Cover and rest dough for 10 minutes. Roll the dough out thinly to about $\frac{1}{8}$ in. and cut in fancy shapes, in matching pairs, removing the centre from one of each pair. Put the biscuits on a greased baking tray in the centre of a moderately hot oven (375 deg. or Gas No. 5) and bake for 10–12 minutes, or until very lightly browned.

Dust the top of each pair of biscuits with icing sugar, spread each base with lemon curd and then sandwich the two together.

Chocolate oatmeal cookies

YOU WILL NEED FOR 36 COOKIES:

3 oz. (or 3 rounded tablespoons) plain flour
pinch of salt
4 oz. butter or margarine
4 oz. (or 4 rounded tablespoons) castor sugar
1 egg
1 teaspoon vanilla essence
1 (4 oz.) packet chocolate chips
1 oz. (or 2 rounded tablespoons) rolled oats

Sift the flour and salt into a square of paper and set aside. Cream together the butter or margarine and sugar until light. Gradually beat in the lightly mixed egg and vanilla essence. Stir in the sifted flour mixture, the chocolate chips and the oats.

Drop the mixture in rounded teaspoonfuls onto a greased baking tray. There should be about 36 spoonfuls, so bake in several batches. Place the tray of cookies just above centre of a moderately hot oven (355 deg. or Gas No. 4) and bake for 12–15 minutes, or until lightly browned.

Melting moments

YOU WILL NEED FOR 13–14 PAIRS:

3 oz. (or 3 rounded tablespoons) plain flour
1 oz. (or 3 level tablespoons) cornflour
pinch of salt
3 oz. butter
1 oz. (or 1 rounded tablespoon) castor sugar
few drops vanilla essence
FOR THE FILLING:
1 oz. butter
2 oz. (or 1 heaped tablespoon) sieved icing sugar
few drops pink colouring
few drops vanilla essence

Sift together the flour, cornflour and salt and set aside. Cream together the butter, sugar and vanilla until very soft. Add half the sifted ingredients and blend well, add the remainder and mix to a smooth dough.

Drop the mixture by teaspoons on to a buttered baking tray not too close to allow for spreading. You should get about 26–28 cookies. Place in the centre of a moderate oven (355 deg. or Gas No. 4) and bake for 15–20 minutes or until just beginning to brown. Remove carefully from the baking tray and allow to cool before filling.

To make the filling. Beat the butter until soft then gradually beat in the sieved icing sugar and a few drops of vanilla essence. Add a few drops of colouring—the filling should be palest pink or leave plain. Sandwich similar sized cookies in pairs with the filling.

163

Melted-fat tea-breads and cookies

Rich cakes and crisp cookies made by this method are ideal for keeping on hand in case visitors call in. Stored in an airtight tin, cakes or loaves will keep up to two weeks—and improve in flavour all the time. Cookies will last up to a week. Don't put cookies in the same tin as the cakes or they will go soft. Be careful to warm fat, sugar and syrup gently—otherwise it will turn into toffee! Never bake these cakes above the centre of the oven; the high percentage of sugar and syrup makes them more liable to burning. Remove from the tin while still hot, otherwise they tend to stick.

Honey cake

YOU WILL NEED FOR 24 SQUARES:

> 5 oz. butter or margarine
> 4 oz. (4 rounded tablespoons) soft brown
>   sugar
> 6 oz. clear honey
> 1 tablespoon water
> 2 eggs
> 7 oz. (or 7 rounded tablespoons) self-raising
>   flour
> blanched almond halves to decorate

Measure butter or margarine, sugar, honey and water into a saucepan. Place over a low heat and stir until the fat has melted. Draw pan off the heat at once and allow to cool until the hand can be held comfortably against the side of the pan. Beat in eggs one at a time. Sift flour on to a piece of paper. Add all at once to the honey mixture and mix thoroughly until smooth—but don't overmix. Pour into a greased and lined oblong baking tin (or you can use a small roasting tin).

Decorate with almond halves, arranging these neatly so that when the baked cake is cut each square has a piece of nut on top.

Place in the centre of a moderate oven (355 deg. or Gas No. 4) and bake for 30–35 minutes or until risen and firm to the touch.

Remove the cake from the tin, leave to cool and then cut in squares.

Malt loaf

YOU WILL NEED:

> 12 oz. (or 12 rounded tablespoons) self-raising flour
> pinch of salt
> 2 oz. (or 2 rounded tablespoons) castor sugar
> 1 oz. (or 1 heaped tablespoon) mixed chopped
>   peel
> 3 oz. (or 3 heaped tablespoons) sultanas, or
>   mixed dried fruit
> ½ pint milk
> 2 tablespoons malt extract
> 1 tablespoon of treacle

Line a large loaf tin with well-greased paper. Sift flour and salt into a large mixing basin. Stir in sugar, peel and fruit.

Into a small saucepan measure milk, malt and treacle and warm gently over a low heat to blend. Make a well in the centre of sifted flour and pour in the warmed liquid. Stir to mix, and then beat well for 1 minute. Pour mixture into the prepared loaf tin, and place in the centre of a moderate oven (355 deg. or Gas No. 4) and bake for $1\frac{1}{4}$ hours.

When baked, brush the top of the hot loaf with a glaze made by boiling together for 2 minutes, 2 tablespoons each of milk, sugar and water.

This loaf is made without fat and is deliciously moist. It should be sliced carefully with a serrated knife and buttered before serving.

Apricot fruit bread

YOU WILL NEED FOR 2 LOAVES:

> 1 lb. dried apricots
> ¾ pint plus 2 tablespoons water
> 12 oz. castor sugar
> 6 oz. lard or vegetable shortening
> 1 level teaspoon ground cinnamon
> 1 level teaspoon ground cloves
> ½ level teaspoon ground nutmeg
> 1 level teaspoon salt
> 2 eggs, lightly mixed
> 1 lb. plain flour
> 1 rounded teaspoon bicarbonate of soda

Grease two large loaf tins and set aside. Snip the apricots into small pieces and simmer in the water with the sugar, lard or vegetable shortening and spices and salt for 5 minutes. Draw the pan off the heat and allow to cool, until hand can be held comfortably against the sides of the pan. Add the lightly mixed eggs, sieved flour and bicarbonate of soda and beat well.

Dividing equally, pour the mixture into the prepared tins. Place in the centre of a moderate oven (355 deg. or Gas No. 4) and bake for 1 hour.

Gingerbread and malt loaf

Gingerbread

YOU WILL NEED:

4 oz. (or 4 rounded tablespoons) plain flour
pinch of salt
½ level teaspoon bicarbonate of soda
1 level teaspoon ground ginger
1 level teaspoon ground cinnamon
1½ oz. white fat
2 oz. (or 2 rounded tablespoons) soft brown sugar
4 oz. mixed syrup and treacle
1 egg
3 tablespoons milk
2 oz. chopped preserved ginger or mixed, dried fruit
1 oz. chopped almonds

Butter and line a 7 in. square baking tin. Sift together flour, salt, bicarbonate of soda, ground ginger and cinnamon into a mixing basin.

In a small pan melt fat, sugar, syrup, and treacle over a low heat, stir until blended and draw pan off the heat. Cool until the hand can be held comfortably against the sides. Add egg and milk, then mix well together and pour into the centre of sifted ingredients. Beat until smooth.

Stir in preserved ginger or dried fruit, pour into the prepared tin and sprinkle with the chopped nuts.

Place in the centre of a moderate oven (355 deg. or Gas No. 4) and bake for 30 minutes or until the gingerbread is risen and firm.

Continental chocolate cake

YOU WILL NEED FOR 6 SERVINGS:

5 oz. plain flour
1 oz. cocoa powder
½ level teaspoon salt
2 level teaspoons baking powder
5 oz. soft brown sugar
2 eggs
6 tablespoons corn oil
6 tablespoons milk
½ teaspoon vanilla essence
FOR THE RUM SYRUP:
2½ oz. lump sugar
2 tablespoons water
1 tablespoon rum
TO DECORATE:
¼ pint double cream
chocolate flake for decoration

Sift the flour, cocoa powder, salt and baking powder into a large mixing basin and add the sugar. Mix together the egg yolks, corn oil, milk and vanilla essence. Pour into the centre of the dry ingredients and beat well to form a smooth batter. Whisk the egg whites until stiff and fold into the mixture.

Pour into a greased and lined 7–8 in. round deep cake tin. Place above centre of a moderate oven (355 deg. or Gas No. 4) and bake for 40–45 minutes. Turn out and allow to cool.

Measure the sugar and water for the syrup into a saucepan. Stir over low heat to dissolve then bring up to the boil and cook briskly for 5 minutes. Draw off the heat and stir in the rum. When the cake is cold return to the tin, pour the hot syrup over the cooled cake and leave overnight. Turn the cake out, coat with whipped cream and decorate with grated chocolate.

Brandy-snaps

YOU WILL NEED FOR 18 BRANDY-SNAPS:

2 oz. (or 2 rounded tablespoons) plain flour
1 level teaspoon ground ginger
finely grated rind of ½ lemon
2 oz. butter or margarine
2 oz. (or 2 rounded tablespoons) moist brown sugar
3 level tablespoons golden syrup
1 teaspoon lemon juice
whipped cream for filling

First sift flour and ginger on to a square of paper and add lemon rind. Measure butter or margarine, sugar and syrup into a medium-sized saucepan. Place over low heat and stir gently until mixture is melted and blended. Stir in the flour mixture, add lemon juice and stir all ingredients thoroughly to mix.

Line a baking tray with a sheet of silicone paper and drop the mixture, half a teaspoon at a time, on to the paper, well apart to allow plenty of room for spreading.

Place on the top shelf in a hot oven (375 deg. or Gas No. 5) and bake for 10 minutes, or until golden brown and bubbly. Remove from oven and leave to cool slightly, then with a palette knife lift each brandy-snap off the paper (you will find they come quite easily off this non-stick paper). Then roll each loosely round the greased handle of a wooden spoon or a greased cream horn tin.

When cool and crisp remove from the mould and fill each with sweetened whipped cream. They can be stored—without cream—in an airtight tin.

Flapjacks

YOU WILL NEED FOR 6–8 FLAPJACKS:

3 oz. butter or margarine
3 oz. (or 3 rounded tablespoons) soft brown sugar
4 oz. rolled oats
pinch of salt

Melt butter or magarine and sugar in a saucepan over low heat, stirring to blend. Draw pan off the heat, stir in the oats and salt and mix well together. Press mixture into a greased 8 in. shallow sponge cake tin. Place in the centre of a moderate oven (355 deg. or Gas No. 4) and bake for 15 minutes. When baked remove from heat, mark 6–8 divisions and allow flapjacks to cool. Take them from the tin and break into pieces where marked.

Yorkshire parkin

YOU WILL NEED:

8 oz. (or 8 rounded tablespoons) plain flour
½ level teaspoon salt
1–2 level teaspoons ground ginger
1 level teaspoon bicarbonate of soda
8 oz. medium oatmeal or 3 level teacupfuls rolled oats
8 oz. treacle
6 oz. lard or vegetable shortening
4 oz. soft brown sugar
1 egg
approximately ¼ pint milk

Sift together in a mixing basin the flour, salt, ground ginger and the bicarbonate of soda. Add the oatmeal or rolled oats and set aside. Measure the treacle, fat, and sugar into a saucepan and stir over low heat until sugar has dissolved and fat is melted. Draw the pan off the heat and pour into the centre of the flour mixture. Add the egg and milk and mix to a smooth batter—stir quickly and mix ingredients thoroughly.

Pour into a greased and lined 8 in. square cake tin. Place in the centre of a moderate oven (355 deg. or Gas No. 4) and bake for 20 minutes. Lower the heat to slow (335 deg. or Gas No. 3) and bake for a further 50–60 minutes. When cooked the parkin will have shrunk back from the sides of the tin. Cool and store in a tin for a week before using.

Ginger nuts

YOU WILL NEED FOR 24 GINGER NUTS:

8 oz. (or 8 rounded tablespoons) plain flour
1 level teaspoon baking powder
2 level teaspoons ground ginger
¼ level teaspoon ground mixed spice
3 oz. butter
2 oz. (or 2 rounded tablespoons) granulated sugar
2 tablespoons golden syrup

Sift together flour, baking powder, ground ginger and spice into a large mixing basin.

Into a small saucepan put butter, sugar and syrup. Stir over a gentle heat until mixture is melted and blended. Draw pan off heat and allow to cool until the hand can be held comfortably against the sides. Pour mixture into the centre of the dry ingredients and mix to a soft dough.

Divide mixture into two halves. Form each half into a long roll and then divide each roll into 12 pieces. Shape each piece into a ball, and roll it in castor sugar. Place on a buttered baking tray, well spaced, and flatten them with the base of a jam jar or tumbler (sugar it to prevent sticking).

Place in the centre of a moderate oven (355 deg. or Gas No. 4) and bake for 10–15 minutes. Cool slightly on the baking tray before removing.

Moist treacle cake

YOU WILL NEED:

6 oz. (6 rounded tablespoons) plain flour
pinch salt
1 level teaspoon ground cinnamon
1 level teaspoon bicarbonate of soda
4 oz. (4 rounded tablespoons) castor sugar
6 oz. (3 tablespoons) black treacle
3 oz. butter
1 egg
¼ pint sour milk (add 1 teaspoon lemon juice to ¼ pint milk)
FOR THE WHIPPED BANANA TOPPING:
1 banana, sliced
1 egg white, unbeaten
pinch salt
1 oz. (1 rounded tablespoon) castor sugar
1 teaspoon lemon juice

Sift the flour, salt, cinnamon and soda on to a square of paper and set aside.

Into a medium-size saucepan, measure the sugar, treacle and butter cut into small pieces, and over a low heat, stirring all the time, heat the mixture until blended together, then draw the pan off the heat and set aside until the hand can be held comfortably against the side of the pan. Add the unbeaten egg and beat in thoroughly, then stir in the soured milk. Sift the flour mixture over the surface and stir in using a flat wire whisk. Pour this mixture into an 11 × 7-inch buttered baking tin, lined with a strip of greased paper, and place in the centre of a moderate oven (355 deg. or Gas No. 4) for 40 minutes, or until the mixture is springy to the touch. Remove from the oven and allow to cool in the tin.

Put all ingredients for the banana topping into an electric liquidiser and blend together on the high speed or whisk by hand. Serve treacle cake, cut in squares topped with banana topping.

Yeast breads

Fresh yeast can usually be bought from a small baker who makes his own bread. Make sure that it's light in colour, with no dark patches; that it is in large pieces and not crumbly; and, most of all, that it smells nice and yeasty.

Cream fresh yeast with a teaspoon of castor sugar and then stir in warm liquid.

Dried yeast is available from most chemists in 1 oz. packets or 4 oz. tins. Remember that ½ oz. dried yeast (or 1 level tablespoon) equals 1 oz. fresh yeast. Dried yeast should be sprinkled over warm liquid (taken from the recipe) in which 1 teaspoon castor sugar has been dissolved. Leave mixture to stand until the liquid froths up like beer—it will take about 10 minutes.

You don't have to prove (or rise) the dough in a warm place. The time can be varied to suit your own time-table:

For a quick rise—½–1 hour in a warm place;
slower rise—1–1½ hours on kitchen table;
overnight—up to 12 hours in a larder.

The dough is sufficiently risen when it has doubled in size and springs back when lightly pressed with a floured finger.

A tough, strong dough is developed by beating and kneading the mixture. There are two main methods of mixing dough. Usual method: dough is mixed well, kneaded and then left to rise in a basin until it is about double in size. After this it is turned on to a floured working surface, knocked flat with the knuckles, kneaded lightly and moulded into shape or put into the baking tins. After shaping it is left to rise once more before being put in a hot oven to bake. Quick method: dough is mixed well, kneaded very thoroughly and then moulded or put straight into tins and left to rise before baking. This is a much quicker method but the resulting texture is slightly coarser.

Few things give a cook more satisfaction than a batch of home-baked bread and buns fresh from the oven. The important thing to remember about yeast is that it is a living cell which produces a gas that expands the dough. The vital word is *warm*—for kitchen temperature, liquid added, utensils used. Extremes of heat and cold will kill yeast before the dough has risen (or 'proved'). When dough has risen sufficiently pop it into a hot oven (450 deg. or Gas No. 8) for the first 5–10 minutes so bread won't over-prove.

Left to right: Cinnamon ring doughnuts, Chelsea buns, hot cross buns, apricot braid, imperial straws and almond crescents

Chelsea buns

YOU WILL NEED FOR 18 BUNS:

- 1 lb. plain flour
- 1 level teaspoon salt
- 1 oz. fresh yeast
- 3 oz. (or 3 rounded tablespoons) castor sugar
- ¼ pint of mixed milk and water
- 2 oz. butter or margarine
- 2 eggs slightly beaten
- FOR THE FILLING:
- 6 oz. mixed dried fruit
- 2 oz. (or 2 rounded tablespoons) brown sugar
- ½ level teaspoon mixed spice
- 1 oz. butter or margarine, melted
- FOR THE TOPPING:
- 2 oz. sifted icing sugar
- hot water to mix

Sift flour and salt into a mixing basin and put in a warm place. Cream together yeast and 1 teaspoon of the sugar, and stir in warmed milk and water. Rub butter or margarine into the sifted flour, add the remainder of the sugar, yeast liquid and eggs. Mix to a dough by hand, and beat (also by hand) on a board for 5 minutes. Put in a mixing basin, cover with a cloth, and leave to prove until doubled in size. Turn the risen dough on to a lightly floured surface, flatten and roll out to an oblong shape about ¼ in. thick, (about 12 in. by 18 in.). Combine together dried fruit, sugar and mixed spice. Brush dough with melted butter or margarine and sprinkle with fruit mixture. Roll up like a swiss roll, starting with one of the long sides. Cut into 1 or 1½-inch slices and place, cut side up, in a greased medium-sized roasting or baking tin. Set aside in a warm place until puffy. Place just above centre in a hot oven (425 deg. or Gas No. 7) and bake for 20–25 minutes. While still hot, top with a glaze made by stirring hot water into the sifted icing sugar.

Cinnamon ring doughnuts

YOU WILL NEED FOR 18–20 RINGS:

- 8 oz. (or 8 rounded tablespoons) plain flour
- pinch of salt
- 1 oz. castor sugar
- 2 oz. butter or margarine
- ½ oz. fresh yeast
- 4 tablespoons milk
- 1 large egg, lightly mixed
- mixed castor sugar and ground cinnamon for coating

Sift flour and salt into a mixing basin, add all but 1 teaspoon of sugar and set in a warm place. Rub in the butter or margarine. Cream the yeast with remaining sugar and stir in warmed milk. Pour the yeast mixture into the centre of the flour, add egg and mix to a soft dough. Beat well by hand for 5 minutes and then set aside in a warm place, covered with a cloth, until risen and doubled in size.

Turn the risen dough on to a lightly floured working surface and knock flat with the knuckles. Knead lightly and roll out a little less than ½ in. thick. Using a 2 in. plain round cutter, stamp out as many rounds as you can. With a 1 in. cutter, remove the centre from each piece of dough to make a ring.

Re-roll all the trimmings to cut as many doughnuts as possible.

Place the rings on a lightly greased baking tray and set aside in a warm place until risen and puffy (about 25–30 minutes).

Deep fry in hot fat, turning them so that they brown evenly.

Drain and roll in mixed castor sugar and cinnamon. Serve while doughnuts are still warm and fresh.

Hot cross buns

YOU WILL NEED FOR 12 BUNS:

- 1 lb. plain flour
- 1 level teaspoon mixed spice
- ½ level teaspoon salt
- 2 oz. butter or margarine
- 4 oz. currants
- 1 oz. chopped mixed peel
- 2 oz. (or 2 rounded tablespoons) castor sugar
- 1 oz. fresh yeast
- 1½ gills (1 teacup) milk.
- 1 large egg, lightly mixed
- FOR THE CROSSES:
- 2 oz. shortcrust pastry or pastry trimmings
- FOR THE GLAZE:
- 2 tablespoons each milk, water and sugar

Into a warm mixing basin sift flour, mixed spice and salt. Rub in butter or margarine, add currants, peel and all but 1 teaspoon of the castor sugar.

Cream together the remaining sugar and yeast and stir in the warmed milk. Add the egg to the yeast liquid, mix lightly, and then pour the mixture into the centre of the dry ingredients.

Mix by hand until you have fairly soft dough.

Turn the dough out on to a lightly-floured board and knead for about 5 minutes.

Return the dough to the mixing basin and leave in a warm place, covered with a cloth, until it has risen and doubled in bulk, (takes about 1–1½ hours).

Turn out the risen dough on to a board, knead lightly and divide into 12 equal portions. Shape into buns and place on a greased baking tray. Cover with a cloth and leave in a warm place for 20–30 minutes, or until the buns look puffy.

To make the crosses roll out the pastry thinly and cut into narrow strips about 2–3 in. long. Brush the risen buns with a little milk and place a pastry cross on each one. Place in the centre of a hot oven (425 deg. or Gas No. 7) and bake for 15–20 minutes.

When the buns are baked but still hot, glaze as follows. Measure the milk, water, and sugar into a saucepan, dissolve over low heat, then boil for about 2 minutes. Brush on while hot.

Apricot braid

YOU WILL NEED:

12 oz. (or 12 rounded tablespoons) plain flour
1 level teaspoon salt
2 oz. butter or margarine
2 oz. dried apricots, snipped in small pieces
2 oz. seedless raisins
finely-grated rind of ½ lemon
1 oz. fresh yeast
1 level teaspoon castor sugar
¼ pint mixed milk and water
1 large egg, lightly mixed
FOR THE TOPPING:
2–3 oz. sifted icing sugar
hot water to mix
2 oz. toasted, flaked almonds

Sift together flour and salt into large mixing basin and set in a warm place. Rub in butter or margarine and then add the dried fruit and finely-grated lemon rind. Cream yeast with the sugar and stir in the warm, mixed milk and water. Pour the yeast liquid into the centre of the dry ingredients, add the egg and mix by hand to a dough.

Beat the dough by hand for 5 minutes. Then turn it on to a lightly floured working surface and knead for another 5 minutes.

Now the dough is thoroughly mixed and ready to shape.

Divide it into five equal pieces.

Roll each one out to a rope about 12 in. long. Plait three of the pieces into a loaf (put a small weight on the start of the plait to hold it). Take care not to stretch the dough. Put the plaited loaf on a greased baking tray. Twist the remaining strips together, and place lengthwise on top. Set the loaf in a warm place until risen and puffy—it will take about 30 minutes. Brush with a little beaten egg and milk and place above centre in a very hot oven (450 deg. or Gas No. 8) and bake for 10 minutes. Lower the heat to 375 deg. or Gas No. 5 and bake for a further 20 minutes. When baked, the bread should sound hollow when tapped.

Blend the icing sugar with enough hot water to make a thin icing. Pour over the loaf and sprinkle the top with the almonds.

Danish almond crescents and imperial straws

YOU WILL NEED FOR 24 PASTRIES:

FOR THE DANISH PASTRY:
1 lb. plain flour
2 level teaspoons salt
2 oz. butter or margarine
3 oz. castor sugar
1½ gills (1 teacup) mixed cold milk and water
1 oz. fresh yeast
8 oz. butter or margarine for folding in

Sift together flour and salt. Beat down the 2 oz. butter or margarine and rub into the flour. Make a well in the centre of the mixture.

Mix sugar with half the liquid and pour into the centre of the flour. Blend rest of the liquid with yeast and pour also into the centre of the flour. Mix to a rough dough.

Turn the dough on to a working surface and knead well until smooth. Cover and rest in a cold place, preferably refrigerator for 1 hour.

After resting, roll out dough to an oblong. Beat down the 8 oz. butter or margarine and shape into a rectangle about ¼ inch thick and just under half the size of dough, and slightly narrower. Place on centre of dough and fold dough over to cover it (let ends overlap slightly, join should be in the middle). Give a half turn clockwise, roll to an oblong, and mark off in thirds. Fold top third to middle and bottom third up over it. Give a half turn clockwise, roll and fold once more. Cover and rest dough for half an hour in a cool place. Give two more turns, rolls and folds, rest again. *For almond crescents* use half the Danish pastry, rolled to about ¼ in. thick and cut into strips 3–4 in. wide. Mark at 3 in. intervals down one long edge. Make similar marks down other long edge but start 1½ in. from corner. Cut pastry into triangles using the marks as guides. Place a small roll of rather soft marzipan on top of each triangle, brush sides lightly with egg and roll up from 3-inch edge to the point. Curl into a crescent, point inwards. Brush with egg. Prove in a warm place until puffy. Place high up in a fairly hot oven (400 deg. or Gas No. 6) and bake for 15–20 minutes. Finish with glacé icing and toasted almonds. *For imperial straws* use half Danish pastry, roll out thinly just under ¼ in. thick. Cut into 3 in. squares, slit the corners and brush lightly with egg. Fold alternate corners over and press in the centre; top with half a glacé cherry. Prove and bake as above.

ALL ABOUT
Rich Fruit Cakes & Icing

Traditional fruit cakes

Rich fruit cakes improve considerably when kept for a time before eating—anything from two to six weeks for a very rich cake. Leave it for 24 hours after baking, then wrap in greaseproof paper and store in a tin. Use carefully cleaned and prepared fruit. Remove the stalks, wash the fruit, then dry thoroughly in a clean cloth. Or you can buy fruit ready cleaned before packing. It is useful to know that any cake recipe without a raising agent, such as baking powder or self-raising flour, may be prepared and left up to 12 hours before cooking. So you can save time by preparing the cake one day and baking it the next.

Preparing the cake tin

Using tin as a guide, cut out one double thickness circle of greaseproof paper for the base and a double strip of greaseproof paper about 2 inches higher than the depth of the tin for the sides. Turn down a margin about 1 inch along one edge of the paper strip and make sloping cuts with scissors along the margin.

Place the long double strip inside the tin with snipped margin lying flat all round the bottom. Put the paper circles on to the base, over this. Brush all over lightly inside with melted butter or margarine.

Lastly, tie a strip of double thickness kitchen foil or brown paper round the outside of the tin for extra protection during the long baking time.

Dundee cake

YOU WILL NEED FOR ONE 8–9 IN. CAKE:

> 10 oz. (or 10 rounded tablespoons) plain flour
> 1½ level teaspoons baking powder
> ½ level teaspoon salt
> 2 oz. (or 2 heaped tablespoons) ground almonds
> 6 oz. butter
> 2 oz. white vegetable fat
> 8 oz. (or 8 rounded tablespoons) soft brown sugar
> 4 large eggs
> finely grated rind of 1 lemon
> ½ teaspoon lemon essence
> 12 oz. sultanas
> 4 oz. glacé cherries, washed and halved
> 4 oz. currants
> 4 oz. candied peel, chopped
> about 18 blanched almonds

Sift together flour, baking powder, and salt, add ground almonds and set aside. Cream together butter, fat and sugar until soft and light. Lightly mix eggs, lemon rind and essence, and gradually beat into creamed mixture a little at a time, adding some of the flour with the last few additions. Using a metal spoon, first fold in remaining flour and then the prepared fruit.

Prepare one 8–9 in. round, deep cake tin (*see instructions*). Spoon in cake mixture and hollow out slightly in the centre, and top neatly with almonds. Place on the shelf below centre of a preheated moderate oven (355 deg. or Gas No. 4) and bake for

Ingredients for a Christmas cake

1 hour. Then lower heat to 310 deg. or Gas No. 2 and bake for a further 2 hours.

Christmas cake

YOU WILL NEED FOR ONE 8 IN. CAKE:

10 oz. (or 10 rounded tablespoons) plain flour
1 level teaspoon mixed spice
1 level teaspoon salt
8 oz. butter
8 oz. (or 8 rounded tablespoons) soft brown sugar
4 large eggs
1 tablespoon black treacle
½ teaspoon vanilla essence
8 oz. currants
8 oz. sultanas
8 oz. seedless raisins
4 oz. candied peel, chopped
4 oz. glacé cherries, washed and cut into quarters
2 oz. blanched almonds, chopped
2 tablespoons brandy or milk to mix

Sift together flour, spice and salt and set aside. Cream together butter and sugar until soft and light. Then gradually beat in the lightly mixed eggs, treacle and vanilla flavouring, adding some of the flour with the last few additions.

Add 1–2 spoons of sifted flour to prepared fruit, then, using a metal spoon, fold in first the remaining flour and then the fruit mixture, chopped almonds and brandy or milk.

Prepare one 8 in. round, deep cake tin (*see instructions*). Spoon in cake mixture and hollow out the centre slightly. Place on the shelf below centre of a preheated warm oven (310 deg. or Gas No. 2) and bake for 1½ hours. Then lower the heat to cool. (290 deg. or Gas No. 1) and bake for a further 2½ hours.

Golden fruit cake

YOU WILL NEED FOR ONE 8–9 IN. ROUND OR 2 LOAF CAKES:

12 oz. (or 12 rounded tablespoons) plain flour
1 level teaspoon salt
10 oz. butter
10 oz. (or 10 rounded tablespoons) castor sugar
5 large eggs
grated rind and juice of 1 large lemon
8 oz. dried apricots, soaked overnight and snipped in pieces
8 oz. glacé cherries washed and halved
8 oz. glacé pineapple, washed and coarsely shredded

Sift flour and salt and set aside. Cream butter and sugar until light in colour. Lightly mix eggs and finely grated lemon rind, then gradually beat into creamed mixture, adding a little of the sifted flour

with the last few additions. Fold in remaining flour, then prepared fruit and lemon juice. Blend well; the mixture should be of a medium-soft consistency.

Prepare one 8–9 in. round, deep cake tin (*see instructions*). Spoon in cake mixture and hollow out the centre slightly. Place in the centre of a preheated warm oven (310 deg. or Gas No. 2) and bake for 1½ hours, lower the heat to cool (290 deg. or Gas No. 1) and bake the cake for a further 2½ hours.

To bake loaf cakes: Spoon half the mixture into a greased and lined large loaf tin—keep remaining mixture aside covered with a cloth. Place in the centre of a warm oven (310 deg. or Gas No. 2) and bake for 1½ hours. Then lower heat to cool (290 deg. or Gas No. 1) and bake for a further 30 minutes. Bake second cake in the same way.

Glacé cherry and sultana cake

YOU WILL NEED FOR ONE 8 IN. CAKE:

10 oz. (or 10 rounded tablespoons) plain flour
1 level teaspoon salt
8 oz. butter
8 oz. (or 8 rounded tablespoons) soft brown or castor sugar
4 large eggs
¼ teaspoon vanilla essence
1 lb. sultanas
1 lb. glacé cherries, washed and halved
2 tablespoons brandy

Sift together the flour and salt and set aside. Prepare the fruit, pat dry and place in a large basin. Add a quarter of the sieved flour mixture to the fruit and mix well.

Cream the butter and sugar until very light and fluffy. Lightly mix the eggs and vanilla essence and gradually beat into the creamed mixture, adding a little of the sieved flour with the last few additions. Fold in the remaining flour, fruit from the basin and the brandy. Stir until blended; the mixture should have a medium soft consistency. Spoon the mixture into a prepared—*see instructions*, 8 in. round deep cake tin and hollow out the centre slightly. Place on the shelf below centre in a warm oven (335 deg. or Gas No. 3) and bake for 1 hour. Lower to slow (310 deg. or Gas No. 2) and bake for a further hour. Then lower the heat to cool (290 deg. or Gas No. 1) for a final hour. When baked a warmed skewer pushed into the centre of the cake should come out cleanly.

Rich walnut cake

YOU WILL NEED FOR ONE 8 IN. CAKE:

    10 oz. (or 10 rounded tablespoons) plain flour
    1 level teaspoon salt
    8 oz. butter
    6 oz. (or 6 rounded tablespoons) castor sugar
    3 tablespoons honey
    4 large eggs
    finely grated rind of 1 orange
    8 oz. walnuts, coarsely chopped
    8 oz. sultanas
    8 oz. seedless raisins
    4 oz. dates, stoned and chopped
    4 oz. candied peel, chopped
    2 tablespoons lemon juice

Sift together flour and salt and set aside. Cream together butter and sugar until light in colour. Mix together honey, eggs and grated orange rind, then gradually beat into the creamed mixture a little at a time, adding some of the flour with the last few additions.

Using a metal spoon, fold in first remaining flour and then prepared nuts, fruit and lemon juice. Prepare one 8 in. round, deep cake tin (*see instructions*). Spoon in cake mixture and hollow out the centre of a preheated slow oven (335 deg. or Gas No. 3) and bake for 1½ hours.

Then lower heat to warm (310 deg. or Gas No. 2) and bake for a further 1½ hours.

Pineapple and walnut cake

YOU WILL NEED FOR ONE 8 IN. CAKE:

    4 oz. shelled walnuts
    8 oz. glacé pineapple
    12 oz. (or 12 rounded tablespoons) plain flour
    little grated nutmeg
    1 level teaspoon salt
    8 oz. butter
    8 oz. (or 8 rounded tablespoons) castor sugar
    5 large eggs
    2 tablespoons milk to mix

Toast the walnuts in a hot oven (400 deg. or Gas No. 6) for a few minutes, then rub off as much brown skin as possible and coarsely chop the nuts. Wash the pineapple to remove any sugary coating, then pat dry and chop coarsely. Sieve the flour, grated nutmeg and salt and set aside.

Cream the butter and sugar until light in colour. Gradually beat in the lightly mixed egg a little at a time, adding some of the sieved flour along with the last few additions. Using a metal spoon fold in first the remaining flour, then the prepared nuts and pineapple and enough milk to mix to a medium soft consistency. Spoon the mixture into a prepared—*see instructions*, 8 in. round deep cake tin and hollow out the centre slightly. Place on the shelf below centre in a moderate oven (355 deg. or Gas No. 4) and bake for 1½–2 hours.

Rich fruit cakes for Weddings, birthdays or Christmas

Cake mixture for other sizes of tins:

This chart will enable you to vary the sizes of your cake layers – and also the number of tiers – but remember that the sizes of a three-tier cake must be carefully balanced. In the table the abbreviation 'tsp' stands for level teaspoon. Baking times are for a cool oven (290 deg. or Gas No. 1)

Square tins	5 in.	6 in.	7 in.	8 in.	9 in.	10 in.	11 in.
Round tins	6 in.	7 in.	8 in.	9 in.	10 in.	11 in.	12 in.
Plain flour	4 oz.	6 oz.	9 oz.	11 oz.	13 oz.	15 oz.	1 lb. 3 oz.
Salt	pinch	pinch	pinch	¼ tsp	¼ tsp	½ tsp	¾ tsp
Spice	¼ tsp	½ tsp	1 tsp	1½ tsp	1½ tsp	2 tsp	3 tsp
Butter	3½ oz.	5 oz.	8 oz.	10 oz.	12 oz.	14 oz.	1 lb. 2 oz.
Sugar	3½ oz.	5 oz.	8 oz.	10 oz.	12 oz.	14 oz.	1 lb. 2 oz.
Eggs	2	3	4	5	6	7	9
Grated lemon rind	½	1	1	2	2½	3	3½
Mixed dried fruit & nuts	1 lb.	1 lb. 6 oz.	2 lb.	2 lb. 10 oz.	3 lb. 4 oz.	3 lb. 12 oz.	5 lb. 4 oz.
Baking time: at cool (290 deg. or Gas No. 1)	3¾–4 hr.	4¼–4½ hr.	4½–4¾ hr.	5–5¼ hr.	5¼–5½ hr.	5½–5¾ hr.	6¼–6½ hr.

Apricot glaze and almond pastes

Putting on the almond paste is the most important stage in icing a cake as this gives you the smooth foundation without which you cannot hope for a professional result. The cake to be covered should be as flat and even in shape as possible. Slight irregularities can be corrected with the almond paste, but a high dome in the centre of the cake should be trimmed level; use a saw-edged knife and slice across. After trimming the cake prepare first the almond paste and then the apricot glaze before proceeding any further. Then brush the cake with apricot glaze. It holds down any loose crumbs and helps almond paste to stick.

Almond paste

YOU WILL NEED TO COVER TOP AND SIDES OF 8–9 IN. CAKE:

6 oz. (or 6 rounded tablespoons) icing sugar
6 oz. (or 6 rounded tablespoons) castor sugar
12 oz. (or 12 heaped tablespoons) ground
    almonds
juice of half a lemon
1 large egg
½ teaspoon vanilla or almond essence or rose
    water

Sift icing sugar into a large mixing basin, add castor sugar and ground almonds. Lightly mix lemon juice, egg and flavouring. Pour into the dry ingredients and, using a fork, mix to a fairly stiff paste. Turn out on to a working surface lightly dusted with castor sugar and knead lightly by hand to a smooth dough.
Avoid overmixing—the warmth of the hands can cause the oil to come out of the almonds, making the paste difficult to roll out. If paste is a little sticky, work in more sugar, or if it is too stiff, a little more lemon juice. Set finished almond paste aside until ready to use.

Apricot glaze

YOU WILL NEED FOR UP TO AN 8 IN. CAKE:

1 heaped tablespoon castor sugar
1 tablespoon water or lemon juice
2 heaped tablespoons sieved apricot jam, (or
    strawberry, plum, gooseberry)

Dissolve sugar in water or lemon juice, then add jam and stir over gentle heat until well mixed. Bring to the boil and simmer gently until the glaze hangs in heavy drops from the spoon; this will take 3–5 minutes. Use hot.

For a large quantity of glaze —necessary for larger cakes. Follow recipe above, using ½ lb. granulated sugar, ¼ pint water and 1 lb. jam; boil for 5–8 minutes. Any surplus glaze can be stored in a glass jar—allow to cool first. Then it may be reheated and used as required.

To cover the cake with almond paste
Divide almond paste into two portions, one third to cover top of the cake and two-thirds for the sides. Dust your working surface with more castor sugar and roll out smaller portion of paste to a circle the size of the top of the cake. If necessary make up the surface of the cake with pieces of marzipan to level it, or take a professional tip and reverse the cake using the flat base as the top. Once you have decided, brush 'top' of the cake with hot apricot glaze and upturn it on to the circle of rolled out almond paste. Press down firmly, and trim away the surplus paste. Add these pieces to remaining paste.
Using a piece of string, measure the circumference of the cake and cut to the exact length—keep this for measuring. Roll out remaining paste to circumference of the cake. To do this, shape almond paste with your hands into a 'rope' the same length. Then flatten this 'rope' with a rolling pin to the depth of the cake. Trim and neaten one long edge of the strip. Brush round the cake with hot jam glaze, then turn cake on its side and lift carefully on to the paste so that the trimmed edge is level with the top of the cake. Roll cake along the strip until the side is completely covered.
Then turn the cake with the almond paste top *downwards* on the sugared working surface.
Trim any paste away from the base or sides and neaten joins. Roll a straight sided jar or tin round the sides to stick paste firmly to the cake. Turn the cake right side up and place on an upturned plate. Cover with greaseproof paper and leave in a cool, dry place 3–7 days.
It is important that almond paste should be allowed to dry out before the royal icing is put on, especially if completed iced cake is likely to be kept for some time. This applies particularly to a Christmas or wedding cake. If this is not done, the oil from the almonds can stain the white icing yellow. Here's a useful tip—if time is short, brush over the almond paste with lightly beaten egg white and leave 24 hours before putting on the royal icing.

Covering a cake with almond paste

Economical almond paste

When making almond paste for economy half the quantity of ground almonds may be substituted with fine semolina or maderia cake crumbs.

Sugar paste

TO COVER TOP ONLY OF 7–8 IN. CAKE:

> 6 oz. white marshmallows
> ½ oz. white vegetable fat
> 12 oz. (or 12 rounded tablespoons) icing sugar, sieved

This may be used instead when almond paste is not popular. Melt the marshmallows in a mixing basin set over a pan of hot water. Stir to mix well, then remove the basin from the heat.
Add the softened white fat and mix well using a wooden spoon. Gradually beat in the sieved icing sugar. When too stiff to use the wooden spoon, turn on to a board and knead in any remaining sugar. Wrap in foil or waxed paper and store in a tin until ready for use. Roll out on a working surface dusted with icing sugar and use to cover cake.
Note This paste does not dry out hard like almond paste.

Vanilla almond paste

YOU WILL NEED TO COVER ONE 7–8 IN. CAKE:

> 1 egg
> 6 oz. (or 6 rounded tablespoons) castor sugar
> ¼ teaspoon almond or vanilla essence
> 6 oz. (or 6 rounded tablespoons) icing sugar, sifted
> 6 oz. (or 6 heaped tablespoons) ground almonds
> **TO COVER ONE 9–10 IN. CAKE:**
> 1 egg plus 1 egg yolk
> 8 oz. (or 8 rounded tablespoons) castor sugar
> 1 teaspoon almond or vanilla essence
> 8 oz. (or 8 rounded tablespoons) icing sugar, sifted
> 8 oz. (or 8 heaped tablespoons) ground almonds

Whisk egg and castor sugar together in a mixing basin set over a pan of hot water until light in colour. Remove basin from the heat and stir in flavouring, then icing sugar and almonds.
Mix with a fork to a rough dough, then turn out on to a working surface dusted with icing sugar and knead until smooth. Wrap in polythene and leave to mature for at least 1 hour before using. Roll out on a working surface dusted with icing sugar, and cover cake in same way as with almond paste.

Use almond paste as a filling for old fashioned simnel cake. Top with more almond paste, decorate with eggs and chickens for Easter.

Simnel cake

YOU WILL NEED FOR ONE 8 IN. CAKE:

> 8 oz. (or 8 rounded tablespoons) plain flour
> ½ level teaspoon salt
> 1 level teaspoon baking powder
> ½ level teaspoon mixed spice
> ½ level teaspoon ground cinnamon
> 6 oz. butter or margarine
> 6 oz. (or 6 rounded tablespoons) castor sugar
> 3 large eggs
> 12 oz. mixed dried fruit
> 4 oz. candied peel, chopped
> juice of 1 lemon
> 2–3 tablespoons milk to mix
> **FOR THE ALMOND PASTE:**
> 8 oz. (or 8 rounded tablespoons) ground almonds
> 10 oz. (or 10 rounded tablespoons) castor sugar
> 1 large egg
> juice of 1 lemon

First prepare almond paste in a mixing basin combine together ground almonds and sugar. Stir in lightly beaten egg and lemon juice and, using a fork, mix first to a rough dough then knead by hand to a smooth paste. Cut off one third of the paste and roll it into a round slightly smaller than the cake tin. Wrap remainder in greaseproof paper and put it in a cool place until cake is baked and ready for using.
Sift flour, salt, baking powder and spices together and set aside. Cream butter and sugar until soft and light, then gradually beat in the lightly mixed eggs, a little at a time, adding some of the sifted flour with the last few additions. Using a metal spoon, fold in the remaining sifted flour, prepared fruit and lemon juice and enough milk to mix to a medium soft consistency.
Line and grease an 8 in. round, deep cake tin and spoon half the mixture into it. Spread level and bang the tin down on the table to exclude all air bubbles. On top of this place the round of almond paste—it should be about half an inch less than the cake tin all round. Spoon in remaining cake mixture and hollow out centre slightly.
Place in the centre of a moderate oven (355 deg. or Gas No. 4) and bake for 1 hour. Then lower the heat to slow (335 deg. or Gas No. 3) and bake for a further 1¾ hours. Leave cake to cool.
To finish the cake
Cut off about a third of the remaining almond paste

and with this shape 11 small eggs. Roll out remainder and cover top of the cake as described previously. With the fingers pinch up the edge, making a border about ½ in. wide, mark this with the prongs of a fork to represent the straw of a nest. Brush with beaten egg and place under a hot grill to brown slightly. Arrange eggs round edge and brown similarly. Decorate with a few chickens and tie a yellow ribbon round the side.

Marzipan modelling

Colour egg-sized pieces of almond paste, *see page 176*, as desired—green for leaves, pink and yellow for flowers—with ordinary colouring, knead until colours are evenly distributed then roll out thinly and shape as indicated in following instructions. Dip fingers in cornflour while shaping and moulding flowers.

Star flowers

Using a medium-sized star-shaped cutter, stamp out pieces from coloured marzipan. Cut half-way to the centre from base of each point to make loose petals. Roll a small ball of contrasting paste and place in the centre of each flower and then press petals round slightly overlapping each other. Shape centre base underneath to a short stem and leave to set firm.

Lily with buds

Stamp out rounds with a small plain or fluted cutter. Roll a small tapering centre from contrasting paste and place on the round with the tip overlapping at top edge. Roll circle round the centre so that the top is open like a lily and the base closed and tapered.

Carnation

Cut long strips about 1 in. deep from thinly rolled pink or yellow marzipan. Flatten out down one side and cut with the prongs of a fork. Roll up from one end, squeeze base shut and open top out to shape like a carnation. Using a fine paint-brush and little darker red or yellow colouring, shade petals.

Rose

Using two shades of the same colour, or yellow and pink, and cut out five small, heart-shaped leaves from thinly rolled marzipan. Flatten top edges with finger and thumb. Curl the first one fairly tightly to make the rose centre, then shape the others round to make the petals. Curve outside petals over slightly for a realistic effect. Press centre base to a stem shape and cut off excess at a slant. Leave to set.

Leaves

Cut heart, holly or spear shapes from thinly-rolled green marzipan. Neaten edges and taper points, then mark in leaf veins, using the back of a knife. Rest rose or holly leaves over a pencil to give a curl and leave to set firm.

Holly berry sprays

Prepare leaves as above. Then roll a little red marzipan into a thin rope, cut into small pieces and roll each into a round ball. Leave to harden, then arrange berries and leaves together in a cluster on the cake surface. Stick with soft icing.

Almond paste for topping cakes

Prepare as in basic recipe. For top and sides double the quantities.

Ingredients	6 in.	7 in.	8 in.	9 in.	10 in.	11 in.	12 in.
Icing sugar (sifted)	3 oz.	4 oz.	5 oz.	5 oz.	6 oz.	7 oz.	8 oz.
Castor sugar	3 oz.	4 oz.	5 oz.	5 oz.	6 oz.	7 oz.	8 oz.
Ground almonds	6 oz.	8 oz.	10 oz.	10 oz.	12 oz.	14 oz.	1 lb. 2 oz.
Eggs	½ small	½ large	1 small	1 small	1 large	2 small	2 large
Almond or vanilla essence	drop	drop	¼ tsp.	¼ tsp.	½ tsp.	½ tsp.	½ tsp.

Royal icing

Unless you're an expert, don't attempt an elaborate icing design—a simple decoration is much more effective. Try practising on an upturned plate before you start work on the cake, and don't get discouraged at the beginning—the more you do the easier it becomes.

Royal icing

YOU WILL NEED TO COAT ONE 8 IN. CAKE:

about 1½ lb. icing sugar
3 large egg whites
1 teaspoon lemon juice
1½ teaspoons glycerine

Sift icing sugar through a fine sieve on to a large square of greaseproof paper. Break egg whites into a mixing basin and beat lightly until just frothy. Do not use eggs that are cold from the refrigerator, allow them to warm up to room temperature. Using a wooden spoon, gradually beat in about half the quantity of sifted sugar. Beat each addition in well before adding the next.

Continue beating until mixture becomes light and fluffy—it may take from 5–10 minutes, but it's worth the effort. Then add lemon juice, glycerine and remaining icing sugar, stirring in a little at a time. Sufficient sugar has been added when the icing holds up in peaks on the spoon—the quantity will vary depending on volume of egg whites. If you leave icing at any time during beating, cover with a damp cloth to prevent any crust forming on top.

Cover prepared icing with a damp cloth and leave for at least one hour before using. After this, you may find it is necessary to add a little more sugar as the icing may have softened a little while standing.

Using an electric mixer

A mixer is a great asset for preparing icing. Crack egg whites into the bowl, and turn mixer on low speed to break up the whites. Then add half the quantity of icing sugar gradually on lowest speed. Raise to a higher speed and beat for 5–8 minutes until light and fluffy.

Remove basin from mixer and beat in lemon juice, glycerine and remaining icing sugar by hand. It's important not to overmix the icing, otherwise too many air bubbles will spoil the surface finish. Allow icing to stand, covered with a damp cloth, for 1½–2 hours before using.

To ice the cake

With tip of a knife spread just a little icing on base of the cake and place on a suitably-sized silver board. Choose one about 2–3 in. larger in diameter than the original cake tin.

Place cake, now stuck to the silver board, on an upturned plate—this makes an excellent turntable for easy icing. Reserve a small amount of icing for the decoration, then spoon remainder on top of the cake. With a spatula or flat, round-bladed knife, spread icing over top and round sides. Smooth top of the cake level, using a circular movement, and holding the spatula upright smooth sides as evenly as possible.

There are two ways of getting the surface really flat. Either dip spatula into hot water, shake off any drips and smooth out any rough surfaces on the icing. Repeat this until the top and sides are smooth. Or, using a metal ruler, dip in hot water, shake to get rid of surplus moisture and, holding it firmly at each end at an angle of 45 degrees, draw it quickly and evenly over top of the cake towards you. Repeat if necessary until top of the cake is flat and smooth. To finish sides, dip a plastic scraper into cold water, shake off any surplus moisture, and, holding it at an angle sloping towards you, place against the side of the cake and revolve the cake. Finish off with a quick movement and repeat if necessary until the side is smooth.

Allow this base coat of icing to dry out before adding any further coats. Store surplus of reserved icing for decoration in a small basin covered with a damp cloth. A second coat of royal icing may be added in the same manner or, alternatively, a thin layer of transparent icing, *see page 182*. Allow finished cake to dry out for at least two days before decorating. This provides a firm base and any badly piped decoration can be carefully scraped off without any damage to the surface icing.

Decorating the cake

It is a good idea to draw your design on a piece of greaseproof paper first before starting on the cake. If you draw pattern to scale—using the cake tin as a guide—it can be placed on the top of the cake and

Clockwise from top left: leaf tube, petal, rose, shell, plain and ribbon

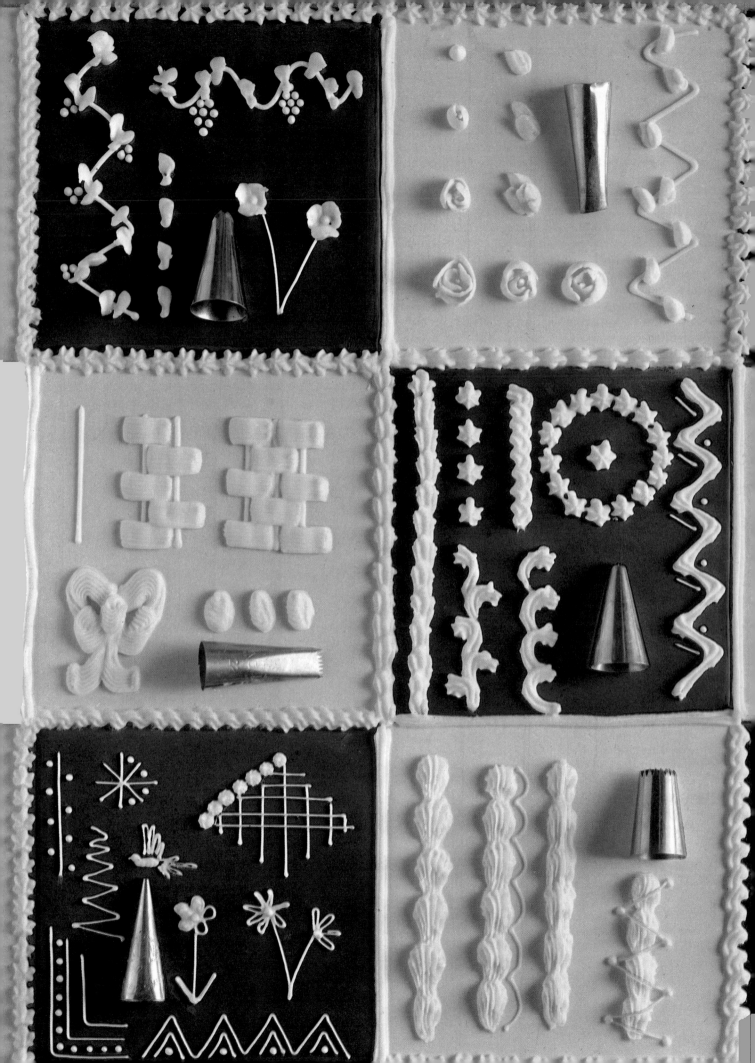

marked through with a clean pin to give a guide for piping.

Colour the icing if necessary before starting work. Add colouring very carefully—use the tip of a snipped straw or buy bottles of colouring with special drip tops.

The consistency of the icing is important—it should be soft enough to pipe easily, but firm enough to hold its shape. After adding colouring it is often necessary to add more icing sugar to stiffen icing again. When using writing pipes, icing can be slightly softer than when using star, or other pipes where piped icing must hold a design.

Prepare a paper piping bag with correct nozzle— and spoon in sufficient icing to half-fill the bag—an over-filled bag will burst easily. Fold over broad end and tuck in the sides. Make sure pipes are clean and free from any hardened icing, especially if the nozzle is very small. Always soak in boiling water after use and dry thoroughly before putting them away.

Begin to pipe close to, but not touching, the surface, and exert an even pressure all the time; the size of decoration depends on the amount of icing forced through the pipe. Stop pressing before lifting the pipe away from the decoration, otherwise you drag up the icing and spoil the design.

Any decoration piped on to the cake badly can be scraped off with a smooth knife blade as long as the surface icing is dry and firm.

It is not essential to have a large number of pipes for decorating. As shown in the colour picture one pipe can be used for several purposes, and a very satisfactory design may be piped using only a No. 3 writing pipe and a No. 6 star pipe.

Writing pipes

Numbers 1, 2 and 3 are fine, medium and thick, in that order. These pipes may be used for straight lines, loops or dots.

Star pipes

Numbers 6, 8, 13, 14, 19 and 21. The number of points in each varies. They may be used for stars, scrolls and shell edging.

Leaf pipes

Numbers 10 and 17. Use for leaves or ribbons of icing.

Ribbon pipes

Numbers 9, 22 and 25 are good for making ribbon or basket work designs. No. 12 is excellent for shell piping.

Petal pipes

Number 58—use for piping flowers. To make them: first pipe small 'knobs' of icing on squares of waxed paper and allow to dry. Place one at a time on an icing nail (or top of a colouring bottle) and, holding petal pipe with wide edge close to the surface, pipe petals round the centre knob. First two or three, then more, to build up the flower.

To make a paper piping bag

Cut a 10 in. square of greaseproof or silicone paper, diagonally across, to form triangles. Fold this, bringing the three points together so that they can be held in the same hand.

Secure points by folding them inwards twice, or use a paper clip to fasten them.

Cut off the tip of the paper cone, so that metal piping nozzle will protrude just a little when it is slipped inside the bag. Bags made from greaseproof paper should be renewed each time; those of silicone paper may be used over again.

Transparent icing

YOU WILL NEED FOR ONE 6–8 IN. CAKE:

> 1 lb. granulated sugar
> ½ pint water
> squeeze of lemon juice

Measure sugar and water together into a saucepan and stir over low heat until sugar has dissolved. Raise heat and bring to the boil. Cook until a temperature of 240 degrees is reached on your sugar thermometer—takes about 5 minutes—or until a small amount spooned into a saucepan of cold water forms a very soft ball.

Draw pan off heat and pour syrup into a clean, wet basin. Add lemon juice and stir gently until mixture becomes cloudy, then pour over cake or first coat of icing.

This icing is ideal for use over a first coat of royal icing and gives an excellent, smooth finish.

Alternative icings
Boiled icing

YOU WILL NEED FOR ONE 8–9 IN. CAKE:

> 1 lb. granulated sugar
> ¼ pint water
> 2 tablespoons lemon juice

Measure sugar and water into a pan, and stir over low heat until sugar has dissolved. Then bring to the boil and cook rapidly until the syrup reaches 240 degrees on a sugar boiling thermometer—about 5 minutes after mixture boils.

Draw pan off the heat and pour syrup into a mixing basin. Add lemon juice and allow to stand 5 minutes. Then stir until the mixture begins to thicken and turn white. When it is thick enough to coat the back of a spoon without running off, pour over the cake and spread quickly where necessary with a palette knife dipped in hot water.

Add any decoration immediately.

Fondant icing

Continue beating until the icing goes quite hard and rough. Turn out on to a working surface and knead until smooth. This icing may be stored in a screw-topped jar. To use, melt over very low heat until soft, add 1–2 tablespoons sugar syrup (dissolve 2 tablespoons sugar in 1 tablespoon water). Pour over cake.

Satin icing paste

YOU WILL NEED TO COVER ONE 8 IN. CAKE:

> 12–16 oz. icing sugar
> pinch cream of tartar
> 1 teaspoon lemon juice
> 1 egg white

Sieve icing sugar and cream of tartar on to a square of greaseproof paper. In a mixing basin lightly mix the lemon juice and egg white, then gradually beat in enough icing sugar to make a stiff paste. Turn on to a clean working surface and knead in remaining icing sugar. Knead for 2–3 minutes until smooth and then set aside, covered with a damp cloth for 1 hour before using.

Roll out on a surface well dusted with icing sugar to a circle large enough to cover the top and a little of the sides of the cake. Place over cake and using the hands—dusted well with icing sugar—mould icing smoothly over top and down sides of the cake. Leave 2–3 days to dry out before decorating.

American frosting

YOU WILL NEED FOR ONE 6–8 IN. CAKE:

> 1 lb. granulated sugar
> ¼ pint water
> 2 large egg whites

Measure sugar and water into a saucepan and stir over low heat until sugar has dissolved completely. Raise heat and bring to the boil. Cook rapidly to a temperature of 240 degrees, if you have a sugar boiling thermometer or until a little, spooned into a saucepan of cold water, forms a soft ball.

Draw pan of boiling syrup off the heat and allow to cool slightly while whisking egg whites until very stiff. Pour syrup slowly on to egg whites, beating all the time. It is easier if someone can add the syrup for you while you whisk. Beat until the frosting is thick and fluffy then spoon on to the cake and spread roughly over the surface. This icing sets very quickly—so any decoration should be added at once. Never try to get a smooth finish with this icing unless you have had a lot of practice.

Royal icing for top and sides.

Follow the basic method.

Ingredients	6 in.	7 in.	8 in.	9 in.	10 in.	11 in.	12 in.
Whites of eggs	1	2	2	3	3	4	4
Icing sugar (sifted)	½ lb.	1 lb.	1 lb.	1½ lb.	1½ lb.	2 lb.	2 lb.
Glycerine	½ tsp.	1 tsp.	1 tsp.	1½ tsp.	1½ tsp.	2 tsp.	2 tsp.
Colouring as required							

For anniversaries and celebrations

Make your cake well in advance so that you can allow plenty of time for the almond paste to dry out before putting on the basic coat of icing; and this must set before piping on a design.

Cakes with a rich fruit base will keep well for many weeks. If, however, you should want a less rich cake, perhaps for children, a Dundee or Madeira recipe would be ideal.

Royal icing is most popular for a complicated decoration since it has a good consistency for piped design.

Design and colour

Take care in the selection of a design. A simple decoration is best unless you have had a good deal of practice. Alternatively, plan a design that can be prepared off the cake and then attached with a little soft royal icing. A good example of this is the birthday cake on page 184, where only the top edge is actually piped on the surface. Either way plan the design *before* you start.

Colour adds a great deal to the finished appearance. Use delicate pastel shades; strong colours should be used only in small quantities.

Add the colouring when the icing is newly made. Use colours that are concentrated so that only a little is required. Too much will soften the icing and make it impossible to use. Yellow, blue and red are the most useful, as most other colours can be mixed from these. Yellow and blue make green, add more blue or yellow according to the shade of green you require. Yellow, blue and red make brown, and red with a little yellow makes a pretty holly red or orange.

Always make sure the icing is of the correct consistency before beginning to pipe, particularly when colouring has been added. The icing should be sufficiently soft to pipe easily yet firm enough to hold its shape. Practise piping inscriptions and rosettes on a plate first, following the design you have chosen. If the icing is too soft empty the bag, return icing to the bowl, and beat in a little more sifted icing sugar. If on the other hand it is too stiff, add a little lemon juice and beat icing thoroughly.

Left to right: designs for wedding, christening, Christmas, birthday and anniversary cakes

Piping separate letters and decorations

This method is particularly useful for names or greetings to be placed on a cake. First trace or draw a simple and clear outline of the design you wish to pipe. It should be the actual size you wish to use. Place design under a sheet of waxed paper and pin down securely with 2 or 3 drawing pins. Using royal icing and a No. 2 plain pipe, pipe the outline only, following the tracing under the paper. When completed move the tracing paper—never the one with the actual piping, and repeat. Follow this procedure as many times as necessary for the decoration, pipe a few extra to allow for breakages.

Now, using the same icing, soften with a little water or lemon juice and spoon back into a paper piping-bag, no tube this time. Snip a tiny piece off the end of the bag and pipe soft icing into the outline, filling it completely. Leave at least 24 hours to set firm then, very carefully, peel away paper. Touch back of each piece with a little soft royal icing and place on the cake surface.

Marzipan modelling

For flowers, leaves and holly berry sprays modelled in marzipan you will find full instructions on page 179.

Sugar paste roses

Any flowers modelled with this paste are stronger than marzipan but are not edible. The whiteness of the paste also allows for more delicate shades of colouring.

Add 1 teaspoon powdered gum tragacanth (available from most chemists) to 1 teacup of royal icing then knead until smooth and blended. Shape a small pointed centre for the rose about 1½ in. high and flatten slightly at the base.

With finger-tips, shape petals from small pieces of icing and pinch the edges until very thin. Dip inside base of petal in a little beaten egg-white and wrap around centre stem of the rose. Continue making petals, small ones at first then larger ones towards the outside. Curve tip of each leaf outwards like a rose.

When finished allow rose to dry until it begins to harden, then cut away from its base. Stick on to the cake with a little beaten egg-white. Cut diamond shapes for leaves and mark leaf veins.

Christmas cake

Using an 8 in. round cake base, cover sides only with green royal icing, reserving a little for decoration. With a No. 2 plain tube and white royal icing, pipe an outline round the sides for fairly large white icicles—*see colour picture*. Using softer royal icing, fill in first the icicles round the sides, then cover the top of the cake completely with white icing. Leave to set firm, then decorate the top with a Christmas tree cut from green marzipan, and pipe green stars on the white surface with reserved green royal icing and No. 1 plain icing tube. Around the base of the cake pipe stars of green royal icing, using a No. 8 star tube.

Alternative decorations

Cover cake with smooth surface of royal icing and pipe a simple design to cover edges, then decorate sides and top with marzipan holly leaves and berries—*see instructions on page 179*. Pipe MERRY CHRISTMAS. Alternatively, frost roughly with American icing and decorate only with a red ribbon bow and a candle or with Christmas figures and trees to make a snow scene.

Anniversary cake

Using a square or round 8 in. cake base, pipe a basket design, using a ribbon tube with serrated edge and royal icing. Pipe around top edge with rosettes, using No. 8 star pipe, and arrange a bunch of marzipan carnations in pink and yellow—*see instructions on page 179*—on the top of the cake. Pipe the number in gold—and place in one corner.

Alternative decorations

Have a plain, smooth finish to the cake and for a golden wedding cake pipe roses in yellow for decoration on top and sides. Around the base of the cake fasten a gold or yellow band. For a silver wedding, pipe a white decoration; add silver horseshoes and leaves and tie a silver band round the cake.

Decorating the celebration cake can be a leisurely job and you needn't worry about the icing becoming hard. All you need to do is keep it in a basin covered with a damp cloth; this will prevent any crust forming on the surface. Icing will keep this way for two or three days and even longer if you put it in a screw-topped jar in the refrigerator.

Birthday cake

Using an 8 in. round cake base, coat top and sides with yellow royal icing. Reserve any extra icing for decoration. To make circus decorations, trace animals, hats and other suitable items from a child's painting book. Outline in red icing, fill in with yellow—*see page 186, for decorations and letters.* Leave to set, then stick high up round sides of the cake with soft royal icing. Pipe a scroll border in yellow icing, using No. 8 star tube, round top edges and tie a yellow ribbon round base of cake. The name can be piped in red, using No. 2 plain tube—*see directions for letters.* For candle-holders pipe whorls of yellow royal icing on to squares of waxed paper, push a red or yellow candle into the centre of each and leave to dry. Peel off the paper and with a little soft icing or beaten egg white stick to cake top.

Alternative decorations

Use other colours and themes, perhaps flowers for a girl, motor cars or animals for a boy—trace the required designs from children's books. For a 21st birthday use a more sophisticated design and include heather sprays, silver horseshoes or piped roses for a girl.

Wedding cake

Using a 12 in. base and an 8 in. tier, cover both with a smooth finish of royal icing. Prepare approximately 14 white piped roses and pipe about 12 or 14 horse-shoes in white—*see instructions on page 186.* With white royal icing and No. 8 star tube, pipe a scroll border around top edge of both cakes. Attach piped roses at intervals—eight round bottom tier and six round the top. With plain No. 2 tube, pipe a loop decoration between flowers—*see picture on page 184*— and plain dots running down from the base of each rose. Tie white satin ribbons round base of each tier, arrange the piped horseshoes at intervals and pipe stars, using No. 8 tube, around base.
Place 3 or 4 pillars in the centre of the lower tier on a thin, silver cake-board, and pipe with royal icing round the base of each to secure firmly. Then place the 8 in. tier on top. If you wish, after covering the cake with almond paste and before coating with royal icing, cut a slice in the cake but do not remove it. Cover with royal icing and mark some sort of pattern for a guide when later cutting the cake. Unless the cake is expected to be very difficult to cut or icing very hard this is not usually necessary.

Alternative decorations

Use a simple design with piped royal icing roses following the design for the christening cake; or pipe a plain scroll border round the top and bottom edges, decorate with silver shoes, horseshoes, sprays of orange blossom, white heather or silver bells. Tie white satin ribbon round the centre of each tier.

Christening cake

Using an 8 in. round cake base, cover with white royal icing. Using a No. 1 or 2 plain tube, pipe a trellis design round the sides, finishing the edges with plain dots. In the centre a cluster of roses enclosed in a dome of raised trellis. For the trellis design, use No. 1 or 2 plain tube, and pipe over the rounded side of 2 or 3 patty or tartlet tins. Lightly grease tins first with vegetable fat. Leave to set firm, then hold tins over a steaming kettle and when loose lift the trellis design off very carefully with two needles. Arrange a pattern of pink roses round the sides and tie a white and pink ribbon round the base of the cake. Place a stork or other suitable decoration in the cake centre with the name of the baby.

Alternative decorations

Pipe in blue or yellow for a boy.

Cutting the cake

After removing tiers (if a wedding cake), and using a strong, sharp knife, cut the cake, whether round or square, completely in half. Cut each half into quarters, then proceed to cut into slices about ½ in. thick and then down into suitable pieces for eating. *Never* attempt to cut slices across the whole cake.

Tying on ribbon

For a really handsome bow, first pin a single length of ribbon round the cake. Then tie a bow separately, using a shorter piece of ribbon, and pin this over the join of the first piece of ribbon.

ALL ABOUT
Pastry

Perfect shortcrust pastry

When preparing pastry everything, including the ingredients, must be kept cool.

Self-raising or plain flour can be used, but plain flour gives a crisper, shorter pastry. It should always be used for a rich shortcrust, where self-raising flour used with egg tends to make the pastry too crumbly and rough.

Always bake pastry in a fairly hot oven, unless a particular recipe instructs otherwise. The richer the pastry the hotter the oven is the general rule.

Work quickly and lightly—over-worked pastry is tough and hard. Once prepared, allow your pastry to rest in a cool place at least 10 minutes before using. This means less shrinkage during baking.

When a recipe says 4 oz. of pastry, it doesn't mean the total weight of the pastry, it means the weight of the flour used. The remaining proportions should be half the weight of fat to flour, and milk or water to mix.

Using the tips of the fingers, gently break the fat into small lumps, then begin to rub it into the flour in order to blend the two together very finely and thoroughly. To 'rub in' means to pick up small handfuls of fat and flour and rub very lightly with the thumbs and fingers so that the mixture falls back through the fingers into the mixing basin. This action not only blends together the fat and flour but also incorporates air which helps to make a light pastry. It's important not to overmix the pastry at any stage, and rubbing in should stop when the mixture looks crumbly.

Add the liquid all at once into the centre of the mixture. Blend, using a fork, until the mixture clings together in a ball, leaving the sides of the mixing basin clean.

Turn the dough on to a lightly-floured surface and knead lightly to make a smooth, fairly stiff dough. Set the pastry to rest for 10 minutes before use.

Plain shortcrust

YOU WILL NEED FOR 4 OZ. PASTRY:

> 4 oz. (or 4 rounded tablespoons) plain flour
> pinch of salt
> 2 oz. mixed fats
> 2 tablespoons milk or water to mix

Sift together flour and salt. Measure the fat on to a plate. Butter or margarine and vegetable fat are the best combination, using equal quantites of each. Using a knife blade, beat down the fats and mix until soft and blended. Add in a lump to the flour.

Sweet shortcrust

YOU WILL NEED FOR 4 OZ. PASTRY:

> 4 oz. (or 4 rounded tablespoons) plain flour
> pinch of salt
> 2 oz. mixed fats
> 1 level tablespoon castor sugar mixed with
> 1½ level tablespoons of milk

Prepare the pastry following basic shortcrust instructions. Use it to make sweet pies, tarts, flans and turnovers.

Ingredients for shortcrust pastry

Rich shortcrust or biscuit crust

YOU WILL NEED FOR 4 OZ. PASTRY:

4 oz. (or 4 rounded tablespoons) plain flour
pinch of salt
2½ oz. butter or margarine
1 oz. castor sugar mixed with
1 tablespoon egg or egg and milk

Prepare the pastry following basic instructions. Use for rich tartlet cases, fruit, flans and biscuit bases.

Cheese pastry

YOU WILL NEED FOR 4 OZ. PASTRY:

4 oz. (or 4 rounded tablespoons) plain flour
pinch of salt and cayenne pepper
2 oz. mixed fats or butter
1 oz. finely grated cheese
2–3 tablespoons milk or egg and milk

Prepare the pastry following basic instructions, adding cheese before liquid. Use for savoury flans and tartlets.

Using the pastry

Always pat the ball of dough into a small edition of the shape you want—this makes for easier working and less waste. Roll out with light, quick, forward, strokes, turning the pastry round as you work but never over—the underneath side, which is always the smoothest, will be the pastry top.

Use as little flour as possible when you work. Flour the rolling pin rather than the pastry. Avoid stretching the pastry as this means shrinkage later on. Preheat the oven to hot, or fairly hot according to the recipes used.

Cheese straws

MAKES 2½–3 DOZEN

Prepare 4 oz. cheese pastry, adding an extra 1 oz. grated cheese (Parmesan is best, Cheddar next). Mix to a stiff dough with beaten egg and milk. Roll pastry until about ¼ in. thick. From one corner cut out about six 1½ in. rings. Cut remaining pastry into 2 in. strips, then into thin straws. Place straws and rings on a greased baking tray and bake in the centre of a hot oven (400 deg. or Gas No. 6) for 8–10 minutes or until pale golden brown. While still warm dip the ends in paprika pepper and slip straws into rings.

Lemon meringue pie

YOU WILL NEED FOR 4 SERVINGS:

4 oz. sweet shortcrust pastry
FOR THE FILLING:
1 oz. (3 heaped teaspoons) cornflour
4 oz. (4 rounded tablespoons) castor sugar
¼ pint water
1 lemon
1 egg yolk
single cream for serving
FOR THE MERINGUE:
1 egg white
1½ oz. (2 level tablespoons) castor sugar

Prepare the pastry following basic instructions. Turn out onto a floured working surface, knead lightly and then roll out to a circle large enough to line a greased 6–7-inch flan case or shallow sponge cake tin. Line tin with pastry and place a piece of crumpled foil in the centre to keep the shape. Place in centre of a hot oven (400 deg. or Gas No. 6). Bake for 10 minutes, removing foil a few minutes before end of cooking time. Place baked flan case on a baking tray and set aside while preparing filling. Measure cornflour and sugar into a small saucepan. Stir in the water gradually and mix well to blend. Add finely grated lemon rind, place over a moderate heat, stirring all the time until thickened and boiling. Cook for 1 minute, then draw pan off heat. Stir in lemon juice and then egg yolk. Pour mixture into prepared pie case. Whisk egg white until stiff, add half sugar and whisk again. Gently fold in remaining sugar and spoon meringue on to pie. Return pie to oven above centre and leave 10–12 minutes until golden brown. Serve warm or chilled with single cream.

Syrup plate tart and jam tarts

YOU WILL NEED FOR 6 SERVINGS:

8 oz. plain (or sweet) shortcrust pastry (use double the
   ingredients in basic recipe)
FOR THE SYRUP FILLING:
3–4 tablespoons golden syrup
2 oz. (or 4 rounded tablespoons) fresh white breadcrumbs
little grated lemon rind
1 tablespoon lemon juice

Using about two-thirds of the pastry for the large tart, roll it out on a lightly floured surface, until about 10 in. in diameter. Grease a 9 in. pie plate and cover it with the pastry. Easiest way to do this is to lie the rolling pin lightly on top of the pastry and fold pastry over it. Lift the pin and lay the pastry on to the pie plate. Press with the thumbs from the centre to exclude air.

Trim away any extra pastry from the edge. To make a pretty edge, make regular slits about 1 in. apart round the pastry rim. Fold each small section in half diagonally.

Gently warm the syrup. Draw the pan off the heat and add all remaining ingredients for the filling. Blend well and pour into the centre of the lined pie plate and spread evenly. Re-roll the pastry trimmings and cut into thin strips. Use these to make a criss-cross lattice topping. Place the pie just above centre in a hot oven (400 deg. or Gas No. 6) and bake for 30 minutes or until pastry is golden brown. If your oven gets very hot you would be well advised to lower the heat to 380 deg. or Gas No. 5 after 20 minutes.

This tart may also have a jam, marmalade or mince-meat filling.

To make the jam tarts: Roll out the remaining pastry very thinly and using a round cutter about 2½ in. diameter, stamp out about 8–9 rounds. Fit into small tart tins, prick the base of each, and add a teaspoonful of jam. Roll out any trimmings thinly and cut narrow strips to decorate the tops.

Place above centre in a fairly hot oven (380 deg. or Gas No. 5) and bake for 15 minutes.

Maids of honour

YOU WILL NEED FOR 12 MAIDS OF HONOUR:

4 oz. sweet shortcrust pastry
little red jam
FOR THE FILLING:
3 oz. (or 3 rounded tablespoons) castor sugar
2 oz. (or 2 heaped tablespoons) ground almonds
1½ oz. butter, melted
½ egg
finely grated rind and juice of 1 lemon

On a lightly floured working surface, roll the pastry out thinly and line 12 tartlet moulds. Place a little red jam in the base of each.

For the filling, mix together the sugar and ground almonds in a small mixing basin. Stir in the melted butter, lightly mixed egg, lemon rind and juice (to measure half an egg, lightly beat one whole egg in a teacup, then measure out half the mixture into your ingredients).

Drop the filling by teaspoonfuls into each lined tartlet case. Place in the centre of a moderately hot oven (380 deg. or Gas No. 5) and bake for 15–20 minutes.

Raisin custard tart

YOU WILL NEED FOR 4 SERVINGS:

4 oz. sweet shortcrust pastry
1 tablespoon seedless raisins
FOR THE FILLING:
2 eggs, slightly beaten
1½ oz. (or 3 level tablespoons) castor sugar
¼ level teaspoon salt
½ teaspoon vanilla essence
½ pint milk
pinch nutmeg

To make this tart you must first bake the pastry blind. Follow these instructions carefully and you shouldn't have any difficulty. Place a lightly greased 7 in. flan ring (plain or fluted) on a greased baking tray. For a pie use a 7 in. shallow sponge cake tin. On a lightly floured surface roll out the pastry and fit in into the ring shape, taking care not to stretch it. Run the rolling pin over the top to cut away the excess pastry. Prick the base of the flan with a fork. (Use a similar method with the sponge tin but cut away excess pastry with a knife)

Line flan or pie with a square of greaseproof paper and over this sprinkle a layer of rice, macaroni or dried haricot beans—store them in a jar and always use them for this purpose. Place in the centre of a hot oven (400 deg. or Gas No. 6) and bake for 8–10 minutes.

To make the filling combine together the eggs, sugar, salt and vanilla essence in a mixing basin. Bring the milk almost up to boiling point, draw the pan off the heat and stir into the egg mixture.

Take the paper and contents out of the baked pastry case and lift off flan ring. Or remove pastry from sponge cake tin. Return the baked case to the baking tray and sprinkle with raisins. Strain the custard filling into the pie shell and sprinkle with grated nutmeg.

Replace the pie just above centre in a very hot oven (445 deg. or Gas No. 8) for about 5 minutes, then reduce the temperature to hot (425 deg. or Gas No. 7) and bake for a further 10–15 minutes or until custard filling has set. Serve cut in wedges either warm or chilled with cream.

Suet crust and raised pies

Suet pastry needs no rubbing in – just add the shredded or finely chopped suet to the flour and stir in the water. Use half the weight of suet to flour and enough liquid to mix to a firm, scone-like dough (about ¼ pint for every 8 oz. flour). Steaming suet puddings give the best results. To steam cover the puddings with double thickness greaseproof paper, fold in a pleat to allow the pudding to rise, and tie tightly.

Have the steamer ready before pudding is mixed. If a proper steamer is not available, the pudding can be partly steamed in an ordinary saucepan – by standing it on an old saucer, rounded side up, with just enough boiling water to reach half-way up the pudding basin.

Cover pan with tightly fitting lid and steam gently for required time; water should be topped up occasionally with extra boiling water. An even quicker method is to pressure cook – follow the manufacturers instructions or general instructions. Place pudding in cooker on the trivet with ¼ pint of boiling water for every ¼ hour's cooking time plus ½ pint.

Cover with a lid and place over moderate heat. Allow to steam for 15 minutes, then bring up to 5 lb. pressure and cook for 35 minutes (if enamel or aluminium bowls are used); for china or oven glass allow extra 10 minutes.

Reduce cooker pressure slowly, then take pudding out of the steamer, leave for 1–2 minutes to allow it to shrink from the sides of the basin before turning it out.

Suet crust pastry

YOU WILL NEED FOR 8 OZ. PASTRY:

8 oz. self-raising flour (or plain flour plus
   1 level teaspoon baking powder)
½ level teaspoon salt
4 oz. shredded or finely chopped beef suet
about ¼ pint water to mix

Sift together the flour (and baking powder if used) and the salt into a mixing basin. Add the suet and stir in the water, enough to mix to a scone-like dough, firm enough to be rolled out. Turn on to a lightly-floured working surface and knead lightly to a smooth dough. The pastry should be used immediately.

Steak, kidney and mushroom pudding

YOU WILL NEED FOR 4 SERVINGS:

8 oz. suet pastry
FOR THE FILLING:
1½ lb. chuck or buttock steak
¼ lb. ox kidney
a little seasoned flour
lard or dripping for frying
1 level teaspoon salt
¼ lb. mushrooms, sliced
1 onion, finely chopped
little stock, or water plus stock cube

Prepare the filling. Trim away any fat and gristle and cut the meat in cubes. With scissors, snip out the core and cut the kidney into pieces. Roll the meat and kidney in seasoned flour and fry quickly in hot fat to seal all the edges. Drain and add the salt, mushrooms and onion.

Prepare the suet pastry as described in the basic recipe. Set aside one quarter of the pastry for the top. Roll out the remainder to a large circle and fit to the base and sides of a well greased 1½–2 pint pudding basin. Allow any extra to overlap the edge. Add the meat mixture to fill the basin and enough stock to moisten. Roll out the reserved piece of pastry to make a lid, damp the edges and fit over the top. Press edges well together to seal, and trim away any excess pastry with a knife.

Cover with greased double thickness greaseproof paper (remember to fold a pleat across the centre to allow the pastry to rise). Tie securely with string and cover with an extra layer of kitchen foil — it's a good idea to make a string handle over the basin to make the pudding easier to handle while hot.

Steam briskly for 3–3½ hours, refilling the steamer with boiling water as required. Serve hot with extra gravy and a vegetable.

This method of lining the basin remains the same for fresh fruit puddings. Use 1–1½ lb. of any fresh fruit in season, plus 4–6 oz. castor sugar and 2–3 tablespoons water. Cover and steam briskly for 2 hours, then serve pudding hot with custard.

Steak, kidney and mushroom pudding, veal and ham pie and miniature pork pie

Syrup layer pudding

YOU WILL NEED FOR 4 SERVINGS:

> 8 oz. suet pastry
> FOR THE FILLING:
> 8 oz. syrup
> 2 oz. fresh white breadcrumbs
> finely grated rind of half a lemon

Make the suet pastry as described in the basic recipe. Divide the pastry into 4 unequal pieces, the smallest being just large enough to cover the base of the basin.

Warm the syrup in a pan over low heat to soften. Draw the pan off the heat and stir in the breadcrumbs and lemon rind.

Grease a 2–pint pudding basin and cover the base with the smallest piece of pastry. Spoon over this a third of the syrup mixture. Roll or pat out the second smallest piece of pastry and place in the basin over the syrup filling. Top with a layer of syrup mixture and a third piece of pastry. Each pastry layer should completely cover the syrup mixture and fit the basin exactly. Top with remaining syrup and final layer of pastry.

Cover with double thickness greased greaseproof paper, folding in a deep pleat to allow for expansion. Tie securely and steam for 2½–3 hours. Turn out and serve with a hot custard sauce.

This pudding is equally delicious made with a filling of jam, mincemeat or marmalade.

Bacon roll

YOU WILL NEED FOR 4 SERVINGS:

> 8 oz. suet pastry
> FOR THE FILLING:
> 1 large onion
> 1 level teaspoon powdered sage
> ½ level teaspoon salt and pinch pepper
> 3 oz. (1 rounded teacup) fresh white breadcrumbs
> 1 oz. margarine
> 4 back bacon rashers

First prepare the filling. Peel and halve the onion. Place it in a pan and cover with cold water, bring to the boil and simmer for 30 minutes. Drain and coarsely chop the onion and add to the sage, salt, pepper and breadcrumbs. Stir in the melted margarine and blend the ingredients lightly with a fork. Trim the bacon rashers and set the filling aside while preparing the roll.

Prepare the pastry as in the basic recipe. Roll out on a lightly-floured surface to an oblong about 12 in. by 8 in. Arrange the bacon rashers over the surface and spread with the stuffing within 1 in. of the edges. Moisten the edges of the pastry and roll into a roly-poly about 8 in. long. Pinch the ends to seal.

Wrap in greased double thickness greaseproof paper, folding the paper in a large pleat the length of the roll to allow for expansion. Then wrap loosely in kitchen foil or in a pudding cloth and tie ends securely. Steam for 2 hours.

Serve slices of the bacon roll with tomato sauce and grilled mushrooms.

Baked suet crust

Prepare the suet pastry as in the basic recipe. On a lightly floured working surface roll out and use as instructed in the recipe you are following. Or use to cover sweet or savoury pies (use tinned or cooked fruit or meat fillings). Place in the centre of a moderately hot oven (380 deg. or Gas No. 5) and bake for 20–25 minutes.

Raised pie or hot water crust is one of the few pastries that needs warmth during mixing. The hot pastry is moulded with the fingers into the desired shape, then filled with a meat mixture and baked. The art of this pastry lies in the moulding. This may be done in a proper raised pie mould, round a 2 lb. jam jar, or simply by hand. Where the pastry is to be shaped by hand without using a mould, it must be slightly stiffer in order to keep its shape while it is being baked. Raised pies are usually eaten cold.

Hot water crust

YOU WILL NEED FOR 12 OZ. PASTRY:

> 12 oz. (or 12 rounded tablespoons) plain flour
> 1 level teaspoon salt
> 4½ oz. lard
> 1½ gills (about 10 good tablespoons) mixed
>   milk and water

Sift together flour and salt into a mixing basin. Set in a warm place while preparing the remaining ingredients. Measure the lard and mixed milk and water into a small saucepan and place over moderate heat. Bring gradually to the boil and when it is boiling rapidly pour *immediately* into the centre of the warmed flour.

Beat well with a wooden spoon until the mixture clings together in a ball, leaving the sides of the basin clean. Turn out on to a wooden board and knead well to a smooth dough.

If the mixture is too soft and hot for moulding, leave to cool a few minutes and it will stiffen up. It's important, however, to work this dough while it is still hot and pliable. If left to get too cold before handling it will crack badly and become difficult to work. Keep the pastry warm and soft, by placing under the hot, upturned mixing basin.

Veal and ham pie in a raised pie mould

YOU WILL NEED FOR 4–6 SERVINGS:

12 oz. hot water crust pastry
FOR THE FILLING:
1–1½ lb. lean veal
½ lb. gammon
1 level teaspoon salt
pinch of pepper
finely grated rind of half a lemon
1 tablespoon chopped parsley
1 hard-boiled egg
1 dessertspoon gelatine dissolved in ¼ pint stock
beaten egg and milk to coat

First prepare the filling. Cut away any fat from the veal and gammon and cut the meat into small pieces. Add the salt, pepper, lemon rind and chopped parsley and set aside while preparing the pastry.

Heavily grease the raised pie mould with lard and place on a well-greased baking tray. Prepare the pastry as in the basic recipe and set aside a small piece for the lid. Knead the remaining pastry out to about ½ in. thick and place in the base of the mould. Using the knuckles, press the pastry from the centre to the sides to get rid of any air bubbles. When the base is covered mould the pastry up the sides. Keep the four fingers of both hands inside the tin and, with the thumbs, press the pastry to the shape of the tin. Make sure there is no thick layer between the base and sides of the mould, and that the pastry has not been pressed too thinly on the sides. Bring the pastry up to overlap the top rim.

Pack in half of the filling, then place the shelled hard-boiled egg in the centre and cover with remaining filling. Roll out reserved piece of pastry for the lid. Damp the edges of the pie and cover with the lid. Press the edges well together to seal, and trim away excess pastry.

Reroll the trimmings and cut leaves. Make a small hole in the centre of the lid, brush the top with beaten egg and milk and arrange leaves. Place in the centre of a hot oven (400 deg. or Gas No. 6). After 20 minutes, lower the heat to moderate (355 deg. or Gas No. 4) and bake for a further 2–2½ hours. During baking, brush occasionally with beaten egg and milk, to make pastry a shiny brown. After 1½ hours, carefully remove the mould, brush the sides of the pie with egg and milk and replace in the oven.

Allow the baked pie to cool, then pour through the hole in the centre cool, but not set, jellied stock.

If you haven't a raised pie mould, shape pastry round a 2 lb. jam jar.

Miniature pork pie

YOU WILL NEED FOR 2 SERVINGS:

FOR THE PASTRY:
4 oz. (or 4 rounded tablespoons) plain flour
½ level teaspoon salt
1½ oz. lard
2 full tablespoons water
FOR THE FILLING:
½ lb. seasoned pork sausage meat
pinch powdered sage
1 hard-boiled egg

To prepare the filling. Add the sage to the sausage meat and with lightly floured hands, shape the meat round the hard-boiled egg.

Prepare the hot water crust pastry following the basic directions. Reserving a small piece for the lid, shape the remainder into a circle.

Flatten out the centre to make the base and shape the edge of the pastry up to start the sides. Pinch the edge between the thumb and first finger. Place the shaped filling in the centre and gradually work the pastry up round the sides to cover it. Roll out the reserved piece to make a lid, damp the edges and cover the pie. Flute the edges in a turret border and decorate with leaves made from pastry trimmings. Make a small hole in the centre and fix a band of greased double thickness greaseproof paper around the sides. Place the pie on a baking tray and brush with beaten egg and milk.

Bake as for the veal and ham pie, but remove the paper band after 30 minutes. Cook for a further 30 minutes (a total of 1 hour).

Serve hot with a green vegetable or grilled tomatoes; or cold with a salad. Each pie can be cut in half and will serve 2 portions.

Rough puff and flaky pastry

These pastries have a crisp, flaky texture and will give your baking a professional touch—though they are surprisingly easy to make! A high proportion of fat is used and the pastry is rolled and folded several times so that it will rise well in a hot oven. Butter gives a good flavour and colour to the pastry, but a mixture of butter or margarine and lard may be used. When preparing the recipes you may use either rough puff or flaky pastry, though I have stated my own preferences. There are four important points to remember: Never make flaky or rough puff pastry at the last moment. It is important that the dough should rest between rollings in a very cool place, otherwise there will be a good deal of shrinkage in the baking. Lemon juice or vinegar is used with the liquid to counteract the richness caused by the high proportion of fat contained in the recipe. All edges must be cut with a sharp knife to release the layers and allow the pastry to rise. This type of rich pastry should always be cooked on a baking tray which has been rinsed with cold water. The steam which will rise from the tray in the hot oven will make the pastry rise better.

Rough puff pastry

YOU WILL NEED FOR 8 OZ. PASTRY:

    8 oz. (or 8 rounded tablespoons) plain flour
    ½ level teaspoon salt
    6 oz. butter or equal quantities mixed margarine and lard
    ¼ pint (about 8 tablespoons) cold water to mix
    1 teaspoon vinegar or lemon juice

Sieve flour and salt into a mixing basin. Cream butter (or blend margarine and lard) until even in texture, then form into lumps about the size of walnuts. If the fat is very soft, cool for a while until it becomes a little firmer.
Add the lumps of fat to the sieved flour, then stir in the mixed water and lemon juice or vinegar. Mix with a round-ended knife until the dough begins to cling together. Draw the mixture together gently

with the fingers and turn out on to a lightly-floured board.
Shape into a rectangle, then roll into an oblong strip. Mark the pastry into thirds, fold one end up and the other down over it—envelope style. Press the ends together to seal.
Give the pastry a half turn clockwise, so that the sealed edges are top and bottom. Repeat the rolling, folding and turning 4 times more, leaving the pastry to rest for at least 10 minutes between each alternate rolling. Then set the finished pastry aside to rest for 20 minutes before you use it.

Cheesy tomato pasties

YOU WILL NEED FOR 8 PASTIES

    8 oz. rough puff pastry
    FOR THE FILLING:
    2 large tomatoes
    1 egg
    1 tablespoon breadcrumbs
    2 oz. (or 4 heaped tablespoons) grated cheese
    1 tablespoon grated onion
    seasoning

Roll the pastry out to an oblong about ¼ in. thick and cut into 8 squares. Leave the pastry to rest and prepare the filling.
To do this, plunge the tomatoes into boiling water for 1 minute, then peel off the skins. Remove the seeds and chop the pulp.
In a mixing basin blend tomato with egg, breadcrumbs, cheese, onion and a seasoning of salt and pepper. Divide the mixture evenly between the pastry squares, putting it in one triangular half. Damp the pastry edges and fold other half over cornerwise.
Press the two edges gently together to seal, mark gently with the prongs of a fork, and then make two slits on the top of each with scissors.
Arrange the pasties on a baking tray which has been rinsed in cold water and place just above centre in a very hot oven (425 deg. or Gas No. 7) and bake for 10 minutes. Reduce the heat to hot (375 deg. or Gas No. 5) and bake for a further 20 minutes.
For a change try sweet pasties made with a filling of stewed or sweetened apple or half a ring of pineapple. They can be eaten hot, or make a delicious addition to a packed lunch.

From the top clockwise: lemon puffs, cheese and tomato pasties, eccles cakes, vanilla slices, sausage rolls and large fruit pie

Fruit pie

YOU WILL NEED FOR 4 SERVINGS:

> 1 lb. fresh fruit (or tinned or bottled fruit)
> 2–3 oz. castor sugar
> 2–3 tablespoons water or fruit juice
> 8 oz. rough puff pastry

Prepare the fruit (use any fresh fruit in season, or tinned or bottled fruit) and place in a 1–1½ pint pie dish—deep and with a rim. Add the sugar and water (use fruit juice if using tinned or bottled fruit).

On a floured board roll the pastry out to a thickness of ¼ in. and make it at least 1½ in. larger than the pie dish all round. Cut off this extra piece and place strips of it on the greased rim of the pie dish. Damp this border and place over it the pastry lid. Press gently round the edge to seal, and trim off any surplus pastry. Flake the edges, using a sharp knife, and mark neatly with the back of the knife.

Place the pie dish on a baking tin, and set on a shelf just above the centre of a very hot oven (425 deg. or Gas No. 7) and bake for 20 minutes. Then lower heat to hot (375 deg. or Gas No. 5) and bake for a further 40 minutes, or until the fruit has cooked through (test with a skewer). Sprinkle with castor sugar and serve hot with cream or custard.

Steak and kidney pie

YOU WILL NEED FOR 4–6 SERVINGS:

> 8 oz. rough puff pastry
> FOR THE FILLING:
> 1½ lb. chuck steak
> 3–4 oz. ox kidney
> seasoned flour
> dripping or vegetable shortening for frying
> salt and pepper
> 1 pint stock or water plus stock cube
> 1 medium onion, sliced
> pinch mixed herbs

Prepare the pastry and set aside. Trim any fat or gristle from the meat and snip the core out of the kidney. Cut the meat into neat pieces. Roll in seasoned flour and fry with onion in the hot fat to brown. Lift the browned meat from the frying pan and place in a saucepan, add a good seasoning of salt and pepper and the hot stock. Bring up to the boil, cover with a lid and simmer gently for 1½–2 hours. Turn the meat into a 1½–2 pint pie dish and add a little of the gravy. On a lightly floured board roll out the pastry and cover the pie as described for fruit pie. Decorate with leaves made from pastry

trimmings. Brush the surface of the pie with beaten egg and milk, set on a baking tray and place in the centre of a hot oven (425 deg. or Gas No. 7). Bake for 30–40 minutes, then lower the heat to moderate (355 deg. or Gas No. 4) and bake for a further 40 minutes to 1 hour.

Eccles cakes

YOU WILL NEED FOR 16 CAKES:

> 8 oz. rough puff pastry
> FOR THE FILLING:
> 1 oz. margarine
> 1 oz. (or 1 rounded tablespoon) brown sugar
> 1 oz. chopped peel
> 4 oz. cleaned currants
> ¼ teaspoon of mixed spice

On a floured board, roll out the pastry thinly to a thickness of about ⅛ in. and leave to stand. Meanwhile prepare the filling. Melt margarine in a pan, then stir in sugar, peel, currants and spice. Cut pastry into 16 rounds, using a 3½–4 in. floured cutter, or use a small saucer as a guide, cutting round the edge with a knife.

Place a spoonful of the filling in the centre of each round. Damp the edge of each of these pastry rounds with water, using the finger-tips then draw up pastry edge and seal.

Turn so that sealed edge is underneath, roll gently into circles about 3–3½ in. across and make three slits with a sharp knife across the top of each. Brush the tops with milk and sprinkle with sugar.

Arrange cakes on a wet baking sheet and place high in a hot oven (425 deg. or Gas No. 7). Bake them for 15–20 minutes until brown.

Flaky pastry

YOU WILL NEED FOR 8 OZ. PASTRY:

> 8 oz. (or 8 rounded tablespoons) plain flour
> ½ level teaspoon salt
> 6 oz. butter or equal quantities margarine and lard
> ¼ pint (about 8 tablespoons) water
> 1 teaspoon vinegar or lemon juice

Sift together flour and salt into a mixing basin and set aside. With a knife beat the fat on a plate until softened (make sure you blend well if using margarine and lard). Spread evenly over the plate and mark into 4 equal portions. Rub one portion into the sieved flour.

Add the water and vinegar or lemon juice and mix to a smooth dough. Leave to rest for 10 minutes before rolling out.

Roll out the dough to an oblong shape, about 3 times as long as it is wide. Mark it into thirds and over the top two-thirds of the dough dot one third of the remaining fat, distributing it in small lumps. Fold the lower uncovered section over the centre and the top down, envelope style. Give pastry a half turn clockwise, seal the edges and roll it out again. Repeat (resting the dough 10 minutes between each turn) until all the fat has been added. Roll and fold once more then leave in a cool place for at least 20 minutes before using.

Vanilla slices

YOU WILL NEED FOR 8 SLICES:

4 oz. flaky pastry
2 tablespoons raspberry jam
FOR THE FILLING:
2 oz. margarine
2 oz. (or 2 rounded tablespoons) castor sugar
4 teaspoons hot water
6 teaspoons cold milk
few drops vanilla essence

Prepare the pastry as in the basic recipe but using half the quantities. Roll out on a lightly-floured surface until pastry is about ¼ in. thick and an oblong shape about 9 in. × 6 in. Trim edges and cut in half lengthwise. Cut each strip across—first in half then into quarters.

Place the pastry strips on a wet baking tray. Brush each with a little milk or beaten egg and milk and place above centre in a very hot oven (450 deg. or Gas No. 8), and bake for 10 minutes, then lower heat to hot (425 deg. or Gas No. 7) and bake for a further 5 minutes. When risen and brown remove from the baking tray and cool before filling.

To prepare the filling, cream together margarine and sugar until light. Beat in hot water one teaspoon at a time. At this stage the mixture will be very soft. Gradually add the milk one teaspoon at a time, beating well between each addition. Flavour with a few drops vanilla essence.

Gently split each cooled pastry slice in half, using a sharp knife. Spread the base first with a little raspberry jam then with the cream filling. Add the top and dredge with icing sugar.

Lemon puff pies

YOU WILL NEED FOR 12–14 PIES:

8 oz. flaky pastry
lemon curd

On a floured board roll out pastry thinly and allow to stand for 10 minutes. Using a 2–2½ in. plain round cutter, stamp 24–28 circles of pastry. Line 12 (or as many as needed) tartlet or bun tins with half the pastry rounds and place a teaspoon of lemon curd in the centre of each.

Damp edges of pastry lids and place over filled bun tins. Gently press pastry edges together to seal. Make two or three slits across the top of each and brush with a little milk or beaten egg and milk. Place fairly high in a very hot oven (425 deg. or Gas No. 7) and bake for 20 minutes or until risen and brown. Cool and dredge with icing sugar.

Use the same method to make mince pies but fill with mincemeat—your own for tip-top flavour.

Sausage rolls

YOU WILL NEED FOR 8–12 ROLLS:

4 oz. flaky pastry
6 oz. pork or beef sausage meat
salt and pepper

Prepare the pastry as in the basic recipe, but using only half the quantity of ingredients given. On a floured board roll the pastry out thinly to an oblong about 12 in. × 6 in. Trim the edges and cut in half lengthwise. Leave to rest in a cool place.

Season the sausage meat and divide into two.

Lightly flour your hands and roll each portion of sausage meat out to a rope as long as each pastry strip. Place one rope of sausage down the centre of each piece of pastry. Damp one long edge of the pastry, fold this over the sausage meat and seal it to the opposite edge. With a sharp knife cut each long roll into four or six sausage rolls. Place on a baking sheet which has been rinsed in cold water and make one or two diagonal slashes on top of each roll. Brush with a little milk or beaten egg and milk. Place above centre in a very hot oven (425 deg. or Gas No. 7) and bake 20 minutes. Larger sausage rolls are delicious for supper, particularly if you heat them gently in the oven just before you serve them.

And a plateful of tiny cocktail sausage rolls will be gobbled down at a party—by children or adults!

Puff and choux pastry

Puff and choux are the crowning achievements of the pastrycook . . . light, delicious and used to make impressive sweet and savoury confections. They look complicated but are not so difficult if you follow the rules. Try to prepare puff pastry early in the day while your kitchen is still cool, then leave it to rest until it is required for baking. Read the recipes through carefully before you start and make sure you have any special tins or cutters required.

Puff pastry

YOU WILL NEED FOR 8 OZ. PASTRY:

8 oz. (or 8 rounded tablespoons) plain strong flour
½ level teaspoon salt
1 oz. white vegetable fat
scant ¼ pint cold water
7 oz. butter or margarine

Sieve flour and salt into a mixing basin. Beat down the white fat and rub into the flour until fine. Add the water all at once and mix to a rough dough, then turn on to a lightly-floured working surface and knead lightly to a smooth dough. Set aside to rest in a cool place.

Beat the butter or margarine thoroughly with a palette knife until well softened, put it on a lightly-floured surface and pat into a fat oblong about 6 in. by 4 in. Roll the rested dough to an oblong about ¼ in. thick, shaping it so that it is ½ in. wider on each side than the butter shape and long enough for the ends to fold to the centre and slightly overlap.

Place the butter shape in the middle and fold both ends of dough into the centre, overlapping to cover the fat completely. Press sides and centre edges to seal and give the dough a half-turn clockwise.

Roll the pastry out quickly and lightly to an oblong about three times as long as it is wide. Mark into three and fold the bottom third up over the centre and the top down over both. Give a half-turn and repeat the rolling and folding.

From left to right: croquembouche, prawn vol-au-vents, cream horns, palmiers, French apricot tart, choux swans, religieuses, éclairs and mille feuille

The pastry has now had two rolls and folds. Wrap it in polythene and leave in a cool place to rest for 20–30 minutes. Give the pastry two more rolls and folds, wrap and rest as before. Finally, give another two rolls and folds (a total of six), wrap up and store in a cool place.

Prawn vol-au-vents

YOU WILL NEED FOR 6 VOL-AU-VENTS:

½ lb. puff pastry
FOR THE FILLING:
2 oz. butter or margarine
2 oz. (or 2 rounded tablespoons) flour
1 pint milk
salt and pepper
1 tablespoon tomato ketchup
¼ teaspoon anchovy essence
8 oz. prepared prawns

First prepare the filling. Melt the butter or margarine in a pan over moderate heat, and stir in the flour. Cook for a few minutes over low heat, but do not allow to brown. Gradually beat in the milk a little at a time, beating well between each addition to get a really smooth sauce. Bring to the boil and cook gently for 5 minutes. Season well with salt and pepper and stir in the ketchup, essence and prepared prawns. Allow to heat through.
Prepare the pastry as in the basic recipe. Roll to at least ¼ in. thick and, using a floured plain 3 in. round cutter, stamp out 12 circles of pastry. Transfer half of these to a baking tray which has been rinsed in cold water and arrange not too close together. Brush with a little beaten egg and milk.
Using a 2 in. plain round cutter, stamp out the centres of remaining 6 pastry rounds. Taking care not to pull them out of shape, put the rings on top of the bases on the baking tin. Seal the two together and carefully brush the tops with a little beaten egg and milk. Place the tiny circles left over round the edge of the baking tin—these will make the lids.
Leave in a cool place to rest for 15–20 minutes. Place just above centre in a hot oven (425 deg. or Gas No. 7) and bake for 15–20 minutes, until well risen and beginning to brown. Remove small pastry lids, lower the heat to 400 deg. or Gas No. 6 and bake for a further 10 minutes or until the vol-au-vents are crisp.
While still warm scoop a little of the softer inside pastry from each vol-au-vent with a teaspoon to allow for a more generous portion of filling. Spoon the hot filling into each case, top with the pastry lid and garnish with a sprig of parsley.

Custard cream

YOU WILL NEED FOR ½ PINT:

3 yolks of egg
3½ oz. castor sugar
1¼ oz. flour
scant ½ pint of milk

Cream the egg yolks and sugar together until white, add the sieved flour, and then gradually stir in the milk. Cook in a double boiler until the custard thickens and comes to the boil. Remove from heat and allow to become thoroughly cold, stirring it occasionally to prevent a skin forming.

French apricot tart

YOU WILL NEED FOR 6–8 SERVINGS:

½ lb. puff pastry
1 large tin apricot halves
a few toasted almonds
FOR THE GLAZE:
2 heaped tablespoons apricot jam sieved
2 tablespoons castor sugar
1 tablespoon water or juice from fruit

Prepare the pastry as in the basic recipe. Roll out on a lightly-floured surface to an oblong about ¼ in. thick, 12–14 in. long and 6–8 in. wide. Trim the edges, then carefully cut a strip about 1 in. wide from the four sides of the pastry. Put remaining oblong piece of pastry on to a baking tray which has been rinsed in cold water and prick all over with a fork. Brush the edges of the pastry with a little beaten egg and milk and arrange the pastry strips, trimming them to fit, to make a border.
Using the blade of a sharp knife, flake and mark the outside edges of the pastry. Score a criss-cross design on top of the border and brush with a little beaten egg and milk. Rest it in a cool place for about 15 minutes before baking.
Place just above centre in a hot oven (425 deg. or Gas No. 7) and bake for 15–20 minutes until well risen and beginning to brown. Lower the heat to (400 deg. or Gas No. 6) and bake for a further 10–15 minutes or until crisp. Remove from the heat and allow to cool.
Arrange the drained apricot halves neatly in the pie case and brush with a little hot apricot glaze.
To make this, measure all the ingredients for the glaze (as *recipe*) into a small saucepan. Heat to dissolve the sugar, then bring to the boil until thick and syrupy. Use while hot and sprinkle with the toasted

almonds. Leave to cool, then cut tart into portions with a sharp knife, and serve with cream.

Cream horns

YOU WILL NEED FOR 12–14 HORNS:

> ½ lb. puff pastry
> ½ pint double cream
> a little chopped angelica for decoration

Prepare the pastry as in the basic recipe. Roll out on a lightly-floured working surface to an oblong about 12–14 in. by 8–10 in. With a sharp knife, trim the edges of the pastry then cut it into ½ in. strips.

Brush the strips with water then take them, one at a time, and starting at the pointed end of a cream horn tin, wrap each strip of pastry, wet side inwards, round the tin, each layer slightly overlapping. Place the covered tins on baking trays which have been rinsed in cold water, with the pastry ends underneath (to stop them unrolling).

Brush with a little beaten egg and milk and set aside to rest in a cool place for 15–20 minutes.

Place just above centre in a hot oven (425 deg. or Gas No. 7) and bake for 15–20 minutes or until well risen and brown. Remove from the oven and gently pull the tins out of each pastry horn.

When cold pipe or spoon whipped cream into each horn and decorate with a little finely-chopped angelica.

Each of these recipes needs only a small amount of pastry so make up ½ lb. as in the basic recipe on page and divide it in half.

Palmiers

YOU WILL NEED FOR 2 DOZEN:

> 4 oz. puff pastry
> granulated sugar

Prepare the pastry as in the basic recipe but give it two extra rolls and folds, sprinkling with *granulated sugar* for these instead of flour. Roll to an oblong about 12 in. by 8 in.

Using a sharp knife, trim the outer edges. Fold both long edges in towards the middle so that they meet. Pat them down firmly. Now fold the pastry in half lengthwise, giving you a pastry strip that is four layers deep and is still 12 in. long.

Cut into ½ in. strips across the width. Turn each strip over on to its side and arrange on a baking tray which has been rinsed in cold water; cut side will be facing you. Do not arrange them closely together as they puff out during baking.

Place above centre in a hot oven (425 deg. or Gas No. 7) and bake for 12 minutes, then turn each

palmier over. Return to oven and bake for a further 5 minutes or until they are golden brown.

Eat when cold and crisp.

For a special treat, sandwich two palmiers together with cream.

Mille feuille

YOU WILL NEED FOR 1 DOZEN:

> 4 oz. puff pastry
> 1–2 tablespoons raspberry jam
> custard cream (*see recipe on page 202*) or use
> ½ pint fresh double cream
> FOR THE ICING:
> 6 oz. sieved icing sugar
> warm water to mix

Prepare the pastry as in the basic recipe. On a lightly-floured board roll it thinly to cover a baking tray about 11 or 12 in. square. Trim the edges and prick all over with a fork. Set aside to rest in a cool place for about 15–20 minutes.

Place baking tin above centre in a hot oven (425 deg. or Gas No. 7) and bake pastry for 10–12 minutes or until crisp and brown. Remove from the heat and cut lengthwise into three equal strips. Set aside to cool before filling.

Prepare the custard cream (if using fresh cream whip until thick). Spread one strip of pastry with the raspberry jam to make the base. Top with a second piece of pastry and spread this with cream. Top with last piece of pastry, flattest side uppermost.

To prepare the icing, sieve the icing sugar into a small mixing basin. Add just enough warm water for a coating consistency. Pour over the top piece of pastry and, using a knife, spread evenly and to the edges. When set firm cut the pastry into smaller slices.

Sugar crisps

Collect together any trimmings from the puff pastry, don't screw them into a ball. Then lay them in strips one on top of the other so that the layers of fat are preserved. Give these trimmings an extra roll and fold sprinkling the table with *granulated sugar* instead of flour.

Roll out thinly and using a 2–2½-inch fluted round cutter, stamp out as many circles as possible. Roll each once again with the pin to an oval shape and place on a baking tray rinsed with cold water. Place above the centre of a hot oven (425 deg. or Gas No. 7) and bake for 12 minutes. Flip over each pastry crisp—return to the oven and bake for a further 5 minutes, until they are golden brown. Eat while warm and crisp—delicious with ice cream.

Choux pastry

Choux pastry is made by beating the flour and salt into the boiling fat. Try to use a plain, strong flour (most large grocer's can supply this). It is very important that you add the flour to the liquid while it is still boiling, and that you beat thoroughly while adding the eggs. This incorporates plenty of air and will give you a lighter pastry. The harder you beat, the better it will be.

Choux pastry

YOU WILL NEED FOR 4 OZ. PASTRY:

2 oz. (or 2 rounded tablespoons) plain strong flour
pinch of salt
2 oz. margarine
¼ pint water
1 level teaspoon castor sugar
2 large eggs

Sift the flour and salt on to a square of paper and leave in a warm, dry place until required. Cut up the fat and put into a medium-sized saucepan with the water and sugar. Bring to a quick rolling boil. Tip the flour in all at once while the pan is still on the heat. Stir to mix and draw the pan off the heat.
Beat the mixture thoroughly until it leaves the sides of the saucepan clean, then allow it to cool until the hand can be comfortably held against the pan. Lightly mix the eggs and beat in gradually. When the eggs have been added the choux paste should appear thick and glossy and just stiff enough to hold its shape when piped.

Eclairs

MAKES 1½ DOZEN:

Spoon choux pastry (*as basic recipe*) into a piping bag (use a cotton or nylon one) fitted with a ½ in. plain piping nozzle. Pipe out 3 in. lengths on to a greased baking sheet. Place above centre in a hot oven (425 deg. or Gas No. 7) and bake for 20 minutes until they are quite crisp and golden brown (if underbaked they will collapse on cooling).

When cold fill with custard cream (*see recipe on page 202*). To do this make a small slit in the sides and use a piping bag and small nozzle; choose the smoothest side for icing, often the underneath is best. Dip this flat side in chocolate or coffee icing (*see recipes*), then hold upright and allow surplus icing to run off. Leave to set firm before arranging in paper cases.

Choux buns

MAKES 2 DOZEN:

Put choux pastry (*as basic recipe*) into a piping bag fitted with a ½ in. plain piping nozzle. On to a greased baking tray pipe out bulbs of the choux pastry not too closely together. Brush the tops of each with a little beaten egg and milk.
Place on the shelf above centre in a hot oven (400 deg. or Gas No. 6) and bake for 20 minutes or until risen, brown and crisp. Remove from the heat and allow to cool.
Fill as for eclairs, using custard cream (*see recipe on page 202*) or whipped fresh cream and dip top in coffee or chocolate icing or finish with a dusting of icing sugar.

Glossy chocolate icing

Into a pan put a rounded tablespoon of cocoa, a rounded tablespoon of granulated sugar and 3 tablespoons water. Stir until boiling and until the sugar has dissolved. Draw the pan off the heat and stir in 6 oz. (or 6 heaped tablespoons) sieved icing sugar to make a thick coating consistency. Use while warm.

Coffee icing

Put 3 tablespoons of very strong black coffee into a pan with 1 rounded tablespoon sugar. Stir over the heat until the sugar has dissolved, then draw the pan off the heat. Stir in enough sieved icing sugar to make a thick coating consistency. Use while warm.

Gâteau St. Honoré

Choux swans

MAKES 2 DOZEN:

Make choux pastry as basic recipe and, reserving a small quantity, pipe out as for choux buns; make the bulbs about the size of half a crown. Using a narrow ¼ in. tube, pipe the rest of the pastry into 'S' shapes to make swans' necks. Make sure you have as many necks as you have buns.

Bake the buns as described. Place the necks to bake just above centre in a hot oven (400 deg. or Gas No. 6) and leave for 10–15 minutes or until brown and crisp.

When the pastry is cool, assemble the swans. Slice the choux buns in half completely, and slice the top half of the bun again to make two wings. Pipe a whorl of whipped cream on the base and replace the two wings, slightly at an angle. Fix the neck into the cream and dust the swan with icing sugar.

Religieuses

YOU WILL NEED FOR 12 RELIGIEUSES:

4 oz. rich shortcrust pastry, *see page 190*
choux pastry (*as basic recipe*)
½ pint whipped cream
coffee and chocolate icing
FOR THE COFFEE BUTTERCREAM:
4 oz. butter
4 oz. (4 heaped tablespoons) sieved icing sugar
1–2 teaspoons coffee essence

Prepare the rich shortcrust pastry, using 4 oz. flour, and roll out to line 12 tartlet tins. Fill each with a little crumpled kitchen foil and 'bake blind' in a hot oven (400 deg. or Gas No. 6) for 10–12 minutes.

Make the choux pastry according to the basic recipe. Following the instructions given for choux buns, pipe out 12 large buns and 12 smaller ones. When cool fill each one with whipped cream or custard cream. Dip the sides and tops of the large buns in chocolate icing and small ones in coffee icing. Leave to set firm.

Prepare the buttercream. Beat the butter until soft and gradually beat in the icing sugar. Then beat in enough coffee essence to give a good flavour. Pipe a little coffee buttercream in the base of each tartlet case and then place a chocolate covered choux bun on top. Pipe a small bulb of buttercream on top of the chocolate icing and place a smaller coffee-iced bun on top. Around the base of each bun pipe a ring of coffee buttercream rosettes.

Gâteau St. Honoré

YOU WILL NEED FOR 6 SERVINGS:

4 oz. rich shortcrust pastry, *see page 190*
choux pastry (*as basic recipe*)
beaten egg and milk for brushing
3 oz. (3 rounded tablespoons) granulated sugar
juice of half a lemon
½ pint double cream
few drops vanilla essence

Prepare the rich shortcrust according to directions and set aside. Prepare choux pastry, *see basic recipe*, and spoon half the mixture into a large piping bag fitted with a ½-inch plain nozzle. Roll the prepared pastry out to a circle and using a dessert plate as a guide, cut out a circle of pastry about 8 inches in diameter. Place the circle of dough on a greased baking tray and prick well with a fork. Brush a 1-inch band round the pastry edge with beaten egg and milk, then pipe a ring of choux pastry about ½-inch in from the edge. Brush with egg and milk, place above centre in a very hot oven (425 deg. or Gas No. 7) and bake for 25 minutes.

Spoon the remainder of the choux pastry into a piping bag fitted with a ¼-inch piping nozzle and on to a greased baking tray, pipe 15 small rounds of pastry about the size of a nut. Brush each with beaten egg and milk and when gâteau base is baked, place the tray of buns on shelf above centre and bake for 20 minutes until risen and crisp.

Allow both gâteau base and choux buns to cool before finishing the cake.

To assemble the gâteau

Measure the sugar and lemon juice into a small saucepan. Stir over moderate heat until sugar has dissolved and then bring up to the boil and cook quickly until a golden brown colour. Draw the pan off the heat and quickly dip the base of each choux bun first in the caramel and then place them round the border of the cake. Fit the buns close together—you will need about 12, depending on the size. When working take care, the caramel is very hot. Spoon a little of the hot caramel onto the top of each choux bun.

Half whip the cream with a few drops of vanilla essence, then add the sugar and whip until thick. Spoon into the centre of the gâteau and chill until ready to serve.

Polkas

YOU WILL NEED FOR 24 POLKAS:

4 oz. rich shortcrust pastry, *see page 190*
beaten egg and milk for brushing
choux pastry (½ *basic recipe*)
FOR THE CHOCOLATE ICING:
3 oz. (3 heaped tablespoons) icing sugar
1 oz. (3 level tablespoons) cocoa powder
1½ oz. vegetable shortening
2 full tablespoons water
2 oz. (2 rounded tablespoons) castor sugar
½ pint double cream
few drops vanilla essence
1 oz. (1 rounded tablespoon) castor sugar
few toasted almonds for decoration

On a lightly floured working surface roll out the prepared rich shortcrust thinly and using a 2–2½-inch round plain cutter, stamp out about 24 circles of pastry. Place on a wetted baking tray, prick each well with the prongs of a fork and brush with beaten egg and milk.
Prepare the choux pastry following basic instructions, and spoon into a piping bag fitted with a ¼-inch plain tube. Pipe a ring of choux paste round the edge of each pastry circle. Brush with beaten egg and place above centre of a hot oven (400 deg. or Gas No. 6) for 14 minutes. Allow to cool then finish as follows.
Prepare the chocolate icing. Sieve the icing sugar and cocoa powder into a mixing basin. Measure the fat, water and sugar into a saucepan and stir over low heat until sugar has dissolved then bring up to the boil. Pour into the centre of the dry ingredients and mix to a smooth icing. Stir until slightly cooled and of a coating consistency, then holding each baked pastry by the pastry base, dip the ring of choux paste in the chocolate icing. Turn right way up and leave to set firm.
Half whip the cream with the vanilla essence, add the sugar and beat until thick. Fill the centre of each 'polka' with whipped cream and sprinkle with almonds.

Croquembouche

YOU WILL NEED FOR 6–8 CROQUEMBOUCHES:

choux pastry (*as basic recipe*)
4 oz. rich shortcrust pastry, *see page 190*
FOR THE CARAMEL:
8 oz. granulated sugar
¼ pint water

Prepare the choux pastry as in the basic recipe. Following the directions for preparing choux buns, pipe out as many buns as you can. Make some larger ones to form the base and some smaller ones for the top. Bake as in choux buns recipe, the smaller ones needing only 15 minutes baking time.
Roll out the rich shortcrust pastry thinly and using an 8 in. plate as a guide, cut out a round of pastry. Lift carefully on to a greased baking tray and prick all over. Place above centre in a hot oven (400 deg. or Gas No. 6) and bake for 10–12 minutes or until crisp and brown.
Fill each of the baked buns with custard cream (*see recipe on page 202*), using a piping bag and small piping nozzle. Set the filled buns aside while preparing the caramel. It is essential that the caramel is used immediately it is cooked, so have everything else ready.
Measure the sugar and water into a medium-sized saucepan and dissolve over low heat. When all the sugar grains are dissolved bring to the boil and cook rapidly until the mixture begins to turn golden brown. When the mixture is evenly brown draw the pan off the heat. Allow the bubbles to subside then hold each bun on the end of a fork and dip it into the hot caramel. It will be very hot so take care not to touch it with your fingers. Beginning with the larger ones, arrange the buns in a pyramid on the pastry base. Pour any remaining caramel over the pyramid. Leave until set firm.
To eat, break the buns apart with two forks and serve with cream.

Savoury petit choux

These are marvellous for cocktail snacks, you can bake them ahead and store in an airtight tin, prepare the fillings and fill them when ready to serve them.
Prepare the basic choux recipe, omitting the sugar from the recipe. Spoon the mixture into a nylon or cotton piping bag fitted with a ¼-inch plain nozzle. Pipe small bulbs of the mixture about 1-inch width onto a greased baking tray. Brush the tops with a little beaten egg and milk and place just above centre in a hot oven (425 deg. or Gas No. 7) and bake for 20 minutes.
Allow the baked choux to cool then using the tip of a knife blade cut a slit in the side of each. Prepare any savoury fillings and spoon into each choux.

ALL ABOUT *Preserving*

Jams, jellies and marmalade

For a large amount of jam you will need a preserving pan. For smaller quantities use your largest strong aluminium saucepan. Jam will boil up to three or four times its original bulk and must have room to boil rapidly for a good set. Use fruit that is just ripe; fruit that is over-ripe won't set properly. Wash it in clear cold water before cooking.

Lightly grease preserving pan with a buttered paper. Add prepared fruit, any water or lemon juice in recipe, and bring slowly to the boil. Reduce heat and simmer gently, stirring occasionally until the fruit is soft and cooked. Put sugar in a dry bowl and set in a warm place.

When fruit is reduced to a thick pulp draw the pan off the heat. Add the warm sugar, stand the pan over *low heat* and stir until the sugar has dissolved, now raise the heat and bring the jam to a rolling boil. Boil quickly, stirring occasionally to prevent sticking, until setting point is reached, usually takes 10–15 minutes. Test after 10 minutes, draw the pan off the heat, and spoon a little of the jam into a clean saucer. Stand in a cool place for a few minutes, and then push the jam gently with the little finger. It is ready if the surface wrinkles. Take the pan off the heat at once and remove any scum.

Ladle the jam into clean, warmed jars, filling well up to the necks. Stand the jars on a tray covered with folded newspapers—a hard cold surface might make them crack. Wipe clean while still warm. Jam may be covered while hot or when cold. Either way place on top a round of waxed paper and then moisten one side of the Cellophane cover, and place it damp side upwards. Pull on tightly and fix with an elastic band. When cold, label and store in a cool, dry, dark place.

Blackcurrant jam

YOU WILL NEED FOR 10 LB.:

4 lb. blackcurrants
3 pints water
6 lb. granulated or preserving sugar

Blackcurrants are rich in pectin, and therefore need more sugar. Using a fork, strip the fruit from the stalks, and place in preserving pan with the water. Simmer until all the currants have broken up, and a thick pulp remains. Add sugar and when it has dissolved boil rapidly and then test for a set.

Strawberry jam

YOU WILL NEED FOR 10 LB.:

6 lb. strawberries (just ripe)
juice of 2 lemons
¾ pint pectin stock *(see below)*
6 lb. granulated or preserving sugar

Hull strawberries and put in preserving pan with lemon juice. Heat gently and when soft—takes about 10 minutes—add sugar. Bring to the boil and cook until setting point is reached—about 10 minutes. Draw the pan off the heat and cool for 15–20 minutes so that the strawberries will be evenly dispersed.

Some strawberries, particularly over-ripe ones, are very low in pectin. In this case extra pectin in the form of gooseberry or redcurrant juice (*see quantity in ingredients*), should be added with the sugar. To make this juice boil 3 lb. gooseberries or redcurrants in 1½ pints water until quite soft, then strain and use.

Making raspberry jam

Raspberry jam

YOU WILL NEED FOR 10 LB.:

 6 lb. raspberries
 6 lb. granulated or preserving sugar

Place hulled raspberries in the preserving pan and heat slowly. No water is necessary, but squash a little of the fruit near the base of the pan to help speed the breaking up process, and then bring to the boil. Simmer about 5 minutes, add sugar and when it has dissolved, boil rapidly for a further 5 minutes, then test for a set.

Plum jam

YOU WILL NEED FOR 10 LB.:

 6 lb. plums (Victoria, golden or greengages)
 1 pint water
 6 lb. granulated or preserving sugar

Wash, halve and stone the plums and put in preserving pan with water. If the stones are difficult to remove, cook plums whole and remove as many stones as possible as they rise to the surface of the pan.
Add the sugar, dissolve and bring to the boil. Boil for 12–15 minutes and then test for a set.
Meanwhile crack about a dozen stones and remove the inner kernels. Blanch them by plunging them into boiling water for 1 minute, then add to the jam at the last minute.

Apricot jam

Follow the recipe for plum jam, using the same quantities of fruit, water and sugar, but boil for 15–20 minutes.

Blackberry and apple jam

YOU WILL NEED FOR 10 LB.:

 4 lb. blackberries
 ½ pint water
 1½ lb. cooking apples
 6 lb. granulated or preserving sugar

Put washed blackberries in preserving pan with half the water and stew until tender. Peel, core and slice the apples, add remaining water and cook until fruit is quite soft. Combine the pulps together;

if a seedless jam is required, sieve the blackberry pulp. Add the sugar, dissolve and boil for a set—takes about 15 minutes.

Gooseberry jam

YOU WILL NEED FOR 10–12 LB.:

 5 lb. green gooseberries
 2 pints water
 6 lb. granulated or preserving sugar

Using a pair of scissors, top and tail the gooseberries. Place in a preserving pan along with the water. Bring slowly to the boil and simmer gently until quite tender—takes about 30 minutes, crushing the fruit with the back of a wooden spoon.
Add the sugar and stir over a low heat until dissolved. Bring to the boil and cook rapidly until setting point is reached—about 10–15 minutes. Draw the pan off the heat and pot quickly.
Note Gooseberries are rich in pectin and can take extra sugar.

Mixed fruit jam

YOU WILL NEED FOR 6–6½ LB.:

 2 lb. green gooseberries
 1 lb. strawberries
 1 lb. raspberries
 ½ pint water
 4 lb. granulated or preserving sugar

Top and tail the gooseberries and place in a saucepan along with the hulled strawberries and raspberries. Add the water and bring up to the boil and simmer gently until the fruit particularly the gooseberries are quite soft, this takes about 30 minutes.
Add the sugar and stir over low heat until the sugar has dissolved. Bring up to the boil and cook rapidly until setting point has been reached, about 10–15 minutes. Draw the pan off the heat, skim and pot quickly.

Jelly

Only fruit rich in pectin—like cooking apples, redcurrants, crab apples or gooseberries—should be used. Wash the fruit but it's not necessary to remove stalks. Cook fruit with water slowly for about 1 hour, then strain through a jelly bag. An easy way is to turn a stool upside down, set a basin underneath and fix the four corners of the jelly bag to the legs. Alternatively, use a large square of double muslin tied firmly over a mixing basin.

Either way scald the cloth first by pouring boiling water through it. Ladle the cooked fruit into the bag and leave to strain several hours or overnight. The strained juice will look quite cloudy. Measure juice into a saucepan and for every 1 pint allow 1 lb. of sugar. Dissolve sugar in juice over low heat and bring to the boil. Boil rapidly and without stirring until setting point is reached—10–20 minutes. Skim and ladle quickly into small, warm jelly jars. Cover as for jam.

Redcurrant jelly

YOU WILL NEED FOR 4 LB.:

4 lb. redcurrants
2 pints water
1 lb. granulated or preserving sugar for every
    pint juice

Wash the redcurrants. Cook in water until soft—about 30 minutes. Strain through a jelly bag overnight and then measure juice back into the pan and add sugar. Dissolve and boil for a set—takes about 10 minutes. Skim and pour into warm, dry, jelly jars. Cover as for jam.

Mint jelly

YOU WILL NEED FOR 3 LB.:

2 lb. green cooking apples
2 pints water
2 tablespoons lemon juice
bunch of well-washed mint
1 lb. granulated or preserving sugar for each
    pint of juice
few drops of green colouring

Wash apples and cut up without peeling. Cook with water and lemon juice and a little mint to a thick pulp. Strain through a jelly bag for several hours or overnight.
Measure the juice back into the pan, add remaining mint, chopped, and the required quantity of sugar and dissolve slowly. Bring to the boil, cook quickly for a set, takes about 10 minutes. Add a few drops of green colouring and pour jelly into dry, warm jars.
The same recipe, without the mint, makes an excellent apple jelly; or crab apples may be used to make a tasty red jelly.

Marmalade

The best marmalade is made from the Seville oranges available in January and February. General rules apply as for jam—the peel can be cut chunky or fine.

Seville orange marmalade

YOU WILL NEED FOR 10 LB.:

3 lb. Seville oranges
juice of 2 lemons
5–6 pints water
6 lb. granulated or preserving sugar

Scrub the fruit, halve and squeeze out juice and pips. Slice the peel, coarsely or finely according to the type of marmalade you prefer. Chop the pith and tie in a muslin bag with the pips.
Place the peel, fruit juice, muslin bag and half the water (use 6 pints for a shallow wide pan and 5 pints for a deep narrow pan) in a mixing basin and leave to soak at least 2 hours or overnight. Add remaining water and bring to the boil. Simmer gently for 2 hours or until the peel is quite soft. Add the sugar and stir until dissolved, then bring to the boil and cook rapidly until setting point is reached—takes about 15–20 minutes.
Draw the pan off the heat and cool for about 15 minutes to distribute peel evenly, then ladle into warm, dry jars. Cover and seal.

Red cherry marmalade

YOU WILL NEED FOR 2 LB.:

1 lb. red cherries
½ lb. raspberries
juice of 1 small lemon
1 lb. preserving or granulated sugar
¼ pint cold water

Wash and stone the cherries and place in a large aluminium saucepan. Sieve the raspberries and add to the cherries, along with the strained lemon juice. Over a moderate heat bring to the boil, and simmer gently for 20–30 minutes, or until the cherries are softened and tender.
Add the sugar and stir continuously over a moderate heat, until the sugar has dissolved, then bring up to the boil and boil rapidly without stirring until setting point is reached, about 10 minutes.
When ready, draw the pan off the heat and skim if necessary, and allow to stand for 5–10 minutes, to allow the cherries to distribute evenly through the jam. Pour into hot jars, cover, seal and label.

Bottled fruit

There are two types of preserving jar, the screw-band type and the clip type. You can also use ordinary jam jars if you buy special metal clips and rubber bands. Examine the jars carefully before you use them and discard any that are cracked or chipped. Metal tops and rubber bands must be renewed each season. Wash and rinse jars thoroughly and leave them upside down to drain. It's not necessary to dry them; fruit slips in more easily if they are wet. Soak rubber bands in a basin of warm water until required.

Select fruit in prime condition; it should be just ripe and without blemishes. Grade it for size so that all the fruit in one bottle will cook evenly. Prepare according to kinds, removing any stalks or leaves.

Blackcurrants: remove the stems but leave on the brown heads.

Gooseberries: use firm green gooseberries and top and tail close to the berry, leaving a small cut surface for fruit syrup to penetrate.

Pears: use ripe dessert pears, or cooking pears stewed first in syrup until tender. Peel and halve the pears and scoop out the cores with a teaspoon. Put into a large bowl of salted cold water (allow 1 level tablespoon salt to 4 pints water) to keep the pears a white colour. Put a plate on the bowl to keep pears under water. Pears are usually bottled in halves and should be well rinsed before being placed in the bottles.

Plums, greengages and damsons: these can be halved, stoned and packed cut side down, or they can be left whole.

Raspberries: bottle as quickly as possible after purchasing.

Rhubarb: use young tender rhubarb and cut into 2 in. lengths for easier packing.

Fruit salad: I find this an extremely useful preserve. Prepare and bottle a selection of fruit including plums, sliced bananas, sliced peaches, pears and green grapes, halved and de-seeded. Don't use fruit with dark skins as these may discolour all the other fruits.

Peaches and apricots: usually halved and peaches are often sliced. Before removing the skins, plunge fruit into boiling water (makes it easier).

Apple pulp: this useful preserve can be served as a sweet with cream or used as a ready-to-serve apple sauce. Wash, peel and core the apples, then put in a very little water with just sufficient sugar to sweeten slightly. Stew fruit to a pulp. Add a little green colouring if liked and spoon into the bottles. Allow about 4 lb. apples for each 1 lb. preserving jar.

Tomatoes: These are useful for adding to soups, stews or casseroles. Use firm ripe tomatoes and remove the skins by plunging fruit quickly into boiling water before peeling. Cut in halves or quarters and pack into jars, cut side down, sprinkling each layer with a mixture of 1 rounded teaspoon each salt and sugar for every 2 lb. tomatoes.

Preserving sugar

Use 4–8 oz. sugar to 1 pint water for most fruit but heavier syrup is pleasant with raspberries, peaches, pears and blackcurrants—for these, allow 12 oz. sugar to 1 pint water.

Measure sugar into a saucepan with half the quantity of water. Stir over low heat to dissolve the sugar and then bring to the boil. Simmer for 1 minute, then draw the pan off the heat and add the remaining water. If boiling syrup is required add all the water at once.

Sterilising with water

Prepare the fruit and pack into the jars. Stand the jars in turn on a plate and fill to overflowing with cool syrup or water. Give the jars a quick twist to remove any air bubbles, cover with rubber band, lid and clip or screw-band. If a screw-band is used, screw up tightly and then unscrew half a turn to allow for expansion—the clip acts as a spring and allows for expansion automatically.

Half fill a large saucepan or preserving pan with cold water and fit a rack or false bottom in it. Place the jars on this, taking care that they do not touch each other, and fill the pan with cold water *to cover the jars completely.* Cover with a lid and turn on the heat very low.

Allow about 1½ hours for the water to come just to simmering point, it should bubble very slightly. Hold it at this temperature for 10–25 minutes according to the fruit.

From the right: fruit salad, gooseberries, plums, greengages and lemon curd

Fruit	Time	Temperature at 1½ hrs.		
Apple pulp	10 min.	165 degrees F.		
Apricots and peaches	15 min.	,,	,,	,,
Damsons	15 min.	,,	,,	,,
Gooseberries	10 min.	,,	,,	,,
Plums	10 min.	,,	,,	,,
Raspberries and soft fruit	10 min.	,,	,,	,,
Rhubarb	10 min.	,,	,,	,,
Pears	20 min.	190 degrees F.		
Tomatoes	25 min.	,,	,,	,,

When the sterilising time is completed, turn off the heat. Lift out the jars with tongs or ladle out enough water to expose the jars halfway down, and lift out with a cloth. Don't stand the jars on a cold surface or they will crack. Put them instead on to a board, folded cloth or newspaper. Screw any metal bands up tightly, and leave to cool without disturbing for 12 hours.

When quite cold remove the clips or screwbands and test the seals by lifting each jar by the lid—the vacuum inside should be strong enough to keep the lid in position. Label and store in a cool dark place. Any bottles that are imperfectly sealed can be re-sterilised at once or opened and the fruit eaten.

Sterilising in the oven

This method is less satisfactory than the water-bath method for apples or pears, as they tend to discolour. There are two basic ways of oven bottling.

Liquid added before sterilisation:

Prepare and pack fruit as before. Cover with cold syrup to within ½ inch of brim of bottle, place rubber rings and covers in position, but do not fix down. Stand bottles on a baking tray (to catch any syrup that overflows) in the oven centre without touching each other. Heat very gradually in a slow oven (240 deg. or Gas No. ¼) and leave for 1½ hours or longer—*see note below*.

The time will vary according to the fruit and the number of jars in the oven.

When tiny pin-head bubbles appear on the fruit or a slight space is noticeable at the bottom of the bottles, the fruit is ready for sealing. Remove the bottles from the oven one at a time, and seal, test and store as water-bath method.

Note A large number of jars in the oven may lengthen the time up to 2½ hours. Pears, apples and tomatoes are best heated for 3 hours.

Liquid added after sterilisation:

Prepare and pack fruit into clean preserving jars. Do not add any liquid. To prevent fruit from scorching, cover with lids or small patty tins, or even a baking tray over all the jars. Place jars on baking sheet in centre of a slow oven (240 deg. or Gas No. ¼) until they are cooked and juice begins to run—¾–1 hour.

If fruit shrinks a good deal, use contents of one jar to top up the others and replace jars in oven for a further 5–10 minutes to complete sterilisation.

Remove jars carefully from oven, place on wooden surface or folded newspaper and fill up with boiling syrup or water. Put on rubber rings and lids and secure immediately with screw-bands or clips. Check screw-bands for tightness a few minutes after cooling. Leave the jars undisturbed until quite cold, then test seals and store as described for the water-bath method.

Fruit cheeses and curds

These are popular preserves with a good flavour. Fruit cheeses are best made when there is a glut of fruit as the proportion of fruit in the recipes is high and can be rather expensive. It makes an excellent and tasty topping for bread or scones or can be used as a sweet accompaniment to hot or cold duck, pork or ham. Home-made lemon curd is infinitely better than shop-bought and sure to be a family favourite.

Damson cheese

YOU WILL NEED FOR ABOUT 3 LB.

3 lb. ripe damsons
3 cloves
1–1½ pints water
sugar as required

Rinse damsons and remove the stalks. Put into a pan with cloves and add water to not quite cover the fruit. Simmer gently until very soft and rub through a nylon sieve. Measure pulp and allow ¾–1 lb. sugar to each pint (according to sharpness required).

Simmer in a heavy pan, stirring frequently until the pulp thickens. This whole process must be carried out very gently, the pulp should not boil. When it's ready, a wooden spoon drawn across the bottom of the pan will show a clean line for a few seconds.

Pot in small hot jars, and cover with waxed papers. When cold, cover and label as for jam.

Apple cheese

YOU WILL NEED FOR ABOUT 2 LB.:

2 lb. cooking apples
1 pint water
finely grated rind and juice of ½ a lemon
1 lb. granulated sugar for each pint of purée

Wipe apples and cut up roughly without removing cores or skins. Put into a pan and add water and grated lemon rind.
Bring to the boil and simmer slowly for about half an hour until the apples are soft and pulpy.
Pass pulp through a sieve and measure the purée into a saucepan. Add sugar, and lemon juice and bring the mixture slowly to the boil, stirring well to dissolve all the sugar. Lower the heat and allow the mixture to cook very gently for about 1–1½ hours until it is very thick, stir the mixture occasionally to prevent scorching.
Pour prepared cheese into small pots and cover, or into a mould which has been rubbed with glycerine. Traditionally the cheese should be turned out of the mould and served on a dish or plate. Or you can serve it straight from the jar.

Honey cheese

YOU WILL NEED FOR 1½ LB.:

1 pint strained honey
4 whole eggs and 2 egg yolks
finely grated rind of 2 lemons and juice of 4 lemons
3 oz. butter

Blend all the ingredients together and stir over low heat until the mixture thickens. Draw pan off heat and pour into small, warm jelly jars. Top with waxed paper circles and cover with Cellophane paper when cold.
This cheese will keep for a year or more if stored in a cool place—makes a delicious filling for home-baked tartlets, cakes and biscuits.

Lemon curd

YOU WILL NEED FOR ABOUT 1½ LB..

4 oz. butter
12 oz. (or 12 rounded tablespoons) granulated sugar
finely grated rind and juice of 3 lemons
9 egg yolks

Combine butter, sugar, lemon rind and juice in a double or heavy saucepan and stir over low heat until sugar has dissolved and butter melted.

Stir in egg yolks and continue stirring over low heat until the mixture is hot and thickened. Do not boil. Remove from the heat and pour into small clean, dry jars. Cover and seal.

Orange curd

Makes 2 lb.: Follow the recipe for lemon curd using 2 oranges and 1 lemon instead of 3 lemons.

Mincemeat

YOU WILL NEED FOR 4½ LB.:

8 oz. stoned raisins
8 oz. sultanas
8 oz. currants
8 oz. apples (weight after peeling and coring)
8 oz. candied lemon peel
4 oz. candied orange peel
4 oz. candied citron peel
1 oz. sweet blanched almonds
8 oz. brown sugar
8 oz. shredded suet
1 level teaspoon mixed spice
½ level teaspoon grated nutmeg
½ level teaspoon salt
finely grated zest and juice of 1 large lemon
4–6 tablespoons rum or brandy

For the best flavour choose large raisins (not the stoneless variety). Most shops sell them already stoned. Again, for flavour, choose candied peel 'caps' rather than ready-cut peel. Scoop out any solid candy sugar before chopping the peel. Almonds may be blanched by dropping into boiling water for 1 minute. Drain and rinse under the cold tap then slip off the loose skins between fingers and thumb and spread out the nuts to dry.
The quickest way to make mincemeat if you have a hand or electric mincer handy is to pass all the fruit, peel and nuts through the coarse blade. (Apples can be minced too). But if no mincer is available the raisins, candied peel and nuts must be chopped finely, and the apple cut into very neat *small* dice. Then mix in all the ingredients thoroughly together, adding rum or brandy to choice. For an extra rich mincemeat up to ¼ pint of spirit may be added.
Pack closely into sterile jars, cover with waxes and then a good moisture-proof cover (plastic snap-on tops, waxed paper or Porosan film are good) and store the mincemeat in a *cool* place until ready to use.
For best results allow mincemeat to mature for at least three weeks. Once opened it is advisable to store mincemeat in the refrigerator to avoid any risk of fermentation.

Bottled and salted vegetables

Best results come with young, fresh vegetables. They cannot be bottled at ordinary temperatures, as with fruit, because most vegetables contain harmful bacteria. To get reliable results and accurate high temperatures you will find it best to use a pressure cooker. Take care to have clean, well-prepared vegetables and time them very accurately.

Preparation

Home-grown vegetables are ideal for bottling, as you need them to be young and fresh. Beetroots, carrots and celery lose their bright, fresh colour because of the high temperatures used. This can be overcome by adding artificial green colouring (use it rather brighter than required in finished results) to the brine.

Wash vegetables in running cold water, all root vegetables should be scrubbed to remove any traces of soil. After washing, trimming or peeling, vegetables must be blanched at once in boiling water for the given time in the chart. This will shrink the vegetables, partly cook them and set the colour.

After this they should be drained well and packed in prepared jars. Make a brine by dissolving 1 oz. kitchen salt—never use table salt, the added starch will make the liquid cloudy—in every quart of water and bring to the boil, add any colouring necessary and use hot.

Asparagus: wash, trim off scales, cut into even lengths, tie in bundles and pack upright.

Beans: remove *broad* beans from pods. Wash and string *French* beans, trim the ends and bottle whole. Wash, string and then slice *runner* beans.

Beetroot: cut off the green tops, blanch whole and then slice or dice as required.

Carrots: wash, scrape and then slice or dice. Very new young carrots can be left whole.

Mushrooms: select small button mushrooms, trim off the stalks and wash in cold water.

Peas: shell and wash.

Parsnips: wash and scrub thoroughly, pare and cut into even lengths.

Green or red peppers: wash and drain, place in a hot oven (450 deg. or Gas No. 8) for 6–8 minutes, then plunge into cold water. Peel off skin, remove seeds and core, then pack whole. No liquid will be needed.

New potatoes: wash, scrub well, grade into even sizes.

Sweetcorn: remove outer husks and the silks, then cut the corn from the cob, taking care to keep the corn whole. A useful vegetable is obtained if sweetcorn and diced green or red peppers are bottled together.

Vegetable macedoine: select a variety of vegetables, prepare according to type, then dice and pack in layers.

Types of jars

Dual purpose Kilner jars with screw caps or ordinary jam jars with snap closures are the best types to use. Check the size your pressure cooker will hold before starting work. Select the jars carefully, discarding any that are chipped or cracked. Wash and stand in hot water ready for use. Scald new rubber bands, rings and lids with boiling water just before use.

Bottling by pressure cooker

Follow the instructions given with your particular pressure cooker, but these are general instructions: Prepare the vegetables as previously instructed and grade according to size in each jar to cook evenly.

Pack the blanched vegetables firmly but not too tightly in clean warm jars up to ½ in. from the shoulder. Fill the jars with hot brine to cover the vegetables and twist the jar sharply to one side to get any air bubbles out. Place on the screw caps or clip tops. With screw caps, screw up tightly and then unscrew half a turn to allow for expansion during bottling; clip tops automatically allow for expansion.

Place the jars in the pressure cooker on the trivet without touching each other. The amount of water in the base of the cooker varies with different cookers, but should be between 1½–2 pints. Add a squeeze of lemon juice or tablespoon of vinegar to save discolouration.

Fix on the cover and heat gently until the steam flows freely from the centre vent. Lower heat and leave to steam for 5 minutes. It is important to steam properly as during this time air is withdrawn from the jars. After 5 minutes place on the 10 lb. indicator weight, bring up the pressure over moderate heat and process according to the time on the chart. Count the time from the minute the required pressure is reached, this is *not* the moment the indicator weight is placed on. Maintain at a steady temperature for required

Beans in salt

time, then turn off the heat and let the cooker cool slowly.

Remove the jars from the cooker, place on a board or folded newspaper (never on a cold surface) and tighten up screw tops. The finished jars may appear to have lost much of the brine but this will not impair the keeping qualities of the vegetables. On no account should the jars be opened to replace the liquid. Leave undisturbed for 24 hours, then test the seals. Label jars and store in a dark, dry place.

Bottling times

Vegetables	Blanching	at 10 lb. pressure
Asparagus	2–3 min.	30–40 min.
Broad beans	5 min.	35–50 min.
French beans	3 min.	35–40 min.
Runner beans	5 min.	35–40 min.
Beetroot	15–20 min.	35–40 min.
Carrots	10 min.	40–50 min.
Celery	6 min.	30–40 min.
Mushrooms	5 min.	35–40 min.
Peas	2–3 min.	40–50 min.
Parsnips	5 min.	40–50 min.
Peppers, red or green	5 min.	35–40 min.
New potatoes	5 min.	40–50 min.
Sweetcorn	3 min.	50–55 min.
Vegetable macedoine	5 min.	40–45 min.

Salting

This is one of the oldest methods of preserving vegetables, and is best suited to green beans and nuts.

Runner beans or French beans: select very fresh young beans, wash, dry and remove the strings.
Leave French beans whole and slice runner beans. For every 3 lb. beans allow 1 lb. kitchen salt. Pack the beans in layers with the salt, beginning and ending with a layer of salt. Press the beans well down and fill the jars to the top. Cover with several layers of brown paper—never use metal lids, the salt will corrode the metal.
After a few days the beans will have shrunk in the jars, and they should be refilled and covered with a fresh layer of salt. It's a good idea to fill a spare jar from which you can top up the main jars. Cover

with brown paper and store in a cool dry place. Before using, wash beans very thoroughly until all the salt is removed (you can soak them in warm water for 2 hours—no longer or they will toughen). Cook in boiling water without any salt until tender, takes about 25–35 minutes.

To salt nuts: choose clean dry nuts, and remove the outer green hull. Discard any which have holes or are withered and pack into a large stone jar—an old-fashioned 6–7 lb. jar is best. Sprinkle layers of salt in between the layers of nuts. Cover with brown paper and store until required.

Serve with a flair

Use your imagination when cooking and serving preserved vegetables. Drain from the jars and put in boiling salted water (except for salted vegetables). Cook until tender—as for fresh vegetables—drain and serve. Toss in melted butter, or season with garlic, or onion salt before serving. Or follow these ideas:

Buttered

Top with savoury butter made by melting butter until golden brown and adding celery seeds or snipped chives or curry powder or a good pinch dried herbs or lemon juice and finely grated Parmesan cheese or chopped parsley or finely grated onion.

Crumb style

Lightly fry 2 oz. (about 1 teacup) fresh white breadcrumbs, in 2 oz. hot butter until golden brown. Add a pinch each of salt and pepper and 1 tablespoon lemon juice or 1 tablespoon grated Parmesan cheese. Stir lightly with a fork and use to top asparagus, carrots or parsnips.

Crunchy

Just before serving vegetables, season with salt and pepper and add a little butter, then sprinkle with any of these:

Slivered toasted almonds: nice on peas, green beans or asparagus.

Crumbled bacon bits: fry until very crisp, then sprinkle over carrots or new potatoes.

Sliced stuffed olives: delicious over carrots, peas or green beans.

Chopped or sieved hard-boiled egg: sprinkle over asparagus.

Snipped parsley: good over anything.

Creamy

Heat ¼ pint single cream over low heat, then season with salt and pepper and add a nut of butter. Pour over asparagus tips, mushrooms, broad beans, carrots, or sweetcorn and sprinkle with grated cheese chopped parsley or paprika.

Scalloped

In a buttered casserole dish arrange layers of cooked vegetables and hot cheese sauce—add a little mustard to accentuate the cheese flavour. Top with buttered fresh breadcrumbs (*see crumb style page 218*) and place just above centre in a hot oven (400 deg. or Gas No. 6) for 5–10 minutes. Serve when vegetables are hot and top has browned.

Mixed

Chopped asparagus with peas or whole kernel corn. Green beans with peas, sliced carrots or celery. Carrots with diced celery, green beans or sweetcorn. Sweetcorn with sliced carrots, mushrooms or shredded peppers. Parsnips with peas or sliced carrots.

Crystallised fruits

Candied and crystallised fruits are expensive to buy so it's very well worth while preparing them at home even though the process is rather a long one.

Method

Use fruits which have a fairly pronounced flavour as the sugar overcomes the more delicate ones. Best results come from using good quality, firm, tinned pineapple chunks or rings, sliced peaches or halved apricots. Using one (1 lb. 11 oz.) tin of fruit the process is as follows.

Drain off syrup from tin and put fruit in a large bowl. Measure syrup and make up to ½ pint with water if necessary. Place in a saucepan with 8 oz. sugar and heat gently until dissolved. Then bring to the boil and pour over fruit. Place a saucer on top to keep fruit submerged and leave for 24 hours.

Pour off syrup and reboil with an extra 2 oz. of the sugar as above. Pour over the fruit and leave for a further 24 hours. Repeat this procedure twice more with an extra 2 oz. of sugar each time.

Strain syrup into a saucepan, add 3 oz. of sugar and stir until dissolved. Add fruit, bring to the boil and simmer for 3–4 minutes. Return to the bowl and leave for 48 hours. Repeat this once or twice again until the syrup has thickened, and then leave the fruit to soak for 3–4 days.

To finish the fruits: drain from the syrup and place on a wire tray. Slip a plate underneath to catch any extra syrup. Place in a very cool oven (240 deg. or Gas No. ¼) and leave for several hours until the surfaces are dry and no longer sticky—turn occasionally so that they dry out evenly. Store in cardboard boxes or jars lined with waxed paper, but do not seal airtight.

Orange peel preserve

Here the method is simpler. Use always the peel from sweet oranges.

Take any quantity of peel and remove as much white pith as possible from the inside. Then cut the peel into ¼ in. strips. Place in a pan, cover with cold water and bring slowly to the boil. Drain off the water, add fresh and reboil—repeat this process two or three times more.

Weigh the cooled peel and place it in a pan, adding to it an equal amount of sugar.

Just cover with water, bring to the boil slowly to dissolve the sugar, and cook gently until peel is tender and clear.

Strain and toss the peel in granulated sugar.

Leave the peel in a warm place to dry for several hours. Then roll in sugar again and store in a screw-topped jar.

If you are using this peel in cakes wash off all the sugary coating first. Otherwise it will sink straight to the bottom of the cake.

Pickles and relishes

Home-made pickles and relishes add zest and flavour to hot and cold meat, savoury pies, salads, sandwiches. They are economical because you can use second grade fruit—cut out any bruised or bad parts first. Never use a metal spoon or sieve, or brass, copper or iron pans when pickling with vinegar; only unchipped enamel-lined or aluminium pans are really safe. Line metal lids with special vinegar-proof paper, or use a synthetic skin such as Porosan.

Pickles

Vegetables should be soaked in brine for 12–24 hours before pickling to extract the water which might otherwise spoil the keeping qualities.

Watery vegetables are 'dry brined', that is, sprinkled with salt; others are put in a solution of ½ lb. salt to ½ gallon water—use kitchen or cooking salt. Malt or cider vinegar give a good flavour, use distilled vinegar for a clear pickle. Or make your own spiced vinegar from the following recipe.

Spiced vinegar

YOU WILL NEED FOR 1 QUART:

    3 in. stick of cinnamon
    6 cloves
    5 pieces of mace
    3 bay leaves
    1 dessertspoon whole allspice
    1 quart of malt vinegar

Tie spices in a piece of muslin and put into a saucepan with vinegar. Bring slowly to boiling point. Remove pan from heat, cover with a lid and leave for 2 hours. Remove spice bag and use vinegar cold.

Pickled beetroot

Boil beetroots whole for 1–1½ hours, then skin and slice or dice them. Do not brine, but pack in jars, cover with spiced vinegar, and seal.

A variety of pickles and relishes in storage jars with lids sealed with melted paraffin wax

Pickled red cabbage

Choose a firm red cabbage and discard outer leaves. Shred rest, sprinkle with salt and leave for 24 hours. Rinse and drain, put in basin and cover with spiced vinegar. Leave a further 24 hours, mixing occasionally, then pack into jars, top up with vinegar, cover and seal.

Pickled onions

Select small pickling onions or shallots, allowing about 4 lb. onions for each quart of spiced vinegar. Cut the ends off neatly, peel and soak in brine solution for 24 hours. Drain and pack tightly into jars. Cover with cold spiced vinegar and store at least 2 months before using.

Pickled eggs

For every 6 eggs used allow 1 pint of spiced vinegar. Prepare the vinegar and allow to cool. Hard boil the eggs, then hold immediately under cold running water and remove shells.
Pack the eggs into wide-necked glass jars with screw lids and cover with cold spiced vinegar. Store in a cool place and leave for 6 weeks before using.

Pickled fruits

Pickled fruits are preserved without brining. They should be cooked gently in spiced vinegar to which sugar has been added. When fruit is tender but still whole, take it out of the vinegar, drain and pack into jars. Cook vinegar until it becomes syrupy, then pour it boiling over the fruit. Cover and seal.

Pickled pears

If possible use small, whole cooking pears. Peel, do not core, leave on the stalk and stick a clove in each. Drop pears into weak brine to prevent discolouration. Add 12 oz. sugar to each quart of spiced vinegar and bring to the boil. Rinse the pears, add to the vinegar and cook very gently until they begin to look transparent. Remove carefully and pack neatly into warmed jars. Boil the vinegar until syrupy, then pour it, boiling, over the fruit.
Cover and seal jars, then store for 2–3 months before using them.

Pickled plums

Use small plums or halve and stone large ones. Proceed as for pickled fruits, using 1 lb. sugar to each quart of spiced vinegar. After removing the cooked fruit boil the vinegar for 15 minutes. Pour into the jars over the fruit and leave until the next day. Then strain and reboil the vinegar for a further 15 minutes and pour over fruit again. Repeat this for four successive days, then cover and seal.

Pickled orange wedges

YOU WILL NEED FOR ABOUT 2 LB.:

4 oranges
water to cover
½ level teaspoon bicarbonate of soda
½ oz. whole allspice
12 whole cloves
3 in. stick of cinnamon
½ oz. bruised ginger
1 pint malt vinegar
1 lb. granulated sugar

Wash and cut each orange into 8 segments, leaving the skin on. Cover them with water and add the bicarbonate of soda. Bring to the boil and simmer for 20 minutes. Tie the spices in muslin, add to vinegar and leave to simmer for 20 minutes in a covered saucepan.
When orange peel is soft, drain off the water. Remove the spice bag and carefully dissolve sugar in the vinegar. Bring to the boil and add the segments of oranges. Cover with a lid and simmer for a further 20 minutes.
Remove orange segments with a draining spoon and put into hot, dry jars. Boil the vinegar and sugar to a syrup and top up the jars. Cover and seal.
Delicious served with cold meat, ham and poultry.

Chutneys

Spices and flavouring can be varied according to individual tastes. With a new recipe make a small trial amount to make sure you like it. A spicy chutney will mellow on storing.
In a covered pan, cook onion and any tough fruit very gently in the vinegar until soft. Then add the spices and other ingredients and finish cooking with the lid off. The finished chutney should be smooth and thick, the vinegar having completely boiled away. Never use a metal spoon or brass, copper or iron pans, only unchipped enamel-lined or aluminium pans are really safe. Bottle as for pickles.

Green tomato chutney

YOU WILL NEED FOR ABOUT 10 LB.:

2 lb. apples
6 lb. green tomatoes
3 lb. onions
1 quart vinegar
3 lb. demerara sugar
12 cloves
1 level teaspoon ground mace
1½ level teaspoons white pepper
1½ level teaspoons cayenne pepper
4 oz. mustard seed
1 oz. (or 2 level tablespoons) salt
1 bay leaf

Wash, core and chop the apples, cut the tomatoes into pieces and peel and chop onions. Simmer these gently in vinegar for 1 hour. Add sugar, bruised cloves, mace, peppers, mustard seed, salt and bay leaf. Simmer gently for 1½ hours or until thick and smooth. Put into hot jars and cover.

Pear chutney

YOU WILL NEED FOR 3 LB.:

3 lb. pears
1 lb. onions
rind and juice of 1 lemon and 1 orange
½ lb. granulated sugar
¼ lb. seedless raisins
½ pint malt vinegar
¼ level teaspoon powdered cloves
1 level teaspoon powdered ginger
1 level teaspoon salt
3 capsicums

Peel and chop pears and onions. Place in a large pan with all other ingredients. Bring slowly to the boil and simmer gently for 2 hours until of a thick and smooth consistency. Remove the capsicums, pour chutney into hot jars and seal.

Apple chutney

YOU WILL NEED FOR ABOUT 6 LB.:

6 lb. sharp apples
1 quart malt vinegar
3 lb. brown sugar
1½ oz. ground ginger
1 level teaspoon mixed spice
¼ level teaspoon cayenne pepper
1 level tablespoon salt
2 lb. sultanas

Wipe, core and chop apples and cook gently in vinegar to a fairly thick pulp. Stir in sugar and remaining ingredients and boil for about 20 minutes without a lid, until thick and smooth—the exact boiling time will depend upon the juiciness of the apples. Stir fairly often to prevent burning. Pour at once into hot jars, filling almost to top, and seal.

Relishes

These are made from chopped mixed fruits and vegetables. Serve them with hot hamburgers, frankfurters, chops or steaks.

Red pepper relish

YOU WILL NEED FOR 5 LB.:

2 dozen sweet red peppers
6 medium-sized onions
1 pint cider or white vinegar
1 lb. granulated sugar
2 level tablespoons salt
2 level tablespoons mustard seed

Halve and de-seed the peppers and mince coarsely with peeled onions. Put in a saucepan with vinegar, sugar, salt and mustard seed. Bring slowly to the boil to dissolve the sugar, then simmer uncovered for 30 minutes until the peppers and onions are soft and the mixture is thick. Pour into hot dry jars and seal.

Tomato and pineapple relish

YOU WILL NEED FOR 5 LB.:

1¾ lb. tomatoes
1 (1 lb. 14 oz.) tin pineapple tid bits, drained
2 teaspoons Worcestershire sauce
3 tablespoons vinegar
1 level teaspoon cinnamon
1 level teaspoon allspice
2 lb. 10 oz. granulated sugar
¼ pint fruit pectin

Cut tomatoes into quarters and simmer in a saucepan for ten minutes. Sieve tomatoes into a clean saucepan and add pineapple, Worcestershire sauce, vinegar, spice and sugar. Stir over low heat, until sugar has dissolved, then bring to the boil, and boil for a further 2 minutes. Draw pan off heat, add fruit pectin. Skim, stir and cool for 5 minutes, then put into pots and seal.

Sauces, Ketchups and syrups

Sauces and ketchups use a lot of fruit, sieved and concentrated into a thick, rich pulp. So be economical and make them when fruit is at its cheapest, at the height of the season.

Tomato ketchup

YOU WILL NEED FOR 5 ½ PINT BOTTLES:

6 lb. ripe tomatoes
½ lb. granulated sugar
¾ oz. (or 1 rounded tablespoon) salt
½ pint white malt vinegar
½ level teaspoon ground ginger
½ level teaspoon mixed spice
½ level teaspoon ground mace
pinch of cayenne pepper

Wash and halve tomatoes and place them in a large saucepan. Cook gently, without a lid, until soft. Using a wooden spoon, rub through a fine sieve into a mixing bowl.
Return pulp to saucepan and add sugar, salt, vinegar, spices and pepper. Cook gently, stirring all the time, to dissolve sugar, then bring to the boil.
Simmer, uncovered, until the pulp is thick and will coat the back of a spoon—about 40 minutes. Pour into warmed sauce bottles to within 1 in. of the tops. Cork with boiled new corks, tying them on loosely with string.
Place the bottles in a large pan, fill with cold water to reach the necks of the bottles and sterilise them, as instructed *see page 227*, for 15 minutes. Remove from the hot water, press in the corks firmly, cool and screw on caps.

Texas hot barbecue sauce

YOU WILL NEED FOR ABOUT 2 BOTTLES:

½ pint tomato ketchup (*see recipe above*)
¼ pint vinegar
1 level teaspoon salt
2 crushed cloves of garlic
2 tablespoons olive oil

Combine all the ingredients together, bring to the boil and simmer gently for 20 minutes. Pour in bottles and sterilise as instructed, *see page 227.*
Serve with steak, chops, frankfurters.

Plum sauce

YOU WILL NEED FOR 4–5 BOTTLES:

4 lb. dark plums
½ lb. onions, finely chopped
½ lb. brown sugar
1 oz. (or 2 level tablespoons) salt
8 cloves
1 oz. mustard seed
FOR THE SPICED VINEGAR:
2 pints malt vinegar
2 rounded teaspoons cloves
1 rounded teaspoon allspice
1 rounded teaspoon black peppercorns
¼ oz. stick cinnamon
¼ oz. root ginger

Place ingredients for spiced vinegar in a saucepan and bring to the boil, draw pan off heat at once and leave to infuse, covered with a lid, for 2–3 hours. Strain and reserve.
Halve and stone the plums and place in a pan with the onion and half the spiced vinegar. Cover with a lid and simmer until very soft and pulpy. Using a wooden spoon, rub the sauce through a very fine sieve into a large mixing basin. Return the pulp to the pan and add the remaining vinegar, sugar and salt. Tie cloves and mustard seed in a muslin bag and add also to the pan.
Simmer with the lid off, stirring occasionally until the sauce is smooth—takes about 1–1½ hours. Pour into clean hot bottles to within 1 in. of the top, cork with boiled new corks, tying them on lightly with string. Sterilise *see page 227* for 15 minutes, cool, seal and store.
This sauce has a sharp flavour and goes particularly well with cold meat, fish and grills.

Mint sauce

½ pint distilled malt vinegar
4 oz. (4 rounded tablespoons) sugar
8 tablespoons chopped mint

Measure the vinegar and sugar into a saucepan and bring up to the boil, stirring to dissolve the sugar. Draw the pan off the heat and add the mint. Pour into the smallest size preserving bottles available, and sterilise—*see page 227*, for 15 minutes.

Piccalilli

YOU WILL NEED FOR 6–7 JARS:

FOR THE BRINE:
1½–2 pints water
¼ lb. salt
FOR THE VEGETABLES:
1 lb. small onions or shallots
1 lb. marrow
1 small cauliflower
½ cucumber
½ lb. French or runner beans
FOR THE SAUCE:
3 oz. (or 3 rounded tablespoons) flour
2 oz. dry mustard
½ oz. tumeric powder
1 quart vinegar

Put the salt in a large mixing basin, add the water and stir until dissolved. Peel and cut up the vegetables into pieces of a suitable size for eating. Leave the onions whole. Add to the brine, cover and leave to steep for 24 hours, then drain.

To prepare the sauce measure the flour, mustard and tumeric into a large pan. Add a little vinegar and blend to a paste. Add the rest of the vinegar and stir over gentle heat until it thickens and boils. Add the drained vegetables and cook gently for 3–4 minutes until warmed through. Pack the vegetables into clean hot pickle jars distributing evenly the various vegetables. Pour in sufficient mustard sauce to cover, clean jars and screw on metal tops, lined with vinegar papers. Store a few weeks before using then serve with cold meat.

Fruit syrups

Fruit syrups make excellent cool drinks with added water or milk. When citrus fruits are used the finely grated rind is included for a good flavour. Grate only the outer zest which contains the flavouring oils, never include the white pith which is bitter and can spoil a delicate flavour. Strawberries, blackberries or raspberries are also good choices for a fruit syrup. Even when processed these syrups will not keep indefinitely and should be used within 2 or 3 months.

Blackberry syrup

YOU WILL NEED FOR 2–3 BOTTLES:

2 lb. blackberries
¾ lb. sugar for each 1 pint of juice

Carefully wash the blackberries. Place them in a small earthenware bowl and set over a pan of boiling water. Leave for about 1 hour, crushing the fruit with a wooden spoon to help extract the juice.

Strain the juice through a scalded muslin cloth and leave overnight to drip. Measure the juice into a pan and add sugar. Stir over low heat until dissolved, then bring to the boil.

Pour into clean, warm bottles to within 1 in. of the tops, and tie on boiled corks lightly with string. Sterilise as below for 30 minutes. Remove from the hot water, and seal and cool.

Fruit syrups are good combined with chilled milk. Add 2–3 tablespoons, according to taste, to a tumbler of milk and stir well.

Lemon syrup

YOU WILL NEED FOR ABOUT 8 BOTTLES:

2 lb. granulated sugar
1 pint water
3 large lemons
1 oz. citric acid powder

Dissolve sugar in water over low heat, and bring to the boil. Draw pan off heat, add lemon juice and finely grated rind and the citric acid. Stir thoroughly and pour into a large jug or mixing basin and leave for 12 hours or overnight.

Strain and pour into clean, dry bottles, filling to within 1 in. of the tops, and loosely tie on the corks. Sterilise, *see page 227*, for 5 minutes. Remove from the water, seal and cool.

To use: measure 2–3 tablespoons into each tumbler and top up with ice cubes, water or soda water and lemon slices.

Orange syrup

YOU WILL NEED FOR ABOUT 7 BOTTLES:

1 pint fresh orange juice (about 8 oranges)
2½ lb. granulated sugar
1½ pints water
1 oz. citric acid powder

Scrub the oranges, finely grate the rind from 4 and set aside. Squeeze out the juice from all the oranges, and if necessary make up to 1 pint with tinned unsweetened orange juice. Measure sugar and water into a saucepan. Add the finely grated orange rind and stir over low heat until the sugar has dissolved. Bring to the boil and draw the pan off the heat. Add the orange juice and citric acid, mix well, strain and pour into

clean, dry bottles, filling to within 1 in. of the tops. Tie on boiled corks loosely with string, and sterilise for 5 minutes. Remove from the water, seal and cool.
To use: $\frac{1}{3}$–$\frac{1}{2}$ fill a tumbler with the syrup and top up with ice cubes, and water or soda water.

Peppermint cordial

YOU WILL NEED FOR 3 BOTTLES:

1 lb. granulated sugar
1 pint water
juice of a lemon
6 drops oil of peppermint
green colouring

Dissolve sugar in water and lemon juice, then strain into a deep saucepan and bring to the boil. Draw pan off heat, add peppermint essence and colouring. Pour into clean, dry bottles and tie the boiled corks loosely. Sterilise as instructions for 30 minutes. Drain from water and cool.
This cordial is nicest served in chilled milk—allow 2 tablespoons per tumbler of milk.

Rose hip syrup

YOU WILL NEED FOR 3–4 BOTTLES:

2 lb. rose hips
4$\frac{1}{2}$ pints water
1 lb. sugar

Remove stalks and mince rose hips. Have ready a pan containing 3 pints boiling water. Place the rose hips in the water, and reboil. Remove from the heat and allow to stand for 15 minutes. Pour the contents into a scalded jelly bag, and allow the bulk of the juice to drip through. Then return the pulp to the saucepan, add 1$\frac{1}{2}$ pints boiling water, reboil and allow to stand again for 10 minutes. Strain as before.
Pour the juice into a clean saucepan and simmer until it measures only 1$\frac{1}{2}$ pints. Add sugar and bring to the boil. Boil for 5 minutes. Pour the syrup while still hot into clean, warm dry bottles to within 1 in. of the tops and tie on boiled corks loosely. Sterilise as instructions for 5 minutes, remove from the water, seal and cool.
Because of its valuable vitamin C content, this syrup is excellent for children either as it is by the spoonful or blended with milk—about 2 tablespoons to each tumbler of milk.

To sterilise sauces or syrups

Pour the mixture into clean, warm bottles to within 1 in. of the tops; this allows for expansion during heating. Cork the bottles with new corks which have been boiled for 15 minutes and tie lightly with fine white string. It's important that the corks should be tied on, otherwise they might blow out during processing and the contents would be lost.
Place the bottles in the deepest saucepan you have, either on a false bottom or on corrugated paper or newspaper. Fill with cold water to within 1 in. of the tops and bring slowly to the boil. Simmer for the required time, then remove from the water. Press the corks in firmly, allow to cool and then screw on the caps.
Sauces and syrups preserved in this way will keep for 2–3 weeks after being opened if they are kept in a cool place. An exception is rose hip syrup which should be used within a week of opening.
Proper sauce bottles, corks and caps can be purchased in England, by post from Fowler Lee and Co., 82 London Street, Reading, Berks.,—send for their catalogues and price list (enclose stamp for return post).

Green tomatoes in ginger syrup

YOU WILL NEED FOR 2–3 JARS:

2 lb. small green tomatoes
12 oz. granulated sugar
1 pint water
4 large pieces of root ginger, bruised well with a
    rolling pin
green colouring

Cut a cross in the base of each tomato, having washed and removed the stalk first. Blanch in boiling water for 5 minutes, then peel off the skins.
Dissolve the sugar in the water and bring the syrup to the boil, then add the ginger. Add the peeled tomatoes and simmer gently in the syrup for 10–15 minutes, or until tender when a skewer runs easily through the core.
Remove tomatoes from the syrup and pack into 1 lb. Kilner jars, then reduce the syrup further by boiling for another 5–10 minutes. Draw the pan off the heat and add a little green colouring. Pour over the bottled tomatoes, then seal with the lid of the Kilner jar.
These are delicious eaten with cold meats of all types, and improve considerably if allowed to mature for a few weeks. To keep longer sterilise, *see instruction*, for 15 minutes.

Home Cooked
Recipes from Abroad

France

Ever since Louis XV heralded a new dish with such delight that he bestowed the Cordon Bleu (an ancient French honour) on its female creator, French cooking has led the world. And justifiably! Nowhere else could they make a crispy delight like Croque Monsieur from bread, ham and cheese. Savoury recipes often use a bouquet garni—parsley, thyme and bay leaf tied together.

Pâté maison

YOU WILL NEED FOR 6–8 SERVINGS:

- ½ lb. chicken livers
- 6 oz. salt pork
- 1 small onion
- 4 oz. fresh white breadcrumbs
- 1 clove garlic, chopped
- 1 level teaspoon salt
- ¼ level teaspoon pepper
- 1 level teaspoon marjoram
- 1 medium-sized egg
- 4 oz. bacon rashers
- 2 oz. butter

Mince chicken livers, pork and onion, add breadcrumbs, garlic, salt, pepper, marjoram and beaten egg—the mixture will be very soft.
Spoon into a well-greased 1 pint pudding basin or pâté dish. Cover with bacon rashers and cook, standing in water in a shallow tin, in a warm oven (355 deg. or Gas No. 4) for 1½ hours. When cooked, remove the pâté from the oven and peel the bacon strips from the top. Cover with greaseproof paper, and stand a weight on top till cold.

Run melted butter over the top and the pâté will keep for up to three days in a refrigerator.
Serve sliced as a starter to a meal, with hot toast and lettuce leaves.

Poulet marengo

(CHICKEN IN A RICH, BROWN SAUCE)

YOU WILL NEED FOR 4 SERVINGS:

- 4 chicken joints
- 2 oz. butter
- 2 tablespoons cooking oil
- 2 onions, finely chopped
- 1 tablespoon flour
- ⅓ pint (or 1 teacup) dry white wine
- 1 tablespoon tomato purée
- bouquet garni
- pepper and salt
- ½ level teaspoon sugar
- ½ lb. button mushrooms, sliced
- croûtons (*see recipe*)

Wipe chicken joints and brown in hot butter and oil in a large frying pan or saucepan.
Remove chicken and add onions to the hot fat. Sauté gently until softened—about 5 minutes. Stir in the flour and cook 1 minute, then add wine, tomato purée, bouquet garni, seasoning and sugar. Stir until boiling and add the chicken joints. Cover pan with a lid and simmer for 1 hour. Add the mushrooms and cook a further 15 minutes. Serve garnished with croûtons (cubes of bread fried until lightly brown).

228

Marquise Alice, tomato hors d'oeuvre and boeuf bourguignon

Poulet Provençale
(CHICKEN OF PROVENCE)

YOU WILL NEED FOR 4 SERVINGS:

4 chicken joints
seasoned flour
2 tablespoons oil for frying
chopped parsley for garnish
FOR THE SAUCE:
1 lb. fresh (or one 15 oz. tin) tomatoes
1 small onion, finely chopped
2 tablespoons oil
1 clove garlic, crushed with a little salt
   and chopped
1 level teaspoon salt
pinch pepper
1 level teaspoon castor sugar
bouquet garni (bay leef, sprig of thyme and
   parsley stalk tied together)
juice of half a lemon

Trim the chicken joints and roll in the seasoned flour. Add skin side down to the hot oil in a frying pan. Brown quickly turning once, then drain and place in a casserole dish. Set aside while preparing the sauce. Plunge the tomatoes in boiling water for 1 minute, drain and peel away the skins. Add, along with the chopped onion and garlic to the hot oil in a saucepan. Fry gently for 5 minutes stirring occasionally. Add the sugar, seasoning and bouquet garni. Cover with a lid and cook very gently for 20 minutes. Draw the pan off the heat and rub the sauce through a sieve. Add lemon juice, check seasoning and pour over the chicken joints.

Cover casserole dish with a lid and place in the centre of a moderate oven (355 deg. or Gas No. 4). Cook for 1 hour until chicken is tender. Sprinkle with chopped parsley and serve.

Boeuf bourguignon
(BEEF IN RED WINE)

YOU WILL NEED FOR 6 SERVINGS:

2 lb. topside beef or chuck or rump steak
1 oz. butter
1 tablespoon cooking oil
1 onion, finely chopped
1 clove garlic, chopped
1 rounded tablespoon flour
½ pint stock
½ pint red wine
bouquet gami
1 lb. button onions, peeled and left whole
¼ lb. button mushrooms
chopped parsley to garnish

Wipe and cut beef into cubes, brown quickly in the hot butter and oil. Drain meat from pan and add onion and garlic to fat.

Sauté gently until soft and beginning to brown. Add meat and sprinkle the flour on top. Stir in the stock and red wine, add the bouquet garni and cover with a lid. Simmer gently for 1 hour.

Then add the button onions—cover and simmer a further 1 hour. About 15 minutes before the cooking time is completed, add the mushrooms, recover and cook for remaining time. Remove the bouquet garni, check the seasoning, and serve sprinkled with chopped parsley.

Poires au vin rouge
(PEARS IN RED WINE)

YOU WILL NEED FOR 4 SERVINGS:

4 lb. small pears
8 oz. (or 8 rounded tablespoons) castor sugar
½ pint water
small pieces of stick cinnamon
¼ pint red wine

Peel pears, but leave whole and with the stalks intact. Place close together in a saucepan with sugar, water and cinnamon. Simmer gently, covered with a lid, for 15 minutes. Remove lid, add red wine and cook for 15 minutes over low heat.

Drain pears and place in a deep serving dish. Continue to boil liquid until reduced to a light syrup. Spoon syrup over pears and chill.

Marquise Alice
(COFFEE CREAM DESSERT)

YOU WILL NEED FOR 6 SERVINGS:

1 tablespoon powdered gelatine
3 tablespoons water
4 egg yolks
2 oz. (or 2 rounded tablespoons) castor sugar
1 pint milk
1 level teaspoon instant coffee
1 packet sponge fingers
rum for flavouring
¼ pint double cream
FOR THE TOPPING:
¼ pint single cream
¼ pint double cream
2–3 tablespoons sieved red jam

Sprinkle the gelatine over the water and leave to soak. In a mixing basin, beat egg yolks and sugar until light and creamy. Stir in warmed milk, place the basin over a pan of hot water and stir until thickened, then add soaked gelatine and stir until dissolved.

Remove basin from heat, mix in coffee flavouring and leave in a cool place until beginning to thicken. Meanwhile, arrange the sponge fingers on a plate and sprinkle with a little rum. Whisk the cream and fold into the cooled custard. Pour half the mixture into a wet shallow cake tin about 8 in. wide. Arrange soaked sponge fingers over the top and pour in remaining mixture. Leave to chill until set firm. Turn on to a plate, whisk the double and single cream together until thick. Reserve half for decoration, and coat the mould smoothly with rest. Place reserved cream in a piping bag and pipe a decoration on top and round the sides *(see colour picture)* add a little colour and pattern with the red jam.

Croque Monsieur

(FRIED SANDWICHES)

YOU WILL NEED FOR 4 SERVINGS:

    8 slices bread, with crusts removed
    4 slices ham
    4 slices Gruyère cheese
    2–3 oz. butter for frying

On four of the bread slices arrange a slice each of ham and cheese. Top with a second slice of bread and trim sides even. Fry sandwiches in plenty of hot butter. When lightly brown, turn and brown the other side. Turn several times, adding more butter if necessary.

Petits fours

These small fancy biscuits and cookies are very delicate, and on the Continent are usually served after a meal with coffee or as a dessert with a mousse or ice cream. These are delicious to eat but a little difficult to make, so follow the directions carefully.

Copeaux

YOU WILL NEED FOR 12–18 COPEAUX:

    3 oz. (or 3 rounded tablespoons) plain flour
    2 egg whites
    pinch salt
    4 oz. (or 4 rounded tablespoons) castor sugar
    3 oz. melted butter, cooled slightly
    few drops vanilla essence

Sift flour on to a piece of paper and set aside. Whisk the egg whites and salt until stiff. Gently fold in sugar, melted butter, flour and vanilla essence.

Using a cotton or nylon piping bag fitted with a ¼ in. tube, pipe in fingers on to a greased and floured baking tray—leave room for them to spread.

Place just above centre in a hot oven (425 deg. or Gas No. 7) and bake for 5–8 minutes, or until golden brown. Remove from the baking tray while still warm and roll round the handle of a wooden spoon to give them an attractive curly shape. Remove when cool and crisp.

Almond macaroons

YOU WILL NEED FOR 24 MACAROONS:

    4 oz. (6 rounded tablespoons) ground almonds
    6 oz. castor sugar
    2 small egg whites, lightly mixed
    ¼ teaspoon almond essence
    granulated sugar

Measure ground almonds and sugar into a mixing basin, beat in the lightly mixed egg whites one at a time, then add almond essence. Beat well until fairly smooth.

Spoon the mixture into a cotton or nylon piping bag, fitted with a ½ in. tube, then pipe on to a baking tray lined with silicone paper—pipe in mounds each the size of a shilling. Sprinkle with sugar.

Place in the centre of a moderate oven (355 deg. or Gas No. 4) and bake for 15 minutes or until firm. Cool for a few minutes, and then lift off the paper.

Tuiles

YOU WILL NEED FOR 12–15 TUILES:

    1–2 oz. finely-shredded or flaked almonds
    2 oz. (or 2 rounded tablespoons) castor sugar
    1 egg white
    1 level tablespoon plain flour
    finely grated rind of ½ lemon or
        few drops almond essence

Mix all the ingredients together and stir thoroughly for one minute. Put small teaspoons of it on to a greased and floured tray, allowing plenty of room for spreading.

Place high up in a hot oven (425 deg. or Gas No. 7) and bake for 5–8 minutes or until they are golden brown.

Remove from the tray very gently with a palette knife, then place over a rolling pin until crisp—this gives them the traditional tuile shape.

Germany

You've never tasted a sausage if you haven't had the smoky, succulent German ones. Buy them from a delicatessen and serve with sauerkraut (cabbage preserved in brine) or pickled vegetables. A German meal usually starts with a thick, warming soup, and finishes with a fairly substantial sweet—cheese, apple or their special fruit cake are top favourites.

Kase torte

(CHEESE CAKE)

YOU WILL NEED FOR 6 SERVINGS:

4–6 digestive biscuits, crushed
1 lb. curd or cottage cheese
3 eggs, separated
4 oz. (or 4 rounded tablespoons) castor sugar
1 oz. (or 3 heaped teaspoons) cornflour
½ teaspoon vanilla essence
1 carton soured cream
FOR THE TOPPING:
1 (14 oz.) tin red cherries or fresh fruit
¼ pint fruit juice
1 level teaspoon arrowroot

Preheat the oven to moderate (310 deg. or Gas No. 2) and make sure it is well heated before putting in the cheese cake.
Lightly butter a 7 in. round cheese cake tin, or use a cake tin with a loose base. Flour lightly and cover base with the crushed biscuit crumbs, press down to make a firm layer. Sieve the cottage cheese and set aside. Using a wooden spoon, beat egg yolks and sugar until light and creamy, stir in cottage cheese, cornflour, vanilla essence and soured cream. Beat until smooth.
Beat egg whites until stiff and fold into the mixture. Spoon into the prepared tin and place on the centre shelf of the oven. Bake for 1½ hours, then turn off the heat and leave the cake in the oven for a further 15–30 minutes. When quite cold, remove from tin.
To decorate: Arrange fruit over the top of the cake. Blend fruit juice and arrowroot and bring to the boil, stirring until thickened. Add a little colouring, if liked, and spoon it over the fruit. Chill before serving.

Wiener schnitzel

(VEAL IN BREADCRUMBS)

YOU WILL NEED FOR 4 SERVINGS:

4 veal escalopes
seasoned flour
1 egg, lightly beaten
fresh white breadcrumbs
1–2 oz. butter for frying

Ask the butcher to beat the veal escalopes very flat. Dip first in a little seasoned flour, then in beaten egg, and lastly in fresh white breadcrumbs. Pat firmly to make a neat coating. Fry in hot butter, turning to brown evenly, until golden brown—takes about 6–8 minutes. Serve very hot with lemon.

Knackwurst und sauerkraut

(SAUSAGES AND SAUERKRAUT)

YOU WILL NEED FOR 4 SERVINGS:

1 lb. tin sauerkraut
½ teaspoon salt
black pepper
¼ teaspoon caraway seeds
1 lb. knackwurst sausages

Remove sauerkraut from tin, drain and place in a pan with boiling water to cover. Cook slowly for 1 hour or until tender, then drain and season with salt and pepper and flavour with caraway seeds.
To cook the knackwurst, bring to the boil about 1–2 in. water in a large pan. Immerse the sausages, cover with a lid and leave to simmer for 10 minutes. Serve with sauerkraut on a hot platter, with German mustard.

Rotkohl mit apfel

(RED CABBAGE WITH APPLE)

YOU WILL NEED FOR 4–6 SERVINGS:

1 (2½ lb.) red cabbage, shredded
⅓ pint boiling water
3 cooking apples, pared, and sliced
1 oz. melted butter or margarine
4 tablespoons vinegar
1½ teaspoons flour
1 oz. (or 1 rounded tablespoon) brown sugar
pinch salt, dash of pepper

Put cabbage in a saucepan, pour over water, bring to the boil and simmer, covered with a lid, for 10 minutes. Add apples and cook for a further 20 minutes or until tender. In a small basin combine butter, vinegar, flour, sugar, salt and pepper, add to mixture and reboil.

Knackwurst with sauerkraut.

Frucht kuchen

(FRUIT CAKE)

YOU WILL NEED FOR 4–6 SERVINGS:

6 oz. (6 rounded tablespoons) flour
pinch of salt
3 level teaspoons baking powder
1 oz. butter
1 oz. white fat
1 oz. (or 1 rounded tablespoon) castor sugar
1 small egg
3 tablespoons milk
little melted butter or margarine
FOR THE TOPPING:
fresh peaches or plums
1 tablespoon castor sugar
½ level teaspoon ground cinnamon
little butter

Sift together flour, salt and baking powder into a mixing basin. Beat down the fats until soft and then rub into the flour. Lightly mix together the sugar, egg and milk and stir in, using a fork to get a scone-like mixture. Set aside for 10 minutes to rest. Turn out on to a lightly floured board and pat out to a circle large enough to fit a 7–8 in. shallow cake tin. Pat dough into buttered tin. Leaving a rim, neatly arrange sliced fruit on the top. Sprinkle over it the mixed sugar and cinnamon. Dot with butter, place in the centre of a hot oven (425 deg. or Gas No. 7) and bake for 15–20 minutes.

Weihnachtsstollen

(YEAST LOAF)

YOU WILL NEED FOR 1 LOAF:

8 oz. (or 8 rounded tablespoons) plain flour
½ oz. fresh (or 2 level teaspoons) dried yeast
4 tablespoons warm milk
2 oz. (or 2 rounded tablespoons) castor sugar
½ oz. butter, melted
1 whole egg
1 egg white
4 oz. dried fruit
beaten egg and milk for brushing
1 oz. icing sugar
FOR THE MARZIPAN FILLING:
3 oz. (or 3 heaped tablespoons) ground almonds
2 oz. (or 2 rounded tablespoons) castor sugar
1 teaspoon rose water
1 egg yolk

To make the dough. Sift the flour into a mixing basin and set aside to warm. Add the yeast to the warm milk with 1 teaspoon of the sugar and stir until dissolved. Add to the sifted flour along with the melted butter, mixed egg and remaining sugar. Knead the dough well, then leave in a warm place, covered with a cloth until risen and double in size.

Meanwhile, prepare the marzipan filling. Combine together the ground almonds and sugar, add the egg yolk and the rose water and mix to a smooth paste. To finish the bread turn the risen dough out on to a floured surface and knead. Roll out to an oval shape twelve inches long and ten inches wide. Place a strip of marzipan down the centre. Brush one side with milk and fold the dough over in half. Seal the edges, cover with a cloth and allow to prove in a warm place until puffy.

Brush with beaten egg yolk and milk. Place in the centre of a moderately hot oven (390 deg. or Gas No. 5) and bake for 25 minutes. Allow to cool and dust with icing sugar.

Wiener apfelkuchen

(APPLE CAKE)

YOU WILL NEED FOR 1 8 IN. CAKE:

6 oz. butter or margarine
6 oz. (or 6 rounded tablespoons) castor sugar
4 large eggs
5 oz. (or 5 heaped tablespoons) self-raising flour
2½ oz. (or 8 level tablespoons) cornflour
grated rind of ½ lemon
¼ level teaspoon salt
4 medium-sized sharp flavoured apples, peeled,
    cored and halved
icing sugar for dusting top
whipped cream for serving

Sift together the flour and cornflour and set aside. In a small saucepan melt the butter or margarine over a very low heat—do not allow to boil. Pour it into a mixing basin, add the sugar and beat well until light. Beat in the eggs, one at a time. Add the salt and enough finely grated lemon rind to taste.

Gradually stir in the sifted flour until the mixture is smooth. Pour half into the base of a buttered 8 in. deep round cake tin. Place on the apple halves, rounded sides upwards and then spoon over the remainder of the mixture, allowing the apple halves to show through slightly.

Place in the centre of a moderate oven (355 deg. or Gas No. 4) and bake for 1 hour. Remove from the tin, and allow to cool, when cold dust heavily with sifted icing sugar. Serve with whipped cream.

Spain

Spaniards don't like their food to be half-hearted. They want plenty of flavour—and plenty of garlic! If you've a delicate palate and find this a bit hard to take, here's a tip. Omit the garlic from the recipe, but crush one clove, rub it round cooking or serving dish and then discard it.

Gazpacho

(COLD SALAD SOUP)

YOU WILL NEED FOR 4 SERVINGS:

    8 tablespoons olive oil
    2 lb. small ripe tomatoes
    2 large Spanish onions, shredded
    2–3 garlic cloves, crushed
    few raw bacon rinds
    2 tablespoons wine vinegar
    ¼ pint dry sherry
    2½ oz. (or 1 teacup) fine white or brown breadcrumbs
    salt and pepper

Heat oil in a large pan, and add tomatoes, onions, garlic, and bacon rinds. Cover liberally with water and bring to the boil. Simmer for at least 1 hour, then rub through a sieve, add vinegar, sherry and breadcrumbs, stir well, add salt and pepper to taste, and chill thoroughly. Serve in soup bowls.

Paella Valenciana

(CHICKEN AND FISH WITH RICE)

YOU WILL NEED FOR 4–6 SERVINGS:

    1 small chicken, cut in quarters
    2–3 tablespoons olive oil
    ½ lb. fresh tomatoes, quartered, or 1 (8 oz.) tin peeled tomatoes
    1 green pepper, de-seeded and shredded
    1 clove garlic, crushed and chopped
    1 (8 oz.) tin tuna fish, flaked
    6–8 scampi
    ½ lb. green peas
    ½ pint water
    pinch of saffron
    8 oz. long grain rice

In a deep, heavy frying pan (the traditional type is often of copper and has two handles), fry the chicken joints in the hot oil until browned. Add the tomatoes, green pepper and garlic and simmer for 5 minutes. Add tuna fish, scampi and peas, stir in the

water and saffron, and bring to the boil. Sprinkle in the rice and simmer gently for 30 minutes until rice and chicken are tender. Draw pan off heat, check seasoning, and let it stand for 5 minutes before serving.

Tortilla

(SPANISH OMELET)

YOU WILL NEED FOR 1–2 SERVINGS:

    3 eggs
    3 teaspoons water
    salt and pepper and pinch of cayenne pepper
    1 dessertspoon olive oil
    1 onion, sliced
    2 tomatoes, sliced
    1 teaspoon tarragon vinegar or lemon juice

Crack the eggs into a mixing basin, season with salt, pepper and cayenne pepper. Add the water and set aside.
Heat the olive oil in a 7 in. omelet or frying pan, add the onion and cook gently until tender—takes about 5 minutes. Then add the tomatoes and cook a further few moments. Stir in the vinegar or lemon juice and the egg mixture. Cook stirring over moderate heat until the egg is beginning to thicken. Allow to brown on the underside, then using a palette knife, turn over and brown on the second side. Because this omelet is bulky, it is served flat.

Zarsuela de mariscos con arroz

(FISH STEW WITH RICE)

YOU WILL NEED FOR 4 SERVINGS:

    3–4 tablespoons olive oil
    2 onions, peeled and finely chopped
    ½ lb. long grain rice
    1 (15 oz.) tin tomatoes
    ¾ pint water
    1 level teaspoon salt and pepper
    ½ lb. rock salmon, cut in pieces
    4 scallops

Heat the olive oil in a large saucepan and add the onion. Cook gently until onions are soft—about 10 minutes. Add the rice and stir until oil has been absorbed then stir in the tomatoes, water and a good seasoning of salt and pepper. Bring up to the boil and simmer gently covered with a lid for 10 minutes. Add the boned rock salmon and the prepared scallops. Cover and cook gently, for a further 15 minutes.
Remove from the heat and stand in a warm place for 5 minutes before serving.

Italy

As befits their volatile temperament, the Italians like variety. They dote on pasta in all its savoury forms—spaghetti, macaroni, lasagna, noodles, adore Pizza pie served hot with wine; and demand lots of fresh fruit and vegetables. Their favourite meat is veal—and they waste not a bone. Often they finish a meal with fruit—but when they do serve a sweet it's usually exotic.

How to cook pasta

Don't try to keep pasta hot. It doesn't improve by being kept waiting, so serve at once. Always use plenty of boiling salted water, as some pastas, among them macaroni and spaghetti, double in bulk.

The pasta should be added gradually to the boiling water, so that the water never actually comes off the boil. If you are cooking long spaghetti, hold bundle by one end and dip the other in the fast-boiling water. Then, as it softens, coil it around the inside of the pan until the whole length is immersed.

Boil fairly rapidly, uncovered, and stir occasionally to prevent sticking. A tablespoon of olive oil added to the water, especially in the case of lasagna or cannelloni, will help to prevent the pieces sticking. Cooking times vary according to thickness, but it's very important that it should not be overcooked. It should be tender, yet firm and a bit chewy. Some varieties may take as little as 2 min. (as with quick cooking egg noodles), or 7 minutes (for quick cooking macaroni). Standard spaghetti and small noodles take about 7–12 minutes, macaroni needs 12–15 minutes and lasagna 15–20 minutes. To test if it is cooked to perfection, lift a strand out with a fork and taste it, or press a piece of the pasta with a fork against the side of the pan—it should break easily and cleanly.

When cooked, drain at once in a colander and then rinse under the hot tap, or in cold water if being used for salads. When drained, use in the recipe as required or toss lightly in melted butter and serve.

Mushroom sauce

YOU WILL NEED FOR 4 SERVINGS:

1 large onion
1 small head celery, scrubbed and shredded
3 oz. butter
1 lb. button mushrooms, trimmed and sliced
3 level teaspoons salt
$\frac{1}{2}$ teaspoon dried mixed herbs
2 level tablespoons flour
1 chicken stock cube
1 pint water
juice of 1 lemon
chopped parsley
grated cheese for serving

Add chopped onion and celery to hot butter in a large saucepan. Cover and cook gently until soft—about 10 minutes. Sprinkle with salt, mixed herbs, and flour and mix well. Dissolve the chicken cube in the almost boiling water. Then stir into the mushrooms along with the strained lemon juice.

Bring to the boil and cook gently, stirring until sauce has thickened. Check seasoning and sprinkle with chopped parsley.

Serve with grated cheese.

Chicken liver sauce

YOU WILL NEED FOR 4 SERVINGS:

1 oz. butter or margarine
2 oz. bacon rashers
1 onion, peeled and finely chopped
4 oz. mushrooms trimmed and sliced
12 oz. chicken livers
1 level tablespoon flour
$\frac{3}{4}$ pint stock or water plus stock cube
1 small ($2\frac{1}{2}$ oz.) tin tomato purée
salt and pepper
1 tablespoon medium or dry sherry (optional)
grated Parmesan for serving

Heat the butter in a medium-sized saucepan and add the trimmed and chopped bacon rashers and the onion. Cook over gentle heat for 10 minutes until onion has softened and is slightly browned.

Trim the livers and slice, then add with mushrooms to the onion and fry quickly for 1–2 minutes to brown. Stir in the flour, then the stock and tomato purée. Season well, cover with a lid and simmer gently for about 30 minutes.

Check seasoning, stir in sherry if used and serve with cooked pasta. Pass grated Parmesan cheese separately.

Pizza pie and spaghetti Bolognese

Bolognese sauce

YOU WILL NEED FOR 4 SERVINGS:

½ lb. minced beef
1 onion, finely chopped
a little cooking oil
tomato sauce, see page 103

Gently sauté minced beef and onion in oil. Stir until meat has browned, then cover with a lid and cook gently for 20 minutes. Drain away all but a spoonful of oil and stir tomato sauce into the meat. Bring to the boil and serve with spaghetti and grated Parmesan cheese.

Pizza

(SAVOURY FLAN)

YOU WILL NEED FOR 2 PIZZA:

FOR THE DOUGH:
8 oz. plain flour
1 level teaspoon salt
½ level teaspoon castor sugar
¼ pint warm water
1 level teaspoon dried yeast
1 dessertspoon olive oil
FOR THE TOPPING:
1 tablespoon olive oil
½ onion, finely chopped
1 (15 oz.) tin tomatoes
1 small bay leaf
½ level teaspoon salt
1 level teaspoon sugar
pinch of pepper
FOR THE GARNISH:
2 oz. grated Parmesan cheese
anchovies and black olives

Sift flour and salt into a bowl. Dissolve sugar in warm water and sprinkle dried yeast over it. Allow to stand until frothy. Add yeast liquid and oil to the flour and mix to a soft dough. Knead on a floured board until smooth and elastic—takes about 5 minutes. Shape dough into a ball and place in a large, greased basin. Set in a warm place to rise, covered with a cloth, until double in size—about 30 minutes.

To make the topping: heat oil in a pan and cook onion until golden brown and soft. Add tomatoes, and all the remaining ingredients except those reserved for garnish. Cover with a lid and cook slowly for about 30 minutes, until thick. Stir occasionally to prevent sticking. Remove the bay leaf and allow mixture to cool.

Turn out the risen dough, flatten with knuckles, and cut into two pieces. Roll into two circles. Place them on greased baking sheets. Nip edges to raise slightly and prick the bases with a fork to prevent air bubbles forming. Set aside for 15 minutes until puffy.

Brush each crust with a little olive oil and spoon over the topping, half on each pizza. Spread to within ½ in. of the edge. Sprinkle with the Parmesan cheese, and garnish with small anchovy fillets and black olive halves.

Place pizza high up in a hot oven (425 deg. or Gas No. 7) and bake for 15–20 minutes, until the crust is browned. Serve hot, cut into 8–10 wedges.

Makes a delicious appetizer served with a glass of red wine.

Osso buco

(VEAL WITH RICE)

YOU WILL NEED FOR 4 SERVINGS:

2 veal hocks (shin)
seasoned flour
1 large carrot
1 medium-sized onion
2 tablespoons olive oil
1 small (15 oz.) tin tomatoes
pinch of mixed herbs
1 pint stock or water plus stock cube
1 teaspoon salt
¼ teaspoon pepper
grated rind of ½ a lemon
chopped parsley
8 oz. long grain rice for serving
1–2 oz. grated Parmesan cheese

Have the veal hocks cut into 3 in. pieces. Toss in seasoned flour. Peel and finely slice the carrot and onion. Heat olive oil in a large saucepan and fry meat and vegetables until brown. Add tomatoes, mixed herbs, stock, salt and pepper. Cover with a lid and cook gently until tender, about 1½ hours. When cooked, add the grated lemon rind and a little chopped parsley. Serve on a base of boiled rice, and sprinkle with Parmesan cheese.

Scallopine di vitello

(VEAL ESCALOPES)

YOU WILL NEED FOR 4 SERVINGS:

4 veal escalopes
seasoned flour
1–2 tablespoons oil for frying
6 oz. mushrooms, sliced
⅓ pint (or 1 teacup) white or red wine
8 oz. long grain rice for serving
Parmesan cheese

Ask your butcher to beat escalopes flat. Coat each lightly with seasoned flour and then fry in the hot oil to brown on both sides. Reduce heat and add mushrooms. Cook gently for 2–3 minutes, then stir in the wine. Cover with a lid and simmer gently for 20 minutes.

To serve, drain the escalopes and mushrooms from the sauce and keep hot. Boil sauce to reduce it a little, then pour over the veal. Serve with boiled rice, and sprinkle with Parmesan cheese.

Pesche ripiene

(STUFFED PEACHES)

YOU WILL NEED FOR 6 SERVINGS:

3 large peaches
6 small rounds sponge cake
FOR THE STUFFING:
2 oz. (or 2 heaped tablespoons) ground almonds
2 oz. (or 2 rounded tablespoons) castor sugar
1 egg yolk
few drops almond essence

Halve and skin the peaches, and remove the stone. Blend together the ingredients for the stuffing and spoon into the hollows of each peach. Place the stuffed peaches in a buttered fireproof dish, cover with a lid and cook in the centre of a moderate oven 355 deg. or Gas No. 4) for 20 minutes.

Serve the hot peaches on rounds of sponge cakes and serve with cream or the following apricot sauce.

Apricot sauce. Measure 2 heaped tablespoons sieved apricot jam into a pan along with the juice of $\frac{1}{2}$ lemon, 1 tablespoon water and 1 level tablespoon castor sugar. Stir till boiling and thickened, this takes about 2 minutes, then pour over the fruit.

Zabaglione

(AN EXOTIC DESSERT CUSTARD)

YOU WILL NEED FOR 4 SERVINGS:

3 egg yolks
4 oz. (or 4 rounded tablespoons) castor sugar
squeeze of lemon juice
6 tablespoons Marsala or sweet sherry

Break egg yolks into a basin and mix lightly. Add sugar, lemon juice and Marsala wine or sweet sherry. Place the mixing basin over a saucepan of boiling water, draw pan off heat. Whisk until mixture is quite thick and fluffy. Remove basin and pour mixture into large goblets or serving glasses. Traditionally, this sweet is served hot, as soon as it is made, but it is equally delicious cold. Either way, serve it with sponge finger biscuits.

Melone ripieno

(STUFFED MELON)

YOU WILL NEED FOR 4 SERVINGS:

1 ripe honeydew melon
$\frac{1}{4}$ lb. raspberries
$\frac{1}{4}$ lb. strawberries
2 bananas
FOR THE SYRUP:
2 oz. (2 rounded tablespoons) castor sugar
3 tablespoons water
1 tablespoon maraschino

For this recipe the melon top is sliced off to make a lid and the rest of the melon is afterwards scooped out to make a bowl for mixed fruit.

Slice off one-third of melon. Either use a knife and make a straight cut, or for a more decorative finish, use a pointed knife and cut, inserting the knife to centre at alternate angles (rather like cutting a grapefruit). Work right round melon back to start. Then lift off lid.

Scoop out and discard melon seeds. Then scoop out melon flesh, cut into chunky pieces and place in a basin. Add hulled and washed raspberries, strawberries and sliced bananas. Set aside to chill while preparing syrup.

Measure sugar and water into a small saucepan. Stir over low heat to dissolve, bring to the boil and simmer for 1 minute. Draw pan off heat, add maraschino and allow to cool.

Then chill with fruit until ready to serve. Add sufficient syrup to fruit to moisten and make some additional juice. Spoon fruit and syrup into melon bowl, heaping it above top. Replace lid and serve with sponge finger biscuits.

Antipasto

(ITALIAN HORS D'OEUVRE)

Arrange on individual dishes a helping of each of the following:-

Tomato salad: skin, slice and dress with oil and vinegar.

Potato salad: mix cooked, diced potato with mayonnaise, chopped chives, mint and parsley. Decorate with one or two strips of anchovies and olive slices.

Peppers: slice off tops and remove core and seeds from green or red peppers. Blanch in hot water and cut in very thin slices. If fresh peppers are not available, canned ones may be used.

Scampi or prawns: allow 1 large scampi or 2 small per person. Toss in a little olive oil and lemon juice and grate a little black pepper over the top.

Denmark

There's no stinting for Danish cooks. The country yields an abundance of rich dairy produce and it is used generously. A Danish housewife would be ashamed to offer a cold table unless it contained a good selection of cold meats, fish and salads—not to mention smørrebrød, the famous open sandwiches which are unrivalled anywhere. With them she likes to serve lager or Schnapps.

Smørrebrød

(DANISH OPEN SANDWICHES)

Use buttered brown, white or rye bread slices as bases. Cover completely with a generous topping. Try these ideas.

Rye bread, buttered, with a slice of ham, garnished with a lettuce leaf, tomato twists and parsley.

Rye bread, buttered, with sliced hard-boiled egg, topped with tomato and garnished with a small sprig of parsley.

On buttered brown bread, spread or slice liver pâté, and top with sliced, sautéed mushrooms and a sprig of parsley, or a rasher of crisply fried bacon.

On brown bread spread Danish blue cheese, top with halved, de-seeded black grapes, and garnish with a sprig of parsley.

Butter a slice of bread, then arrange a lettuce leaf base, and top with prawns and mayonnaise, if liked. Garnish with a lemon twist and a sprig of parsley.

Or any cold meat or cold cooked vegetables can be mixed with mayonnaise, flavoured with curry powder and then arranged on brown bread with base of lettuce.

Frikadeller

(DANISH MEAT BALLS)

YOU WILL NEED FOR 3–4 SERVINGS:

½ lb. beef
½ lb. pork
1 medium-sized onion
flour for mixing (see recipe)
1 egg
1 level teaspoon salt
1 small bottle soda water or milk
butter for frying

Discard fat and mince meat two or three times with the onion; (you may, if you prefer, use veal and pork or beef instead). Mix well in a basin and then pat evenly over base of mixing bowl. Spoon one quarter of the mixture to the side and fill space with flour. Blend flour with all the meat and stir in egg, seasoning and enough soda water or milk for a fairly soft mixture.

At this stage a little should be tasted to see if the seasoning is correct. Do this by dropping a teaspoon of the mixture into boiling water. Cook for 5 minutes. Correct the seasoning if necessary, and continue with the recipe.

Drop the mixture by tablespoons into hot butter in a frying pan—you should get about 6–8.

Fry over moderate heat on both sides until well browned, this takes about 20 minutes.

Serve hot with seasonable vegetables, they are especially nice with mushrooms, peas, beans or spinach and potatoes tossed in brown sugar and butter. Serve also with a brown sauce, or browned butter (add extra butter to the frying pan and pour over).

Frikadeller are delicious cold, if sliced and arranged on an open sandwich with fried bacon rashers, mushrooms, pickled onions or a fried egg.

Mini Frikadeller are ideal for cocktail snacks. Prepare the mixture as above but drop in teaspoons into the hot butter and cook for about 5–10 minutes.

When cooked, spike on cocktail sticks with cooked mushrooms, tiny sausages or pickled cucumber.

Fildisur fløde

(HERRINGS IN SOUR CREAM)

YOU WILL NEED FOR 4 SERVINGS:

4–6 salted herring fillets
milk (see recipe)
1 carton soured cream
1 tablespoon chopped chives
Pumpernickel bread for serving

Cut herring fillets into small pieces and soak overnight in enough milk to cover.

Next day drain and place fillets in a small basin, add soured cream and chives. Toss to mix and then leave to marinate for 2–3 hours. Serve with slices of buttered Pumpernickel bread, brown bread or toast.

Orange and chocolate layer cake and a selection of smørrebrød

Rødgrød med fløde

(FRUIT JELLY)

YOU WILL NEED FOR 4–6 SERVINGS:

½ lb. red currants or rhubarb
½ lb. raspberries
1 pint water
about 2 level tablespoons cornflour
   to thicken *(see recipe)*
6 oz. (or 6 rounded tablespoons) castor sugar

Wash and trim fruit, then cook gently in water until soft. Drain off juice (use up fruit with ice cream) and for every ½ pint juice, blend 1 level tablespoon of cornflour with a little water to a thin paste.
Pour juice into a pan, add sugar and bring to the boil. Remove from heat, and stir in blended cornflour. Stir continuously over moderate heat till thickened and boiling. Pour into a serving dish and serve warm or cold with top of the milk or cream.

Chokolade appelsin lagkage

(CHOCOLATE AND ORANGE CAKE)

YOU WILL NEED FOR 10 SLICES:

8 oz. (or 8 rounded tablespoons) self-raising
   flour
3 oz. (or 3 rounded tablespoons) cocoa powder
8 oz. Danish butter
10 oz. (or 10 rounded tablespoons) castor sugar
2 eggs
⅓ pint (or 1 teacup) buttermilk
FOR THE BUTTERCREAM:
8 oz. Danish unsalted butter
6 oz. (or 6 heaped tablespoons) icing sugar
juice of ½ an orange
mandarin or fresh orange segments for decoration

Sift together the flour and cocoa powder and set aside. Cream the butter and sugar until soft and then gradually beat in the eggs. Add the butter-milk and fold in the sifted flour mixture.
Spoon it into 2 buttered 8–9 in. round sponge cake tins.
Place in the centre of a moderate oven (355 deg. or Gas No. 4) and bake for 40 minutes.
Cream butter until soft and gradually add the sifted icing sugar. Beat in the orange juice, blending thoroughly. When cake is baked and cooled, slice the layers and sandwich together with half the buttercream. Coat sides and top with remainder, and decorate with mandarin or fresh orange segments.

Chokolade nøddekage

(CHOCOLATE LAYER MERINGUE)

YOU WILL NEED FOR 4–6 SERVINGS:

3 egg whites
4 oz. (or 4 rounded tablespoons) castor sugar
1 oz. (or 1 rounded tablespoon) cocoa
½ pint double cream
¼ lb. hazel nuts or toasted, flaked almonds

Mark out three 8 in. circles on separate sheets of silicone paper and place each on a baking tray.
Whisk egg whites until they stand up in peaks, then gradually whisk in castor sugar. Fold in sifted cocoa powder, and spread meringue out on prepared baking trays, keeping within marked circles. Bake in the centre, and on the shelf below, of a very slow oven (200 deg. or Gas No. ¼) for 3 hours or until completely dried out.
Remove from oven and cool; then remove from the paper. Sandwich together with whipped cream and nuts. Leave to stand for 2–3 hours before serving to allow meringue to soften a little.

Ablekage

(DANISH APPLE CHARLOTTE)

YOU WILL NEED FOR 4 SERVINGS:

5–6 oz. butter
4 oz. (or 2 level teacups) fresh white
   breadcrumbs
4 oz. (or 4 rounded tablespoons) castor sugar
½ pint sweetened apple purée
¼ pint single cream for serving

Heat butter or margarine in a large frying pan. Combine breadcrumbs and sugar and add to hot fat. Fry, stirring all the time, until breadcrumbs are browned and crisp and all butter or margarine has been absorbed. Draw pan off heat.
Over base of a buttered 1½-pint baking or pie dish, sprinkle one third of the crumbs. Top with half apple purée and then another layer of the crumbs. Spoon remaining apple purée over pie and top with crumbs.
Place in centre of a moderate oven (355 deg. or Gas No. 4) and bake for 30 minutes. Serve warm or chilled with the single cream.

Greece

The Greeks are an insular race with their own highly individual customs and recipes. The three chosen here are among the most popular of their traditional dishes. They are not difficult to make and are subtle enough to appeal to an English palate.

Taramosalata

(COD'S ROE PÂTÉ)

YOU WILL NEED FOR 4–6 SERVINGS:

    8 oz. smoked cod's roe
    5–6 tablespoons olive oil
    1 tablespoon lemon juice pepper
    1 level teaspoon chives, finely chopped
    1 level tablespoon parsley, finely chopped

Remove outer skin carefully, and chop cod's roe into small pieces; place in a bowl with 1 tablespoon of olive oil. Leave 5–10 minutes.
Pass roe through a fine sieve, and beat until smooth. Gradually beat in the remaining oil and lemon juice, one tablespoon at a time, until mixture is of a creamy consistency. Add a shake of pepper, chives and parsley. Allow to stand a short time before serving.
This pâté is nicest served with hot toast as a starter to a meal.

Moussaka

(AUBERGINES AND CHEESE)

YOU WILL NEED FOR 6 SERVINGS:

    5 tablespoons cooking oil
    1 lb. minced beef or lamb
    1 large onion, chopped
    1 teaspoon salt and pinch of pepper
    2 teaspoons tomato paste
    3 tablespoons stock or water
    4 aubergines
    6 oz. grated cheese
    FOR THE SAUCE:
    1 oz. butter
    1 oz. (or 1 rounded tablespoon) flour
    ½ pint milk
    salt and pepper

Heat 1 tablespoon of the oil. Add meat and onion and brown. Add salt and pepper, stir in tomato paste and stock or water. Bring to boil and simmer, covered with a lid, for 30 minutes. Peel and thinly slice the aubergines and fry lightly in remaining oil.
Put a layer of cooked aubergines in the base of a large ovenproof dish and sprinkle thickly with some of the grated cheese. Cover with a second layer of aubergines and more cheese. Top with meat mixture and another layer of aubergines and cheese, reserving approximately 1 oz. of the cheese.
To prepare the sauce, melt butter, stir in flour and cook gently for 1–2 minutes. Add milk and bring to the boil, stirring all the time. Season with salt and pepper, pour over prepared moussaka. Top with remaining cheese. Place casserole dish in the centre of a moderate oven (355 deg. or Gas No. 4), and bake for 30 minutes or until bubbling brown.

Halva

(SYRUP SOAKED CAKE)

YOU WILL NEED FOR 16 PIECES:

    1 lb. fine semolina
    4 oz. whole almonds, skinned
    1 level teaspoon ground cinnamon
    6 oz. butter
    8 oz. (or 8 rounded tablespoons) castor sugar
    4 eggs
    FOR THE SYRUP:
    8 oz. (or 8 rounded tablespoons) castor sugar
    1 pint water
    juice of half a lemon

Mix together the semolina, finely chopped almonds and cinnamon and set aside. Cream the butter and sugar until light. Add the eggs, one at a time, beating the mixture well each time. Fold in the semolina and spoon into a buttered and lined 7 in. shallow square baking tin. Place in the middle of a very moderate oven (335 deg. or Gas No. 3) and bake for 40–45 minutes.
Meanwhile prepare the syrup. Dissolve the sugar in the water over low heat. Add the lemon juice and bring up to the boil. Simmer for 2–3 minutes then draw the pan off the heat. When the cake is cooked, turn out of the tin, remove paper and spoon over some of the hot syrup. Continue adding syrup until it has all been absorbed. When cold cut the cake in squares and serve with Turkish coffee.

India

Say 'curry' and you think of India. Most British cooks have no idea of the variety there is in curry—it can be subtle or highly spiced, mild or very hot. If you are adventurous you can make your own curry powder but it's easier to buy a well-known brand—some have as many as 50 different ingredients in them.

Curry powder

Grind finely together 2 tablespoons each of tumeric, cumin and coriander seeds; 1 tablespoon each of powdered ginger and ground pepper; 2 teaspoons each of fenugreek, chillies, cardamom seeds and mace; and 1 teaspoon each of mustard seeds, cloves and poppy seeds. Store in a screw-topped jar.

Curries can be made from fish, meat, eggs or vegetables; the best flavour is achieved when the main ingredient is gently simmered in the curry sauce. It is important to add a little sweetness with mango chutney or brown sugar to counteract the harshness of some curry flavours. Curry sauce should be thin to soak well into the rice served with it. When serving, put boiled rice first on to the plate and spoon curry and sauce on top. Curry sauce can be prepared well ahead of time. Long, slow cooking improves the flavour, as does keeping it overnight.

Basic curry sauce

YOU WILL NEED FOR ABOUT 1 PINT:

1½ oz. margarine
1 small onion, finely chopped
½ cooking apple, finely chopped
2–4 level tablespoons curry powder
1 level tablespoon plain flour
1 pint stock or water
1 teaspoon curry paste (optional)
1 tablespoon chopped mango chutney
1 tablespoon moist brown sugar
juice of ½ a lemon
½ level teaspoon salt
1 oz. sultanas

Melt fat in a heavy pan, add onion and apple and cook gently for 5–6 minutes. Stir in curry powder and flour and gradually stir in stock or water and bring to the boil. Add remaining ingredients, cover with lid and simmer for 20–30 minutes.
Use for any of the following:

Curried eggs

TO SERVE 4

Halve 8 hard-boiled eggs and arrange in a hot dish. Pour over the cooked sauce, garnish with gherkins and serve with boiled rice.

Curried prawns

TO SERVE 4

Add 8 oz. prepared prawns to the cooked sauce and allow the mixture to simmer for a further 10–15 minutes to heat through.
Serve in a ring of plain boiled rice, garnished with a few whole prawns and wedges of lemon.

Curried beef

TO SERVE 4

After the sauce has been prepared, but before simmering, pour it over 1½ lb. fresh chuck steak, cut in cubes and arranged in a casserole dish. Cover with a lid and cook in a very moderate oven (335 deg. or Gas No. 3) for 2 hours. Serve with boiled rice.

Chicken curry

TO SERVE 4

Make the sauce, but before simmering, pour it over 4 fresh chicken joints. Cover pan with a lid and simmer for 1 hour. Serve with boiled rice.

Boiled rice

Always use the long grain or patna rice because the grains stay fluffy and separate. Rice is very easy to cook. Allow about 2 oz. rice per person.
In boiling water: add washed rice to a large pan of boiling salted water, sprinkling it in slowly so that the water does not come off the boil. Boil fairly rapidly for 8–10 minutes, or until a grain pressed between the fingers has no hard core.
Drain at once through a sieve and rinse under hot water. The rice may be returned to the pan or a warm

oven and allowed to steam dry for a few minutes. Toss with a fork to stop grains sticking together.

In cold water: Measure 1 teacup rice (4 oz.—enough for 2 persons) into a saucepan (lightly buttered to stop rice sticking to the bottom) with 2 cups of water and 1 level teaspoon salt. Cover pan with a lid and cook gently for 20 minutes or until the rice has absorbed all the water and is tender. Draw pan off heat, toss grains with a fork and serve at once.

Garnishes and side dishes

Gherkins, pickled onions, sweet chutney, fresh grated coconut, red or green chillies (hot—so should be used with great caution). These are only a few of the side dishes for curries. In Britain it's rare to serve more than half a dozen side dishes, but in India, especially at a banquet, there are many more.

Poppadams: tasty, wafer-thin biscuits which are usually fried, though they may also be grilled. Delicious hot, with curry and rice.

Bombay duck: a dried fish which has rather an offensive smell uncooked, but is quite different when fried in fat or cooked in the oven until crisp, and then crumbled over the curry.

Banana: skin and chop and mix at once with a little lemon juice.

Cucumber: peel and chop neatly and mix with a little lemon juice and a pinch of sugar.

Diced tomato: skin, halve and de-seed two tomatoes. Dice and mix gently with a pinch of sugar, seasoning and a little lemon juice.

Sweet and sour pineapple and almonds: heat 1 rounded tablespoon sugar in a small pan until golden and melted. Cool for 1 minute then add 1 tablespoon vinegar, stir in 1 level teaspoon cornflour blended with 4 tablespoons pineapple juice, taken from a tin of pineapple chunks. Cook, stirring until thickened and clear, then stir in some roasted, blanched almonds and some chopped pineapple.

Chapatti

YOU WILL NEED FOR 4 SERVINGS:

> 6 oz. wholemeal flour
> ½ level teaspoon salt
> water to mix

Place flour and salt in a mixing basin. Gradually add enough water, a little at a time, to mix to a stiff but not wet dough. Rub the mixture with fingers while adding liquid to get an even texture. Knead well with knuckles until smooth and elastic. If possible set aside to rest for 1 hour before using.

Divide into 4 and shape each piece into a small ball. Using plenty of extra wholemeal flour (it is important that the dough should not stick) roll each piece thinly to a circle about ¼ in. thick.

Place in an ungreased, hot, heavy frying pan. Brown lightly on either side, then place under a pre-heated grill, discarding rack and using the pan of the grill as a base.

Now the chapatti will quickly puff up. Be sure to turn them once so that they will rise evenly.

Serve the chapatti immediately, while hot, with butter if liked. Delicious with curry.

Indian rice

YOU WILL NEED FOR 4 SERVINGS:

> 1½ pints water
> 2 level teaspoons salt
> 8 oz. long grain rice
> 6 cloves
> 1 piece of stick cinnamon
> 3 bay leaves
> 4 whole black peppercorns
> pinch saffron
> ½ oz. butter

Measure the water and salt into a saucepan. Bring up to the boil, add the rice and remaining ingredients except butter. Stir until re-boiling then cook rapidly for 10–12 minutes, until rice grains are soft.

Drain, removing only cinnamon and bay leaves. Place rice in a hot serving dish, add the butter and toss.

Sweet chutney

YOU WILL NEED FOR 6–8 SERVINGS:

> 3 onions, peeled and cut in quarters
> 1 clove of garlic, crushed with salt
> 6 apples, peeled and finely chopped
> 8 oz. soft brown sugar
> 1 level teaspoon salt
> ¼ level teaspoon ground cinnamon
> 1 teaspoon cumin seed
> 2 oz. seedless raisins
> 1 level teaspoon ground ginger
> ⅓ pint (1 teacupful) vinegar

Pass the onion and garlic through a mincer into a saucepan. Add all remaining ingredients and bring slowly up to the boil. Simmer gently for 45 minutes to 1 hour until the mixture is thick and pulpy. Draw the pan off the heat, cool and chill before serving.

China

Clear soup usually begins an informal Chinese meal and it is followed by one or two meat dishes, an egg or fish dish and one or two vegetable dishes—plus a bowl of rice, naturally. Rice is the staple food of the Chinese and a number of dishes are served with it. In wealthier families when up to a dozen separate dishes are served during each meal, rice merely acts as a 'buffer' to the rich and tasty dishes, all served at the same time. If you are a beginner keep the courses down to two and add a bowl of crispy noodles. To finish the meal you can't beat a bowl of lychees (fresh if available, otherwise tinned) and China tea.

Chinese ingredients

Bamboo shoots: lend a firm, crisp texture to meat and vegetables. Available tinned, they are usually about 3 in. long and ready for use.

Bean sprouts: crunchy and yellow-white, they have tiny yellow buds at one end, and are tinned in water with husks removed ready for use.

Ginger: the Chinese prefer fresh young ginger roots, but where these are not available use preserved ginger in syrup—wash off the syrup and slice ginger finely. Two or three thin slices will give sufficient flavour.

Soy sauce: this is used more than almost any other single flavouring ingredient. It adds flavour and a certain amount of salt. It is quite correct to add soy sauce to your plate of cooked food, if you like it, even if it is not one of the original ingredients.

Water chestnuts: buy these in tins, cleaned and neatly peeled. They don't have a great deal of flavour, but add an unusual crisp and crunchy texture to dishes. Water chestnuts may be sliced in thin circles or cut in tiny cubes.

Cornflour: produces the clear, translucent sauces for which Chinese cooks are renowned. Always blend the cornflour first with a little cold water before adding to any hot liquid to avoid lumps.

Cooking oil: use vegetable oils, preferably soya bean or corn oil (the latter is more easily obtained).

Chicken chop suey

YOU WILL NEED FOR 4 SERVINGS:

1 (2–2½ lb.) chicken
2 pints boiling salted water
1 onion, sliced
2–3 stalks celery, sliced
1 green pepper, chopped
3 tablespoons soy sauce
1 (1 lb.) tin bean sprouts
2 level tablespoons cornflour
salt and pepper
8 oz. patna rice for serving

Plunge chicken into boiling salted water, cover with a lid and simmer gently for 1 hour or until tender. Drain, remove meat from carcass, cut it into small pieces and set aside.
Measure 1 pint of the chicken broth into a large saucepan and add the onion, celery and green pepper. Bring to the boil, cover with a lid and simmer for 10 minutes or until vegetables are tender. Stir in soy sauce, drained bean sprouts and the reserved chicken meat. Simmer 3–4 minutes to heat very thoroughly. Blend cornflour to a smooth, thin paste with seasoning and 2 dessertspoons cold water, and stir into chicken mixture. Stir until thickened and boiling. Serve with boiled rice.

Sweet and sour pork

YOU WILL NEED FOR 4 SERVINGS:

1 lb. lean pork
vegetable fat or lard for frying
FOR THE SWEET AND SOUR SAUCE:
1 (12 oz.) tin pineapple chunks
4 tablespoons vinegar
3 oz. (or 3 rounded tablespoons) soft brown sugar
1 tablespoon soy sauce
¼ level teaspoon salt
2 level tablespoons cornflour
1 small green pepper, de-seeded and thinly sliced
1 small onion, thinly sliced

Remove any fat from pork and cut meat into cubes. Fry in a little hot fat until it is golden brown on all sides.
Drain pineapple from the tin and reserve syrup, making it up to ½ pint with water. Combine this with vinegar, brown sugar, soy sauce and salt. Measure cornflour into a large saucepan and moisten with a little of the liquid, stirring to a smooth paste. Then stir in remaining liquid. Cook over moderate heat, stirring constantly, until thickened and clear. Add meat, cover with a lid and cook for 1 hour or until meat is tender.

Add the sliced pepper, onion and pineapple and cook for a further 15 minutes.
Serve the dish with plenty of boiled or fried rice.

Prawns and cucumber

YOU WILL NEED FOR 4 SERVINGS:

1 (8 oz.) packet frozen prawns
1 tablespoon sherry
1 level teaspoon salt
1 level teaspoon sugar
1 whole cucumber
2 tablespoons cooking oil
2 level teaspoons cornflour blended with ¼ pint water
1 level tablespoon chopped chives or parsley

Marinate prawns in sherry, salt and sugar. Peel cucumber, quarter lengthwise, and cut into 1-inch pieces. Heat 1 tablespoon oil and sauté cucumber about 3–5 minutes until transparent. Drain and set aside. Add a further tablespoon oil to pan and sauté prawns, stir in the marinade and cornflour blend and cook until thickened. Add cucumber and re-heat. Serve garnished with chopped chives or parsley.

Fried rice

TO SERVE 4

Heat 1 tablespoon oil in a saucepan, add 1 finely chopped onion and 8 oz. patna rice. Fry over moderate heat, stirring well until the rice is golden brown, then stir in 1 pint stock, or water plus stock cube. Cook, covered with a lid, for 20 minutes until rice is tender and liquid absorbed. Season and serve.

Fried crispy noodles

YOU WILL NEED FOR 4 SERVINGS:

8 oz. noodles
boiling, salted water
oil for deep frying

Cook noodles in plenty of boiling salted water for 5 minutes. Drain and rinse in cold water, then drain again until as dry as possible. Put noodles in a frying basket, plunge into hot fat, and fry for about 5 minutes or until crisp and golden brown. Drain well and serve.

Chinese fritters

YOU WILL NEED FOR 8 FRITTERS:

1 (10 oz.) tin bean sprouts
1 (7½ oz.) tin crab
2 eggs
salt and pepper
oil for frying
FOR THE SAUCE:
1 small packet frozen peas
1 level tablespoon cornflour
1 level tablespoon castor sugar
½ pint water
3 tablespoons soy sauce

Drain the liquid from the tin of beans, break crab flesh into pieces, discarding any bone or sinews. Lightly whisk the eggs in a basin, add a good seasoning of salt and pepper, bean sprouts and crab flesh.
Heat enough oil to cover the bottom of a frying pan and drop in tablespoons of the egg mixture. Fry until golden brown over moderately hot heat then turn and brown on the other side. Drain and keep hot while preparing the sauce.
Put peas to cook according to packet directions and drain. Measure the cornflour and sugar into a saucepan. Gradually stir in the water blending the ingredients, then add the soy sauce. Bring up to the boil over moderate heat, stirring all the time until thickened and boiling. Add cooked peas and serve with the fritters.

Almond cakes

YOU WILL NEED FOR 12 CAKES:

3 oz. (3 rounded tablespoons) plain flour
¼ level teaspoon baking powder
pinch salt
1 oz. ground almonds
2 oz. (2 rounded tablespoons) castor sugar
2 tablespoons oil
¼ teaspoon almond essence
½ lightly mixed egg
12 blanched almonds

Sieve the flour, baking powder and salt into a mixing basin. Add the ground almonds and sugar and mix well. Hollow out the centre of the mixture, and add the oil, essence and egg. Mix together kneading to a stiff mixture. Shape into 12 balls and roll each into a round. Place on a greased baking tray and press flat. Place a blanched almond into the centre of each cookie and place in the centre of a moderate oven (355 deg. or Gas No. 4). Bake for 25 minutes or until golden brown.

ALL ABOUT
Hot & Cold
Drinks

Whether making coffee, mixing simple cool drinks or more elaborate party punches, prepare them properly—never skimping on ingredients. Serve cold drinks looking gay, attractively garnished and thoroughly chilled, and hot drinks really hot in appropriate mugs, goblets or glasses.

Hot coffee

There are several methods of making coffee and many different blends of coffee to select from. The best plan is to try out various methods and blends and then stick to the one you like best.

Always ask for medium ground coffee unless you specifically require a fine or coarsely ground mixture. Generally speaking a lighter roast is the best for a breakfast coffee, try an American or Kenya blend. As a rule continental blends are stronger and more suitable for after dinner coffee, beware of any cheap mixtures with added chicory which can taste bitter. In the following methods quantities are for 1 pint of coffee, enough to serve 4 cups with hot milk added.

Jug: measure 1½–2 oz. (or 2 heaped tablespoons) medium ground coffee into a heated jug. Add a pinch of salt and allow the grounds to warm gently to draw out the flavour. Measure 1 pint of cold water into a kettle and bring to the boil. Pour immediately over the coffee, stir well, cover with a cloth or a saucer and leave to infuse for 4–5 minutes. Strain it through muslin into a heated coffee pot or second jug.

Saucepan: measure 1½–2 oz. of medium ground coffee into a saucepan, add a pinch of salt and 1 pint of cold water. Stir well and bring just to the boil. Remove from the heat immediately, stir again cover with a lid and set aside in a warm place to infuse 4–5 minutes. Strain into a heated coffee pot or jug, and serve.

Percolator: measure 1 pint of cold water into the lower part of the percolator and 1½–2 oz. medium ground coffee into the top perforated section. Heat gently and when the water boils allow it to bubble through the coffee for about 6 minutes. Remove from the heat and serve.

Cona: Pour approximately 1 pint water into the jug base of the cona coffee maker. Insert the funnel firmly into the neck of the jug. Make sure a space is left between the base of the funnel and the bottom of the jug. Place in the glass drainer. Into the funnel measure 1½–2 oz. medium ground coffee. Make sure the bottom of the jug is dry and set over the heat. Either over a gas flame or on an electric plate with a protective mat. Leave over moderate heat and in a few moments, with the exception of a small quantity, the water will boil up into the funnel and infuse the coffee. Leave for 1 minute then draw the jug off the heat and allow the water to return to the jug base. Remove the funnel and use the jug for serving.

Filtered: Heat the coffee pot and filter top thoroughly with hot water. Place a filter paper in, and measure required fine ground coffee into the top and set over the coffee pot, the quantity depends on the size of the pot. Pour sufficient boiling water into the top to fill. Cover with the lid and allow the water to drain through into the pot below. Refill again with boiling water, the number of times depends on the size of the pot. Remove the filter top, place the lid on the pot and serve.

Orangeade cooler, ginger champagne, fizzy lemonade, iced coffee, mulled wine and raspberry flip

'Instant': For an after dinner coffee use one of the strong blends of instant coffee. Allow 1 teaspoon, more or less, per cup of coffee.

Irish coffee

Warm a ¼ pint glass goblet for each serving and pour in a measure of Irish whiskey and 1 level tablespoon sugar. Top up to within 1 in. of the top of the goblet with a strong hot black coffee, stir to dissolve the sugar. Holding the rounded side of a dessertspoon upwards close to the level of the coffee, slowly pour very lightly whipped double cream on to the spoon over the coffee. Do not stir after the cream has been added and serve at once.

Hot chocolate

YOU WILL NEED FOR 4 SERVINGS:

    1 (4 oz.) packet chocolate chips
    2 tablespoons water
    1 pint milk

Empty the contents of the packet of chocolate chips into a 1½ pint saucepan. Add the water and stir over very low heat, until melted and smooth. Draw the pan off the heat and gradually stir in the milk. Reheat until hot but do not allow to boil. Serve in mugs, topped with a spoonful of whipped cream or marshmallows, if liked.

Blackcurrant drink

Into tall mugs measure 2–3 tablespoons blackcurrant cordial and the juice of half a lemon. Add 1 teaspoon sugar and fill up with boiling water. Serve very hot.

Honey toddy

Into mugs measure 1 tablespoon honey and the juice of half a lemon. Top up with boiling water, stir well and serve topped with a slice of lemon.

Ice cool in summer

A cool drink in a tall frosty glass is just the thing on hot summer days. Keep a few basic ingredients in the larder and they can be fixed in a jiffy. It's a good idea to keep a bottle of sugar syrup handy for sweetening summer drinks. Prepare this by dissolving 8 oz. granulated sugar in ¼ pint water over a low heat. Bring up to the boil, then draw off the heat, cool and store in a bottle. Stir into any fruit drinks according to taste.

Orangeade cooler

YOU WILL NEED FOR 4–6 GLASSES:

    1 large tin orange juice
    2 oz. castor sugar
    few snipped mint leaves
    3 tablespoons lime juice
    1 pint lemonade

Measure half the quantity of orange juice into a saucepan and bring to the boil. Remove from the heat and stir in the sugar and mint leaves. Leave to cool. Add the remaining orange juice and lime juice and pour into a large jug. Just before serving add the lemonade. Pour into ice-filled glasses and decorate with a sprig of mint.

Cidercup

Mix together equal parts of cider, lemonade, and undiluted lemon or orange squash. Pour into a jug and add chopped apple, orange slices and mint leaves for garnish, chill then serve.

Ginger champagne

YOU WILL NEED FOR 6–8 GLASSES:

    6 oz. castor sugar
    ½ pint water
    1 tin grapefruit juice
    juice of two fresh oranges
    4–6 small ginger ales

Measure the sugar and water into a small pan. Bring to the boil slowly, stirring to dissolve the sugar. Simmer gently for 15 minutes Remove from the heat, cool and add the fruit juices and ginger ale. Chill and serve.

Iced tea

Make tea in your usual way, but slightly stronger, and add a pinch of powdered cloves (or two whole cloves) while the tea is brewing. Stand the pot aside to cool.

Strain the tea into a large jug containing plenty of ice. Serve in tumblers with a wedge of lemon—which should be squeezed into the tea—castor sugar for sweetening and a couple of straws.

Iced tea punch

YOU WILL NEED FOR 6 GLASSES:

1½ pints boiling water
2 tablespoons tea leaves
juice of 2 lemons
juice of 3 oranges
4 rounded tablespoons castor sugar
2 small bottles ginger ale
orange slices and mint to decorate

Pour the boiling water over the tea. Cover and let stand for 5 minutes. Stir and strain into a deep jug. Add lemon and orange juice and stir in the sugar. Chill well.
When ready to serve, fill 6 tumblers with ice cubes, and divide the tea mixture among the glasses. Fill to the top with ginger ale and decorate with a slice of orange and sprig of mint.

Iced coffee

YOU WILL NEED FOR 4 GLASSES:

1 rounded dessertspoon instant coffee
¼ pint hot water
ice cubes
1 pint chilled milk
sugar to taste

Dissolve instant coffee in hot water. Place plenty of ice cubes in large jug and add the dissolved coffee. Add milk and enough sugar to sweeten. Stir well to mix and then serve.

Ice cream sodas

These are wonderful on a really hot day, especially if the topping-up liquid is chilled until cold in the refrigerator.

Raspberry flip

In tall glasses spoon raspberry ripple or vanilla ice cream on crushed fresh raspberries. Top up with soda water. Serve with straws and spoons.

Cola quickie

In tall glasses place 2 tablespoons single cream, add several scoops of chocolate ice cream and top up with coca-cola.

Coffee cooler

Measure into a saucepan 2 tablespoons instant coffee powder, 3 oz. castor sugar and 1 pint water. Bring slowly to the boil, stirring and simmer gently for 10 minutes. Remove from the heat and chill well. Place scoops of coffee ice cream in 4–5 tall glasses. Pour the coffee syrup over and top up with soda water.

Strawberry soda

Crush 1 small punnet of fresh strawberries with a little castor sugar and spoon into 4 tall glasses. Into each glass stir 1 tablespoon single cream, add a scoop of vanilla ice cream and top with ginger ale.

Gay garnishes
Garnished ice cubes

Pour water into a freezing tray until about two thirds full and allow it to freeze. Place any of the following on top of the cubes and pour on just enough water to cover and freeze again. Small sections of orange or lemon slices, red or green maraschino cherries, tinned pineapple chunks.

Garnishes for glasses

Hang small bunches of grapes over the edge, or decorate with orange or lemon slices. Garnish with twists of cucumber peel or fruit kebabs made by spearing pieces of fruit on cocktail sticks. Use cinnamon sticks as stirrers.

Flavoured ice cubes

Instead of water, freeze tinned pineapple juice, which adds flavour while it melts.

Frosty rims

To frost the rims of your glasses dip the edges of each into lemon juice and then castor sugar. Leave to dry a little.

Syrups

Here's a smart idea for a smart Mother who knows that her family are very likely to demand cold, thirst-quenching drinks when she's least expecting it. These syrups can be prepared ahead of time, stored in a bottle and diluted into a drink when required.

Lemon syrup

YOU WILL NEED FOR 1 PINT:

1 lb. castor sugar
1 pint water
1 oz. citric acid powder (obtainable from a chemist)
2 teaspoons lemon essence

Measure the sugar and water into a pan and bring slowly to the boil. Stir gently to dissolve all the sugar and simmer for 5 minutes.
Remove from the heat and pour into a large jug or bowl and leave to cool. Add citric acid and lemon essence. To use, measure 1–2 tablespoons into a glass with a few ice cubes, and top up with cold water.

Chocolate syrup

YOU WILL NEED FOR ½ PINT:

4 oz. unsweetened chocolate
½ pint water
6 oz. castor sugar
¼ level teaspoon salt
½ teaspoon vanilla essence

Place the chocolate and water into a small saucepan and over very low heat, stir until melted and blended. Add the sugar and bring slowly to the boil, stirring occasionally. Simmer for 2 minutes. Remove from the heat and add the salt and vanilla. Cool before storing. To use, dilute 2–3 tablespoons of syrup in each glass of milk.

Coffee syrup

YOU WILL NEED FOR ¾ PINT:

8 oz. (or 8 rounded tablespoons) castor sugar
4 heaped tablespoons instant coffee
½ pint boiling water

Measure sugar and coffee into a saucepan. Add water and stir until dissolved. Bring to the boil, and simmer for 2 minutes without stirring. Draw off heat and allow to cool, then pour into a bottle and store in a refrigerator. Measure 4–6 tablespoons coffee syrup into a jug, add plenty of ice cubes and 1 pint of cold milk.

Fizzy lemon syrup

YOU WILL NEED FOR 2 PINTS:

1½ pints boiling water
8 oz. (or 8 rounded tablespoons) castor sugar
1 oz. tartaric acid powder
2 teaspoons lemon essence
1 egg white

This delicious lemon syrup makes a marvellous stand-by for quick drinks. Prepare it ahead and keep stored in your refrigerator. Pour boiling water over sugar and stir occasionally until dissolved. Set aside to cool. Add tartaric acid and lemon essence (both obtainable at chemists) and a well whisked egg white. Bottle and store in a cool place.
To serve, measure 2–3 tablespoons syrup and ½ salt spoon bicarbonate of soda into tall tumbler. Add ice cubes if wished and top up with cold water.

To use the syrups

Mocha milk shake: Measure 2 tablespoons chocolate syrup and 2 tablespoons coffee syrup (or use 2 teaspoons instant coffee) into each glass. Top up with milk, stirring it in gradually.

Frosted chocolate: Into a tall tumbler measure 3 tablespoons chocolate syrup. Fill one third of the glass with cold milk and stir to blend the syrup. Add a scoop of chocolate ice cream and fill to the top with more milk.

Old-fashioned ginger beer

This is an old fashioned recipe making ginger beer from a yeast plant. Keep the plant in a bottle or jar in the light but not on a hot, too sunny window sill. Place 2 oz. baker's yeast or 1 oz. good dried yeast in a jar, add 2 cups of water, 2 teaspoons of sugar and 2 teaspoons of ground ginger. A plant has now been made from which ginger beer can be made as follows:

Feed daily for 7 days with 1 teaspoon of ground ginger and 1 teaspoon of sugar.
To make the drink, strain through muslin and add to the liquid the juice of 2 lemons, 2 pints of

boiling water and 1 lb. of sugar. Make up to 1 gallon with cold water. Keep 3 hours before bottling. Store in a cool place and keep for 14 days before serving, making sure the bottles are well corked.

Party punches and mulled wine

When there's a crowd, serve a fruit punch, wine cup or mulled wine, they look exciting especially if garnished with lots of prepared fruit and are a reasonably inexpensive way of offering refreshment to a large crowd. Use any good inexpensive wines and add a variety of liqueurs, port, sherry, Madeira, brandy or fruit juice as you like. You can invent all sorts of interesting recipes yourself by carefully selecting the ingredients and tasting as you go along. Don't be tempted to spin out the wine cup by diluting with too much soft drink, or soda water.

Fruit punch

YOU WILL NEED FOR 18–20 GLASSES:

½ lb. castor sugar
¼ pint water
1 large (19 oz.) tin orange juice
1 large (19 oz.) tin pineapple juice
1 small tin pure lemon juice
2 quarts ginger beer
orange and lemon slices for garnish

Measure the sugar and water into a saucepan. Stir to dissolve the sugar and then bring to the boil. Simmer for 5 minutes. Remove from the heat and add the fruit juices and pour into a large bowl. Allow to chill. Just before serving gently stir in the ginger beer and a few orange and lemon slices.

Summer wine cup 1

YOU WILL NEED FOR 14–16 GLASSES:

8 oz. strawberries
1 tablespoon castor sugar
juice of 3 lemons
1 miniature orange Curaço or Cointreau
2 tablespoons brandy
ice cubes
1 bottle claret
1 bottle Sauternes
½–1 pint soda water
sprigs of mint for serving

Wash, hull and slice the strawberries in half. Place in the base of a large serving bowl along with the sugar, lemon juice, liqueur and brandy. Leave to stand for a while. Add the ice cubes and wines and just before serving add the soda water. Ladle into goblets and serve with sprigs of mint.

Summer wine cup 2

YOU WILL NEED FOR 18–20 GLASSES:

1 bottle claret
1 bottle vintage cider
2 liqueur glasses Cointreau, Kirsch or Grand Marnier
dash bitters
1 bottle champagne cider or fizzy lemonade
ice cubes
sliced apple, orange and banana to decorate

Blend together the claret, vintage cider, liqueur and bitters in a punch bowl and chill well for ½–1 hour. Just before serving, stir in the champagne cider or fizzy lemonade, ice cubes and sliced fresh fruit.

White wine cup

YOU WILL NEED FOR 18 GLASSES:

2 bottles Graves (or other dry white wine)
1 pint (or ½ quart bottle) ginger beer
2 measures brandy

In a large china or punch bowl blend all the wines together and stir gently to mix. Ladle into a jug and serve, making more when necessary.

Party wine cup

YOU WILL NEED FOR 30 GLASSES:

6 bottles lemonade
6 bottles dry white wine, (try Spanish Graves)
2 bottles lemon squash
3 apples
1 (16 oz.) tin red cherries
2 bananas

In a large china mixing basin or punch bowl mix together the lemonade, wine and lemon squash. Peel, core and slice the apples, add to the wine cup along with the stoned and halved cherries and the peeled and sliced bananas.

Note To make the wine cup go further, add 1 bottle champagne cider which hardly alters the flavour.

This quantity served 30 people, allowing several glasses each for the evening.

Mulled wine

YOU WILL NEED FOR 12 GLASSES:

 2 bottles inexpensive red wine
 2 oz. brown sugar
 4 cloves stuck in half an orange
 small stick cinnamon
 juice of half an orange and one lemon
 lemon slices to decorate

In a large enamel saucepan, combine all ingredients except lemon slices and bring almost to boiling point. Lower the heat and infuse for 10 minutes, then pour into a punch bowl.

Decorate the edges of the bowl with lemon slices, ridge the lemon rind with the prongs of a fork, before slicing.

If you haven't a punch bowl, use a large earthenware mixing basin or fruit bowl and a kitchen ladle. Serve warm wine in goblets with a slice of lemon in each.

Party punch

YOU WILL NEED FOR 30 GLASSES:

 1 bottle gin
 1 bottle lemonade
 4–6 bottles Merrydown cider
 1 lb. apples, 2–3 bananas, 4 oranges

In a large punch bowl mix together the gin, lemonade and cider, according to strength required. Prepare and slice the fruit. Float fruit in the punch, mix and ladle into goblets.

Index

255